I0889715

Alfred Kromołowski

TO TELL THE WHOLE TRUTH

A Holocaust Testimony from Częstochowa

This book was published under the auspices of
The Center for Research on the Holocaust in Poland,
generously supported by the Aaron Gutwirth Fund and the
Danek Gertner Yad Vashem Scholarship.

Alfred Kromołowski

TO TELL THE WHOLE TRUTH

A Holocaust Testimony from Częstochowa

Translated from the Polish by Dr. Richard Fagot

יד ושם
YAD VASHEM
THE WORLD HOLOCAUST REMEMBRANCE CENTER

THE INTERNATIONAL INSTITUTE FOR HOLOCAUST RESEARCH

The Center for Research on the Holocaust in Poland

Alfred Kromołowski

To Tell the Whole Truth

A Holocaust Testimony from Częstochowa

Academic Editor: Dmitry Kolotilenko

Language and Production Editor: Adina Mendelsohn

© 2026 All rights to the English edition reserved to Yad Vashem
P.O.B. 3477, Jerusalem 9103401, Israel
yadvashem.store@yadvashem.org.il
www.yadvashem.org

The publisher has made every effort to trace the copyright holders and to obtain permission to reproduce copyrighted material included in this book. Any inadvertent errors or omissions will be rectified at the earliest opportunity.

This book may not be reproduced, in whole or in part, in any form, without written permission from the publisher.

Responsibility for the opinions expressed in this publication is solely that of the author.

Unless otherwise indicated, all photos in this publication are in the public domain or courtesy of the Kromołowski family.

On the cover: Alfred Kromołowski, 1948; Alfred Kromołowski's metal prisoner tag, bearing prisoner number 1678.
Courtesy of the Kromołowski family.

ISBN 978-965-308-721-7

Typesetting: Hava Salzman
Printed in Israel by Ayalon Printing

The publication of these exceptional memoirs,
brought to fruition after many years of intensive efforts
and forty years after the passing of our father,
is an act of remembrance for our beloved parents,
Alfred and Róża (Monhajt) Kromołowski
—survivors of the Częstochowa ghetto
and the HASAG labor camp.

Halina (Kromołowska) Hamou and Jerzy Kromołowski

CONTENTS

A FAMILY TRIBUTE

In dedication

To the memory of the very sizable family of Alfred Kromołowski, almost all of whom perished tragically along the path of torment, devised with diabolical planning by the Nazis.

To the memory of the Jewish community of Częstochowa—a once vibrant and thriving community of 48,000 people, including locals, refugees, and deportees, which was utterly erased and cruelly destroyed before the indifferent eyes of the world, and to the remembrance of Jewish life, so vivid and full of spirit, a life that once existed but is no more, forever mourned by the author until his final day.

To the few survivors, who emerged from that inferno, deeply scarred by sheerly unimaginable horrors; who went on to rejoin the bustling stream of life, to build new families and raise children. The nightmare they endured bound them together as one family, with a shared but deeply concealed understanding inaccessible to those who were not there.

And finally, to the second, third, and future generations of these survivors—so that they may know, remember, refuse to forget, and guard the vow: Never Again. Especially now, hardly a century after these unprecedented events took place, as a new antisemitic wave raises its hideous head yet again.

Halina (Kromołowska) Hamou, Jerusalem, Israel
Jerzy Kromołowski, Los Angeles, USA

FOREWORD

Alfred Adam Kromołowski, son of Jakub and Stefa (Szewa) Kromołowski (née Górska), a Holocaust survivor, testifies to the life events he experienced, his family's earlier history, as well as to the broader context of Jewish communal life in Poland. Kromołowski's memoir combines personal testimony with historical documentation, offering a multifaceted account of the Jewish community of Częstochowa in Poland before, during, and after the Holocaust. He chronicles the prewar environment, the legal and social structures that shaped the Jewish community's predicament, and the aftermath of the Holocaust in postwar Poland. Unlike diaries, which record experiences and emotions in the moment, Kromołowski's memoir weaves hindsight and retrospective analysis into his testimony: the reader is immersed in the period's ambience, yet is often reminded of the author's retrospective vantage point.

The book spans three generations of Kromołowski's family, tracing their history alongside the evolution of Jewish communal life in Częstochowa. It begins with their experience at the end of the nineteenth century, when Poland was still partitioned and the area in which they lived was subject to Russian rule. He then traces their experiences during World War I, the political and social challenges of the interwar Second Polish Republic, the descent into the darkness of the Holocaust, as well as the author's postwar legal work and communal life. It also includes his reflections on memory, justice, and Polish–Jewish relations.

Częstochowa was one of the centers of Jewish life in Poland. Founded around 1765 with fewer than 100 residents, its Jewish community had grown to 28,486—20.62 percent of the total population of the city—on the eve of World War II. Jews played a significant role in the city's cultural life and economy. In the realm of culture and education, the community operated schools, synagogues, and charitable institutions. In the economic realm, many worked in trade, crafts, finance, and small industry. Wealthier Jewish families owned businesses and lived in central neighborhoods. By 1925, Jews owned the majority of Częstochowa's 136 factories, including seventeen large-scale textile plants employing around 15,000 workers. The factories in Częstochowa used heavy machinery; for example, Szymon Neuman and Markusfeld's Warta linen factory, which by 1929 employed 2,250 workers, used steam-driven looms. Jewish-owned industry reportedly exceeded the value of non-Jewish-owned industry by one-third. The Great Depression of 1929 and growing intergroup tensions, however, devastated the Jewish middle class.[1]

A Vanished World

The memoir opens with an evocation of that bygone era—a vivid portrait of nineteenth-century Jewish life in Poland. Kromołowski recounts the family traditions, religious celebrations, and communal solidarity of the shtetl. His descriptions of holiday rituals—reciting *Ma Nishtana* at Passover, reading the *haggadah* aloud with family, partaking in the solemn *kol nidrei* service and the symbolic *kapparot* ritual on the eve of Yom Kippur, listening to the stories of elders—convey the language, humor, idioms and the intimate rhythms of a vanished world.

Kromołowski's narrative style moves seamlessly between modes. At times, he evokes a literary, even romantic atmosphere—especially when recounting his family's history or scenes of Jewish communal life. These moments are rich in sentiment and character, often shaped by the tone of nostalgic storytelling rooted in Yiddishkeit. Yet much of the memoir adopts a more historical, even legal, voice: events are dated, battles named, numbers cited, and background developments carefully woven

1 Mark W. Kiel, *The Jews of Częstochowa: The Life and Death of a Community, a Concise History* (Berlin and Boston: Walter de Gruyter GmbH & Co KG, 2022), p. 115.

into the storyline. His descriptions of people—especially Jewish figures from his own family or community as well as those he learned about from others—are presented with care and evaluation. The footnotes provide information on key figures mentioned by Kromołowski, with a focus on those relevant to Częstochowa and to the author's testimony. Other names have nevertheless been included, even when details of those people are unknown or less relevant, as they remain an essential part of his memories, reflecting the people who shaped his life and experiences. This stylistic hybridity gives the memoir its layered texture, blending emotional memory with documentary support.

Alongside affectionate recollections of the past, the memoir also recounts anti-Jewish incidents, such as the arson that destroyed his family's mill, and he also references the delicate balance that existed between Jews, Poles, and other ethnic groups. Kromołowski suggests that major pogroms—such as those of 1881–1884 and 1903–1906 across the Pale of Settlement—contributed to the atmosphere of insecurity and volatility that surrounded Jewish communities in the Russian Empire. In the author's view, these violent outbreaks, though often sparked by local events, reflected deeper structural tensions. In reconstructing the early instances of anti-Jewish violence in Częstochowa itself—notably in 1902 and 1919—Kromołowski draws on contemporary newspaper reports and postwar Yizkor books, as well as on his family's memory.

In Częstochowa

Following the burning of their mill during Passover of 1884, Kromołowski's maternal grandparents, Chana and Abram Górski, moved from the village of Mirów to the city of Częstochowa. This marked a turning point, shared by many Jewish families during this time: the transition from traditional shtetl life to the aspirations and challenges of urban modernity. In this increasingly industrialized environment, Kromołowski's father made every effort to run a successful business: a soap factory. All the while, he had to navigate the challenges of the volatile political landscape of the newly emerging Second Polish Republic, which appeared on the political map after more than a century (1772–1918) of Poland's subjugation to foreign powers. Kromołowski's survey of national figures that dominated the political scene at the time—Józef Piłsudski, Kazimierz Sosnkowski, Jędrzej Moraczewski, Wincenty Witos, Ignacy Daszyński, and others—

provides valuable historical background for readers of this English edition. He traces the interplay between Polish national ideologies and the mounting pressures faced by the Jewish community, all within the framework of his own family's experience during this turbulent yet formative era in Poland.

In 1935, Kromołowski graduated from the University of Warsaw with a master's degree in law. His career in Warsaw was met with many obstacles that he attributed to antisemitism—a conclusion shaped by his broader observations of the promotion of discriminatory policies in interwar Poland. Kromołowski reflects on the intensifying nationalistic atmosphere confronting Jewish students and professionals that sought to limit Jewish access to higher education and professional advancement.

Kromołowski was socially and politically active, joining the popular Jewish Scouts' organization during his school years. In the fourth grade, he decided to leave the movement, and with several friends, he cofounded a local branch of the Bnei Zion Zionist organization. Through his involvement in such organizations, he also offers a valuable survey of prewar Jewish communal and political life in Częstochowa, capturing the organizational richness and ideological diversity that characterized the Jewish public sphere before 1939. For example, he talks about the activities of the Labor Zionists, General Zionists, the Bund, and Agudat Israel, among others, and their role in shaping communal identity, educational and welfare institutions, and political consciousness. The picture that emerges shows Częstochowa's Jewish population as deeply engaged with questions of cultural direction, religious affiliation, and national identity.

The Holocaust in Częstochowa: Personal Testimony and Historical Record

Kromołowski's reconstruction of events during the Holocaust draws not only on memory but also on extensive sources that he consulted after the war. These include Yizkor books, historical documents, and broader historical research. While the core of his testimony is rooted in personal experience and direct observation, many of the contextual details and broader reflections are informed by secondary sources. In such instances, this edition provides clarifying footnotes that cite parallel evidence, offers factual elaboration, or refers the reader to relevant scholarship.

The Holocaust years constitute the core of Kromołowski's memoir, a valuable testimony to the ordeal of Częstochowa's Jewish community.

From December 1939 to September 1942, Kromołowski served as a tax clerk in the Department of Trade and Commerce of the Częstochowa Council of Elders (Judenrat). At the end of September 1942, during a selection, his life was saved by Judenrat member Maurycy Kopiński. In the newly created Small Ghetto, Kromołowski worked in the Judenrat's housing office. From both a personal and professional perspective, he gives a detailed and harrowing account of the destruction of Jewish life in the city, tracing the daily realities of the ghetto, forced labor, and fear. His description of the ghetto's liquidation—especially the mass deportations of 1942 to Treblinka extermination camp—captures both the logistical scope, as well as the personal and collective trauma of a community being rapidly and systematically erased.

While Kromołowski's story is shaped by his specific circumstances, in many respects it also echoes the experiences of countless other Jewish families in occupied Poland. Like many, his family initially attempted to flee Częstochowa, but was forced to return and shift into survival mode within the confines of the city, and later of the ghetto. His account of imprisonment, forced labor, and repeated brushes with death during selections, deportations to death camps, and mass murders at the murder site follows a trajectory that is familiar from other testimonies about other communities. Many of the broader details he recounts—about conditions in the ghetto, networks of resistance, and connections with other ghettos and movements across Poland—are echoed by other survivor accounts. In cases where he lacked direct or intimate knowledge, Kromołowski supplements his testimony with collective memory. Kromołowski's account of the Holocaust is also crucial, among other reasons, for his careful geographic descriptions of events. His detailed recollections of neighborhoods, buildings, and intersections provide a descriptive map of the vanishing environment and community.

Perhaps one of Kromołowski's most important contributions to our understanding of the Holocaust in Częstochowa is the detailed picture he presents of the inner workings of the Częstochowa ghetto and the HASAG forced labor camp. Kromołowski's legal training became a tool for survival during the Holocaust. His administrative roles in the ghetto gave him insight into its inner workings, but they also exposed him to the moral and practical dilemmas of Jewish leadership under occupation. He accuses the Judenrat of "servility to the Germans, often at the expense of the Jewish population." His critique extends to all "informers, confidants, and henchmen" who collaborated with the German authorities in the hope of saving themselves. At the same time, he believes that the Częstochowa

Council of Elders was among the more liberal Judenräte in occupied Poland, and that, despite its limitations, it managed to create relatively bearable conditions for the ghetto's population, especially in the earlier period. His reflections are thus marked by both moral criticism and recognition of the tragic complexity of Jewish leadership under Nazi occupation.

Once he resolved to resist actively—taking action to hide from selections, devising bold evasions, or speaking audaciously to German officials in life-or-death moments—he managed not only to escape death but also, at times, to protect his family members and others around him. At the same time, he acknowledges what so many testimonies attest to: that survival was often arbitrary, determined as much by fleeting opportunity or sheer chance as by planning or courage. In spite of personal audacity, relationships, and initiative, the fate of Jews remained uncertain and haphazard.

As in the prewar and postwar sections of the memoir, Kromołowski's account of the Holocaust years interweaves personal testimony with broader historical developments. He notes major wartime events—the advance of the Red Army, the turning point at Stalingrad, and the opening of the Western Front—not as distant episodes, but as developments that affected the mood and expectations within the ghetto. These references do not overwhelm the personal dimension of the narrative but serve to situate it within the larger chronology of the war, allowing the reader to trace how external events intersected with daily life in occupied Częstochowa.

After the war, Kromołowski devoted himself to communal and legal work. From 1949 he served as a board member of the Jewish Culture and Art Society in Częstochowa. He also served as legal secretary of the Association of Polish Jews in the city and participated in the local Commission for Documenting German War Crimes. In recognition of his service, he received multiple diplomas and commendations from Jewish organizations and the local Polish authorities. His postwar efforts to hold perpetrators accountable became a key part of his legacy. He testified in the 1946 trial of Heinrich Köster, a senior figure in the Częstochowa forced labor camp and a sergeant in the Schutzpolizei, who was convicted for the murder of hundreds of Jewish prisoners. In 1973, Kromołowski also gave testimony against Walter Fasold, the German engineer and production chief at the HASAG ammunition factory. Through these actions, Kromołowski continued to serve as a witness, determined that memory be accompanied by justice.

Despite his traumatic experiences during the Holocaust, he made the decision to stay in Poland, determined to try to rebuild his life in the homeland of his birth. As one of the few members of his family to survive, he sought to continue his existence as a Jew and a Pole, honoring and preserving the memory of his family in the country where they had lived for generations. Yet the postwar environment denied him this possibility: hostility, bureaucratic obstacles, and societal rejection gradually pushed him out of communist-ruled Poland, forcing him once again to uproot his life. The traumatic antisemitic events of March 1968 left a deep impact on Kromołowski and his wife and influenced their decision to later leave Poland and settle in Copenhagen, Denmark. There he devoted himself to painting and writing his memoirs, which are now preserved in their original form in the Yad Vashem Archives in Jerusalem, Israel.

This experience of secondary trauma—having endured the horrors of persecution only to be forced to leave his home country—profoundly shaped his worldview. Throughout his memoir, one can clearly see the imprint of these experiences: a tension between attachment to homeland and alienation, a drive to memorialize lost family and culture, and an ambivalent attitude toward his native country—an inner conflict with the society to which he belonged and from which he was excluded at the same time. In the final chapter of his memoir, Kromołowski reflects not only on what was lost but on what is required for Jewish continuity. His conclusion is that Jewish survival depends on sovereignty, autonomy, and armed self-defense. His Zionist conviction emerges as a moral lesson drawn from the trajectory of Jewish history as he experienced and interpreted it.

Lastly, this memoir offers an important contribution to our understanding of the Holocaust in Częstochowa, and it will serve as a valuable source for any such future study. Kromołowski's testimony, grounded in memory and informed by legal insight, preserves both personal and communal history—a voice that urges remembrance, reckoning, and the responsibility to bear witness.

Dmitry Kolotilenko

Family Tree

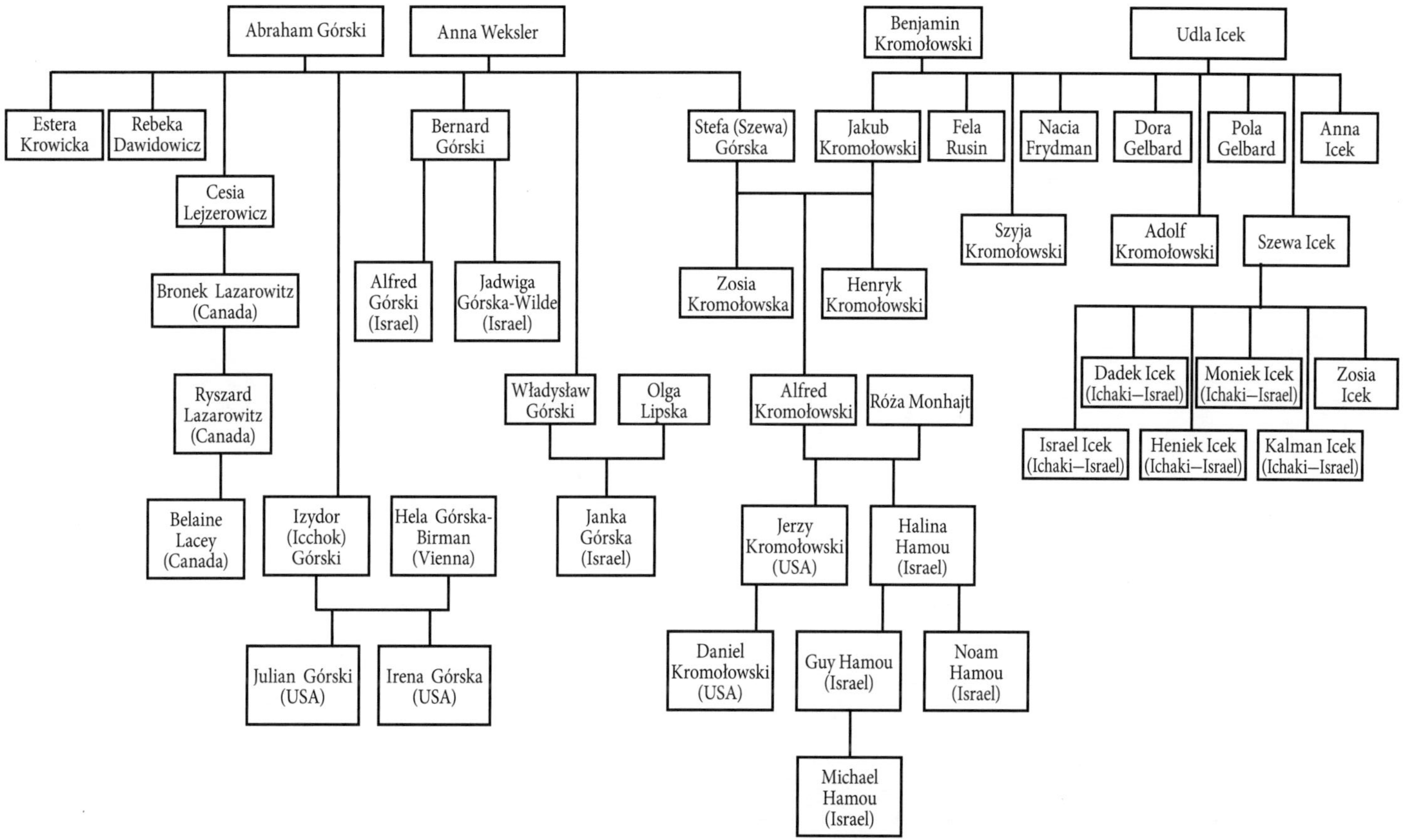
Abraham Górski
Anna Weksler
Benjamin Kromołowski
Udla Icek
Estera Krowicka
Rebeka Dawidowicz
Cesia Lejzerowicz
Bronek Lazarowitz (Canada)
Ryszard Lazarowitz (Canada)
Belaine Lacey (Canada)
Izydor (Icchok) Górski
Hela Górska-Birman (Vienna)
Julian Górski (USA)
Irena Górska (USA)
Bernard Górski
Alfred Górski (Israel)
Jadwiga Górska-Wilde (Israel)
Władysław Górski
Olga Lipska
Janka Górska (Israel)
Stefa (Szewa) Górska
Jakub Kromołowski
Zosia Kromołowska
Henryk Kromołowski
Alfred Kromołowski
Róża Monhajt
Jerzy Kromołowski (USA)
Halina Hamou (Israel)
Daniel Kromołowski (USA)
Guy Hamou (Israel)
Noam Hamou (Israel)
Michael Hamou (Israel)
Fela Rusin
Szyja Kromołowski
Nacia Frydman
Dora Gelbard
Adolf Kromołowski
Pola Gelbard
Anna Icek
Szewa Icek
Dadek Icek (Ichaki–Israel)
Moniek Icek (Ichaki–Israel)
Zosia Icek
Israel Icek (Ichaki–Israel)
Heniek Icek (Ichaki–Israel)
Kalman Icek (Ichaki–Israel)

CHAPTER ONE

MY MOTHER'S ROOTS

In the little village of Mirów near Częstochowa lived a Jewish miller and his family. The nearby Pilica River flowed lazily, with green meadows and grasslands stretching over its banks, and in the distance, the forest grew dark and vanished from sight only at the horizon itself. Near the river stood a wooden mill, sturdily built, and it was here where the foamy water plummeted with a crash from a high weir to turn the huge, creaking, mill wheel. Next to the mill, in a small orchard, stood a one-story house, wooden like the mill, built on a foundation of square limestone, with large windows equipped with wrought-iron shutters.

The miller, a Jew of tall stature and slim build with a swarthy face framed by a small black beard, was just closing the mill door with the help of a burly young assistant with a thick moustache. He put the keys in his coat pocket and said goodbye to his worker.

"Be well, Jan," the miller said. "We will not work tomorrow and the day after tomorrow, because it's our Easter holiday.[1] There will be no work

1 The Jewish holiday of Passover (Pesach) commemorates the biblical story of the Exodus from Egypt. In the Jewish Diaspora, Passover lasts eight days. During this period, Jews refrain from eating bread and instead consume only unleavened

in the following days either, and we will resume business as usual only on Wednesday next week."

The young miller shook hands with his boss and said in a low voice, "I know it's your Easter, and you are not allowed to eat bread." Looking around, he then added, "But watch out, dear Abram. Beware of Piotrowski, as he's your great enemy. I heard from the peasants that he's threatening to set your place on fire, because you're ruining him. His mill is now working only twice a week; the peasants prefer to mill with you, since you're cheaper and you don't cheat them."

The miller stood there, somewhat troubled. With his head bowed, he rubbed his thick black beard and said, "My dear Jan! Everything is in God's hands, and I believe that He will not abandon me or my family. Farewell! May God be with you!"

Deep in thought, he walked slowly toward his house, where a short, stocky woman wearing a black wig stood out front, anxiously awaiting her husband's return from work so they could start preparations for the festive Passover meal. His house and the mill stood a little off to the side, but the other mill—belonging to the peasant Piotrowski—was visible a few hundred steps away, hidden among trees and bushes, rising on a hill by the same river. Abram's mill had been a thorn in his side for years.

Abram Górski was my grandfather. He married Chana Weksler, my grandmother, in 1873, and they settled in the town of Działoszyn on the Warta River,[2] where my great-grandfather, Herszel (Hersz) Górski, ran a large silk-weaving mill. He was a wealthy man, one of the pioneers of the textile industry in Poland and the founder of a silk and cotton factory.[3] He took care to ensure that his only son Abram received a thorough education, both secular and talmudic.[4] His two daughters had a French governess and spoke fluent French, which was quite rare among Jewish families living in the Polish territories at that time.

flatbread (*matza*), to commemorate the haste of the Exodus from Egypt, when the Israelites left so quickly that their dough did not have time to rise.

2 Działoszyn is located some 40 kilometers northwest of Częstochowa.

3 The textile industry became a prominent occupation among Jews in Eastern Europe in the nineteenth century. In Częstochowa itself, Jews played an important economic role and contributed much to the industrial development of the city. According to Mark Kiel, fourteen of the twenty factories established between 1870 and 1895 were set up by Jews. See Kiel, *The Jews of Częstochowa*, p. XVI.

4 Talmudic education refers to a traditional Jewish education that emphasizes critical analysis, debate, and discussion of the Talmud and related texts.

After a few years of marriage, when my grandparents already had four children, they decided it was time to start an independent life, away from the support of their parents with whom they had been living until then. It was decided that as Abram had been helping his father run the textile factory, a mill would be bought for him in the village of Mirów, taking advantage of an opportunity that serendipitously came their way. It was there, in a newly purchased house adjacent to the mill, where the young couple and their children would make their home and try their luck on their own. The broker in this transaction was my grandmother's father, Weksler, a wealthy farmowner in Pińczów, near Kielce.

The mill had previously belonged to Nosalski, a recently deceased villager of Mirów, whose wife had decided to move permanently to Częstochowa, where her adult daughters were living. With the joint funds contributed by Weksler and Hersz Górski, the property in Mirów, along with the adjacent orchard and several morgens[5] of cultivated land, were purchased in around 1878. Without delay, the family moved to Mirów. As was customary at the time, the parents gave the newly minted millers several hundred rubles[6] for an auspicious start, and they threw a lavish party for the prominent residents of Mirów to introduce themselves to their neighbors, drinking a *l'chaim*[7] with them before each person rushed back to his own home.

5 A morga is an old measurement of land that was used in the nineteenth century. In Congress Kingdom of Poland, it equalled 0.5598 hectares. See "Morga," Encyklopedia PWN, Wydawnictwo Naukowe PWN, https://encyklopedia.pwn.pl/szukaj/morga%20.html (accessed August 18, 2025).

6 The ruble was the currency of the Russian Empire. Poland was partitioned three times in the second half of the eighteenth century (in 1772, 1792, and 1795) between the Kingdom of Prussia (Prussia), the Habsburg Empire (Austria), and the Russian Empire (Russia). Within the Russian partition, a dependent Polish state named the Congress Kingdom of Poland—otherwise known as Congress Poland—was created by the Congress of Vienna in 1815. Częstochowa, along with other towns and villages mentioned by Kromołowski, were located in the Kingdom of Poland and remained under the rule of the Russian Empire until after World War I, when Poland regained its national independence as the Republic of Poland in 1918. The Polish monetary system in the Russian partition underwent various phases of reformation and russification, and in the 1840s and 1850s, it was integrated into the Russian monetary system, essentially losing its national distinctness and independence. For more on this, see Wojciech Morawski, *Zarys powszechnej historii pieniądza i bankowości* (Warsaw: Wydaw. Trio, 2002), pp. 259–261.

7 *L'chaim* is a Jewish toast meaning "to life."

Abram Górski, a wise, educated, and intelligent man who spoke Polish,[8] quickly won the hearts of the peasants of Mirów, thanks to his innate tact and gentle character. The new miller's honesty coupled with his reasonable prices won him customers, and the mill steadily prospered. This state of affairs lasted a few years, and my grandparents' led a thriving and happy life. The children grew up, and the mill earned enough money to ensure a good living for the family.

Their neighbor, the drunkard Piotrowski, encountered more and more trouble as he tried to compete with Abram Górski's well-run mill. Piotrowski often cheated with the scales and stole flour from the peasants, so they soon preferred to take their grain to Górski's mill. Sensing an approaching economic disaster, Piotrowski resorted to the familiar arsenal of propaganda tactics. At every opportunity, he told the local peasants that Abram Górski was a Jew, that the Jews had murdered Jesus Christ,[9] and that for Passover they baked *matzos* (unleavened bread) with the blood of innocent Christian children.[10] However, this did only minor harm to my grandfather and his milling business. Most of the peasants laughed, nodded, and said that Abramek[11] was a decent jewboy. He doesn't cheat, he grinds cheaply, and, if needed, he'll write an application in Russian and a letter in Polish for them. And, he even holds educated discussions with Reverend Kasprzak, the local priest, about the Old Testament. And so, life went on.

8 Most Jews spoke Yiddish as their mother tongue, but high proficiency in Polish and Russian offered social and economic benefits. Of course, knowledge of Polish served better integration and acceptance among Poles. For linguistic data of the population in Poland in 1913, see Andrzej Jezierski and Andrzej Wyczański, eds., *Historia Polski w liczbach: Państwo, społeczeństwo*, vol. 1 (Warsaw: Główny Urząd Statystyczny, 2003), p. 186.

9 The "deicide accusation"—the false notion that Jews were collectively responsible for the crucifixion of Jesus—exerted long-term influence in Europe. It was formally renounced by the Roman Catholic Church only at the Second Vatican Council (1962–1965). At the grassroots level, it was a common anti-Jewish motif at the time, as described by Kromołowski, and it still persists in some segments of Polish society. On anti-Jewish attitudes, see the data and explanations provided by Marek Kucia, Marta Duch-Dyngosz, and Mateusz Magierowski, "Anti-Semitism in Poland: Survey Results and a Qualitative Study of Catholic Communities," *Nationalities Papers*, 42:1 (2014), pp. 8–36.

10 At various points in history, beginning in the Middle Ages, Jews were falsely accused of using the blood of Christian children to bake *matza* for the Passover holiday. This anti-Jewish trope is known as the blood libel.

11 Deminutive of Abram and Abraham.

It was the spring of 1884, and the eve of the Jewish holiday of Passover was approaching. As tradition dictates, Jews sit down to a *seder*, a ceremonial supper, during which they retell for the umpteenth time the story of the joyous redemption of the Jewish people and how Moses led them out of slavery in Egypt.[12] Jews celebrate this fortunate event by a week-long holiday eating only *matzos*, not bread, to commemorate the fact that their ancestors fleeing Egypt had no time to bake bread for the journey and only had time to mix raw dough, which they baked in the scorching sun during their escape before eating it.[13]

My grandmother, Chana Górski, prepared the *seder* feast, threw out and burned the *humetz*[14] and all remains of bread and flour the house, and carefully swept and cleaned the entire home. She took out the dishes that were kept separately and intended for use only during the holidays—kitchen utensils, plates, and tableware—and awaited her husband's arrival. Abram Górski, dressed in his finest clothes, returned with his three sons from the prayer service held in Mirów's synagogue, and the entire family sat down at the festively decorated table, as my grandfather began celebrating the *seder* according to the order sanctified by centuries of tradition. It was a warm April evening. Amid the surrounding silence of Mirów, candles were lit only in the Jewish homes, and voices were heard in prayer and song. Herszel, the eldest son of Abram, began to ask the four questions of the Passover *seder* and, turning to his father, sang in a thin, boyish voice, just as he had been taught in the *heder*.[15]

12 The *haggadah* is the text read at the Passover *seder* (Heb: order, referring to the ceremonial meal) to fulfill the commandment that every Jew must tell their children the story from the Book of Exodus. See Exodus 13:8.

13 See Exodus 12:39.

14 *Humetz* (or *hametz*) refers to foods containing leavening agents, which are forbidden during the Passover holiday.

15 *Heder* was the primary Jewish elementary education system in Eastern Europe from the Middle Ages, instilling religious and cultural values through the study of Torah, Mishna, Talmud, and liturgy. From the nineteenth century, modernization challenged its traditional role. Enlightenment, nationalism, and increased access to secular education further reduced its prevalence. At the same time "progressive" and Zionist *heders* emerged. Despite these shifts, the traditional *heder* remained central in Orthodox communities. See Mordechai Zalkin, "Heder," YIVO Encyclopedia of Jews in Eastern Europe, https://encyclopedia.yivo.org/article/31 (accessed August 18, 2025); David Roskies, *Heder: Primary Education among East European Jews: A Selected and Annotated Bibliography of Published Sources* (New York: Jewish Theological Seminary of America, 1977); Steven J. Zipperstein, "Transforming the

"Tell me, father, how is this Passover night different from all other nights of the year?"[16]

Suddenly, loud noises were heard outside, and the darkness of the April night was shot through with flashes. Someone knocked hard, and shouts rang out.

"It's on fire! Górski's mill is on fire!"

The mill was burning like a torch, the dried wood consumed in a flash. The roof was already on fire, and the flames were spreading with surprising speed. The peasants were only able to rescue the house, dousing its roof with water drawn from the river, preventing the house from burning down while sparks were flying everywhere. By the time the fire brigade from nearby Niegowa arrived, the mill had already burned to the ground, and only the blackened mill wheel, creaking and whimpering, kept turning assiduously. That was how my grandfather's milling career in the village of Mirów came to an end. It was his first defeat in life.

There was no doubt that the perpetrator of the fire was the miller Piotrowski, and every honest person in Mirów lamented the misfortune of Abram Górski and his great loss. But nothing could be done. There was no evidence of Piotrowski's guilt. The next day, the community head accompanied by a constable arrived, jotted down some notes, questioned Górski and the peasants living in the neighborhood, nodded their heads, and left. It was a sad Passover for Abram Górski and his family. Everything he had achieved through years of hard work was lost, including a good deal of property, and he had to come to terms with this fact. At the time, neither insurance nor compensation were available.

After a few days, Hersz Górski and Weksler—my grandparents' fathers—came to Mirów, and after some deliberation, they decided that the remaining house and the land should be sold, and that my grandfather and his family should move to nearby Częstochowa and start again from scratch. A few months later, they managed to sell the ruins of the mill, which had turned to ashes, together with the house and the land for an absurdly low price, and the whole family departed Mirów for Częstochowa in hired carts. With that money, and with the help of his still-wealthy

Heder: Maskilic Politics in Imperial Russia," in Ada Rapoport-Albert and Steven Zipperstein, eds., *Jewish History: Essays in Honour of Chimen Abramsky* (London: Peter Halban, 1988), pp. 87–109.

16 The question, "How is this night different from all other nights?" is from the Four Questions (*Ma Nishtana*) traditionally asked by the youngest at the Passover *seder* to prompt the retelling of the story of the Exodus.

parents, Abram Górski rented a store on Prosta Street, adjacent to the Old Market Square,[17] in the commercial quarter of the city. It was a small store, accessed by three wooden stairs and located just opposite the side wall of St. Zygmunt's Church. Today, there is no trace left of Prosta Street because it was destroyed, along with all the neighboring streets in the Jewish quarter, during the Holocaust.

In the Old Market Square, in a house owned by a man named Liberman, my grandfather rented an apartment consisting of three rooms and a kitchen, which was swiftly furnished and decorated. It was a short distance from the apartment to the store, and early each morning, my grandfather, after saying his morning prayers, hurried to his newly opened store, over which hung the sign "Abram Górski—Textile Goods." The shelves bent under the weight of textiles piled there—various kinds of percale, linens, silks, head scarves worn by village women, and many other fabrics used in what was then known as the elbow-length (referring to the traditional unit of measurement based on the human arm) or mercerized goods industry. The store became very popular; it was attractive and always full of shoppers, mostly peasants from neighboring villages and towns. Its busiest days were Tuesdays and Fridays, when great fairs were held in Częstochowa. Grandfather was assisted by his wife, Chana, and in a short time, the business flourished, generating a good income.

The years passed quickly, the children grew up, and life proceeded smoothly. Their Jewish home was quite bourgeois. Grandfather, being a more progressive Jew, did not wear a long coat and covered his head with a hat rather than the black yarmulke commonly worn by Polish Jews. On Saturdays and holidays, he would don his top hat and go with his sons to the nearby synagogue on Nadrzeczna Street, where he had a permanent seat in the second row of pews, affixed with a metal plaque bearing his name and surname. This synagogue, the Old Synagogue (*Dy Ałte Shul*), was burned to the ground and desecrated in 1939 by German thugs.[18]

17 In Poland, it was common for Jews to reside close to the city's market square.

18 The Old Synagogue was situated at 32 Nadrzeczna. It was ransacked and desecrated in September 1939, and it was completely destroyed on June 25, 1943, during the liquidation of the Small Ghetto. See "Old Synagogue," The World Society of Częstochowa Jews and Their Descendants, https://www.czestochowajews.org/old-czestochowa/old-synagogue/ (accessed August 18, 2025); Kiel, *The Jews of Częstochowa*, p. 32.

The Old Synagogue, Częstochowa.

My grandfather Abram subscribed to the Hebrew magazine *Hatsefira*[19] and the Polish-language, Zionist-oriented magazine *Izraelita*,[20] and read them with great care. He was a man of deep values,

19 *Hatsefira* was the first Hebrew newspaper in Poland, founded in Warsaw and issued in the years 1862 and then later between 1874 and 1931. It was founded by Hayim Zelig Słonimski and was later revitalized by Nahum Sokolow. Initially serving conservative Polish Jewry with news and scientific content, it became a leading platform for Hebrew literature and Zionist debates. *Hatsefira* initially approached Zionism cautiously but shifted under Nahum Sokolow, who, inspired by the First Zionist Congress in 1897, became a strong supporter of Theodor Herzl and political Zionism. He used the paper to promote Zionism among religious circles, notably through his influential articles "Le-Maranan ve-rabanan" (1899–1901). Despite its influence, factors such as censorship, financial struggles, and World War I led to its closure in 1931. See Avner Holtzman, "Tsefirah, Ha-," YIVO Encyclopedia of Jews in Eastern Europe, https://encyclopedia.yivo.org/article/109 (accessed August 18, 2025).

20 *Izraelita* (1866–1915) was the longest-running Polish-Jewish journal, which was published in Polish by reformist Jews in Warsaw. Initially focused on Judaism and modernization, it later expanded to address broader cultural, social, and literary topics. Despite low circulation and limited appeal among the Jewish masses, it became an important platform for ideological debates, voicing opposition to antisemitism and promoting religious reform and modern education. Under Szmul Hirsz Peltyn (1831–1896), it emphasized assimilation and Polish patriotism,

impeccable character traits, great knowledge, wisdom, and exceptional gentleness. He was well liked and respected among the Jewish bourgeoisie of Częstochowa, where he was known as Avrumele. The Górskis had eight children—four sons and four daughters. My mother was the seventh child and was therefore named Sheva, which means "seven" in Hebrew. She was the youngest daughter and was followed by the youngest son, Icchok Górski.

Later, the eldest child, Hersz, later called Henryk,[21] moved to Łódź, where he worked as a salesman for a large textile company.[22] He got married, but sadly died childess at a young age, plunging the entire family into grief. I only know him from a photograph that was in the family album at my parents' home. I have often looked at the image of my uncle who died prematurely, with his curly mustache and luxuriant mop of hair, his handsome face framed by a short beard. To honor his memory, my younger brother was named Henryk, and tragically, he too died prematurely, just like his namesake.

My grandparents' eldest daughter, Rywka, was married at the age of twenty to a wealthy merchant, a coal wholesaler known in the Jewish quarter of Częstochowa as Jankiel Kojlenhendler.[23] His real name was Dawidowicz, and he owned two houses on Garncarska Street. Of my grandparents' remaining children, their son Wolf (Władek), ran a factory manufacturing plaster and onyx products in Częstochowa. He mainly produced figurines of various Catholic saints, which attracted eager customers as the famous Pauline monastery of Jasna Góra—with the image of the Black Maiden[24] that was said to produce miracles and heal all kinds of ailments—was located in the city. The monastery was a regular pilgrimage

but later editors, including Nahum Sokolow (1859–1936), embraced Zionist ideas. Izraelita nurtured a vibrant intellectual milieu and played a key role in integrating Jewish themes into Polish literature and culture. See Magda Opalski, "Izraelita," YIVO Encyclopedia of Jews in Eastern Europe, https://encyclopedia.yivo.org/article/1774 (accessed August 18, 2025); Marian Fuks, *Prasa żydowska w Warszawie, 1823–1939* (Warsaw: Państwowe Wydawnictwo Naukowe, 1979), pp. 85–103.

21 A Polish varient of the name Hersz.

22 Łódź was an industrial center, with over one-third of its population being Jewish. Before the war, it had the second largest Jewish community in Poland, after Warsaw.

23 The name Kojlenhendler means coal seller in Yiddish.

24 This is widely known as the Black Madonna. It refers to the revered icon of the Virgin Mary housed at the Jasna Góra Monastery in Częstochowa, and serves as a major pilgrimage site in Poland and a symbol of Polish Catholicism.

site for countless Catholics from all over the country and abroad, and the pilgrims would buy various religious artifacts and statues of saints, which were consecrated by the monks as an object of special religious reverence.

Bernard Górski, the second son, moved to Łódź, married and settled in the town of Konin. Under strange circumstances, he was captured by the Germans during World War I and taken to an internment camp in Germany on a charge of espionage. He was later released and settled permanently in Berlin, where he ran a bookstore. After Hitler came to power, Bernard Górski was forcibly displaced by the Germans. He was taken to the Polish border and was in a displaced persons camp in Zbąszyń.[25]

Aunt Cywia married a merchant from Praszka,[26] Dawid Lejzerowicz, leaving the three youngest children living at my grandparents' house: Estera, Sheva—my mother, also known as Stefcia or Stefa—and Icchok. Uncle Icchok attended the Edelist public school[27] before leaving for further studies at the Lampowski trade school in Pabianice, near Łódź, since only a very small percentage of Jewish youth were accepted into high schools in Częstochowa at that time.

The nineteenth century was drawing to a close, and the new century was promising to be turbulent in the Polish lands, occupied at the time by tsarist Russia. In 1894, Nicholas II Romanov ascended the throne and initiated the expansion of Russian imperialism in the Far East. The advances made by Russia—including the capture of Port Arthur, the occupation of Manchuria, and the strengthening of Russian influence in Persia—caused concern among ruling circles in both England and Japan, who then formed an Anglo-Japanese alliance against Russia. A war with Japan was thus imminent.[28]

25 Jews of Polish nationality were expelled from Germany in October 1938, and were interned in Zbąszyń, Poland, close to the German border. The deportations to this camp followed a Polish decree rescinding all passports of Polish residents unless a special reentry permit was granted, which Germany then used as a pretext to expel Jews. At the end of negotiations, some were allowed to return briefly to Germany to settle their affairs, while others were permitted by the Polish authorities to leave the town and relocate elsewhere in Poland. See Bonnie M. Harris, "From German Jews to Polish Refugees: Germany's Polenaktion and the Zbąszyn Deportations of October 1938," *Kwartalnik Historii Żydów*, 230 (2009), pp. 175–205.

26 Praszka is a town in Poland, located in Olesno County, Opole Voivodeship.

27 Kromołowski later refers to the Edelist school that he himself attended on Spadkowa (Spadek) Street.

28 Russia lost the Russo-Japanese War of 1904–1905.

At the same time, organized movements of factory workers in Russia and the Polish territories began to demand improvements in the extremely difficult working conditions, an increase of their very low wages, and an end to the ruthless exploitation of the industrial proletariat. The tsarist government, fearing any kind of social change and freedom movements, and to divert the attention of the working class from social and existential issues as well as independence slogans, began organizing pogroms against the Jews, pointing to them as the source of all evil.[29]

Under the aegis of the tsarist government, two organizations were set up in Russia: The Black Sotnia[30] and the Brotherhood of Michael the Archangel.[31] Both specialized in inciting riots against the Jewish population, sowing hatred against Jews, and directly organizing anti-Jewish pogroms. The favored slogan of these pogroms was "*beey Zhydov—spasaj Rassyju*" (Beat the Jews—Save Russia). Incidentally, this slogan was also used later, when the tsarist satraps were replaced by the communist-red satraps of the Soviet Union. At that time, pogroms against Jews in the Russian territories were commonplace, and Jewish blood was spilled in abundance. The bloodiest of these pogroms took place in Kiev, Kishinev, and Zhitomir.[32]

There was not a single city, town, or village with Jewish inhabitants in the entire Russian Empire that was not touched by the bloody tentacles of the pogromists. Jews were murdered, wounded, and beaten bloody, and

29 The first mass pogroms had already begun following the assassination of Alexander II in 1881.

30 The Black Sotnia (or the Black Hundred, Russian: Chyornaya sotnya) was a reactionary, monarchist and ultranationalist antisemitic movement in Russia, active in 1905–1917.

31 The Russian People's Union of St. Michael the Archangel was an ultranationalist, monarchist organization in early twentieth-century Russia, which was active as part of the Black Hundred movement. It advocated for loyalty to the tsar, Orthodox Christianity, and a vision of Russian ethnic supremacy.

32 During the Kishinev pogrom in 1903, fifty Jews were murdered. The pogroms during the years 1905–1907 followed the failed 1905 revolution. Hundreds of Jews were murdered by counterrevolutionary elements in places such as Odessa and Kiev. On May 11, in Zhitomir, violence erupted when Jews were falsely accused of using the tsar's portrait for target practice. Groups associated with the Black Hundred attacked the Jews. Twenty-nine Jews were killed, and 150 were wounded. See Antony Polonsky, *The Jews in Poland and Russia, vol. 2: 1881 to 1914* (Oxford and Portland: Littman Library of Jewish Civilization, 2010), pp. 54–55. On the Kishinev pogrom, see also Steven Zipperstein, *Pogrom: Kishinev and the Tilt of History* (New York: Liveright, 2018).

their property was robbed or destroyed. The atmosphere grew increasingly tense in Russia surrounding the trial against the Russian Jew Beilis, organized and provoked by the Black Sotnia. Beilis was falsely accused of ritual murder, but was found innocent during the court process. He was accused of murdering a Christian baby and draining the blood from its body, which he then allegedly used to bake Passover *matzos*. The child, who had been hidden by the provocateurs, was soon found alive and healthy.[33]

Similar pogroms began to spread into the Polish lands, where there was no lack of reactionary forces among both the aristocracy and antisemitic Polish bourgeoisie, for whom the Jews' domination in the country's economic life was the proverbial salt in the wound. These higher social spheres also looked on with horror at the ever-growing masses of workers becoming increasingly vocal in their demands for an improvement in working conditions, democratization of political life, and independence from occupation by the tsarist regime.

Under these somewhat favorable conditions for anti-Jewish violence, the Polish National Democrats, together with a major segment of the clergy—under the protection of the tsarist administration—organized a pogrom in Częstochowa in 1902.[34] It was Monday,

33 The Beilis Affair (1911–1913) was a high-profile trial in the Russian Empire where Mendl Beilis, a Jewish factory superintendent, was falsely accused of ritually murdering a Christian boy, Andrei Yushchinsky, in Kiev. However, Kromołowski is mistaken: The boy was indeed murdered and his body was found mutilated. The trial, fueled by antisemitism, aimed to propagate the blood-libel myth. Despite state efforts to secure a conviction, Beilis was acquitted due to absence of evidence and to Beilis's strong alibi. The incident highlighted deep societal antisemitism in Tsarist Russia. The murder was committed by a criminal gang seeking to cover up their activities. Evidence pointed to Vera Cheberyak, who was arrested by the Bolsheviks in 1918 for the boy's murder and the fabrication of the case against Mendl Beilis. See Robert Weinberg, *Blood Libel in Late Imperial Russia: The Ritual Murder Trial of Mendel Beilis* (Bloomington: Indiana University Press, 2014). pp. 1–3; Elissa Bemporad, "The Afterlife of the Beilis Affair: The Blood Libel in the Soviet Union," in Elissa Bemporad, *Legacy of Blood: Jews, Pogroms, and Ritual Murder in the Lands of the Soviets* (New York: Oxford University Press, 2019), pp. 36–37.

34 In what follows, Kromołowski attempts to reconstruct the events of May 1902 based on the newspaper report published in *Arbayter Shtimme*, 30 (October 1902). An English translation of the newspaper report can be found in Mark Liber (supplemented by Shimkha Lev), "The 'Rabunek'—The Pogrom in 1902," in Raphael Mahler, ed., *The Jews of Czestochowa* (Częstochowa, Poland), tr. Gloria Berkenstat Freund, https://www.jewishgen.org/yizkor/czestochowa1/

August 11, 1902, the eve of the Jewish fast day of Tisha B'Av, the anniversary of the destruction of the Temple in Jerusalem by the Romans and the loss of Jewish independence in the ancient Land of Israel. On this day, Jews usually gather in synagogues and sprinkle ash on their heads as a sign of mourning, and they sit on low stools or directly on the floor as a sign of repentance.

On the morning of the eve of Tisha B'Av in 1902, however, a few Jews were quaralling, and a Christian woman was beaten up in the Old Market Square in Częstochowa. As a result of the brawl, the woman sustained physical injuries and was taken to a hospital. All those involved were known burglars and thieves in the city—both the Jews and the Polish woman. The latter had been convicted of three burglaries and had served prison sentences. As far as the Jewish thieves were concerned, the Jewish community had already asked the police and administrative authorities several times to permanently remove them from the town. A few hours after the scuffle, news spread around town that the woman who had been beaten up had died of her wounds, supposedly promoted by biased hospital doctors, supporters of National Democracy—an ultra-nationalist party in Poland, whose platform was to expel Jews from the country.[35] The truth was that, after treating her superficial wounds, the beaten woman was discharged from the hospital in good health and sent home.

Just then, crowds of both Polish hooligans and workers leaving the factories for their lunch break began to gather in the streets where the Jewish residents lived. Also among the crowd were large numbers of unemployed people, many of whom were in Częstochowa at that time due to the prevailing economic crisis. In the Old Market Square, the crowd started to throw stones at Jewish stallholders, smashing their stalls and stands, and robbing and destroying their goods. Passersby with a Jewish appearance were beaten. Jewish merchants began to hastily close their stores.

All at once there was unbelievable panic, a blend of different sounds: screams of beaten Jews, the clang of smashed shop windows, and the crowds rushing to smash stores and plunder goods. Jewish dwellings were broken into and furniture was destroyed. Jews were beaten and tortured.

czestochowa1.html, pp. 166–170 (accessed August 18, 2025). English translation of the original Yiddish, *Tshenstokhover yidn* (New York: United Czestochower Relief Committee and Ladies Auxiliary, 1947).

35 National Democracy (Endecja), a right-wing nationalist movement in Poland that stressed Polish national and Catholic identity, opposed socialism and minorities' influence, and was a major rival to Piłsudski's camp before and after 1918.

Accompanying their screams, quilts and pillows were torn apart in the hope of finding hidden treasures inside. Jews hid in cellars and attics, and whoever had a kind Polish neighbor tried to seek shelter there. From the Old Market Square, the crowd of angry hooligans ran to almost every Jewish street. There, too, stores and apartments were robbed, and every Jewish passerby was beaten bloody.

It was not until about seven o'clock in the evening that police and military patrols—in very small numbers—appeared on the streets. However, even these patrols were afraid of the enraged crowd, withdrawing in panic after only a short time. Eventually, the crowd slowly dwindled and began to disperse. It was said that in the early hours of that day, the mayor and the chief of police unofficially warned their Jewish acquaintances against riots. They told the Jews that a pogrom was being organized in Częstochowa and advised them not to show themselves in the district near Jasna Góra, where three days earlier, a religious ceremony combined with a procession had taken place to consecrate the newly built monastery tower after a recent fire.

The pogrom continued the next day too, and was met with complete passivity on the part of the police, the Russian authorities, and the general Polish population. Even more than on the previous day, masses of ruffians and factory workers gathered on the Warta riverbank, and from there, with shouts calling for beating the Jews, they set off toward the nearby Garncarska, Nadrzeczna, and Krakowska Streets—where the largest number of Jewish stores and workshops were located—as well as the Old and New Markets. Again, as on the previous day, the crowd smashed stores, robbed and destroyed goods, got drunk on wine and vodka taken from the smashed Jewish liquor stores, and attacked Jewish passersby, dragging Jews out of their apartments and beating them mercilessly.

The situation was tragic. Representatives of the Jewish community tried intervening with the Russian authorities, but the military chief refused to receive the delegation and ordered that these representatives be informed he was not in his office. In turn, the Jewish representatives alerted the governor in Piotrków by telegraph. Finally, in the afternoon hours, Russian soldiers appeared on the streets of the city, although not in very large numbers as the Częstochowa garrison was away on maneuvers. An army detachment stood in the courtyard of St. Zygmunt's Church, at the junction of Old and New Market Squares, and the soldiers began to chase the mob away, beating them with rifle butts. However, although chased away from one place, they gathered in another, continuing their campaign of destruction and massacre as they dragged the Jews out of their apartments.

The army moved to a different position, surrounding the alley leading from the New Market to the wealthier districts of the city, where banks, an exchange office, wealthier stores, and the Russian state bank were located. The enraged mobs now began to douse Jewish stores with kerosene and burn them, carry away whole sacks of goods, and rob Jewish dwellings. Once again, feathers from ripped pillows and quilts flew in the streets, and the screams of the tortured inhabitants could be heard everywhere. Goldman's wholesale store, Miętkiewicz's paint store, and Bem's and Gold's manufacturing stores were completely destroyed and looted.

Data about this pogrom can be found on the pages of the Yiddish-language newspaper, *Arbayter Shtimme*, which published the exact course of events some time after the Częstochowa pogrom, in October 1902.[36] In the relevant descriptions of the pogrom in the newspaper, we read:

> Toward the evening of the second day of the pogrom, the situation in the Jewish quarter of the city looked hopeless. Panic-stricken fear gripped the Jews of Częstochowa. It was clear that the pogrom had been organized on purpose and with the obvious support of the local administration. The richer Jews began to leave the city at night, escaping to nearby towns. What was striking during this pogrom was that not a single sign of protest was uttered, not a single warning signal from Polish society, from the Polish intelligentsia and clergy. And yet it was doubtless that the Russian administration clearly wanted to inflame and deepen the hatred that the Polish society had for their fellow Jewish citizens, to revive and stoke the already not inconsiderable antisemitism, and in this way more easily rule and direct the conquered country, according to the old Roman proverb *divide et impera*—divide and rule. On the contrary, The Polish intelligentsia clearly took the side of the thugs who took part in the pogrom, although they knew very well that these were irresponsible hooligans, primitive people without any scruples or sense of morality, and most often simply criminals and various kinds of social lowlifes.

We further read in *Arbayter Shtimme*:

> It was a fact that when a Jewish woman who had been beaten to the point of blood, and who was semi-conscious, was taken by a passerby to a hospital, she turned for medical help to a well-known

36 *Arbayter Shtimme*, 30 (October 1902).

> doctor in Częstochowa, Dr. Władysław Biegański, who was just passing by, but she met with his categorical refusal to provide help. Another victim of the pogrom, a Jew whose arm was broken by the rabble, was also refused medical help. He went to a well-known surgeon in Częstochowa, Dr. Wrześniowski, asking him to take care of his wounds, but the doctor refused to help. Thus, the pogrom action, organized and supported by the Polish society, became a national mission, a crusade against the Jews, and blessed by the Catholic clergy.[37]

Paciorkowski, a well-known lawyer in Częstochowa, met a Jewish acquaintance on the street on the second day of the pogrom and said to him with a sneer: "So, our people are beating your folks!" Then, he turned and walked away without shaking the Jew's hand in farewell.[38]

Rather than fading, the pogrom continued to spread devastation on the third day. Around noon, groups of workers leaving the factories joined all sorts of troublemakers and moved as a unified crowd to the Old Market and the Jewish streets, where they began throwing stones at the windows of the Old Synagogue on Nadrzeczna Street and breaking the entrance door. However, complete desecration was prevented by a group of Jewish porters and butchers armed with rods and axes, who resolutely stood up to the mob of outlaws, declaring that they would not hesitate to cause bloodshed in defense of the synagogue. The defenders of the synagogue were led by a Jewish porter known for his strength, nicknamed Majer Riz (Mayer the Strongman). The group managed to stave off the crowd, who stopped destroying the synagogue and moved on.

In addition, the Jewish butchers threatened to mow down anyone who tried to rob their butcher shops on Targowa Street, and thanks to this effort, Targowa Street survived this devastation, and no Jewish butcher shop or apartment on this street suffered even the slightest damage. Krygier, the owner of a house on Krakowska Street, who, it should be noted, was a Christian, stood in front of the house with a revolver in his hand, threatening to shoot any mobster who dared to plunder his property.

But these sporadic attempts at resistance did not dampen the lust for plunder and the shedding of Jewish blood in any way, and the pogrom raged through the Jewish streets on the third day with even greater force and hatred. Jews continued to be beaten, goods were looted, and apartments were

37 Ibid.

38 Ibid.

ransacked. Total anarchy prevailed in the Jewish streets. Power had passed into the hands of the crowd, and nothing seemed likely to calm things down.

My mother told me about our family's experiences during this pogrom, as well as her own impressions of the massacre. I remember her telling me that my grandfather, who owned a factory store on Prosta Street, located in the center of the Jewish quarter just off the Old Market, was already an elderly, sick man at that time. He barely left the house, and the store was mostly run by my grandmother and my mother, who was still a young woman of twenty-one. Grandfather suffered from heart problems and immediately felt worse when he heard about the outbreak of the atrocities. The store was closed, and the residents looked out of their windows in horror, wringing their hands at the scenes taking place in the streets below. From the windows of Grandfather's apartment, you could see the mob prowling the Old Market Square—the epicenter of the pogrom.

At first, by a lucky coincidence, my grandfather's store survived the carnage. However, on the third day of the pogrom, after the crowd had been chased away by the Jewish porters, they moved on to the stores in the Old Market Square and the New Market Square, as well as those on Prosta Street and Warszawska Street, and the doors of my grandfather's store were broken, the store windows were smashed, and the crowd rushed inside and robbed almost all the goods remaining in the store. However, the previous evening, when there was temporary calm in the Jewish quarter, Grandfather had organized a rescue operation with the help of his household members and relatives, whereby they managed to move a considerable amount of goods to a safe place. Had he not done so, the family would have been left without any means of livelihood, as was the case for many Jewish families who became paupers overnight because of the pogrom.

Terrified by the events unfolding on the streets and in the face of ever-increasing danger, my grandfather's family and neighbors discussed the current events, full of fear for their lives. After the goods had been rescued the previous night, Liberman—his closest neighbor and owner of the house where my family lived—came to visit my grandfather. He looked anxiously out the window and said, "I cannot understand why the Russian authorities tolerate this anarchy; after all, this crowd could turn against the Russians in a flash."

That day, my grandfather was very depressed and felt ill. He sat down opposite Liberman and said in a weak voice, "I think that the authorities must finally put an end to this anarchy. It is in their own best interests, but until this happens, many of us may lose our health or even our lives, because nobody can predict what this wild and rowdy mob may finally provoke. This is, sadly enough, the fate of our nation deprived of its own homeland." My grandfather continued:

> You see now, the only way out for us Jews is to strive to return to our old, lost country, to [Ottoman-ruled] Palestine, our historical homeland. Expelled from there centuries ago, we have every right to return and create a state there that would not only give us, the victims of pogroms, shelter, but also teach us to oppose our enemies, who will certainly not be absent there either. Only such a solution to the so-called Jewish question would bring future Jewish generations freedom and the right to develop in their own land without constant fear and discrimination. The Zionists are right, and I believe that someday in the future the plans to rebuild Jewish statehood in [Ottoman-ruled] Palestine will be realized and maybe with God's help my grandchildren will live to see that time come true.[39]

The words of my grandfather, Avrumele Górski, spoken in 1902 during the raging anti-Jewish pogrom in Częstochowa, proved to be prophetic. Forty-six years later, the Jewish State of Israel was established, and I, his grandson, lived to see the moment when an Israeli soldier with a rifle in his hand stood guard over the independence of the Jewish state and the security of its people, and was able to demonstrate more than once that the enemy, stretching out an armed hand to destroy the Jewish people, would be ingloriously defeated. By that time, however, a sea of Jewish blood and tears had already been shed.

Returning to the events of the tragic Częstochowa pogrom, hunger became a frequent companion in Jewish dwellings, as it was increasingly difficult to procure food. People were fearful of going out to buy groceries, lest they become victims of the criminals who roamed everywhere with impunity. Shopping was thus done under the cover of darkness and with considerable difficulty. The braver ones ran to neighboring Christian shopkeepers and paid exorbitant prices for the most basic provisions.

39 Kromołowski's grandfather echoes the ongoing debate of this period. Theodor Herzl, considered the father of the modern Zionist movement, advocated for Zionism in his 1896 treatise *Der Judenstaat* as what he saw as a modern "solution to the Jewish question." He argued that the creation of an independent Jewish state—preferably in the then Ottoman-ruled Palestine—would rescue Jews from the growing menace of antisemitism.

Around three o'clock in the afternoon on the third day of the pogrom, there was a breakthrough in the seemingly hopeless situation. The governor from Piotrków and the tsarist prosecutor from Warsaw both arrived in Częstochowa. A detachment of Cossacks,[40] renowned for their ruthlessness and cruelty, was brought in from Będzin. Sixty regular policemen arrived from Łódź. These forces, together with the local soldiers, police, and border guards, constituted a serious military corps capable of suppressing the pogrom. Apparently, the Russian authorities understood that the pogrom could, at any point, turn into a revolt against the tsarist authorities and therefore decided—not in the interest of the Jewish population but out of fear for their own skins—to quell the pogrom by force.

The main Russian forces were positioned at the exit of the New Market, toward First Avenue. The police ordered the hooligans to disperse—a call that was repeated many times but to no avail. The robbery of stores continued; the breaking into homes and beating of Jews did not cease. All of a sudden, someone in the crowd shouted, "Down with the Moscovites," while someone else intoned the Polish national anthem.[41] The mob took up the chant, and a hail of stones fell on the Russian soldiers standing with guns at their feet. A Russian command followed, and the troops fired several warning shots into the air. However, the stone throwing did not stop, and the crowd began to violently push the soldiers. A rifle salvo was then fired into the crowd, and at the same moment, Cossacks on horseback rushed through the gates of all the neighboring houses, beating people right and left with their hackles and sabers.

Finally, the crowd scattered, panic broke out, and whoever was able to do so ran away or hid from the charging Cossacks inside the gateways of the houses. Two dead and many wounded remained in the Market Square. Soldiers and policemen rushed forward, chasing the thugs and arresting many of them. Those arrested were led to the police station, called *cyrkuł*,[42]

40 In the nineteenth century and at the beginning of the twentieth century, the tsars used Cossacks extensively in military actions, especially in suppressing revolutionary activities. In this case, the pogrom was also perceived as a rebellious outburst that had to be suppressed.

41 The song "Jeszcze Polska nie zginęła" (Poland Is Not Yet Lost), also known as "Mazurek Dąbrowskiego" (Dąbrowski's Mazurka) was written in 1797 by Józef Wybicki and became the national anthem of Poland from 1927.

42 *Cyrkuł* comes from the French word *cercle*, meaning district—for example, an administrative or a police district. See Joachim Stefan Bartoszewicz, *Podręczny*

and subsequently imprisoned. Some hours later, there was complete calm. The streets and squares were deserted, with only military patrols and Cossacks on horseback roaming the town. That day, no one dared to venture outside, and the Jewish quarter was plunged into silence.

The following days brought further calm. Military and police patrols were still in sight, but the Cossacks were nowhere to be seen. Life began returning slowly to its normal state in the Jewish neighborhood. Hesitantly, people began to open their stores again, set up stalls, and trade in what they had left and what had been saved from robbery. Those bloody days experienced by the Jewish population of Częstochowa resulted in 120 looted and smashed Jewish stores, a tremendous number of beaten and wounded Jewish men and women, many plundered Jewish apartments and much ruined equipment, and most importantly—and worst of all—an ever-deeper chasm of hatred and enmity between the Polish and Jewish populations. In addition, two of the pogrom's instigators had been killed by soldiers, with many wounded taken to the hospital. While many of those arrested were prosecuted for battery and robbery, and some were deprived of the goods and household possessions they had stolen from the Jews, the treatment of the defendants was very lenient, and they ended up with minor sentences—no more than two or three months in jail.

The events in Częstochowa were not made public in either the local or foreign press.[43] Polish society also remained silent about the pogrom. However, it was impossible to erase the sad memory of these events from Jewish hearts and minds, nor the events of that first pogrom in the city from the pages of history. It represented a frightening manifestation of out-of-control antisemitism, and the strange solidarity between Polish-Christian society and the savage bands of social outcasts and criminals.

In August 1904, my grandfather, Abram Górski, died and was buried in the Jewish cemetery on Olsztyńska Street in Częstochowa. His death was a source of sorrow not only for the bereaved family but also for a large part of the Jewish community, which prided itself on this noble, honorable, and educated man, whose honesty and integrity were legendary. After my grandfather's death, the youngest of his sons,

słownik polityczny: do użytku posłów, urzędników państwowych, członków ciał samorządowych i wyborców (Warsaw: nakł. Księgarni Perzyński, Niklewicz i S-ka, 1923), p. 113.

43 See "Anti-Semitic Outbreak," *The New York Times*, September 14, 1902. On responses to the pogrom, see Mahler, *The Jews of Czestochowa* (Częstochowa, Poland), pp. 45–46.

Icchok, returned from Pabianice to the family home. He had graduated from a trade school, and for a time, he ran his father's haberdashery store. However, it soon turned out that he had much broader interests than dealing in trade and dry goods.

Influenced by the example of his peers, he quickly threw himself into political activity, joining the Zionist–Socialist Party of Jewish Workers,[44] which was very popular at that time among progressive Jewish youth. Very soon he became one of the leaders of this organization in Częstochowa, along with Józef Kruk, Broniatowski, Szymon Prusicki, Aleksander Tempel, and others.[45] The party strove to raise awareness among members of the Jewish proletariat and fight for socialist ideals, including to shorten the workday, improve the working conditions and wages of factory workers, and abolish exploitation of the working class. At the same time, among the broad masses of the Jewish population, they actively promoted and organized immigration to Mandatory Palestine, aiming to create a democratic Jewish state founded on socialist principles. Of course, this activity was illegal in the tsarist territories; operating secretly, its members were constantly exposed to persecution, and, if caught, were imprisoned or exiled to Siberia. The Jewish middle class also looked unfavorably on the young revolutionaries, who often came from wealthy and religious families.

Alexei Nikolayevich Michaluk—a so-called *prystav*,[46] or commissar, posted to the county of Częstochowa, responsible for the entire Old Town where the Jewish ghetto[47] of old Częstochowa was located—inflicted terror among this politicized youth and, incidentally, also among the local Jewish merchants. Michaluk was a man of powerful physique, with a red, bloodshot face and a prominent, blue-tinged nose. His small, gray, piercing eyes resembled those of a piglet and seemed to penetrate deeply when confronting an interlocutor or delinquent. When he spoke, he would stroke his long, drooping mustache. On Fridays,

44 The local group in Częstochowa followed the broader Workers-Zionist movement (Poalei Zion), and after 1919 reorganized as "United" following a Warsaw unification conference; the party later split and dwindled amid emigration, economic crisis, communist infiltration, and state repression.

45 On the Zionist–Socialist Workers' Party in Częstochowa, see Mahler, *The Jews of Czestochowa* (Częstochowa, Poland), pp. 115–122.

46 *Prystav* refers to a rank in the tsarist administrative system, in this case a police rank.

47 The word "ghetto" is used here to refer to the area where Jews resided—the Jewish quarter—rather than a place of forced residency.

he would visit the Jewish stores under the pretext of checking sanitary conditions. He usually entered the store supporting himself by the sides, lightly striking the shop counter with his knout[48] while speaking an odd mix of Russian, Polish, and Yiddish: "Nu, skażi mienia, far wus zdies tak brudno, czort z toboju Chana Mojsiejewicz! Ja tiebie muszę zakryt etyj zasranyj magazin. Ich mus sastawit protokol. Ja slieczał szto twoj Icek eto izwiestnyj socjalist i ja jewo w tiurmu! Ej wy Jewreje!" [Nu, tell me, the devil be with you, Chana Moisiejewich, why is your shop so dirty. I must shut down this shit business of yours. I must write a report. And also, it came to my ears that your Itzik is a well-known socialist, and I will put him in prison. You damned Jews!]

Upon hearing such a rant, the merchant in question, bowing low, would take a ruble from the folds of his shawl and, squinting kindly, would slip it into the Moskal's[49] hand, assuring him that his store was always clean. The merchant would then add that his Itzik has always been a pious and good fellow, who spends his days with the *rebbe*, studying Talmud, and that politics, God forbid, has never entered his head. Then, the *prystav*, placated with the bribe, would hide the ruble in the deep pocket of his huge pants and leave the store, still threatening the merchant with the knout and clanking his medals—among which was the Tsar's medal "for suppressing the Polish rebellion"—that proudly occupied a place of honor. And off he went to repeat exactly the same scene in the next Jewish store, usually with an equally successful result. In this manner, Michaluk regularly extracted considerable sums of money from the Jewish merchants. Yet, at times, he could also be extremely dangerous.

Surrounded by a swarm of spies, recruited mostly from all kinds of lowlifes, including the scum of the Jewish community, Michaluk was always well informed and aware of the political affiliations of the inhabitants of his district. He also knew who belonged to the Zionist–Socialist party. He did not hesitate to put many of its members in prison, sparing no effort to have them exiled to Siberia. He considered it his holy duty to catch the party leaders *in flagrante delicto* at an illegal meeting.

Icchok Górski and his comrades knew this and were thus wary of Michaluk and his informants. At one well-concealed meeting of the party leaders, one of its chairmen, Dr. Józef Kruk, suggested to his friends that they consider assassinating the detested *prystav*. After being approved,

48 This is referring to a type of whip historically used in Russia.

49 Moskal refers to a Russian (originally Muscovite), often used pejoratively in Polish/Ukrainian contexts to indicate an oppressor or outsider.

the implementation of such a plan was delegated to two members of the organization—employees of the celluloid plant, who volunteered to carry out the mission.

It was decided to carry out this dangerous, albeit carefully conceived, plan in the first days of December 1904. One sunny morning, Michaluk left his apartment in Zielona Street, situated in a calm and scarcely populated quarter of the city. No one else was out walking at such an early hour. A horse-drawn carriage approached from the direction of Teatralna Street,[50] and inside sat the two assassins, disguised as wealthy merchants dressed in furs and with magnificent fur hats on their heads. The merchants bowed politely at the sight of the slow-moving *prystav*, and when the carriage passed Michaluk—who did not suspect anything—they suddenly threw a grenade, which exploded with a loud bang. Michaluk fell to the ground, while the coachman—also a party comrade in disguise—spurred the horses forward, and the carriage swiftly disappeared around a bend in the street. The assassination attempt was only partially successful. Michaluk was quite seriously wounded but recovered after several months of treatment in a hospital. The next day, the assassins were sent abroad by the party via Herby, near Częstochowa, a Russian–German border point.

After his recovery, Michaluk was transferred to Sosnowiec.[51] However, this coup achieved its intended effect. The party's esteem in the Częstochowa area increased considerably, and the tsarist police were pale with fear. As a result, they increased the local military garrison and fortified police forces. News of the assassination attempt echoed throughout the country, inspiring hope for an improvement in the political situation in Congress Kingdom of Poland—the Russian part of divided

50 Today this area includes al. Wolności and Kościuszki (Liberty and Kościuszko Avenues).

51 While an account of this specific assassination attempt was not widely reported, there were a number of attempts on senior police officers in Częstochowa during 1904–1905. On November 12, 1904, chief of police Alexander von Nehrlich was stabbed and died a few weeks later. See the Polish daily newspaper *Górnoślązak*, January 8, 1905. See also the online article written by historian Juliusz Sętowski, "Człowiek roku 1904—Wincenty Makowski," Co/Gdzie/Kiedy W Częstochowie Portal kulturalny, https://www.cgk.czestochowa.pl/blog/artykuly-autorzy (accessed August 18, 2025). On June 24, 1905, his successor Popow was on his way home when he was deafened by a bomb thrown in his direction. See the Piotrków newspaper Tydzień, 1905, no. 27, p. 3; Tomasz Andrzej Nowak, "Częstochowa na łamach piotrkowskiego 'Tygodnia' (1873–1906)," *Ziemia Częstochowska*, 45, pp. 61–129, specifically p. 110.

Poland[52]—and the living conditions of the proletariat. In Częstochowa, many large and small manufacturing plants were in operation at that time, mainly in the metal and celluloid industry. A considerable number of Jewish workers were employed in Wajnberg's celluloid-products factory, Landau's celluloid factory, as well as Markusfeld's so-called Malarnia Painter's House, producing paint and wallpaper.[53]

There and in many other factories, Icchok Górski and his comrades campaigned to raise awareness and organized trade unions, which put more and more demands on the employers to improve the workers' conditions and standard of living. If the employers refused to accept these demands, they threatened with a strike. The period preceding the revolution of 1905 was stormy,[54] and Icchok Górski appeared at many workers' rallies, which typically resulted in public demonstrations. He was a celebrated figure among the Częstochowa proletariat, but also well known to the tsarist police.[55]

52 See footnote 6 in this chapter.

53 Many Jewish families, such as the Geislers, Grossmans, Kohns, Landaus, Oderfelds, and Markusfelds, contributed to the development of industry, commerce, and banking in Częstochowa. See Jakób (Yaakov) Lewit, "Industry in Częstochowa—Its Creation and Development," in M. Schutzman, *Sefer Czenstochow*, vol. 1 (Hebrew and Yiddish) (Jerusalem, 1967/68), pp. 401–412. For an English translation, see https://www.jewishgen.org/yizkor/Czestochowa6/cze1_401.html (accessed August 18, 2025); Jerzy Mizgalski, "The Political Identity of Jews in the Nineteenth and Twentieth Centuries as Reflected in the History, Heritage, and Cultural Identity of Częstochowa Jews," in *The Jews of Częstochowa–Coexistence–Holocaust–Memory*, Conference Proceedings of the American Association for Polish-Jewish Studies (Częstochowa: Wyższa Szkoła Pedagogiczna w Częstochowie, in collaboration with the Archiwum Państwowe w Częstochowie and the Żydowski Instytut Historyczny w Warszawie, 2004), p. 45.

54 The Russian Revolution of 1905 forced Tsar Nicholas II to introduce government reforms and attempt a transition from autocracy to constitutional monarchy. Social and political discontent affected Congress Poland and other areas under Russian rule. On January 9 (Julian calendar) or January 22 (Gregorian calendar), 1905, a peaceful demonstration marching toward the Winter Palace in St. Petersburg was met with gunfire from tsarist troops, resulting in a massacre of the demonstrators, a day known as Bloody Sunday.

55 The tsarist regime established the Okhrana (Department for Protecting the Public Security and Order) in 1881 following the assassination of Tsar Alexander II. This secret police force was tasked with combating political terrorism and monitoring revolutionary movements throughout the Russian Empire until its collapse in 1917.

It was common knowledge that Górski was one of the organizers of the assassination attempt on Michaluk. He was also known for being one of the party's activists who had formed a workers' self-defense group with a considerable stock of small arms and ammunition at their disposal. The weapons warehouse was well hidden and known only to the top management, which included Górski. The weapons were acquired through Polish activists of the PPS (Polish Socialist Party), with whom the Zionist socialists remained in close contact and cooperation.[56] The weapons were brought to the Old Town from the suburb of Jasna Góra, mostly by women, hidden in food baskets. Sometimes, at the request of her brother, my mother carried weapons for the party in this way—in great secrecy from the rest of the family.

In the spring of 1905, the long-expected Russo-Japanese War broke out. In an attempt to launch a rescue campaign for the besieged Port Arthur, Russian troops were repulsed in several bloody battles, the most important of which was the Battle of Mukden (March 1–10, 1905). The Russian fleet, which had made its way to the Pacific Ocean, was destroyed in the famous Battle of Tsushima on May 28, 1905. Thanks to the diplomatic skills of the Russian minister Sergei Witte, the warring parties—under strong pressure from the United States—ended the hostilities at meetings held in Portsmouth, New Hampshire, on September 5, 1905. While Russia emerged from the war with honor, it was still forced to withdraw from Manchuria and cede part of Sakhalin to Japan, give up the tenancy of Port Arthur, and agree to and recognize Japan's influence in Korea.

The fiasco of the war intensified the revolutionary turmoil within the country, forcing Tsar Nicholas II to declare the principles of the Constitution on October 30. Not satisfied with this step, which they considered inadequate, the revolutionary parties called for a general strike that not only included blue-collar workers but also railroad and postal officials. All means of communication were brought to a complete standstill. There was social disorder in the rural areas of the Baltic provinces; in Finland as well as Congress Poland, violent revolutionary and separatist–nationalist sentiment was also strengthened.

56 The Polish Socialist Party (Polska Partia Socjalistyczna, PPS), founded in 1892, was a major political movement advocating socialism, workers' rights, and Polish independence during the partitions. It played a significant role in political activism, including strikes and uprisings, and was influential in regaining Polish sovereignty in 1918.

Against this background, sociopolitical changes and revolutionary parties with socialist leanings, such as the PPS, the Bund, and the Zionist–Socialist Party, appeared in Częstochowa—similar to the rest of the country—and significantly intensified their political activity. Rallies, demonstrations, and strikes were an almost daily occurrence. Essentially, this entire period of turmoil was the revolution of 1905.

There was also a general strike in Częstochowa, which encompassed not only public transport, railroads, and post offices, but it also shut down offices, factories, numerous institutions, and the school system. Pupils in governmental high schools tore the buttons off their school uniforms on which the tsarist Russian eagle was engraved, demanding to introduce a broad school reform to include abolishing the existing harsh discipline, ending the system of spying on pupils, and introducing Polish language classes. They also demanded political reforms, such as democratization and the inclusion of representatives of all population sectors in the Russian empire in the parliament and state institutions.

The violent political movements led to the establishment of the first Duma (parliament) in 1906. However, the parties in this Duma presented such a radical front that it was dissolved after a few months. The Russian government was then taken over by Stolypin,[57] who dissolved the second Duma in 1907, and held elections for a third Duma based on a revised electoral law. The third Duma consisted mostly of government parties. In an effort to strip the radical intelligentsia of its influence over the peasantry, Stolypin carried out a land reform that allowed peasants to own land individually, but he restricted press freedom, ruthlessly repressed revolutionaries, and organized pogroms against Jews.[58] The victory of Stolypin's reactionary

57 Pyotr Arkadyevich Stolypin (1862–1911) was a Russian politician who served as the third prime minister and the interior minister of the Russian Empire from 1906 until his assassination in 1911. Known for his efforts to suppress revolutionary activity and implement agrarian reforms, Stolypin aimed to modernize Russia by strengthening the peasantry through land ownership reforms, fostering a loyal middle class. Despite his initiatives, he faced strong opposition from revolutionaries and conservatives and was assassinated in 1911 by Dmitry Bogrov, a revolutionary of Jewish origin.

58 The relationship between the Jews and Stolypin was complex. Stolypin was, in fact, determined to ease the conditions of Jews in the Russian Empire. Thus, in August 1906, his government intended to pass a bill removing many anti-Jewish restrictions, but the tsar refused to ratify it. See Polonsky, *The Jews in Poland and Russia*, vol. 2, pp. 63–64; Abraham Ascher, "Prime Minister PA Stolypin and His 'Jewish' Adviser," *Journal of Contemporary History*, 30:3 (1995), pp. 513–532.

measures resulted in increased Russian nationalism in Congress Poland as well, which meant that in Polish territories, widespread persecution of the people occurred, followed by many new serious hardships.

During this period of heightened political and social conflict, deep despair prevailed among Jewish merchants, stallholders, and fruit sellers in Częstochowa. Adding to their grief was a gang of Jewish thugs who terrorized the lives of the merchants, extorting substantial sums from shopkeepers and stallholders in exchange for protection and the possibility of making a living peacefully. A few mobsters would come to the store or stall—usually on market days—and demand money. If the merchants refused, a long whistle would be blown and a whole gang of their comrades would appear, scatter the goods on the ground and trample them underfoot, overturn the stall or demolish the store, before finally taking the goods with them as they disappeared.

The merchants usually, and without hesitation, paid the demanded ransom out of fear of these far worse consequences—their lesson learned from previous traumas. Moreover, this extortion was carried out with complete impunity, because the gangsters collaborated with the tsarist police. The gang spied on behalf of the police, reported on upcoming party meetings and plans for various political actions, and gave the police the names of the party leaders, who were subsequently arrested. In this way, the Szliwa band—as it was known among the Jewish population of Częstochowa after its leader, Icik Szliwa—had on its conscience many Zionist–Socialist Party activists who were active in the local area. Szymon Beker and Kopel Gerichter, among others, were sentenced to several years of imprisonment. At the request of Icchok Górski, the party court sentenced the leaders of this band—Icik Szliwa and Moszek Paca—to death. Górski organized the plan to crush the gang and carry out the party's sentence. My mother related the course of events to me.

One day in May 1905, a group of fighters from the workers' self-defense group—recruited mostly from workers at the Wajnberg factory—under the command of Icchok Górski surrounded the Old Market Square in Częstochowa. The fighters were armed with revolvers and clubs, and waited for Szliwa's gang to withdraw to safety after having extorted their ransom. One of the band leaders—Moszek Paca—approached, walking along the sidewalk in the direction of Lichter's leather store. He walked slowly with his hands in his pockets and his cap pulled low over his eyes. Two fighters standing on that sidewalk let Paca pass and then fired two revolver shots at him at close range. One bullet hit him in the hand and the other in the neck. Paca fell down, bleeding profusely. After a moment he got up, walked a few steps, and fell to the ground again. Then one of the fighters fired a third, fatal shot at him. Moszek Paca died on the spot.

The leader of the band, Icik Szliwa, noticed that something had happened and hid among the peasants who were trading cattle at the market. When the police arrived soon after, Szliwa ran out and sought protection among the policemen, who surrounded him and led him out of harm's way. For the next few days, Szliwa ventured out only when accompanied by police officers, before departing for somewhere in Silesia. A few months later, however, he returned to Częstochowa and, with renewed confidence, stopped relying on police protection. Then, one day in August, the secret Jewish militia caught up with him in the street and fired shots, killing this traitor who for many years had been the terror of the city—especially of the Jewish population.

After the deaths of Szliwa and Paca, the activities of this terrorist gang came to an end, and its remaining members left the city for fear of retaliation from the secret Jewish militia. The police, despite diligent searches, did not find any trace of the fighters who had carried out the party's sentence to execute Szliwa and Paca. The liquidation of this dangerous band was one of the significant successes achieved by the Zionist–Socialist Party against the backdrop of the revolutionary turmoil of 1905.

After the general strike, Kruk and Górski called a meeting of the party's executive committee in one of their apartments on Targowa Street to discuss the matter of joining a planned demonstration and rally organized by the PPS. It was a warm late September evening, and the windows of the ground-floor apartment, where the meeting was held, were wide open. The party's delegates were beginning to arrive. Suddenly, Hela Birman, a brave and dedicated comrade who was standing in the street below to safeguard the meeting, came to the window and shouted that policemen were approaching before quickly disappearing into the darkness. Those already present quickly gathered up the papers lying on the table and began to flee, some through the door, others through the window, onto the street. Almost everyone managed to escape, but the police—who had already managed to surround the street and the house where the meeting was held—caught Icchok Górski, who was about to jump out of the window. He received several blows to the head with a rifle butt, lost consciousness, and was taken to jail. The family was filled with despair—Górski was in danger of being sent to Siberia. Immediate efforts were made to free him from temporary arrest.

Since it was possible to bribe the tsarist police to settle the matter, the rubles poured in. Górski's sister Sheva (my mother)—then twenty-two years old and on whose young head the upkeep of the house rested after the recent death of her father (my grandfather) Abram Górski, and who was mainly occupied with running the store—went to the governorate in Piotrków, where she attempted to secure her brother's release. With the help of Jewish intermediaries who were well-versed in the workings of the office, she tried to present the foiled party meeting as an ordinary social gathering of a few friends, who, by the way, were almost all sons of wealthy merchant families. Most likely, these interventions and efforts would have been in vain, because my uncle was known to the police as an avowed socialist and party activist. But Icchok Górski was incredibly lucky. Exactly at that time, a son was born to Tsar Nikolai II, and amnesty was proclaimed for political convicts in honor of the *tsarevich*[59] throughout the entire Russian empire. Thanks to this general amnesty, Górski was released nearly two months after his arrest.

While in prison in Piotrków, Górski met several influential activists from the PPS. Thanks to them, he was able to secure an excellent job as a clerk with the Vienna-Herby railway company following his release. He was the first Jewish railroad official on Polish soil. While working at the border station in Herby, near Częstochowa, he was able to organize arms smuggling on behalf of the party and took charge of smuggling endangered members of allied socialist parties to Germany and Austria. The National Democracy circles in Częstochowa could not accept the fact that a Jew held such a prominent position in the railroad administration, and in one of their publications, the *Bocian*, they included a caricature of Górski with a large nose and a bent back, wearing an official railroad cap. The drawing was accompanied by a vicious antisemitic poem.

Sometime later, Górski, whose revolutionary activity on the Herby railroad was already known to the tsarist police—especially because he organized the first trade union of railroad workers on Polish territory—was dismissed from his job, despite the efforts of one of the company's senior officials, Balabanov, a sympathizer of the revolutionary movement. In 1907, Górski left for Estonia and entered the Faculty of Law at the University of Dorpat.[60] There, Górski was again drawn into political work, but despite agitation from his colleagues who were part of the Social Democracy of the Kingdom of Poland and Lithuania, he remained faithful to Zionist–Socialist ideals, maintaining lively contact with an activist from Warsaw as well as with party comrades

59 A title referring to the male heir of the tsar.

60 Modern-day city of Tartu.

who remained in Częstochowa, such as Dr. J. Kruk, Aron Singalewski, Rafał Federman, and others. He wrote the following to his good friend Kruk in Yiddish:

> Dear Józef No. 1 [this was how a prominent party activist was addressed in political circles],
>
> I breathe freely here in Dorpat. We gather completely openly and without any repression from the tolerant Estonian administration. I am in very close contact with socialist activists from the SDKPiL, and we have endless discussions with Russian socialists from the Social Democratic Party of Workers of Russia who reside here. I have met a very interesting and very promising young Russian student, L. Bronstein [Trotsky],[61] whom I admire for his ideological fervor, vivid intelligence, and extraordinary oratory aptitude. However, I cannot come to terms with his radical views and ideas of permanent world revolution based on the dictatorship of the proletariat. He and his comrades are striving to bring about a world revolution by violent means and to seize power by a bloody coup. This could lead to incredible bloodshed and the eradication of the educated class. A vacuum will be created, and then what? Although a Jew, the Jewish cause does not concern him at all. He is opposed to Zionism and counteracts it in all its forms and claims that the creation of a Jewish state in [Ottoman-ruled] Palestine, even with a socialist face, is a daydream and sheer anachronistic fantasy. While he is ready to respect our views, he maintains that with time they must become more radical and merge with SDKPiL. What do you think? Greetings to all comrades and friends.
>
> Your Icchok[62]

Due to a lack of money to continue his studies in Dorpat, my uncle Icchok was forced to return to Poland and, for a time, lived and worked in Łódź. Finally, at the request of his party comrades, he returned to Częstochowa

61 Leon Trotsky (born Lev Davidovich Bronstein, 1879–1940) was a Marxist revolutionary, theorist, and key leader in the Russian Revolution of 1917. He played a central role in founding the Red Army and was a leading figure in the early Soviet government. After losing in a power struggle with Stalin, he was exiled and later assassinated in Mexico.

62 The author reconstructed the content of this letter based on what he was told.

and once again threw himself into the hazardous currents of political activism.

At that time, the city was shaken by a serious fire that had engulfed Landau's factory. Five young Jewish women employed in the production of celluloid toys were killed, and a large number of severely burned workers were hospitalized.[63] The fire broke out as a result of the complete disregard for basic fire safety measures by the factory owners. The flammable celluloid caused the fire to consume the entire factory in an instant. It burned like a torch. The girls were working on the upper floors of the building and could not escape to safety. The Jewish socialist parties in Częstochowa organized both a funeral for the victims and a general strike by Jewish workers of the local industrial plants. The funeral essentially became an extended general workers' demonstration.

During this funeral, which was attended by thousands, rallies and demonstrations were held with flags, placards, and banners. The funeral procession passed through the Jewish district on its way to the Jewish cemetery on Olsztyńska Street. Activists from workers' organizations addressed the crowds over the open graves, and among them, Icchok Górski spoke on behalf of the Zionist–Socialist Party. This speech, delivered in front of a huge crowd of striking workers, was widely quoted by the city's inhabitants and, naturally, was brought to the attention of the tsarist administration. In his speech, Górski publicly spoke out against the Stolypin reactionary measures and the tsarist regime, and demanded reforms and improved working conditions for factory workers.

And so, a few days after the strike and the funeral, the police arrested Górski. Deportation to Siberia was seemingly inevitable. Again, all possible means were used to save my uncle, and the party began to act. They managed to bribe the prison doctor, and Górski was taken to the Panna Maria Hospital, located on Second Avenue, next to the railroad bridge. It was easier to visit him here, and the party leadership often held meetings at his bedside. They decided to take advantage of the fact that there was no police supervision at Górski's bedside—he was declared "severely ill"—to prepare his escape abroad, which was his only available option. His political crime was clear, and the sentence of deportation to Siberia hung over my uncle's head.

63 According to Mark Kiel, five women and two men were killed. They may have been Poles, since Landau had switched from employing some Jews to only employing Poles. See Kiel, *The Jews of Częstochowa*, p. 50.

Arrangements were made for Górski to be placed in a separate ward. He was outfitted with street clothing and a fur coat, which were carefully concealed. One winter evening, Górski, dressed in the elegant clothes, donning a wealthy man's fur coat and fur hat, pressed down on the door handle to his hospital room and quietly walked out into the corridor. It was visitors' day, and the hospital was full of people visiting their sick relatives and friends until late in the evening. Górski looked like a wealthy, well-dressed merchant, so it did not occur to anyone that he was a patient—let alone a prisoner under special hospital supervision. The nurse who had been commissioned by the hospital management to care for and observe this sick man had been bribed and sent elsewhere on purpose at the time of the escape. Also bribed was the hospital doorman guarding the front door. Górski walked down the corridor toward the exit with such confidence and nonchalance that the doorman didn't even notice him, taking him for one of the visitors.

Right next to the hospital building, a party comrade and my mother, Stefa Górska, were waiting in a carriage. Uncle got in, and the carriage set off, joining the normal traffic on this always busy main artery of the city, and headed toward the train station located next to the hospital. There was no need to wait long at the station, as the hospital escape had been organized so meticulously that there was a train ready to leave immediately for Herby. The whole group calmly entered the train compartment, and everyone breathed a sigh of relief when the train departed. It was a success. At the station in Herby, it was time to say goodbye. With the help of smugglers who were well trained in such expeditions, Górski—equipped with a false passport—was successfully smuggled across the green border[64] to nearby Lubliniec, which was part of the German Reich at the time.[65] From there, without any interference and with a false passport in his pocket, he arrived in Vienna, where, after completing his university studies, he held several prominent positions at a banking firm. There, he also met his wife and party comrade Hela Birman, with whom he had two children: a daughter Irena and a son Julian.

64 Green border (*zielona granica*) refers to an unguarded stretch of a state border, typically through forests, the kind used for clandestine crossings.

65 This is referring to the Second Reich—the German Empire between the unification of Germany in 1871 and the establishment of the Weimar Republic in 1918.

CHAPTER TWO

MY FATHER'S ROOTS

During this politically charged period, an ironware merchant lived in Częstochowa. He was a tall, heavyset, and powerful Jew who did not have an easy life and barely earned enough money to support his large family: his wife Udla and their eight children—three sons and five daughters. Much of his distress stemmed from the prospect of dowries for his daughters, without which, as we know, it was very difficult for a Jewish girl to find a decent husband. This merchant's hair was bright red, like a carrot. He also had a long red beard, lightly streaked with gray, and from under his thick, bushy eyebrows, two bright, squinty green eyes peered out at the world.

The whole family lived in three rooms on the middle floor of a house owned by Fimsi—commonly nicknamed "Devil"—on Warszawska Street, not far from Plac Trzech Krzyży (Three Crosses Square). The merchant referred to himself as a trader in the iron business, although this occupation was a little unusual for those times and was not yet firmly established. He did not have a store, and the goods he traded, as he used to say, "stayed with the people."[1] He was known among the townspeople of

1 He stored his goods with others.

Częstochowa as *der gayler Yume* (red-haired Benjamin), and his trading activity was based on the fact that he had excellent knowledge of the area and good connections. He knew which of the numerous large and small manufacturers in the city urgently needed a metal press, steam boiler, milling machine, lathe machine, or any other equipment for their plant, and also who had similar machines—used, of course—for sale. Then, the transaction was simple and required only two steps: to convince both the person who had the machine to sell it cheaply and the person who wanted to acquire the machine to buy it for a high price. And our red-haired Benjamin had mastered, developed, and perfected this ability to sell.

He also possessed other qualities invaluable to his profession. He had a phenomenal memory and could fluently recite entire verses by heart from the holy Torah, and he also had an uncommon wit and ability to put any misanthropist in a good mood. Thanks to his near-fluent Polish, he was able to recruit Christian clientele. He also had deep Talmudic knowledge, which he had acquired during his time in yeshivot as a youth in Bolesławiec, where he was born.

His late father Kalman from Bolesławiec, of blessed memory, used to tell him: "Remember, son, our holy Torah is such an impenetrable treasury of all knowledge, that the man who possesses this knowledge is worth as if he had the gold of the entire world at his disposal." So it was for this reason that he considered himself a wealthy man, although there were times when, instead of stuffing himself with a wonderful carp, he and his family had nothing to eat on Saturday but miserable herrings. Nevertheless, his good humor never abandoned him, he was always full of ideas and positive thoughts, and a smile often crowned his red-bearded face.

The Jewish New Year (Rosh Hashana) and the Day of Atonement (Yom Kippur) were approaching. It was accepted that for these holidays, every self-respecting Jewish family had to stock up on a decent number of fine hens and roosters. The poultry was used for two purposes: to feed a large family (may no evil eye harm it), but also to fulfill the ritual of sacrifice (*khapores*),[2] because on Yom Kippur, God writes in his book of judgments who will live and who will die in the coming year. According to custom, pious Jews on Yom Kippur eve take a hen or a rooster, circle it around their head several times, and read a prayer in which they ask that God, in His mercy, will grant life to the praying Jew and, instead, sentence the bird held in his hand to death; the unfortunate bird must die anyway to

2 In Hebrew, *kappara* (pl. *kapparot*) meaning the expiation of sins.

feed the family with its tasty meat.[3] So, there was a great demand for fowl during that season. The peasants coming to the city to sell their wares in the farmers' markets would therefore hike up the prices and try to sell their merchandise at an exorbitant profit.

This year, however, Benjamin decided to put an end to these villagers' greed and their exploitation of the religious custom to boost their earnings. Early one morning, he gathered his family together and went with his wife and daughters to the Warsaw turnpike,[4] through which peasants with hens had to pass on their way to the city's markets. There, after giving them specific instructions, he lined up his wife and daughters by the roadside, each at a distance of a few dozen meters from one another. He himself stood further away—the last one in the row.

A peasant woman approached, carrying baskets full of clucking poultry in both hands. Benjamin's daughter Fajgla approached her and said, "So, pretty woman, you have roosters for sale? And how much do you want for this rooster?"

"Let's have a ruble for these two roosters," replied the peasant woman.

Fajgla took the two roosters in her hands, waved them over her head, and said, "No, my dear. I won't buy them, because they have already been swung!"

The peasant woman looked around with bulging eyes, not understanding what the Jewess had just said. She put both roosters back in the basket and continued on her way. The same conversation repeated itself a few dozen steps further on where Benjamin's wife stood. She also spoke to the woman, and, after looking at the roosters and swinging them over her head several times, she said, "No, I will not buy them, they have already been swung." Similar scenes continued to play out even further away, where Benjamin's other daughters—and he had five in total—stood. Each one repeated the same adage: "They have already been swung."

The peasant woman, greatly confused, was convinced that her poultry had some major defect, making it unsuitable to sell for the Jewish holidays, which she knew were approaching and therefore Jews should be eager to buy all kinds of poultry. Finally, the villager was about to reach Benjamin—the originator of the idea. Approaching the peasant woman with a confident

3 According to the custom, the sins of a person committed during the year are symbolically transferred to a fowl.

4 Warszawska Street in Częstochowa begins at Ignacy Daszyński Square (Plac Daszyńskiego) in the city center and runs in a northeastern direction through Stare Miasto (Old Town) and Wyczerpy-Aniołów.

step and without any introduction, he took the best two roosters out of the basket, weighed them in his hand, looked at them carefully, and said:

"You know, housewife, they have already been well swung!"

The woman looked at the red-haired Jew with obvious embarrassment and asked, "And what does it mean, that they have been swung?"

"They are already useless for Jews for the feast, because someone has already swung them over his head," Benjamin explained with conviction.

"I already know that they have been swung," said the somewhat dumbfounded peasant woman. "Some Jewish women were standing on the road here and were shaking and spinning them, but maybe the merchant would at least give 25 kopeyki for them?"

"How many birds do you have there?" Benjamin asked.

"I have five hens and five roosters," answered the shaken peasant woman in an uncertain voice.

"So, I can buy all these already swung roosters and hens for half a ruble," said Benjamin. "Well? Want it or not?"

"If you say they have been swung already, then let it be for half a ruble," replied the woman, bewildered and already tired of this bargaining.

The red-haired Benjamin took the half ruble from his pocket, pressed it into the woman's hand, placed the fowl in a sack he had prepared in advance, threw it on his back, and said, "Well, you are lucky, because for me it does not matter whether they have been swung or not." And off he went on his way, groaning under the weight of the birds fluttering in the sack.

New Market Square, Częstochowa.

The story about the roosters spread around town, eliciting much-needed laughter among the Jewish citizens during those troubled and turbulent times.

Apparently, God had written in his book of predictions for the coming year an auspicious judgment for Benjamin and his family. A month after the Jewish New Year feast, he was contacted by a young and already very wealthy industrialist by the name of Alfred Kohn,[5] who was expanding his paper factory located on the shores of the Warta River, next to Strażacka Street. Benjamin, smiling and pleased with himself as usual, was greeted by Kohn who was seated at his spacious desk in the paper mill's office.

"I know that you are a trader and broker in the purchase and sale of various machines. Now I urgently need a large steam boiler and a steam engine for my factory. Can you deliver these machines to me, and, if so, when?"

Benjamin looked at the young industrialist, stroked his red beard, and asked, "At how many atmospheres in pressure should this boiler be set?"

"I need a 100-atmosphere steam boiler and a steam-driven piston or turbine engine," replied Kohn.

"Is it enough for you to have a turbine engine with a valve gear, or must it have slide-joints?" asked Benjamin professionally, well versed in the details of his profession.

"It's enough to have a valve gear, as long as both machines are in good condition," said Kohn.

Benjamin bowed his head slightly before looking at Kohn, and said, "All right, Mr. Kohn, I have the machines and can deliver them to you within a month, but I can't give you a definite price yet! For now, you can give me a deposit, let's say 2,000 rubles. But I must tell you in advance that such machines are quite expensive."

"All right," said Kohn. "Write me a receipt."

Kohn opened the desk cabinet, took out a bundle of 100-ruble

5 Alfred Kohn (1880–1943) was a technology engineer and co-owner of the Paper and Mills Factory in Częstochowa, Poland. He was actively involved in social initiatives, including supporting the Dobroczynność Charitable Society for Jews and participating in the Częstochowa branch of the Polish Red Cross. Following the outbreak of World War II in 1939, Kohn fled to the Soviet Union, where he died on November 1, 1943, in Korostielówka, Mołotarski District. See Juliusz Sętkowski, ed., *Częstochowa Jews: A Biographical Dictionary* (Częstochowa: Muzeum Częstochowskie, 2020), English translation by Andrew Rajcher, https://www.czestochowajews.org/history/biographical-dictionary/ (accessed November 19, 2025), p. 240.

banknotes, counted 2,000 rubles, put away the receipt signed by Benjamin, and handed the redheaded merchant the fresh, rustling notes. Benjamin swallowed hard, his throat completely dry from excitement. He put the money in his pocket with the casual ease of a seasoned financier and thought to himself, "Good God, I've never had such a sum of money in my hand before. And anyway, where am I going to get the machines that this assimilated Jewish *shaigets*,[6] wants from me? God give me strength to keep my composure here and not shout out loud in joy!"

But he smiled at Kohn, shook his hand goodbye, and said, "Mr. Kohn, I will report to you within two weeks to discuss the matter of transporting the machines and their final price."

Then he bowed and left the industrialist's office with a shaky step. He walked home mightily excited, thinking, "Is this a dream or reality? Should he pinch his cheeks to be sure? Benjamin, Kalman's son, do you know what 2,000 rubles and the prospect of a great income mean today in these hard times? After all, you can buy a cow for twelve rubles, and for 1,000 rubles you can buy a lord's manor and a couple of dozen morgens of arable land."

Deep in thought, he arrived home. He sat down heavily on a chair at the table, supporting his head in his hands, and remained motionless. His wife Udla anxiously regarded her always-cheerful husband, and thought, "Maybe, God forbid, he is sick?" She gave her husband a glass of tea, and after Benjamin had taken two sips, he related the whole story of the deal he had made with Kohn. They talked and deliberated for a long time. The next day, Benjamin left for Dąbrowa Górnicza,[7] where he had friends who were merchants and brokers. Some time later, the redheaded merchant regaled the whole story of this complicated but fortunate transaction to his friend, Jossele Bem, sparing no detail and concluding, "You see, my dear Jossele, with God's will, also a stick can shoot, as it already happened in the Sinai desert when Moses obtained water from a rock by a stroke of his stick, to satiate the thirsty 600,000 fleeing slaves."[8]

"My prayers for a good new year were apparently heard, because in Dąbrowa, after much concern and endeavors, I managed to purchase from one of the mines the steam boiler and steam engine that Kohn needed.

6 A non-Jewish man (Yiddish), often derogatory.

7 Dąbrowa Górnicza is located some 60 kilometers south of Częstochowa.

8 Exodus 17:1–7 recounts the episode in which the Israelites, traveling through the desert, complained of thirst, and God instructed Moses to draw water from a rock to provide for the people.

The machines were in quite good condition and had just been taken out of production in the mining industry because the management had purchased a more modern machine in Germany. I can only tell you that after paying the cost of buying and transporting all these machines, I had 4,000 rubles left on the clean side of the business, may I be so healthy along with my wife and my children. But now I'm so tired and overworked, and I feel so old after the hardships and tension of these last two months, that I must go to the magistrate straightaway!"

Puzzled, Jossele Bem looked at Benjamin and asked, "What do you mean? I don't understand! What does all your business and your fatigue have to do with the magistrate?"

Benjamin, staring at Jossele with his merry green eyes and stroking his red beard, said, "Well, I'm still a redhead now, but I feel that I'm getting old and soon will be gray after what I've been through lately. So I need to register at the magistrate's office to let them know that I'm the same man who was first a redhead, then went gray, and eventually ended up with a white beard and all white hair. When a man's hair color changes, he becomes a completely different person!"

That's just how this man was, Benjamin son of Kalman—or Kalmy as they called him in Yiddish. And this was my grandfather, Benjamin Kromołowski, a well-known iron merchant in Częstochowa.

Shortly afterward, with the money he had earned from Kohn, my grandfather purchased from Henig—a wealthy man living on Sportowa Street—a large plot of land with a house opposite Ogrodowa Street. There he established a new enterprise, a warehouse for old iron and non-ferrous metals, offering everything in the field of applied metallurgy—from construction iron and secondhand machinery to screws, rivets, and bolts of every size and design. The ironware was laid out in whole heaps, partly under a roof and partly in the open air, and people could wander among these goods until they found what they needed. There were all sorts of rails, filament wires, and ramshackle machines, but also different metal plates, sheet metal, corrugated plates—anything a buyer of ironware could want. The business prospered and, in time, my grandfather became a wealthy man. As he had predicted, he quickly turned gray. He grew old but remained a busy businessman who told jokes at every opportunity, laced with the occasional Hebrew verse from the Talmud.

But let us not overlook the chronological course of events, nor forget that we are now talking about the early years of the twentieth century. Częstochowa's Jewish population had only recently been shaken by a tragic pogrom when news reached them of a new pogrom in Białystok that had terrible consequences and numerous Jewish victims.[9] The Jewish population of Częstochowa lived in constant fear lest the catastrophic events, which were still fresh in their memory, would happen again.

At that time, my grandfather was still busy establishing his ironware business and had little time to attend to his children, who were already growing up. Of his three sons, Szyja and Adolf were twins. They were as similar to each other as two drops of water, and it was extremely difficult to tell them apart. They were both red-haired, dressed alike, and were the same height—only their temperament was different. Szyja was cheerful and jovial—just like his father—enjoyed playing cards, and used a billiards cue so masterfully that few could match him in the game, which was very popular at the time. On the other hand, Adolf—who was called Abia at home—was a quiet, placid, less versatile young man. Although he was not as outgoing as his brother, he, too, was by no means averse to the pleasures of the world, and was very fond of billiards and cards. He was much less interested in books, both secular and religious.

One day, Adolf agreed to play billiards at Kalma Rajcher's place on First Avenue. He had been persuaded to compete against Majorczyk, a local representative of the golden youth, who was extremely adept at billiards and played the game professionally as one of his other—rather suspicious—sources of income. The game was to be played for money: half a ruble per game. Adolf was playing very poorly and was losing game after game. He had already lost a few rubles. Wanting to take revenge and win back what he had lost, he played on and on with pitiful results. It looked like it was turning into a real disaster—after all, a ruble in those days was quite a sum of money.

Just married, Adolf's young wife was waiting at home for money to do her shopping for the approaching *Shabbes* (Sabbath). The game was being watched by a few spectators, among them the young Jotuś Szaja, the son of a metalwork factory owner in Częstochowa. Jotuś Szaja was a great friend of Szyja, Adolf's twin. Seeing what was going on, he quietly sneaked out of the billiard room to look for Szyja to tell him about Adolf's debacle, and to try in some way to prevent any further downfall. He quickly found him sitting in a nearby café. Szaja had a little stutter,

9 During the pogroms in Białystok—June 14–16, 1906 (Gregorian calendar) or June 1–3 (Julian calendar)—estimates of fatalities range between 70 and 200 killed. According to Polonsky 200 were killed, and 700 were injured. See Polonsky, *The Jews in Poland and Russia*, vol. 2, p. 62.

which was more pronounced when he was nervous. Reaching Szyja, he grabbed him by the hand.

"Listen, your brother A-A-A..."

"What?" Szyja asked impatiently.

"Adolf," Jotuś Szaja, gasping for air, finally exclaimed, "is losing at billiards to Majorczyk."

Szyja got up from the chair and said to the messenger of these bad tidings,"Go to Adolf and give him this note, but in such a way that Majorczyk won't notice."

He wrote a few sentences on a piece of paper taken from his pocket. Jotuś Szaja ran as fast as he could back to the billiard room and managed to slip Adolf the note from his brother. Soon after, Adolf, who had already lost a lot of money but was nevertheless grinning, took off his jacket, hung it on the back of a chair, and said to Majorczyk, "Listen, Majorczyk, we're going to take a little break. I have to go to the bathroom."

Majorczyk, who already had a few rubles in his pocket and was feeling quite satisfied as he ordered a beer, agreed. After some time, it was Szyja who returned from the bathroom instead of Adolf. He was wearing a shirt, tie, and Adolf's suspenders, so even the sharpest eye could not distinguish him from his twin brother. He calmly took the billiard cue in his hand and resumed the game. Majorczyk began to rapidly lose game after game.

Szyja not only recovered the money lost by his brother but won two more games to the astonishment of Majorczyk, who began to suspect that something was amiss and was looking intently at his victorius conqueror. However, he did not protest, as he was not at all sure whether he was playing against Adolf or the formidable billiard player, Szyja. Majorczyk was clearly upset by the loss, and offered to end the game, to which Szyja gladly agreed. The fans were amused by this event and pleased with the final outcome. Nobody liked Majorczyk, who was rumored to be a pimp. Jotuś Szaja approached him and said, "Well, Ma-ma-jorczyk, you've been lucky today."

"And why?" asked the golden young man.

"Well, you didn't play for your pants, or you would have been walking down the streets naked," answered Szaja before leaving with Szyja, dressed in Adolf's jacket. Now Majorczyk was sure that his opponent had been Szyja, but with no proof, he had to accept the defeat, biting his lip in anger.

The twin brothers' adventures, however, did not end there. Adolf was waiting in the café—just as he had agreed with his brother—and he was not in the best of moods. He didn't know what the outcome of the billiard game would be, and he felt bad about the money he had lost. He imagined returning home with empty pockets while his wife waited for the much-needed money. It was late, night had fallen, the café was slowly emptying, and the owner was preparing to close, but Szyja had still not arrived. Eventually, he had no choice but to leave. Adolf, wearing Szyja's jacket, looked nervously into the billiard room. Seeing that none of his friends were there, he staggered home, his head full of dire thoughts.

Meanwhile, Szyja, feeling quite pleased with himself because of his newly won victory, said goodbye to his friend Jotuś Szaja. But instead of going home, he turned abruptly toward Targowa Street, where Adolf lived with his newly married wife, Regina. He went upstairs and knocked on the door. It was late at night. Regina opened the door for him, taking him for Adolf, and grumbled about her husband leaving her alone barely two months after they had got married and coming home so late at night. Overcome with grievance, she went back to bed. Szyja then deliberately positioned himself—undressed!—in bed next to his brother's wife. Regina, not noticing any difference at all and already a bit smitten, moved closer to her faux-husband.

Suddenly, there was a timid knock on the door. Regina, surprised and a little alarmed, leapt out of bed, put on her dressing-gown, lit a candle, and opened the door. Adolf stood on the doorstep, embarrassed, and he started to explain and apologize for coming home late. Finally, he entered the bedroom and saw a figure lying in his bed, with only his reddish hair sticking out from under the blanket. Adolf pulled back the covers and saw his brother, who laughed out loud and said with a triumphant expression, "Imagine that your wife took me for you and saw absolutely no difference. I have long wanted to find out if our resemblance is so great that it can mislead even your own wife. Don't be angry, it was just an innocent prank, but very enjoyable for me."

All three of them laughed heartily, and the brothers began to report their adventures in the billiard room and about misleading Majorczyk. Neither of them mentioned a word about Adolf's loss and how the almost vanished money had been saved. Regina brought some cakes and tea, and when Adolf quietly took the rubles and handed them to his wife with a lordly expression, they were all quite satisfied. They sat at the table for a long time while Szyja told jokes, imitating his friends' voices so well that Regina almost fell out of her chair laughing.

It goes without saying that this whole story really happened and remained a family secret that nobody knew about for a long time. I am the first to divulge this secret because I want to remain faithful to the

pledge I made to myself: to tell the whole truth, and nothing but the truth, in these memoirs.

A year later, Adolf and his young wife Regina moved to America. Regina had an uncle in New York named Rusek, who had made a considerable fortune in trade and had established a large department store in the Bronx. Rusek wrote that he had spent some time in Klondike, where he had been a gold miner and was lucky enough to find a considerable amount of gold on his plot of land, which he used to open a store. He had made quite a fortune from his trade and now he needed trustworthy and honest people to help him in his department store. He promised to hire Adolf and Regina as soon as they arrived, assuring them that they would not regret it.

There was nothing for the young couple to deliberate about. The offer was enticing and very beneficial to them. Adolf had no profession, and nothing more than a miserable and uncertain future awaited him in his country of birth—all the more so following the events of the recent years, the persecution of the Jewish population, and the rapidly spreading antisemitism. The poorer Jewish classes were immigrating to America more and more, and massive numbers of people were leaving Russia and the Congress Kingdom of Poland every year.[10]

Soon, their ship tickets arrived from New York, along with some money from Rusek for the journey. One bright day, Adolf and Regina, with tears in their eyes, said goodbye to their family and left for Hamburg, from where they sailed on a ship with hundreds of other Jewish emigrants to the land where slogans of freedom, equality, and brotherhood—as Rusek had maintained in his letters—were a fact and not utopia. Back in my grandfather's house, the older daughters got married, as did Szyja, who tried his luck in trade. Of the sons, only the youngest son, Jakub, remained at home.

At the time of these events, Jakub was twenty years old. He had long since left the *heder* where he had received his talmudic education. Not without his father's objections, he shed the long *kittel* (robe) and black *yarmulka* (skullcap) traditionally worn by *Hasidim* who remained faithful

10 Between 1881 and 1914, 2.4 million Jews left the Russian Empire, of which 80 percent moved to the United States. See Yannay Spitzer, "Pogroms, Networks, and Migration: The Jewish Migration from the Russian Empire to the United States, 1881–1914," *Maurice Falk Institute for Economic Research in Israel, Discussion Paper Series* (2021), pp. 1–83; Gerald Sorin, *A Time for Building: The Third Migration, 1880–1920* (Baltimore: Johns Hopkins University Press, 1995).

to Jewish tradition and were completely isolated from the outside world. Under the influence of his progressive colleagues and friends, Jakub studied secular sciences and quickly became Europeanized.

He was a young man, gifted by nature with uncommon physical strength and courage. More than average height, well-built, and muscular, he enjoyed doing calisthenics and even tried his hand at athletics. His physical prowess earned him the respect of his opponents, and, valuing his personal dignity and possessing courage, he proved a dangerous target for the Polish street urchins and rascals who used to start fights with the Jewish youth. Unlike others, he was not afraid of being accosted, did not run away from his attackers, and responded to insults and attacks with his fists. He could easily deal with two or even three thugs at a time. When he deemed it necessary to intervene—and when verbal arguments did not help—he resorted to using his fists, and with just a few blows, he knocked even the most dangerous Polish brutes to the ground. However, he tried to avoid fights, and entered into confrontations only when there was no other way out—the use of physical force became an act of self-defense.

One day, Jakub was walking along Dojazd Street, where the railroad station was located. He was on his way to pick up a wagon with scrap metal from Sosnowiec for his father's iron depository. The wagon needed to be unloaded and the scrap metal taken by horse-drawn carts to the local Hantke ironworks in Raków. Jakub was helping his father run the depot. It was a rainy autumn day. The local Rabbi Asz,[11] accompanied by his *shammes*[12] Aron Pelc, was walking on the opposite sidewalk. The rabbi, although not yet old, was highly respected in Jewish religious circles. He was part of the *Haskala*, the Jewish Enlightenment movement, and because of his position as head of the local Jewish community, he wore a top hat. At the same time, a carriage was driving down the street and, in a flash, the cab driver—a heavyset, mustached peasant—raised his whip and knocked

11 Nachum Asz (1858–1936) served as the rabbi of Częstochowa and was an active member of the city council. He was deeply involved in charitable work, heading the committee to aid Jewish victims of pogroms in the Russian Empire and serving as vice president of Linas Hatzedek (The Society to Aid Poor and Sick Jews). He actively advocated against efforts to ban ritual slaughter in the state of Poland. See Sętkowski, *Częstochowa Jews: A Biographical Dictionary*, pp. 25–27; "Rabbi Nachum Asz—Chief Rabbi of Częstochowa," The World Society of Częstochowa Jews and their Descendants, https://www.czestochowajews.org/old-czestochowa/rabbi-nachum-asz/ (accessed August 18, 2025).

12 A warden or assistant rabbi in synagogue services.

the hat off the rabbi's head. The rabbi was terrified and grabbed his head, while the *shammes*—equally terrified and apparently fearing even worse consequences—abandoned the rabbi and ran away, seeking shelter in the nearest gateway. The rabbi stood in the street with his bare head, calling for help.

An earlier photograph of Rabbi Asz in 1894.

Jakub leapt across the street toward the carriage, grabbed the horse by the bridle at a run, and brought it to a stop. With a single blow of his fist, he knocked the cab driver off his seat and onto the road. At lightning speed, he lifted the cab driver from the ground with both hands and delivered several blows to his face—so hard that the cab driver started to bleed. Holding the driver by the collar of his overcoat, Jakub ordered him to pick up the rabbi's mud-stained top hat. He was so beaten and terrified by this unexpected intervention that the driver did not even think about resisting. He obediently lifted the rabbi's hat from the ground. Then, Jakub shouted in his ear, "Clean the mud off the hat, you rascal, or I will knock out the rest of your teeth!"

The order was obeyed without objection. Using both his hands and the hem of his coat, the cab driver cleaned the mud off the dirty hat.

"And now," said Jakub, "hand over the hat, apologize to the rabbi, and kiss his hand."

This order was also scrupulously followed by the stupefied and frightened carriage driver. Held firmly by the collar, he bowed to the rabbi, mumbled something, kissed the rabbi on the sleeve of his overcoat, and handed him the now clean and shiny top hat. After that, with a powerful kick to the buttocks, the driver was left lying on the road, stretched out in the mud.

Jakub took the rabbi's hand and calmly escorted the clergyman—who was very shaken by the incident—to his house nearby, on the same street. Apparently, the brave and bold behavior of the Jewish young man was accepted by the Polish bystanders, who could not be accused of philosemitism: None of them reacted with the slightest word or gesture to the sight of the beaten carriage driver.

Soon after this event, which became well known within the Jewish community, the Staniewski Brothers' circus arrived in Częstochowa. The main attraction at the circus was the wrestling—the so-called French fights, modeled on the wrestling rules of the ancient Greeks and Romans. Grips were limited to the upper half of the body, and wrestlers were divided into categories, so they only fought others of the same weight. The circus featured wrestlers belonging to different weight categories, the most famous of whom was the Estonian student Possof, fighting in the lightweight division. Posters were displayed in the streets, inviting people to the wrestling matches and announcing that the winner of the lightweight category would face an amateur—if such a brave person could be found among the town's inhabitants.

Jakub was a great fan of wrestling matches, so he often went with his friends to the circus, especially when Possof was competing. One day, after the circus fights had finished, a friend of his named Haftka suggested that Jakub should enter himself as the amateur competitor. At first, Jakub categorically rejected this idea for the sake of his parents, who would surely be against the idea that the son of pious Jewish merchants would be performing in the circus like a clown. The whole family would have been outraged. But when his friends proposed that he wrestle anonymously as a black-masked wrestler and they all began to urge him on, Jakub started to warm to the idea of facing a professional athlete of Possof's stature. He finally agreed. His friends gave their word that the whole affair would remain secret so that no one from Jakub's family would find out who was hiding beneath the black mask. Jakub felt confident physically and had already tried his hand at wrestling with other amateurs in the meadows near the Zawada barracks.[13] He usually emerged the winner. The temptation was great for a young man secure in his own strength, and Jakub became determined to fight.

A week later, on Saturday evening, Jakub and his friends went to the circus again for the final bout in the lightweight category. Possof was to compete for the championship title against the Italian athlete Caldi, and the winner would then fight an amateur from the audience—if anyone came forward and agreed to take part. There was a lot of tension among the friends because no final decision had been made, and no one knew whether Jakub would decide to participate. Jakub was wearing black gym shorts, and he had a black mask in his pocket.

After a few decisive moves, Possof lifted Caldi up and put him on his shoulders. The referee announced Possof's victory amid resounding applause. The athlete bowed to all sides, and the referee presented him with the lightweight winner's sash and medal as the orchestra played fanfare. After a few moments, the referee announced that now Possof would fight an amateur in the lightweight category and waited for a contender to come forward. The circus director stepped into the middle of the ring and announced that the management had set a cash prize of twenty-five rubles for any volunteer contender if he succeeded in defeating the lightweight champion Frederick Possof, student from Estonia, in the French fight.

Again, there was silence. Samek Haftka and Borzykowski, who sat closest to Jakub, looked at him expectantly. Jakub thought to himself, "What the hell, you have to try your hand. What will be, will be. Twenty-five rubles is not a trifle, after all." And so, he swiftly produced the mask from his pocket and put it on. He checked if the elastic was tight around his head, then got up from his seat and moved toward the middle of the circus ring. Applause broke out, and Staniewski shook hands with Jakub, who asked for his name, whether he agreed to fight Possof at his own

13 The Zawada Barracks, built by Karol Zawada on his estate in Częstochowa, were a Polish military installation during the interwar period. They housed the 27th Infantry Regiment, which was part of Corps District No. IV. The barracks were located on Gen. J. H. Dąbrowskiego Street. Today, the site no longer serves a military purpose—the main building is now used by the Częstochowa University of Technology (Politechnika Częstochowska). For a historical overview, see Juliusz Sętowski, "Spacer z Julkiem: koszary Zawady," https://cgk.czestochowa.pl/miesiecznikartykul/188 (accessed November 19, 2025).

risk, and whether he would fight in a mask. Jakub explained that he was not willing to disclose his name and wanted to fight in a mask under the pseudonym Black Mask, but he would absolutely accept the risk of the fight. Staniewski smiled and invited Jakub backstage to prepare for the fight. The three of them left.

Jakub undressed, leaving only his shorts and the mask on his face. He pulled his bootlaces tighter and waited. He was more than a little nervous. It was the first time in his life that he would be performing in public, in a circus, as an amateur athlete. He was already beginning to regret giving in to his friends' pleas and yielding to his own aspiration to try his hand at fighting a trained professional athlete.

"It will be a shame if Possof effortlessly throws me to the mat right away and people laugh at me uproariously. But it's too late for regrets. It will look even stranger if I withdrew now. Let it be, then—let God's will be done. I should be of good cheer and fight."

After a moment, Staniewski, the referee dressed in white shorts and a shirt of the same color, and Possof, sporting a mocking smile, appeared. Both opponents were weighed—Possof weighed in at 74 kilograms, while Jakub weighed 1 kilogram less. The referee agreed to the fight.

As the orchestra played the "Gladiator's March," all four men stepped into the middle of the ring. Staniewski gave a hand signal, the music stopped, and he announced that the amateur from Częstochowa called Black Mask would fight the lightweight champion Frederick Possof. The fight would be in French style. If the amateur managed to defeat Possof and pin him down—as confirmed by the referee—he would receive a prize of twenty-five rubles.

The orchestra resumed the march, and the two wrestlers faced each other. Possof was slightly taller than Jakub and more muscular, but Jakub's fine physique was equally impressive. Possof removed his master's sash and remained, like his opponent, dressed only in shorts, bare to the waist. The mocking smile was still firmly in place. He raised both hands and, with a sudden movement, gripped Jakub, trying to lift him and throw him down onto the mat. Jakub, however, stood planted on his outstretched legs. He jerked and, with a violent movement of his whole body, managed to escape Possof's grip and broke free. Possof wobbled slightly on his feet. Then, both Jakub's hands latched on to Possof's belt, whose spread legs bent slightly at the knees before he suddenly collapsed. Jakub's whole body buckled and leaned forward as the muscles of his legs, arms, and shoulders tensed, and as Possof's legs crumpled—his body in Jakub's powerful grip—he then hit the mat. Jakub lay on top of Possof, pressing him tightly into the mat with his arms and legs spread wide. Possof was lying on his back for a moment before he picked himself up, turned around, fell to his knees, and made rapid movements with his back and hands to knock his opponent off him. The two opponents fought for some time, but now, Possof was lying motionless on his knees, as if gathering strength to attack again.

Jakub realized that if he let his opponent get up from the mat, he would lose his chance of victory. He suddenly put both hands on Possof's neck, just beneath his shoulders, holding him in the iron grip of his arms. This was a dangerous wrestling grip called the "double Nelson," making it very difficult to extricate oneself from because it actually paralyzed the person's shoulder, neck, and head movements, and restricted breathing. The whole audience froze in tense anticipation. The spectators craned their necks to closely observe the intriguing fight. Possof tried desperately to free himself from the firm double Nelson grip, which was suffocating him, but the masked amateur volunteer didn't let go. All of a sudden, with a violent movement of his arms and entire body while still immobilizing the upper part of his opponent's body, Jakub threw Possof on his right side and placed him—partly suffocated and weakened—onto his back. The man was lying flat on the mat, panting heavily and pressed under the weight of Jakub's body and his taut legs and arms. Possof lay horizontal on the mat, and although he flapped his legs around, he could not get up. The entire audience howled, and the applause intensified. The referee blew his whistle, signaling the end of the fight.

Finally, Jakub released his grip, got up, and helped Possof to his feet. The man stood up, out of breath and gasping for air, but no longer smiling derisively. He shook hands with his opponent and quickly left the ring. The Black Mask's victory was complete, and to thunderous applause, the referee announced his win publicly, and Staniewski paid Jakub his prize money.

Jakub returned to his friends and discussed the fight with them. He was amazed; without any special effort, he had managed to beat the famous lightweight champion, whose strength, technical skills, and great wrestling experience turned out to be just a circus trick. There was no end to the congratulations, and the group of friends—together with the winner—left the Staniewski circus tent in the best of spirits.

The following year, Jakub appeared as a conscript before a military commission. The doctor who examined him was full of praise for Jakub's health and physical condition, which effectively meant he was accepted into the ranks of Tsar Nikolai's army. Shortly thereafter, Jakub said goodbye to his family and friends and left for the hinterlands of the

Russian Empire assigned to the artillery. He first served in Kazan, then in Kaluga, and finally in Orenburg in the Ural Mountains. From there, he was sent to noncommissioned officer's school, from which he graduated shortly before the outbreak of the Russo-Japanese war with the rank of senior artilleryman. He sent his parents a photograph of himself in a long artillery uniform, wearing a skewed cap, standing with his chest forward, and smiling under a short mustache, with his leg extended forward in high boots with spurs and holding the handle of a slightly curved sabre. On the epaulettes were freshly earned corporal's stripes. I remember him from his photograph, which I often saw as a child in the family album.

Jakub later fought against the Japanese at Port Arthur[14] and participated in the great battle of Makden.[15] When the Russian army of His Imperial Highness got a hiding and the retreat began, Jakub found himself, together with his regiment of mounted artillery, in the depths of the All-Russian *Gasudarstwo*[16] and strengthened his position as gunner on the hill called Putilovskaya Sopka,[17] from where he fired on the advancing Japanese infantry. Here, he was wounded by a grenade fragment and fell to the ground with a badly bleeding leg, and, after losing consciousness, he rolled down the hill. He was taken to a hospital near Tashkent, where he recovered and stayed until the end of the war before he was discharged. He was honored in the daily order and awarded a medal for bravery on the battlefield. He was also promoted to *zwodniy fayerverker*,[18] with his rank displayed on his epaulettes. Still suffering from a slight limp, he finally arrived at his parents' home with a military escort in the middle of 1906.

14 The Battle of Port Arthur (February 8–9, 1904) marked the beginning of the Russo-Japanese War (1904–1905).

15 The Battle of Mukden (February 20 to March 10, 1905) was the most decisive major land battle of the Russo-Japanese War, in which Russia suffered a major defeat near Mukden in Manchuria.

16 Kromołowski likely alludes to the Russian epithet *Vserossiyskiy* ("all-Russian"). *Gasudarstwo* means state. The epithet *Vserossiyskiy* was part of the title of the tsar: Imperator i Samoderzhets Vserossiyskiy ("All-Russian Emperor and Autocrat"—i.e., emperor and sovereign over all of Russia). Kromołowski uses the adjective to emphasize here that Jakub was far away from Poland, deep inside the vast Russian Empire.

17 In English: Putilov Hill. This refers to a battle that took place around Novgorod Hill and Putilov Hill in October 1904 as part of the Russo-Japanese War.

18 This is a military rank for noncommissioned officers in the artillery of the Russian and several other armies.

For some time, he held on to his military glory and paraded through the streets of Częstochowa in the artillery's long greatcoat, uniform, cap, and clanking spurs. Eventually, however, Jakub got bored with his war adventures and realized that it was high time to return to civilian life, particularly because being part of the Tsar's army did not earn any popularity within the Jewish community, which always treated service in the Russian army as a scourge. Jews tried as hard as they could in every possible way—legal or otherwise—to evade Foni's service, as the Russians were teasingly called by the Jewish population. So, Jakub returned to civilian life and to his duties in his father's ironworks shop. He also began looking for a job to gain independence from his parents, find a profession of his own, and establish his position in society. One evening, Benjamin sat down with his son at the family dining table and, in his customary philosophical manner, began to discuss his son's professional options. Analyzing various occupations, their pros and cons, and their usefulness to people, he finally concluded that the least chosen—and therefore the most lucrative—is an occupation that involves keeping things clean.

"People nowadays," said Jakub's father, "are very careful about cleanliness, they bathe often, wash several times a day, and wash their underwear. Every man must now have a clean, white, starched collar. They wear white half-shirts, cuffs, women wear white aprons, clean underwear, and they need soap to wash, so soap has a future, and it is best to be a soap maker. First produce soap on a small scale, then on a larger scale, and finally build a big soap factory and become its prosperous manager. Money allows us to live. It is our weapon against the enemies who constantly want to destroy and punish us. We had the misfortune to have Jesus Christ born to our people, whom the Romans crucified and whom Christianity recognized as its God.[19] We don't have an army, we don't have cannons or rifles. We don't have a state. So, we must have something else to defend ourselves. That is our tried-and-true Jewish weapon over the centuries—money. Get busy making money, because money has saved many a Jewish life before."

Benjamin did not even ask his son's permission regarding this choice of profession and sent him to learn from a man named Goldach, who was the only person in Częstochowa who produced laundry soap. Goldach was a short, round, and lively Jew with a healthy, deep-red complexion. He had a thin black beard and smelled of tallow and various perfumed

19 This alludes to the deicide accusation explained earlier.

oils with which he sprinkled his products to increase their commercial value. When boiling soap in a large cauldron, he would add water in abundance. For every bucket of water added, he would chant the reason why he was doing so.

"One bucket for my wife's health, the second for my children's health, the third for Aunt Rayzla's health, and the next for Grandma Golda-Pessia."

And when he placed a large amount of water in the cauldron, thus reducing the quality of his excellent—as he maintained—product, he then poured one last bucket of water for the health of his pupil and successor, Jakub.

During this time, professional matchmakers also began to visit Benjamin with marriage proposals for his youngest son, saying, "The young man has already left the army. Healthy, thank God. He must be married, because a young man should not stay a bachelor for too long." Jakub's parents also wanted him to get married, establish a family, and live independently, according to the Jewish religion.[20]

Among the many matchmakers[21] who visited his parents with marriage proposals, the old and experienced matchmaker Anszel was particularly active. One Saturday evening, Anszel appeared once again. The summer evening was warm and humid, and as he sat down at the table, he took a large red handkerchief out of his pocket and wiped his sweat-soaked forehead. He had a large nose, reddened by the constant use of snuff, and a long gray beard, which he would often jerk nervously to bring the end of his beard to his mouth to chew on.

After a long silence, sipping the tea he had been served and taking a bite of honey cake, Anszel made his matrimonial offer. It concerned a pretty young woman from a good Jewish home who ran a large dry goods store for her widowed mother. She was allegedly clever, had a 1,000-rubles cash dowry, and was an excellent housekeeper.

"She is a kosher Jewish maiden," Anszel the matchmaker praised his "merchandise from a decent kosher home. Just close your eyes and

20 See Genesis 2:24.

21 The role of a *shadhan* (matchmaker) in Jewish tradition, particularly within Orthodox and ultra-Orthodox communities, is to facilitate marriages by introducing prospective brides and grooms, considering factors such as family background—including its socioeconomic status—religious observance, and compatibility. This practice is rooted in the value of marriage as a central tenet of Jewish life and often involves formal negotiations and arrangements between the two families.

agree, and I will make sure that the bride and her family agree. And we will arrange a *kouck*."[22]

Anszel finished extolling the virtues of this "kosher bride"—Sheva, the daughter of Avramel (Abram) Górski, a merchant from the Old Market who had died several years earlier. When Benjamin and Urla heard this, they grinned in satisfaction and unanimously decided that this proposal was indeed tempting and worthy of the highest attention.

So, after a few more visits from Anszel, a *kouck* between the young couple was arranged on neutral ground. The encounter was short and rather formal, with the young couple exchanging a few sentences. Jakub told the young woman about an episode from his recent military service, and she, looking quite attractive in her fashionable gray outfit and matching hat on her raven-black hair, expressed her opinion on the horrors of all wars and the need to ensure peaceful and cultured existence for the war-torn nations of the globe.

However, the decision was to be made at a higher level. After the meeting between Jakub's parents, Benjamin and Urla, and the bride's mother, Chana Górska, and her older brother, the wealthy industrialist Władek Górski who represented his younger sister on behalf of their deceased father, it was decided to hold the wedding without delay.

On February 7, 1907, the elaborate wedding of Sheva (Stefa) Górska and Jakub took place in the large Harmonia Hall on Strażacka Street. The hall was in Fogel's house, which had been specially adapted to be rented out for Jewish weddings. A large procession of wedding guests gathered there, with family members and friends of the young couple present. The wedding ceremony took place in the middle of the hall under a beautifully embroidered synagogue canopy and lit by the light of hundreds of candles. The wedding was conducted by Nachum Asz, the chief rabbi of Częstochowa—the same rabbi who had been rescued by Jakub from the Polish cab driver's antisemitic attack several years earlier. The famous Szmulewicz brothers band played for the guests. The tables were heavily laden with food and drink, and the wedding guests were served by several waiters in tailcoats, led by the well-known chef Pupa, whose face was defined by two miniscule, black, ever-frightened eyes and a potato-shaped nose protruding from the center of his round, plump face, which was framed by short black stubble, hard like reeds. The dances were led by Rubieński, a principal ballet master and dance instructor in the city.

22 A *kouck* is the first encounter of a young couple.

After midnight, the groom—who was already a little intoxicated—ordered the band to play the Russian *trepak*. To the delight of the the amused and clapping audience, he danced this spirited Cossack dance alone, full of expression, with all the obligatory *prysiudy* and heel knocks.[23]

These newlyweds described here are my parents, Stefa Górska and Jakub Kromołowski.

Stefa (Sheva) Górska.

Jakub Kromołowski.

23 *Trepak* is a traditional Russian and Ukrainian folk dance characterized by its energetic movements, including stomping, squatting (*prysyadka*), and dynamic leg kicks.

CHAPTER THREE

WORLD WAR I

I was five or six years old, and I remember the events as if through a veil of fog. My father was sitting on the steps leading up to the house at 7 First Avenue, which was owned by the Rozencwajgs and where we lived at the time. Father was surrounded by several members of our family, and my mother was there as well, wiping her tears with a handkerchief. Everyone advised my father to stay at home and not to go anywhere—not to join the Russian army—because the German army would surely arrive in no time. According to the news circulating around town, the Germans had already crossed the border at Herby, a dozen or so kilometers away from our town, and was advancing without encountering any resistance at all.

Father couldn't make up his mind and frequently changed his decision. He would decide to stay, so I would take his boots to his room and bring him his slippers, which apparently conveyed a sense of peace and family warmth. Then he would suddenly decide to leave, which meant that I would again run to his room and bring him his leather boots instead. Finally, he made a decision. "If I stay and the Russian army pushes the Germans out of the country, the Russians may shoot me for desertion. I don't want to take the risk." He then kissed my mother and me, shook hands with his relatives, picked up his suitcase, and proceeded to the railroad station to go to war aboard one of the last trains departing for Warsaw.

It was August 1914. As a reservist in the Russian army, Father had received a mobilization order instructing him to report to one of the artillery regiments stationed in Siedlce.[1] The morning after he left, my mother and I stood in front of the gate to our house and saw a troop of Russian Cossacks galloping in retreat down the alley toward Warszawska Street. An hour later, the vanguard of the German army entered our town, along with trucks filled with soldiers wearing field-gray coats and spiked helmets on their heads, as well as cavalry units with lances and pennants blowing in the wind. I breathed in the unfamiliar smell of gasoline wafting through the morning air. Since then, I have always associated the smell of gasoline with the German army occupying our city.

This left me, my mother, and my two younger siblings at the mercy of Father's business partner in the small soap factory on Nadrzeczna Street. Before he left, my father had received a promise from his partner—and brother-in-law, for that matter—that he would take care of our family, and that my mother would replace her husband in the business. But Mother, burdened with three small children, realized that she would not be able to devote much time to her work in the soap shop, which required a strong male hand.

The youngest of us, my little brother Henio,[2] was born on April 14, 1914, which made him only a few months old when Father left. My sister Zosia,[3] born on October 10, 1910, was four years old. I was the eldest, and therefore often accompanied my mother on her errands and was sent to do shopping—I was very proud of this. At that time, we had a maid who had been with us for many years, and she was very devoted to our family. We had nicknamed her Janowa, but her name was actually Antonina Padla. She was an elderly woman, and not long after my father left, she became seriously ill and died in the hospital. I recall what a hard blow her death was for my mother, who took care of the funeral arrangements, since Janowa was completely alone. As she was a Catholic, we followed her coffin to St. Zygmunt's Church[4] for a memorial service, and then proceeded to the Kule Cemetery[5] for her burial.

1 Siedlce is a city in eastern Poland, located in the Masovian Voivodeship some 90 kilometers east of Warsaw.

2 From the Polish name Henryk.

3 From the Polish name Zofia.

4 Kościół św. Zygmunta (St. Zygmunt's Church) is a historic church in Częstochowa, located in the city center, in the Old Town.

5 Kule Cemetery in Częstochowa is located on a small hill, in the northern part of Częstochowa.

So, it was just the four of us, and my mother shouldered the burden of supporting and raising her three young offspring. She was still a young woman—no more than thirty-two years old—with enough energy to assert her rights as co-owner of a prosperous soap factory during the war period. With three small children to care for, she could not devote much time to working in the factory; nevertheless, she often visited the premises. At first, everything turned out quite well as far as our material needs were concerned. Osajasz, my father's business partner, told Mother that he was releasing her from her obligation to work at the factory, and instead, as she was part-owner of the business, he would pay her a weekly salary, which Mother believed would cover our living expenses.

However, as time went by, this salary began to shrink, and payments became increasingly infrequent, eventually reduced to a tiny, almost symbolic sum. Mother was forced to find extra income to cover our constantly growing expenses. She found a cheap source of German textile goods and would distribute them around the apartments of wealthy merchant families, and earned money for our upkeep in this way. From early in the morning, she would run around with these packages, climbing flights of stairs and spending long hours outside the house, hard at work.

Mother found a bigger and more comfortable apartment for us in Hasklowicz's house on Kopernika Street.[6] Grandmother Górska, who had been widowed many years earlier following the death of our grandfather, Abram Górski, came to live with us, making it possible for Mother to go out and work because Grandma took care of us and the household.

The first year of the war was coming to an end. We initially received letters from Father quite often, and once, a relative of ours even sent us some money from Warsaw. In the accompanying letter, this relative wrote that during Father's stay in Warsaw, he had left us some money, which he was now forwarding to us. He sent us greetings from Father. Then, suddenly, we stopped hearing from my father and received no news of him.

Meanwhile, the war was raging, the bloodiest slaughter that Europe had ever experienced. The outbreak of the war was caused by Germany, which sought to gain new markets and to divide the world in its favor.

6 Kopernika Street (formerly Żelazna Street) was one of the central streets in Częstochowa, intersecting with Wolności Avenue. The Hasklowicz house, located at 3 Kopernika Street, was owned by Jakub Hasklowicz (1863–1943), a stonemason and proprietor of a stonemasonry workshop. See Sętkowski, *Częstochowa Jews: A Biographical Dictionary*, pp. 199–200.

There were two adversarial camps: a triple alliance of the so-called Central Powers—Germany, Austria-Hungary, and Italy—and a triple alliance called the Allied Powers— Great Britain, France, and Russia. Italy soon withdrew, leaving the two empires of Germany and Austria-Hungary in their alliance.[7]

Events moved very quickly after the assassination of the Austrian heir to the throne, Archduke Franz Ferdinand, in Sarajevo on July 28, 1914. Austro-Hungary declared war on Serbia on July 28, Germany declared a state of war with Russia on August 1, and with France on August 3. The Austro-Hungarian empire declared war on Russia on August 6, and Britain and Serbia declared war on Germany.[8] Italy remained neutral.

On the Western Front, the invasion of German troops into neutral Belgium sparked the action there. The French Army went on the offensive in Alsace on August 7 and took over Lorraine on August 18. However, the right flank of the German army broke through the Belgian army's resistance and entered France. Here, the Germans were successful in the battles of Charleroi, Mons, and Le Cateau, and reached as far as the Marne River, east of Paris. However, they were repelled at the Battle of the Marne and retreated to the Aisne-Verdun River line,[9] where they engaged in prolonged positional fighting.

Meanwhile, on the Eastern Front, the Germans captured a large area of the Polish Kingdom, including Częstochowa. The Russians suffered significant defeats at Tannenberg and at the Masurian Lakes. On September 28, the German and Austro-Hungarian armies went on the offensive in the direction of Warsaw and Dęblin, and the battle near Lódź in November and December was again lost by the Russians.[10] After the defeat suffered

7 A number of factors contributed to the outbreak of World War I. For more information on World War I in general, see Michael Howard, *The First World War* (Oxford: Oxford University Press, 2002). On the causes, see pp. 1–31.

8 Great Britain declared war on Germany on August 4, 1914, while Serbia, in fact, did not formally declare war on Germany in August 1914.

9 The Germans retreated to the Aisne River. Verdun was not part of the German defensive line after the Battle of the Marne.

10 In the Battle of Łódź from November 11 to December 6, 1914, the Russian armies were severely mauled and nearly encircled, but they managed to extricate themselves. In turn, the German army found itself in great danger. The Russians avoided encirclement and inflicted heavy casualties on the Germans, though they conceded some territory.

at Kraków[11] and Limanowa,[12] the Russian army began to retreat, and it was again beaten in East Prussia and at Przemyśl. Disruption of the front line near Gorlice triggered the general retreat of Russians from Polish territories.[13]

At the same time these events were taking place on the Eastern Front, the Germans were using deadly gas for the first time in the history of wars on the Western Front, and soon, both sides were engaging in chemical warfare. Italy joined the Allies, while the German-Austrian army, supported by Bulgaria, crushed the Serbian army in Kosovo (October 19–23).

The war broke out on the Eastern and Western Fronts simultaneously. It was mostly long-lasting, positional fighting, and for months, huge masses of troops on both fronts remained in the trenches, firing at each other with artillery and machine guns. A naval front also developed at this time, and the Germans began to use submarines to sink Allied ships as well as commercial vessels, including those of neutral countries.[14] Within less than a year following the outbreak of war, the German and Austro-Hungarian armies had occupied all Polish territories. The Germans set up their civil and military administration there, and the occupied Polish areas were known as Generalgouvernement Warschau.[15]

Families with larger apartments were ordered to house German officers, and at my aunt's house on Strażacka Street, a Lieutenant Dr. Heinemann was billeted. He was a German Jew, and most surprisingly, he was an extremely pious man who strictly followed the laws of Jewish faith. Dr. Heinemann liked me very much, and when I came to visit my aunt, he

11 The Battle of Kraków took place on the Eastern Front during World War I from November 16 to November 28, 1914. The outcome was indecisive, and the Austro-Hungarian army launched a counteroffensive at Limanowa-Łapanów.

12 The Battle of Limanowa-Łapanów (December 1 to December 13, 1914) between the Austro-Hungarian army and the Russian army took place near the town of Limanowa 40 kilometers southeast of Kraków.

13 The Russians initially captured the Austro-Hungarian fortress of Przemyśl in March 1915 but lost it during their retreat following the Central Powers' Gorlice-Tarnów Offensive in May–July 1915.

14 Submarines played an important role for the first time during World War I. Both the British and the Germans used submarines against enemy warships from the outset. Regarding merchant ships, people on board were allowed to evacuate before the ship was sunk. Eventually, the Germans adopted so-called unrestricted submarine warfare, sinking nonmilitary ships without warning. The British sought to counter this threat by escorting merchant ship convoys.

15 Warschau was an administrative district created by the German Empire during World War I (October 18, 1915–November 11, 1918).

would invite me into his room and treat me to cakes and chocolate. There were not many sweets in my mother's house at that time, so I devoured Heinemann's delicacies and listened to his stories about the family he had left behind in Berlin. He had a son about my age, whom he missed very much, and he often showed me his photograph. He spoke to me in German but tried to make it resemble Yiddish, which I understood well because my mother spoke it with Grandmother Górska. Dr. Heinemann called me Jadek, and every Friday, he took me to the local synagogue, where he had his permanent seat and placed his appointment card on the lectern. He prayed fervently from a Hebrew-German prayer book and recited the weekday prayers wearing a *tallit* and *tefillin*.[16]

On Passover eve, Dr. Heinemann would shake all the bread crumbs out of the pockets of his uniform and sweep the room with a goose feather and wooden spoon to methodically remove the *humetz* from all the room's nooks and crannies, which he would then burn in the yard. During the holiday, he ate only *matzos*. My aunt kept a kosher kitchen—as did my mother—strictly observing the dietary laws for cooking food and separating *milhick* (dairy) and *flayshik* (meaty)[17] dishes so as not to prepare them in the same pot or serve them on the same plate.

My friendship with Dr. Heinemann made a huge impression on me. More than once, I tried on his military cap—which, of course, was far too big on me—and fiddled with the silver epaulettes of his uniform. I was proud when German soldiers saluted him in the street when we walked together to synagogue services on Friday or Saturday. He also comforted me, telling me that the war would soon be over, my father would return home safe and sound, and everything would be as it was before. He said he was praying for my father's swift return home.

Around that time, my sister Zosia was ill with a middle ear infection and was suffering badly. A high fever and severe headaches prevented her from sleeping. The child moaned in pain, and my mother was in despair. We needed a doctor to come, but it was not easy to find a doctor in our town due to the war. I immediately ran to Dr. Heinemann and told him about our dilemma. He promised that he would help. And indeed, that evening, Dr. Heinemann came to our apartment with another doctor in tow, a fat

16 A *tallit* is a fringed prayer showl worn by religious Jews. *Tefillin* (phylacteries) are a set of small, black leather boxes with leather straps, which contain scrolls of parchment inscribed with verses from the Torah. They are worn by adult Jewish men during weekday morning prayers.

17 *Milhik* is derived from the Yiddish *milch*, meaning milk. *Flayshik* is derived from the Yiddish *fleish*, meaning meat or flesh.

German dressed in a military uniform. His name was Freudenthal. He was an army laryngologist and a hospital colleague of my friend Heinemann. They both examined my sister, and Freudenthal looked at my sister's ear through a special mirror. He put some eardrops into her ear, leaving us with a bottle of drops and instructing us to use it from time to time. Both doctors also diagnosed Zosia with anemia due to lack of proper nourishment. They prescribed some medicine and advised my mother on how to nourish her. They left us sweets and refused to take any payment.

Many years later, after my tragic experiences during World War II, I compared the Germans of Hitler's time with the Germans I had encountered during my childhood. I could not understand how this nation could have undergone such an immense transformation and degeneration in just twenty years. What powers of hell had turned this nation of Heinemanns and Freudenthals into a nation of torturers and executors who murdered in cold blood 6 million European Jews, including 3.5 million Polish Jews, without any rational and objectively justifiable reason?[18]

I don't remember who taught me to read and write. Maybe it was my mother, or maybe our distant relative Jadzia Kajzer, who often visited us in those days and, at my mother's request, took care of my education. As a seven- or eight-year-old boy, I spent a lot of time reading books—stories and fairy tales, but I was most fascinated by travel and historical novels. I became acquainted with books by Stanisław Przybyszewski[19] and, among others, with the character of Colonel Joselewicz in his novel *Berek Joselewicz*,[20] in which this financial agent of Bishop Massalski[21]

18 Many Holocaust survivors expressed the same kind of question in their testimonies. Indeed, after the outbreak of World War II in 1939—the invasion of Poland by Germany on September 1 and by the Soviet Union on September 17—many Jews had the opportunity to escape Nazi occupation and cross over into Soviet-controlled territory. While some left the German-occupied territory, others decided to stay. Drawing on personal experience and recalling that the German rule during World War I was tolerant toward Jews, many preferred to stay put rather than face the potential dangers of living under Soviet rule.

19 Stanisław Przybyszewski (1868–1927) was a Polish novelist, dramatist, and poet associated with the decadent school.

20 The reference is probably to *Berek pod Kockiem* (1911), a novel authored by Walery Zygmunt Lucjan Przyborowski, whose pen name was Zygmunt Lucjan Sulima.

21 Berek Joselewicz (1764–1809) was in the service of Prince Massalski, bishop of Vilna. Joselewicz was a Polish–Jewish colonel of the Polish army who led a Jewish cavalry regiment during the Kościuszko Uprising in 1794 against the Russian and Prussian domination.

created a Jewish cavalry regiment, fought against the Muscovites during the Kościuszko Uprising, and died in the Battle of Kock.[22]

Later, in my mature years—when I lived in Poland after the war, in the so-called people's democracy[23]—I wondered why this novel by Przybyszewski, which celebrated the life and death of a Jewish–Polish patriot and the struggle of his numerous Jewish soldiers who gave their lives for Poland, was never reprinted. Maybe it was the postwar antisemitism that was the obstacle, or maybe it was fear of the Russians, against whose occupation Berek Joselewicz fought to liberate Poland. Perhaps reprinting this book could have been interpreted as a call for an uprising against the current Russian occupation—an occupation that was admittedly informal but very real in postwar Poland as well as many other countries in the Eastern Bloc.[24] I also read the novel *Olszynka Grochowska* by Przybyszewski, also not reprinted after the war, probably for the same reasons. *Gulliver's Travels*, *Robinson Crusoe*, and Jule Verne's books were some of my favorites. I would go regularly to the Wiedza Library on Teatralna Street, where Mrs. Kosińska, the librarian there at the time, was well acquainted with my interests in history and travel books.

My weakness since early childhood was arithmetic. Learning to count came easily to me, but addition, subtraction, and other mathematical operations were much harder. My cousin tried to drill the principles of arithmetic into my head but decided I was a blockhead and that I wouldn't grow up to be any good. And so, from my earliest years, I had no desire to learn and felt a paralyzing fear of any kind of mathematics.

I remember that when I was four or five years old, my mother and Hela Birman—my future Aunt Górska—decided that it would be best to send me to *freblówka* (kindergarten). So, one day, they took me to the nursery school run by Miss Madzia Zalcman at 32 Second Avenue. When I noticed the teacher and the lines of white banks and racks, I made such a shriek and broke down crying so desperately that I had to be hastily taken home again.

22 The Battle of Kock was fought on May 7, 1809.

23 This is a reference to the postwar communist-ruled Poland.

24 The Eastern Bloc—also known as the Communist Bloc, the Socialist Bloc, and the Soviet Bloc—was the coalition of communist states aligned with the Soviet Union during the Cold War between the United States and the Soviet Union between 1947 and 1991.

For some time, I attended the Edelist school[25] on Spadkowa Street,[26] but one day, for some transgression of school discipline, the teacher administered corporal punishment, hitting my knuckles several times with a ruler. I began to howl in pain and fear, and ran home. Requests and threats to return to school did not help, and I never went back to the Edelist school.

One day my mother brought home a teacher who was supposed to teach me Hebrew prayers as well as reading and writing in Yiddish. He was an old Jew with a long grayish beard and rabbit-like red eyes. His name was Kozioł, which means goat in Polish, and his appearance indeed resembled this useful domestic animal. He was constantly shaking his beard during the lesson, as he tried to familiarize me with the Hebrew letters. After some time, when he had succeeded in teaching me the letters, he would blissfully fall asleep, leaning with one of his arms on the table, while I recited in boredom the assigned text, inserting sarcastic remarks about my *melamed*.[27] The goat would then abruptly awaken from his sleep, and then—just in case—he would utter, "*Od hankivaynu nazad!*" meaning that I had to repeat the text from the word *hankivaynu* onward. Then, he would drink the glass of tea that my mother usually put on the table for him, and the lesson was over. My Hebrew education did not last very long, but I remembered the word *hamayr* (donkey) well, an epithet that Kozioł frequently bestowed on me.

In the meantime, the war was still raging and severe deprivation took hold of our home. We moved to a smaller apartment at 4 Spadek Street, the Besser's house. My mother struggled to earn a living, and it became increasingly problematic to feed the family. There was a general food shortage, and the Germans introduced rationing. Everything was sold with ration cards or vouchers. There were more and more substitutes. Bread, or *popularka*, was also sold with ration cards, as was sugar, flour, meat, and

25 In 1902–1903, a *heder* was established in Częstochowa for children of impoverished families, inspired by the Talmudic principle that great Torah scholars often emerge from poverty. Led by Reb Dawid Icyk Edelist and other activists, the school grew rapidly, reaching 400 students by 1907–1908. Despite financial challenges and opposition from local *melamdim* (teachers), the school became an official school under the name Mahzikey Hadas. In 1910, with donations and a gifted plot of land at 68 Nadrzeczna, the foundation stone of a two-story building was laid. The building was supposed to house the school and a study hall. See Schutzman, *Sefer Czenstochow*, vol. 1, pp. 549–554.

26 This is referring to Spadek Street, often known as Spadkowa Street before the war.

27 *Melamed* means teacher.

so on. The sugar was yellow and hardly sweet, and the bread was black, clay-like, and sticky. Drinks were sweetened with saccharine. The food had no nutritional value, and we ate mainly potatoes, which were also difficult to acquire.

At first, Mother would take us to the countryside for the summer, where it was easier to get food, especially bread that the peasants baked themselves. It was real, unadulterated bread spread with real butter, which was a true delicacy for us in those difficult times. It was also easier to get eggs, which my mother gave us to eat after our long period of hunger in the city. The village we stayed in was called Ostrowy, located a dozen or so kilometers from our town.[28] Mother rented a cottage consisting of a room and a kitchen from a farmer named Cierpiał, who moved with his family into the barn during that time. This cottage was located on the edge of the village, right by the forest, and was completely enveloped by the greenery of the trees. Here, we breathed the fresh forest air, running along the pine forest and meadows smelling of grass.

After a few weeks in the countryside, we regained our strength and health, and our anemic Zosia once again had rosy cheeks. Mother often left for the day because she was still working as a peddler, so Grandma Górska stayed with us in the village. Our other grandmother, Urla, was not very active and rarely visited us, not showing much concern for her grandchildren's hardships and misfortunes. We did not see our grandfather, Benjamin, at all—he was a total stranger to us, even though he was doing well and still ran his old ironware store on the same street as the one we lived on. Despite the ongoing war, the merchant trade in the German-occupied territories was flourishing. The nearby open German border made cross-border communication possible and encouraged merchants from Polish areas to trade with Germany. Industrial goods, textiles, machines, and tools were imported to Poland, while coal, iron ore, wood, and food were exported to Germany for the fighting German armies and the civilian population.

The cleverer Jewish merchants became rich, like my much older and already married cousin Chaim Dawidowicz—he changed his name to Joachim—who became very wealthy from the wholesale coal trade. My mother's brother Władek Górski, married to Olga Lipska, also made money in the wood and forest trade. Our soap factory was prosperous as well, but my mother was not allowed to enter it and no income came from this source.

28 Ostrowy nad Okszą, located some 20 kilometers north of Częstochowa.

Mother was very tired from running up and down stairs and carrying packages, and she often cried bitterly. With her waning strength, her earnings were low and often insufficient to cover our expenses, especially the expensive apartment rent. Once, Mother sent me to get money from our partner, who informed me that if Mother signed over her share in the factory, we would get the money. Mother, however, refused to give in to this ultimatum, believing that my father would eventually return from the war. Our associate and the rest of the family, on the other hand, did not seem to share this opinion: They believed my father was dead. The fate of my mother and her young children apparently did not interest them, and there was not even the slightest sign of protest.

I also burst into tears more than once when I was sent by my mother to collect the money owed to her. I encountered constant resistance and intransigence from our business partner, whose wife, after all, was my father's sister. This was the first time I was confronted face to face with human greed and a lack of morality and decency. From then on, our relations with my father's family completely broke down, and despite our very precarious financial situation, my mother did not sign the demanded act of surrender. Occasionally, we received money for Grandmother Górska, who lived with us, and from my uncle Icchok Górski in Vienna. Grandmother Górska would always give this money to my mother.

During the war, my Uncle Icchok worked in an Austrian military office as a censor. Being fully proficient in Russian and German, he censored letters written by Russian prisoners of war who were being held in Austrian POW camps, visited these camps, and was in contact with the International Red Cross. He was especially interested in the fate of Polish prisoners, particularly if they were from Częstochowa. He continued to play an active role in the Viennese socialist organizations, specifically the Austrian Zionist–Socialist organization. He and his comrades published the magazine *Freiland* in German and closely cooperated with the main socialist leaders in Vienna at that time, especially Israel Zangwill, one of the leaders of the Jewish Socialist Territorial organization, as well as Borochow, Trotsky, and the leader of the Polish PPS, Daszyński.

During this time, Uncle Icchok was president of the Socialist Students' Association and an employee of a cooperative workers' bank in Vienna. He searched tirelessly for my father. One day, a letter arrived from my uncle in which he wrote how he had learned—through one of the Russian prisoners of war from Częstochowa—that our father was alive and serving in the artillery with the rank of sergeant. It is hard to describe our joy. Mother seemed renewed in spirit and hope that father would come back. Our partner went pale. A short time later, my uncle sent a letter from Father to Mother, which he had received through the International Red Cross. The letter was dated 1916, and in it my father reported that he had been wounded but had recovered and returned to active duty.

During that time, I passed the entrance exam to the Wacław Płodowski Gymnasium in Częstochowa and began my schooling. My mother gave me a schoolbag (*raniec*). Donning a school cap in the shape of a French cap—or a *nocnik* (potty) in student dialect—I marched every morning to 19 Teatralna Street, where our school was located. My mother was very proud of me and assured my relatives and friends that I would surely grow up to be a lawyer. She supported this claim by pointing out that I talked a lot and convincingly, and that I spoke quite freely—something my mother bluntly described as mouthy. In this respect, my mother's assumption was prophetic, because many years later, after graduating from the Faculty of Law and completing the required training, I indeed became an attorney.

Returning to my memories, however, I admit that in school I moved from class to class without much difficulty. I found learning to be easy, and I even somehow managed with arithmetic, although I did not like the subject. I found the multiplication tables difficult to learn by heart. But I admired the works of Karl May and his heroes Winnetou, Old Shatterhand, and Haji Halef.[29] Those were good times for me, when my childish imagination invented ideas of travel and adventure to exciting, unknown countries.

In the meantime, not nearly as ambitious and much less exotic, my mother would often send me to relatives who could afford to take their children to the countryside during summer vacations. One summer, I stayed with my Uncle Górski in Ostrowy, and together with my slightly older cousin, we went on trips to the forest with a group of scouts. We played hide-and-seek games and wandered around the surrounding meadows, pitched tents in campsites, and were on the lookout. We would light campfires and bake potatoes. After such expeditions, my appetite was enormous, unlike that of my cousins, and I caused a real sensation by throwing down two or even three plates of cabbage soup with fried potatoes during dinner. In the

29 Karl Friedrich May (1842–1912) was a German author of adventure novels set in the American Old West and the Orient. His most famous works include the Winnetou series, which features a Native-American hero named Winnetou, and Old Shatterhand, the German protagonist who is his close friend. Haji Halef is a character from May's Oriental novels.

process, I managed to compensate for my poor nutrition caused by the lack of provisions at home.

The year 1917 rolled around. I was a pupil in the first or perhaps second year of school, when great changes occurred. The Germans still occupied Polish territory, but they began showing some anxiety and behaving with much less arrogance. People started whispering about great changes in Russia and about the approaching end of the war, and about the Americans joining the war on the side of the Allies. German troops returning to their country began to pass through our town. In tattered uniforms and torn shoes, the soldiers looked miserable, discouraged, dejected, and completely lacking in the Prussian drill they had displayed at the beginning of the conflict.

One day, our teacher Mr. Smolarkiewicz told us that the tsar had been overthrown in Russia and a revolution had broken out. The newspapers were also full of news about workers and peasants coming to power in Russia. The leaders of the Russian Revolution were frequently mentioned: Lenin, Trotsky, and Felix Dzerzhinsky, a Polish revolutionary who was said to use two revolvers to shoot the enemies of the revolution.[30] When news came of the execution of Tsar Nicholas II and his family,[31] my mother told us that now the war was probably over, and my father would return home. Events moved quickly, and almost every day brought dramatic news that left people open-mouthed. After the fall of the absolute power in the three empires occupying Poland,[32] it looked like we were on the verge of a free

30 Lenin, Trotsky, and Dzerzhinsky were key figures in the Russian Revolution and the early Soviet state. Vladimir Lenin (1870–1924) was the leader of the Bolshevik Party and the architect of the October Revolution in 1917. Leon Trotsky (1879–1940), a prominent Bolshevik revolutionary, was Lenin's close ally. Trotsky advocated for permanent revolution but was later sidelined by Stalin, ultimately being exiled and assassinated. Felix Dzerzhinsky (1877–1926) was the founder of the Soviet secret police, the VChK (often abbreviated as Cheka—the All-Russian Extraordinary Commission), and played a central role in crushing opposition and implementing state repression during the early years of Soviet rule, especially during the so-called Red Terror (1918–1922).

31 Following the Russian Revolution of 1917 and the subsequent Bolshevik takeover, Tsar Nicholas II, along with his wife Alexandra and their five children, were detained by the Bolsheviks. They were initially held under house arrest in various locations until they were moved to Ekaterinburg. On the night of July 16–17, 1918, Tsar Nicholas II, his wife, their children, and some of their loyal servants were murdered by the Bolsheviks in the basement of the Ipatiev House.

32 The Russian, Austrian, and German Empires.

and democratic Poland, with a liberal, tolerant regime free of oppression. People felt the breath of freedom.

Newspapers brought news of the defeat of the Central Powers, of the revolution that had also broken out in Germany, and of the abdication of the German Emperor William II Hohenzollern, who fled with his family to Holland, settled in Dorn, and chopped wood out of boredom. In Austria, where Karl Habsburg had ruled after the death of Franz Joseph, riots broke out, resulting in the collapse of the Austro-Hungarian empire.[33] The Habsburgs abdicated, and the democrats came to power. Democratic states were beginning to form on the ruins of former empires.

In October and November 1918, the disarming of the German troops began throughout Poland. I was nine years old then and saw with my own eyes in our town how middle-school boys from higher grades, brandishing old pistols and wearing red-and-white bands on their sleeves, were stopping heavily armed Germans who generally did not put up any resistance and without a murmur allowed themselves to be disarmed and arrested. The Germans soon began to flee, and one day in Częstochowa, the civilian militia appeared on the streets armed with German rifles under the command of a Polish officer named Belina Prażmowski.[34] Meanwhile, in Germany, a revolution was brewing, and the communists gained great influence. Their leaders were Rosa Luxemburg, a Jewish woman from Zamość, and Karl Liebknecht.[35]

33 Karl I became emperor of Austria and king of Hungary after the death of Franz Joseph in 1916. However, his reign coincided with the collapse of the Austro-Hungarian Empire, which was caused by military defeats in World War I, economic instability, and rising nationalism. Despite Karl I's attempts at reforms and peace negotiations, the empire disintegrated by the end of the war in 1918, leading to the establishment of nation-states in Austria and Hungary.

34 Władysław Zygmunt Belina-Prażmowski (1888–1938) was a Polish cavalryman, colonel, and politician. A member of the paramilitary organizations Związek Walki Czynnej and Związek Strzelecki, he served under Józef Piłsudski during World War I, becoming one of the first Polish soldiers to enter Russian-held Polish territory.

35 Rosa Luxemburg (1871–1919) was a Jewish-born Polish-German revolutionary and Marxist theorist, known for her advocacy of a socialist revolution and her opposition to World War I. She cofounded the Spartacist League and played a key role in the German Revolution of 1918–1919, calling for radical socialist change. Karl Liebknecht (1871–1919) was a German socialist politician, a member of the Socialist Party, and a staunch opponent of the war. Together, Luxemburg and Liebknecht led the Spartacist Uprising in Berlin, which was crushed by the German government, and both were murdered in January 1919.

The collapsing thrones in Europe stimulated the revival aspirations of a number of nations, which for over 100 years had been under the thumb of the Russian, German, and Austrian Empires. A movement toward new statehood began to rise in Poland. A decisive role in the creation of Polish independence was played by Józef Piłsudski's brigades.[36] These legions—composed of Russians, Austrians, and Germans—initially fought beside and in agreement with the Central Alliance against Russia, because Austria and Germany had pledged to create an independent Polish state.

However, when Germany demanded that the legions swear an oath of allegiance, Piłsudski and his chief of staff Sosnkowski[37] refused. Piłsudski and Sosnkowski were placed in the Magdeburg Fortress, and the legionnaires were interned by the German forces in camps in Szczypiorno and Beniaminów. They were part of the First Brigade of the Legions. Now that the Austro-Hungarian monarchy had collapsed, the released legionnaires began to organize under the leadership of Józef Piłsudski and Sosnkowski, who had been freed from Magdeburg. Also returning to Poland were legionnaires who had fought under the Austrians on the Italian front and under General Zieliński in Bukovina. Upon his return to Warsaw, Piłsudski used these legions to form the nucleus of a regular Polish army. The Allied governments agreed to the creation of a Polish army in France under the aegis of the Polish National Committee, under the command of Józef Haller, known as the Hallerians.[38]

US President Woodrow Wilson, in his declaration of January 22, 1917, acknowledged Poland's right to independence, and the same was announced by the provisional Russian government on March 30,

36 Józef Klemens Piłsudski (1867–1935) was a Polish statesman who served as chief of state (1918–1922) and the first marshal of Poland (from 1920). He played a crucial role in shaping Poland's foreign policy after World War I and is regarded as a key figure in the establishment of the Second Polish Republic in 1918. Piłsudski continued to exercise significant influence as Minister of Military Affairs and de facto leader from 1926 until his death in 1935.

37 General Kazimierz Sosnkowski (1885–1969) was a Polish independence fighter, general, diplomat, and architect.

38 Józef Haller von Hallenburg (1873–1960) was a Polish lieutenant general and legionary in the Polish Legions during World War I. He was instrumental in organizing and leading the Polish army in France, the Blue Army, which was created with the support of the French government to fight for Poland's independence. Haller brought the Blue Army—also known as Haller's army—back to Poland in 1919, where they played a crucial role in the Polish–Soviet War and the defense of the newly reestablished Polish state.

1917. Until Piłsudski's return from Magdeburg, the Polish territories were formally ruled by the Regency Council,[39] composed of the Warsaw Archbishop Cardinal Aleksander Kakowski,[40] Prince Zdzisław Lubomirski,[41] and Józef Ostrowski,[42] but Warsaw was ruled by the German, General von Besseler.[43] The council members demanded the fulfillment of Austria's and Germany's proclamation of the creation of an independent Polish state. After the Germans fled from Warsaw at the end of the war, Piłsudski took power from the Regency Council and appointed a civilian cabinet with Jędrzej Moraczewski as prime minister, while Piłsudski became chief of state. The principle of equality for all citizens before the law was proclaimed, and after years of persecution and pogroms, it looked as if the Jews in the areas of the reborn Polish state would also enjoy full civil rights, especially since thousands of Jewish legionaries and many Jewish officers had fought side by side with Poles in Piłsudski's legions, shed blood, and given their lives for the rebirth of their Polish homeland. But, alas, how differently fate directed the course of events! What actually transpired was not fate, but rather human hatred coming to the fore.

Meanwhile, in the fall of 1918, on the eve of Rosh Hashanah (the Jewish New Year), my father came home from the war. This holiday was full of joy for our battered family. After four years of absence, he was a complete stranger to us children. He had to reacquaint himself with us, since when he left, we were all just a few years old—the youngest still an infant. Father was thirty-seven when he returned home, but he looked much older. His hair was almost entirely gray and thinning, his face thin and peaked. His health was also impaired. Father noticed the scarcity in our home and wanted to hear about our fate during his four-year absence. He

39 The Rada Regencyjna was a provisional Polish authority established by the German and Austro-Hungarian occupation forces in October 1917. It was intended to serve as the nucleus of a future Polish state, though its powers were strictly limited.

40 Cardinal Aleksander Kakowski was an Archbishop of Warsaw and a leading figure of the Polish Catholic Church, serving as one of the three members of the Regency Council (1917–1918).

41 Prince Zdzisław Lubomirski was a conservative politician, mayor of Warsaw, and member of the Regency Council during the German occupation.

42 Józef Ostrowski was a landowner and politician who served as a member of the Regency Council.

43 General Hans von Beseler served as governor of the Government General of Warsaw of the German occupied part of the Kingdom of Poland during World War I.

was extremely upset when he heard of our loneliness and poverty during that time. He did not come home empty-handed, however. After being discharged from the army, he had taken up soap making in Russia and made some money from it. He invested it in Russian gold coins, which had not lost their value even after the 1917 revolution.

After our joyous New Year's holiday at home together, my father went to the soap-making factory on Nadrzeczna Street. He had to break into it because his partner—fearing my father's wrath—had not appeared. He divided up all the raw materials and goods, setting aside his share. Then, my father's partner and my grandparents arrived. My father became enraged and painted a vivid picture of his starving children and hardworking wife, describing the harm they had done to him and his family before throwing my grandparents out. The two partners then sat down at the table, and after settling accounts and informally dissolving their partnership—which had not stood the test of time—my father took his share of the goods, the partner took his, and the factory closed.

Father threw himself into business, and after some time, he joined a large-scale steam soap factory established on the premises owned by Dziubas and Fiszel, where several local soap factories formed a joint company called the Society of United Soap Factories—Dziubas, Fiszel & Co. My father became a director of this company and, under pressure from his family, took on his former partner—who had been left destitute—as a shareholder, even putting up part of the contribution for him. My parents did well, prosperity returned to our home, and my mother devoted herself entirely to running the household and raising her children.

During his spare time, my father would tell us about his wartime adventures and the dangers he faced. In particular, Father told us about his experiences at the front, when he managed to save a cannon with ammunition from the advancing Germans, for which he received a prestigious military decoration from Tsar Nicholas II—the Cross of St. George, 3rd degree—and a promotion to the rank of a sergeant. My father's actions during the war were described in the military newspaper *Yevreyskaya Nedyela*, published for Jewish soldiers of the Russian army. It also featured a picture of him with the cross pinned to his chest. My father brought both the newspaper and the cross back with him from Russia and proudly showed them to us and any guests, who always enjoyed hearing his stories.

As mentioned earlier, my father was injured during the war. In 1916, a piece of shrapnel hit my father in the back, damaging his lung. He spent a long time recuperating in the hospital and was discharged from the army by the medical commission due to his poor health. He went to live in Vitebsk, where he made a living through trade before returning to his profession of soap making, which was in short supply in Russia during the war and even more so after the revolution, during which my father was in St. Petersburg. In 1918, when the Bolshevik authorities allowed the repatriation of Polish citizens who had served in the Russian army, my father returned home with whatever money he had earned in Russia.

Meanwhile, historical events followed quickly one after another, and a new war broke out, this time with Bolshevik Russia. The Red Army, who were occupying the territory evacuated by the Germans, advanced as far as the borders of the former Kingdom of Poland. The Polish army under Piłsudski's command took the offensive on April 19, 1919, and captured Vilna (Wilno, Vilnius), then Belarus, Volhynia, and Podolia, and on May 8, 1920, they entered Kiev. Piłsudski's plan was to establish a Lithuanian and Ukrainian state in those territories, linked to Poland by a federation. In this spirit, he issued a proclamation to the population of the former Grand Duchy of Lithuania and Ukraine, and entered into an alliance with Ataman Petliura, a Ukrainian and notorious nationalist, infamous for his numerous pogroms against Jews.[44]

However, the Bolshevik army broke through the Polish front between the Dniester and Dnieper Rivers around June 8, encircling and capturing the rear units of the Polish army, which began to rapidly retreat at an accelerated rate. The Bolsheviks captured Vilna and entered Polish territory proper, while the second Bolshevik army threatened Lwów.[45] The Bolshevik army was followed by an exile Polish government composed of Polish communists, which was supposed to take control of the country. It was a dangerous situation for Poland. All political party

44 Symon Petliura (1879–1926), was the Commander of the Ukrainian People's Army (UNA) and leader of the Ukrainian People's Republic (UNR) during the Ukrainian War of Independence, which was part of the wider Russian Civil War (1917–1922). Petliura's personal responsibility for the pogroms has been a matter of debate among historians. Antony Polonsky notes that on the one hand Petliura was willing to support Jewish self-defense groups. But on the other, he tolerated anti-Jewish violence perpetrated by some within the Ukrainian armed forces. See Polonsky, *The Jews in Poland and Russia*, vol. 2, pp. 34–37. On pogroms, see Jeffrey Veidlinger, *In the Midst of Civilized Europe: The Pogroms of 1918–1921 and the Onset of the Holocaust* (London: Picador, 2021).

45 The Red Army's offensive gained momentum throughout June and July 1920. Forces under Mikhail Tukhachevsky in the north and Semyon Budyonny's 1st Cavalry Army in the south achieved significant breakthroughs.

disputes were postponed, even the conspiratorial schemes of the Polish ultra-nationalists—the so-called National Democracy (Endecja), led by the eminent Polish antisemite Roman Dmowski.[46] A Council of State Defense was created. The government was taken over by a coalition cabinet headed by the People's Party leader Wincenty Witos[47] and Socialist Party leader Ignacy Daszyński.[48] The army was strengthened by volunteers from Poland and abroad. Józef Haller's Polish army, which had been formed in France, was sent to Poland to fight against the Bolsheviks.[49] The same happened with Polish units created in Poznań.[50] Both these volunteer armies were known for their hostile attitude toward Jews, whom the antisemitic propaganda identified with the Bolsheviks. Nevertheless, many Polish Jews joined the Polish army during its formation and took part in the fighting against the Bolsheviks. France rushed to Poland's aid, sending military equipment along with a group of officers headed by General Weygand. Among this group of officers was also a young officer named Charles de Gaulle.[51]

Under the influence of Polish nationalist propaganda, antisemitic tendencies intensified, and were deliberately blown up by members of the National Democracy, who were also against the left wing, against the

46 Roman Stanisław Dmowski (1864–1939) was a Polish politician, and co-founder and chief ideologue of the National Democracy (Endecja) political movement. He was regarded as a key figure in the Polish nationalist movement who marginalized other ethnic groups including Jews.

47 Wincenty Witos (1874–1945) was a Polish politician, leader of the People's Party (Polskie Stronnictwo Ludowe, PSL), and prime minister of Poland. A key figure in the interwar period, he advocated for agrarian reforms and was a proponent of democratic governance. He served as prime minister three times, including during the Polish–Soviet War.

48 Ignacy Daszyński (1866–1936) was a Polish socialist politician, co-founder of the Polish Social Democratic Party (Polska Partia Socjalno-Demokratyczna, PPSD), and advocate for workers' rights and social reforms. In 1920, he served as deputy prime minister in the Government of National Defense (Rząd Obrony Narodowej) led by Wincenty Witos during the Polish–Soviet War.

49 After arriving from France, from May 1919, Józef Haller's Polish army first fought against Ukrainian forces in the Polish–Ukrainian War (November 1918 to–July 1919) before engaging in the Polish–Bolshevik War, as stated above.

50 This is a reference to the so-called Poznań Volunteer Death's Battalion (Batalion Śmierci) formed in 1919.

51 Charles de Gaulle (1890–1970) was the leader of the Free French Forces during World War II and president of France from 1959 to 1969.

People's Party (Ludowce), and against Piłsudski, who ideologically came from the ranks of the Polish Socialist Party (PPS). The Endecja and other antisemites of various stripes—supported in part by the Catholic clergy—spread false rumors about the Jews. The term *Judokomuna*[52] had already been coined by then. Jews were identified with communists and Bolsheviks, and they were accused of wanting to introduce Bolshevism in Poland, of shooting Polish soldiers in Vilna, Lwów, and Pinsk from around the corners of houses, of conducting pro-Bolshevik propaganda, and of being their allies in the Polish territories. They were allegedly responsible for instigating economic upheaval, raising prices, speculating, exploiting the Polish people, impoverishing Poland, and causing unemployment. Essentially, the Jews were blamed for all economic failures of the new government, as well as for the invasion of Poland by the Bolsheviks and for the ensuing war with them.

This tactic of dealing with the Jews was not new and can be traced back to the Middle Ages, when Jews were murdered for all failures, for famine, for spreading epidemics, and for enemy invasions. And this very same method had recently been used effectively in Poland under tsarist rule, as well as in tsarist Russia, where, as we know, organizations existed implicitly to spread hatred against Jews and organize pogroms, for example, Black Sotnia. Now, Polish antisemites were reaching for the same weapon of demonization, hatred, and collective responsibility of the Jews. Polish newspapers took on the task of disseminating antisemitic propaganda and inciting pogroms. And the results of this were quick to appear. Nationalist mobs began to beat, murder, and rob Jews and their property already in those first days of freedom. Pogroms broke out in many Polish areas—in Lwów, Vilna, Pińsk, Białystok,[53] as well as in countless poor towns on Ukrainian and Polish lands that had been seized by Polish soldiers and their allied rabble of Ukrainian Haydamaks,[54] which were now flowing with Jewish blood.

52 Or *Żydokomuna* (Judeo-Bolshevism) is an antisemitic stereotype suggesting that Jews were collectively aligned with the Soviet Union in promoting communism in Poland, or that there was a Jewish conspiracy behind it. The term is associated with the broader "Jewish world conspiracy" myth and was used to justify antisemitic violence and discrimination.

53 The pogroms in Lwów (1918), Vilna (1919), and Pińsk (1919) were violent antisemitic attacks targeting Jewish communities before and after World War I, and during the Polish–Bolshevik War. Fueled by the myth of *Żydokomuna*, the pogroms resulted in the murder of many Jews and in the looting of their property in these cities.On the Białystok pogrom, see earlier.

54 The term Haydamaks originally referred to eighteenth-century Ukrainian peasants

In our city, this antisemitic incitement was fronted by the newspapers *Goniec Częstochowski*,[55] edited by the well-known antisemite Wilkoszewski, and the *Kurier Częstochowski*.[56] On May 27, 1919,[57] Hallerians in blue uniforms with cornets atop their heads and Poznanians—Polish troops on their way to Warsaw—stopped in Częstochowa, heading for the front against the Bolshevik army. Coming home from school that day, I saw the streets were full of soldiers accosting passersby that looked Jewish, cutting off their beards while kicking and beating them haphazardly, not sparing any part of the body. Jews fled in panic and hid in their apartments. Stores and stalls were closed hurriedly. The mood in the town was tense. At about two o'clock in the afternoon, a false rumor spread through the town that Jews were shooting at the soldiers of Haller's formation, and that a Hallerian soldier had been killed by a Jew.[58] In reality, no one in the city had fired a shot, and no shot had been heard.[59] The false rumor had been spread by antisemitic elements to incite a pogrom.

and Cossacks who revolted against Polish landowners. Here it is used metaphorically to describe Ukrainians involved in antisemitic pogroms, portraying them as violent, unruly, and hostile toward Jews.

55 *Goniec Częstochowski* was a Polish daily newspaper published in Częstochowa from 1906 to 1939, known for its right-wing nationalist orientation. It covered local and national news, politics, and culture until its closure during the German occupation in World War II.

56 *Kurier Częstochowski* was another local Polish newspaper.

57 What follows is the description of the second anti-Jewish pogrom in Częstochowa, taken by Kromołowski mainly from *Chenstochower Tageblat* (May 28, 1919), as he himself mentions. For a reconstruction of the pogrom, see Wiesław Paszkowski, "Pogrom w Częstochowie 27 maja 1919 r. w świetle relacji żydowskich," in *Pogromy Żydów na ziemiach polskich w XIX i XX wieku vol. 2, Studia przypadków (do 1939 roku)* (Warsaw: Instytut Historii PAN, 2019) pp. 263–283. There are some differences between Kromołowski's and Paszkowski's reconstruction and interpretation of events.

58 The allegation that violence erupted because a Jew shot at a Hallerian soldier—thereby assigning part of the responsibility for the pogrom to the Jews—was published in a local newspaper on May 29. See "Krwawe zajścia w Częstochowie. Obfite plony prowokacji komunistyczno-niemieckiej," *Goniec Częstochowski*, May 29, 1919, p. 3, https://zbiory.biblioteka.czest.pl/czasopisma/goniec_czestochowski/1919/Goniec_Czestochowski_Nr_113_1919.pdf/ (accessed August 18, 2025).

59 According to an account in a Polish newspaper, soldier Stanisław Dziadecki sustained a minor head wound without seeing the shooter. Someone insinuated that it was a Jew. See ibid.

A Jewish feldsher, or medic, named Mosze Nasanowicz living at 18 Second Avenue, was approached by two policemen, who demanded that he come with them to help a Jew who had been wounded by the Hallerians. Nasanowicz packed his feldsher's equipment and bandages and headed off with the policemen toward the Old Town. When the men working in the alleys saw a Jew being led away by two policemen, they started whispering among themselves. Soon, the workers started shouting that the police were taking away the Jew who killed a Polish soldier. Before the policemen realized what was happening, and before they had managed to explain who the Jew was and where they were heading, the crowd of workers attacked the totally innocent Nasanowicz. He was beaten with spades and pickaxes. The feldsher, knocked to the ground, was brutally murdered in front of the accompanying policemen. Again, innocent Jewish blood was shed.

Having had a taste of blood, the mob rushed toward the Jewish quarter and started mercilessly beating Jewish passersby, smashing and robbing stores and stalls, and breaking into Jewish homes. Bed linen was ripped apart, furnishings were broken, money was stolen, and destruction was all around. The Jewish stalls in both the Old and New Markets were looted and burned. The mob then began to storm the door of the old synagogue on Nadrzeczna Street, and when it gave way, the mob rushed inside. There, they took apart the pews, desecrated the altar, broke the Torah crowns, and tore the parchment scrolls to pieces, scattering its shreds on the ground.

The mob, led by soldiers from Haller's army, then moved on to the ritual slaughterhouse next to the old synagogue. Hearing the crowd breaking into the synagogue courtyard, the ritual slaughterers (*shohetim*) Nehemia Gotlib, Joszua Bergman, and Mosze Działowski took refuge in the apartment of the Christian synagogue janitor. However, the hordes also attacked this apartment, breaking and destroying its furniture. They dragged Nehemia Gotlib out into the courtyard, where he was beaten to death with rods and stones, until his brain flowed from his shattered skull. The other two ritual slaughterers managed to escape. They stole 1,200 Marks from Gotlib's corpse. He left behind a wife and six children.

After they murdered Gotlib, the mob burst into Bergman's apartment where he was beaten until he lost consciousness. He was taken to the hospital in a serious condition. The synagogue *shamash* (beadle), Machel Rozenberg, and his wife and son were also beaten. At 34 Nadrzeczna Street, the mob broke into the apartment of Jankiel Gelbard, who was beaten and robbed of 700 Marks. At 38 Nadrzeczna Street, Finkelsztajn and Dukat were severely beaten and robbed. The crowd then rushed to 11 Mostowa Street. Moszek Brokman was dragged out of his home, beaten, and kicked until he fell lifeless to the ground. Brokman's family, too, was attacked, and his apartment was robbed. Nothing was left intact. In the Old Market Square, hooligans, Haller's soldiers, and the soldiers from Poznań captured Hershel Działoszyński, who was savagely beaten with rods and kicked while on the ground until he died, his skull shattered.

Another crowd of pogromists, consisting of workers, soldiers, and students from local high schools, waited on Dojazd Street, near the railroad station for the arrival of a train from Kielce. The mob rushed at the Jewish passengers, beating them mercilessly before snatching their suitcases and packages. A man named Faktor from Piotrków and Majer Wertelojm from Włoszczowa were beaten until they bled and were robbed of all their belongings. Wertelojm had come to Częstochowa to report for military service and was beaten unconscious. The thugs also ripped off his gold watch and took it. Mordka Epelbaum—who lived at 39 Warszawska Street—along with his wife and son, tried to take shelter in the Kaliski Hotel. The owner did not want to let him in and pushed him out onto the street, announcing that it was right to beat up Jews. Epelbaum's son lost an eye after he was hit so hard with a blunt instrument by a student at Sudejko's gymnasium.

In addition, Alta Zajdman, a fifteen-year-old girl, was attacked and received a blow to the head, subsequently suffering from mental illness. Shmul Frajman was beaten and wounded by Hallerians while having his beard cut. Likewise, Josef Broniatowski was wounded while having his beard and whiskers cut. He was beaten bloody, and his apartment was robbed. The 400 Marks that were in his pocket were taken. Mordka Sznajder was also attacked, and his apartment robbed. Moszek Grinberg was struck repeatedly on the head. Moszek Buchman was beaten as students from the Koźmiński Gymnasium kicked him mercilessly while he was lying on the ground. Mendel Pejsak was hit all over his body using rods. These were only a few examples.

The pogrom continued. Jews were murdered, beaten, and robbed with no response from the municipal and police authorities. The police chief, Belina Prażmowski, riding his horse, tried to disperse the mob, but he was dragged from the horse, while the policemen standing nearby remained completely impassive. They fled, taking their commander with them.

Anszel Cymerman, a baker's apprentice, tried to fight his attackers and was struck on the head multiple times with an ax. Bleeding and unconscious, he was taken to the hospital, where he was pronounced dead from his wounds. More than thirty Jewish apartments were totally plundered and devastated. Fifty Jewish families, whose stores were entirely robbed, were left without any means of subsistence. Klingberg's and Kamioner's wood warehouses were set on fire by these hooligans and burned to the ground. A number of seriously wounded Jews lay in hospitals: A. Pławner, M. Szapiro, J. Częstochowski, Grynblat, Dr. Ignacy Szrajber—a gymnasium professor—L. Birenbaum, and Abramowiczowa. A grenade was thrown into Dr. L. Kohn's apartment. Moreover, the premises of Jewish institutions were plundered and demolished: the *beit hamidrash* (house of study) on Nadrzeczna Street, the Jewish gymnasium on Dąbrowskiego Street, the People's Bank at 7 First Avenue, and the Association of Jewish Craftsmen at 12 First Avenue. Windows were broken in both the Old and New Synagogues.

The funerals of five victims[60] of the pogrom took place on May 29, 1919, with many thousands of Jews participating. The corpse of the murdered medic Nasanowicz was brought out from the Virgin Mary Hospital on Second Avenue. The funeral procession then continued through the old town and stopped by the Jewish Hospital in Zawodzie. From there, the bodies of the four other murdered Jews were collected, and amidst the weeping of the funeral goers and the wailing of the families, the funeral procession headed toward the Jewish cemetery on Olsztyńska Street. The funeral was attended by members of the Jewish religious community, the students, teachers, and principal of the Jewish high school, as well as the well-known historian Prof. Majer Bałaban. Dr. Apolinary Hartglas, a Jewish member of the Polish Parliament, was also present.

The dead were buried in the first row of the cemetery, in a place of honor. There were no speeches, only funeral prayers. The crowds cried over the bodies of the innocent victims. The grief and emotion were so great that even the Polish policemen surrounding the procession shed sympathetic tears. Five more corpses buried in a common grave had now been added to the numerous victims of pogroms and murders on Polish territory. It seems that the only protest expressed by Polish society against the bloody events of Częstochowa was a telegram sent by the chairman of the Polish trade unions, Professor Józef Dziuba, to the Ministry of Internal Affairs in Warsaw. In it he condemned the passivity of the central and local authorities, as well as the police, during the pogrom, and he also

60 According to the official report of the Jewish community, five men were killed, twenty-three were seriously injured, and forty-four were lightly injured. See Paszkowski, *Pogrom w Częstochowie*, p. 275.

condemned the immoral perpetrators of the pogrom—the antisemites from the Endecja movement.[61]

The Częstochowa pogrom caused deep indignation around the world. Jews living abroad—especially in the United States—raised an alarming cry of protest, both in the American press and in numerous memoranda addressed to the Polish government. From the farthest corners of the globe came telegrams from the countrymen of Częstochowa to their relatives, inquiring about their health and safety. In addition, Jewish representatives filed interpellations regarding the pogrom. At the meeting of the Częstochowa City Council, Jewish councilmen proposed a rigorous investigation and the harsh punishment of those found guilty. They demanded that Haller's army and the Poznanian fighters be immediately expelled from the city, and that all soldiers who took part in the pogrom be held accountable for their actions. The motion was proposed and supported by the alderman Rafał Federman; however, it failed to pass because the majority of the Polish councilmen were members of antisemitic parties and voted against it. All the Jewish councilors left the meeting hall in protest.

The history of the Jews in the Polish lands was written in blood and tears,[62] and the tragedy of Częstochowa was another link in the neverending chain of atrocities, killing, hatred, and persecution that had repeatedly afflicted the Jewish citizens for over 1,000 years. Propelled by fierce antisemitism and hostility, its zealous propagators and leaders constituted a segment of the Polish intelligentsia and the Polish Catholic clergy. They were among the instigators of spilled Jewish blood, finding an eager and willing audience among the mobs and hooligans.

61 Paszkowski argues that violence erupted due to a number of specific factors, which were triggered by the shooting of a Polish soldier, escalated due to police ineffectiveness, and culminated in violent mob actions. Ibid., pp. 282–283.

62 This perception of the history of Jews in Poland is reflected to a certain extent in Jewish collective memory. Jewish–Polish relations are often perceived as traumatic, characterized by Polish hostility and violence toward Jews. Actual outbursts of anti-Jewish violence before, during, and after the Holocaust reinforced these negative perceptions in Jewish collective memory. However, if one looks at the 1,000-year long history of the Jews in Poland—notwithstanding anti-Jewish perceptions, beliefs, and behaviors—it was also characterized by rapid demographic development of the Jewish population alongside the extensive development of Jewish social institutions and active economic participation. For a comprehensive account of Jews in Poland and Polish society, consult Antony Polonsky, *The Jews in Poland and Russia*, vol. 1 (1350–1881), vol. 2 (1881–1914), vol. 3 (1914–2008) (Oxford and Portland: Littman Library of Jewish Civilization, 2010–2012).

As mentioned, the Częstochowa pogrom was prepared and inspired by the National Democrats and all forms of antisemites.[63] The columns of *Goniec Częstochowski* and *Kurier Częstochowski* had long since been filled with unfounded accusations against the Jews, who were allegedly the cause of the economic crisis as well as all the social and political disasters that had befallen Poland at the dawn of independence—including the intention to establish Bolshevism in Poland.

From the pulpits of churches, parts of the Polish clergy called for a reckoning with the Jews, whom they accused of bringing the Bolsheviks to Poland with the goal of eliminating Christianity. The slogan spouted by Polish antisemites during those years was "The *Żydokomuna* is the eternal enemy of Christianity, Catholicism, and Poland."[64] This seed of hatred fell on fertile soil, and the result was a series of pogroms against Jews, one of which took place in Częstochowa. This happened despite the fact that, at the same time, tens of thousands of Jewish soldiers were fighting in the ranks of the Polish army against the Bolsheviks, offering their blood and lives for Poland.

The same rampant antisemitism that had unleashed anti-Jewish pogroms immediately after World War I—calling for a crusade against Polish Jews for aligning themselves with the Bolsheviks and wanting to bring Communism to Poland—continued its deed of hatred against the few survivors of the Nazi death camps immediately after Poland regained freedom after World War II. For a change, however, the Polish antisemites of the 1960s dressed themselves in the red hats of Gomułka-Moczar Communism and did not hesitate to use antisemitic slogans; this time, of course, not because they were *Żydokomuna*, but because they were capitalists, Zionists, nationalists, and the so-called fifth column of global imperialism. Once again, Polish Jews were stripped of their honor and faith, and were considered enemies of the People's Republic of Poland. Jewish university students were beaten, imprisoned, and expelled en masse from the universities, Jews were dismissed from their jobs, and even people in the highest state positions were deprived of bread. Again, anti-

63 See Paszkowski's reconstruction in *Pogrom w Częstochowie*, pp. 282–283.

64 On the the attitude of the Catholic Church toward Jews—by examining the Catholic Press in the interwar period—see Anna Landau-Czajka, "The Image of the Jew in the Catholic Press during the Second Republic," in Antony Polonsky, Jerzy Tomaszewski, and Ezra Mendelsohn, eds., *Polin: Studies in Polish Jewry*, vol. 8: *Jews in Independent Poland, 1918–1939* (Liverpool: Liverpool University Press, 1994), pp. 146–175.

Jewish leaflets were distributed and there were calls for a crackdown on Jews. This led to a massive exodus of the remnants of Polish Jewry from the country between 1968 and 1978, for whose freedom and independence they had fought with the partisans, behind the walls of the burning Jewish ghetto in Warsaw, and in the ranks of the Polish People's Army on the trail from Lenino to Berlin.[65]

At the time of this pogrom in our town in 1919, I was a ten-year-old boy—still a child. But the image of those Polish soldiers, wearing cornets featuring an eagle emblem, who rushed into our yard with shouts of "beat the Jew" will stay with me for the rest of my life. Nor will I ever forget how, with a smile of triumph, they ordered our janitor Antoni to pump water from the well to rinse Jewish blood from their hands.

65 In March 1968, following the severance of diplomatic ties with Israel following the Six-Day War, Gomułka's government launched an aggressive public campaign against Jews, labeling them Zionists who pose an internal threat to Poland. A comprehensive list of all Polish citizens of Jewish descent was prepared, and Jews were systematically removed from public service roles, including academic and educational positions. They faced pressure to leave the country, and over the subsequent two years, approximately 25,000 Jews left, reducing Poland's Holocaust-devastated Jewish population to only 5,000–10,000. On the persecution of Jews in postwar Poland under Władysław Gomułka, secretary-general of the Communist Party's government, see David Engel, "Poland since 1939," YIVO Encyclopedia of Jews in Eastern Europe, https://encyclopedia.yivo.org/article/18 (accessed August 18, 2025).

CHAPTER FOUR

THE INTERWAR PERIOD

Following the bloody pogroms of 1919–1920, Polish Jews began to turn with increasing attention toward Mandatory Palestine, where the seeds of Jewish statehood were beginning to form. Lord Balfour's declaration on November 2, 1917, on behalf of the British government, exercising the League of Nations mandate in Mandatory Palestine and announcing the creation of a Jewish national home, played a key role in the spontaneous emergence of the idea of founding an independent state there. This was an official endorsement of Zionist ideology, a movement aimed at reviving Jewish statehood in *Eretz Israel*, initiated by Dr. Theodor Herzl and accepted by the Zionist Congress in Basel in 1897.[1] Zionism became very popular among Jewish youth in those years so abundantly saturated with Jewish blood. The Jewish Scouts' organizations—traditionally with no political affiliation—began their restructure to become Hashomer Hatzair at this time.[2]

1 Theodor Herzl (1860–1904) was an Austro-Hungarian Jewish journalist, writer, political thinker and activist, founder of the Zionist Organization, and advocate for Jewish immigration to the Land of Israel to establish a Jewish state.

2 Hashomer Hatzair (The Young Guard) is a socialist-Zionist youth movement originating from the Kingdom of Galicia and Lodomeria, Austria-Hungary, on the

Like many of my peers, I belonged to the Maccabi Jewish Scouts' association. Its headquarters were on Teatralna Street, next to the building known as "House of the Prince," where a well-known Jewish philanthropist named Henryk Markusfeld had granted young people use of a several-room apartment on the first floor of his home, along with the possibility to gather in the large courtyard and garden. I was a member of the Young Wolves Squad—the youngest *shomrim*, or members—and our instructor was Wilek Leslau, a student at the Jewish junior high school.[3] Our organization was made up of girls and boys between the ages of ten and fourteen. The older Zionist youth who strived to immigrate to *Eretz Israel* to cultivate the arid land there were affiliated with the Hechalutz organization, where they intensively learned about agriculture and farming.[4]

We came to the meetings dressed in scout uniforms made of a heavy, green fabric: knee-length shorts, shirts, and green, knee-high socks. A scout hat à la Robert Baden Powell,[5] and a blue scarf completed the look.

eve of World War I. It focused on educating Jewish youth in socialist ideology, fostering a connection to Jewish culture and Zionism, and promoting collective living and agricultural labor. The movement played a significant role in the Jewish settlement in Mandatory Palestine and has since evolved into an international movement advocating for social justice, environmentalism, and progressive values, alongside its commitment to Zionism and Jewish identity.

3 Wolf Wilek Leslau (1906–2006) was a semitologist and Zionist. Leslau attended a *heder* and studied in a yeshiva in Częstochowa. He joined Hashomer Hatzair and became one of its leaders in Częstochowa. See Sętkowski, *Częstochowa Jews: A Biographical Dictionary*, pp. 295–296.

4 Hechalutz was a pioneering Zionist movement that emerged during the First Aliya (1882–1903) and the Second Aliya (1904–1914), but gained momentum only from 1917 onward—the year of the Balfour Declaration, the Russian Revolution, and the emergence of nation-states in Eastern Europe. It focused on promoting Jewish immigration to the Land of Israel and on agricultural settlement. It played a crucial role in the establishment of Jewish agricultural communities (*kibbutzim*) and helped lay the groundwork for the formation of the State of Israel. Hechalutz members were at the forefront of the Jewish defense in the Diaspora, including in the ghettos where the Jews were concentrated by the Nazis as part of "the Final Solution of the Jewish Question." See Israel Oppenheim, "Hechalutz," The YIVO Encyclopedia of Jews in Eastern Europe, https://encyclopedia.yivo.org/article/1688 (accessed August 15, 2025).

5 This is referring to a broad-brimmed, high-crowned hat with a distinctive pinched Montana-peak shape. Worn by Robert Baden-Powell, the founder of the Scout movement, it became an iconic part of the early Scout's uniforms.

A great delight for us was the Lag Ba'Omer[6] celebration of spring and harvest. On that day, our entire *ken*[7] would go on a trip out of town, usually to the Błeszno estate that belonged to the Jewish Rozenbaum family. Lined up in rows of four, with a banner unfurled and an orchestra consisting of snare drummers and clarinet players, we marched through the city. At the head was our leader at that time, Jermek Gitler,[8] a law student. Our march looked quite impressive as we walked in unison. In the middle of the street and along the sidewalks, passersby would stop and watch us. Once, when we were marching through the main part of our city, I heard a fragment of a conversation between two locals with characteristic Sarmatian mustaches who were looking at us.

"What is this parade, my friend?" one asked the other.

"It's the Jewish army going to [Mandatory] Palestine to fight the Arabs," explained the other with mock seriousness.

Hearing those taunts of our Polish compatriots, I could not imagine that a time would come when in the land of our forefathers, in *Eretz Israel*, a Jewish army would indeed arise to defend the reborn state and its citizens from enemies. But at that time, the nucleus of such an army was already being formed in Mandatory Palestine. Jewish pioneers—*halutzim*—were leaving their families and the ghettos of the Diaspora and immigrating in ever-increasing numbers to Mandatory Palestine, the historical homeland from which the Jewish people had been driven out in ancient times by Roman violence. There, they devoted themselves to hard labor and reclaiming every inch of land from the firm grip of the rocky, sandy deserts.

With rifles on their backs, they drained the swamps, which were a source of malaria, planted eucalyptus trees to keep the volatile sands at bay, and on the ever-increasing amount of land purchased by the national

6 Lag Ba'omer is a Jewish holiday marked by various customs, including outdoor celebrations, bonfires, picnics, and parades. For Zionists, the holiday also served to commemorate the Bar Kohba revolt against the Romans.

7 A *ken* is the name of a unit or branch within a Jewish youth organization. It means nest in Hebrew.

8 Jeremiasz Gitler (1903–1943) was a lawyer and Zionist activist from Łódź and was the cofounder of Hashomer Hatzair in Częstochowa. He became a member of the Judenrat and later its deputy head before being murdered with his family in 1943 at the Częstochowa Jewish Cemetery during the execution of the Jewish intelligentsia. See Sętkowski, *Częstochowa Jews: A Biographical Dictionary*, p. 159.

land funds[9] (at that time, the nucleus), they created—as if by a miracle—blooming orange orchards and gardens out of the arid sand and stone. Agricultural settlements (*kibbutzim*) were established, and the brand new Jewish city of Tel Aviv was created. All this took place amidst constant fighting with hordes of Arabs, who attacked Jewish homes and stealthily shot at *kibbutz* inhabitants, seeing how the flourishing fertile tracts of land that, thanks to the arduous efforts of the *halutzim*, turned under their nose from the wasteland and desert to fertile acres and blooming orchards.

I was probably in the fourth grade of junior high school when I thought I was too old for scouting and traded in the short shorts in favor of long men's pants. At that time, together with several friends, we founded the Young Zionist Circle. Our organization was called Bnei Zion[10] (Children of Zion), and it was headquartered in the local Zionist association's premises on Piłsudskiego Street, in someone called Winer's house, across from the train station. In a short time, our circle grew to include several dozen Jewish girls and boys. Alongside me, the founders included Natan (Nachum) Klarman, Karol Kałużyński, and Leon Rozensztajn. The members of our organization were mainly local school students, but there were also young craftsmen trainees or trade workers. For some time, I served as chairman of this Zionist youth organization, and later Klarman—then a student at the local Jewish high school—was elected.

My involvement in this youth organization consumed a lot of time, to the significant detriment of my performance in school. There were meetings, lectures, and talks about the history of Zionism, Jewish history, and the current political situation of Jews around the world. There were heated discussions, and various conflicting political views within the Zionist movement competed with each other; representatives of Poalei

9 Keren Kayemet LeYisrael (Jewish National Fund) and Keren Hayesod (United Israel Appeal) are both crucial fundraising organizations in the history of Zionism. Keren Kayemet was established in 1901 to buy and develop land for Jewish settlement in the Land of Israel, while Keren Hayesod, founded in 1920, focused on securing financial support for Zionist activities and Jewish immigration. Together, they were instrumental in building the infrastructure of the Jewish state.

10 Bnei Zion was a Zionist organization in Poland that promoted Jewish national identity, Hebrew culture, and immigration to *Eretz Israel*. Active in the early twentieth century, it focused on education, youth engagement, and support for the Zionist cause, operating alongside other Zionist movements like Poalei Zion and Mizrachi.

Zion, Hitahdut, and the Revisionist Zionists,[11] who looked up to their leader Vladimir (Ze'ev) Jabotinsky,[12] presented their arguments.

We were also involved in raising funds to purchase and develop land in Mandatory Palestine through various campaigns, including Keren Hayesod and Keren Kayemet. The collection and distribution of the blue money-collection boxes of Keren Kayemet that were placed in numerous Jewish homes especially required a lot of work. It was a vibrant organizational life that contributed not only to mental development, but also to character formation and the setting of life goals. Many of my comrades from Bnei Zion—later renamed Herzliya—went on to join the left-wing Gordonia[13] and immigrated to *Eretz Israel*, thereby realizing their political credo. Many of them still live and work in Israel.

My parents frowned upon my involvement in youth movement work, and they were not wrong, because my school work suffered. There came a point when I had to choose between the organization and school. I realized that, at least at this stage of my life, they could not go hand in hand.

The realities of life had a decisive impact on my choice. The day before the May 1 celebration (workers' day), the police arrived at our organization's premises in the middle of one of our regular social meetings. I happened to be the speaker, presenting on various topics in Jewish history. There were around a dozen of us, both boys and girls, all approximately fourteen years old. The police surrounded us, and their superior, Police Chief Kuczyński, accused us of being communists

11 Poalei Zion was a socialist Zionist movement advocating for Jewish labor rights and the establishment of a Jewish state in *Eretz Israel* through socialist principles. Hitachdut was a labor Zionist organization that combined socialist and practical settlement ideals, emphasizing cooperative agriculture and aliya. Revisionist Zionists, led by Ze'ev Jabotinsky, opposed socialist Zionism and promoted a more militant, nationalist approach, advocating for a Jewish state with a strong Jewish military force.

12 Vladimir (Ze'ev) Jabotinsky (1880–1940) was a prominent Zionist leader and writer who advocated for Jewish self-defense and the establishment of a Jewish state in *Eretz Israel*. In 1923, Jabotinsky founded the Betar youth movement, promoting discipline, pride (*hadar*), and military training. In 1925, he established the World Union of Zionist Revisionists, which soon broke away from the World Zionist Organization under his leadership.

13 The Gordonia movement's principles were founded on the ideas of Aaron David Gordon, which centered on the redemption of the Land of Israel and the Jewish people through manual agrarian labor and living on the revived Land of Israel.

holding a meeting to organize a May Day parade. My assurances and solemn declaration that we were, in fact, members of a Zionist youth organization, recognized by law, fell on deaf ears. With guns pointed at us and surrounded by a platoon of police officers, we were taken to the nearby police station on Krakowska Street, where we were subjected to a thorough personal search. Of course, no communist propaganda papers or revolutionary leaflets were found. However, my Latin notebook, which I had with me, caused some consternation: one of the policemen mistook it for a collection of secret communist codes, but this matter was soon cleared up.

Nevertheless, we were all kept under arrest for the entire night. Only on the following day did the members of the board of directors of the Zionist organization come to the police station to offer explanations. The chairman of the Jewish religious community, Samuel Goldsztajn, provided a security deposit, which was apparently enough, because we were all released. I was afraid that news of my arrest would reach my school's administration, which could lead to unpleasant consequences. But somehow, everything worked out well, without attracting attention. Following this distressing incident, I decided to suspend my activities in the Zionist organization until I had finished school.

On December 9, 1922, Gabriel Narutowicz was elected president of the Republic of Poland thanks to the votes from the left and national minorities (including Jews). The Polish right wing, led by the antisemitic National Democrats, reacted to this election with the greatest resentment, claiming that the head of state had been elected by non-Polish votes. On December 11, crowds of demonstrators attacked the new president on his way to the Sejm (the Polish parliament), and on December 16, he was assassinated by the painter Eligiusz Niewiadomski[14] with a pistol shot. At this critical moment, the reins of government were seized by General Władysław Sikorski,[15] who stabilized the country through multiple

14 Eligiusz Niewiadomski (1869–1923) was a Polish painter, art critic, and right-wing nationalist who assassinated Poland's first president, Gabriel Narutowicz, on December 16, 1922.

15 General Władysław Sikorski (1881–1943) was a Polish military leader and politician, serving as prime minister (1922–1923) after the assassination of President Narutowicz, helping to stabilize Poland. He later became prime minister of the Polish government-in-exile (1939–1943) and commander in chief of the Polish armed forces during World War II, before dying in a mysterious plane crash in Gibraltar.

measures, before the election of a new president, the cooperative activist Stanisław Wojciechowski.[16]

Shortly thereafter, the right wing, in conjunction with the People's Movement, overthrew Sikorski's government. The new goverment, with the Polish People's Party activist Wincenty Witos as prime minister, failed to control inflation and the economic problems. Piłsudski's supporters came to power, after he himself withdrew from political life and settled on the sidelines at his estate in Sulejówek. A general strike of workers and working intelligentsia broke out, and bloody fights between workers and the army took place in the streets of Kraków.[17] The government was taken over by Grabski, who carried out a currency reform.[18] Instead of the Polish mark, which had been severely devalued by inflation (a box of matches cost 1,000 marks), he introduced the Polish złoty. This somewhat stabilized the economic situation, and he also set up Bank Polski and essentially won the trust of the nation. However, in 1925, the economic crisis returned, and budget shortages shook the Polish złoty. After numerous cabinet rearrangements and turbulence in April 1926, Piłsudski led his loyal troops into Warsaw. After a three-day battle supported by the socialists, he forced the government and the president to resign.

On May 31, 1926, the Sejm accepted Piłsudski's proposal to elect Professor Ignacy Mościcki as president. After Piłsudski's May coup d'etat, the Sejm was pushed into the background; the real power was exercised by Piłsudski, who held the office of prime minister, then minister of military affairs. He ruled with the help of the party of former legionaries and military men he had created, the BBWR (Non-Party Bloc for Cooperation with the Government) or the Sanacja movement. Piłsudski obtained a loan for Poland from the United States, stabilized the currency, and, most importantly, steadied Poland's internal situation, ensuring peace, order, and security for all its citizens. Piłsudski lessened the influence of National

16 Stanisław Wojciechowski (1869–1953) was the president of Poland from 1922 to 1926. His presidency ended when he was overthrown in Piłsudski's May Coup of 1926.

17 This refers to the Kraków riot on November 6, 1923, when a general strike led to violent clashes between workers and the military.

18 Władysław Grabski (1874–1938) was a Polish politician and economist, best known for his 1924 currency reform, which replaced the hyperinflated Polish mark with the złoty, and for the establishment of the Bank Polski. He served twice as prime minister (1920, 1923–1925) and played a key role in Poland's early economic policies.

Democracy—a stronghold of reaction and antisemitism—curbed the influence of political parties, and, in fact, established a dictatorship by filling all key positions with BBWR party members.

Admittedly, the period of his rule—his dictatorial actions notwithstanding—was a success.[19] He led Poland out of the economic crisis, ensured domestic peace, and created work, despite the dissolution of the Sejm and the arrest of the opposition leaders, who were imprisoned in a military camp in Brest-on-the-Bug.[20] BBWR remained the sole political power ruling Poland for many years, strictly following the will of its leader Piłsudski, whose title was elevated to the rank of marshal of the state. Former military officers (colonels) were successively appointed as prime ministers—Walery Sławek, A. Prystor, and others—but throughout the entire ten-year period of the party's rule, it was Piłsudski's will that was ultimately imprinted on Poland's political life. For the Jews of Poland, it was also a time of peace and security, free from persecution and pogroms.

During this period of political transformation, my maternal grandmother, Chana Górska, died after a long illness. She lived to a quite advanced age, but spent the last years of her life sick in bed. Two years later, my paternal grandfather Benjamin Kromołowski died as well. They were both buried in the Jewish cemetery on Olsztyńska Street. When I finally visited this cemetery after the Nazi massacre, I did not find any traces of their graves. The Germans devastated and desecrated this cemetery, taking the more valuable monuments to Germany or else selling them to the local population. My grandfather died in his apartment in Spadkowa Street in the house belonging to Szperling, lovingly cared for by my grandmother, Udla, and his family.

My father told me that shortly before his death, Grandfather was visited by his friends from the *chevra kadisha* (burial society) of which he was a long-time member. They sat by the side of his bed and comforted him as much as they could, telling him that on the journey of every mortal, everyone must dance this last dance. Then, my grandfather, whose wit did not leave him even in the final moments of his life, said in

19 The duality of Piłsudski's rule, which contained both authoritarian and universal components, is portrayed in Joshua Zimmermann's book *Jozef Pilsudski: Founding Father of Modern Poland* (Cambridge: Harvard University Press, 2022). As Kromołowski states, in spite of his authoritarian tendencies, Piłsudski combatted antisemitism and handled major crises of the newly born Polish state.

20 In September 1930, party leaders were imprisoned in the fortress of Brześć. They were later released.

a weak voice, "I would gladly give the musicians a tip, so that someone else would dance this dance for me." My grandfather died shortly after. Fate spared him the tragic experiences that befell his wife, Udla, who at the age of eighty-three, went with my entire family to the trains, holding the hand of her eldest daughter Fela, where they were deported to the Treblinka extermination camp, to a martyr's death, like millions of Polish Jews murdered by the Germans.

During this time, my Aunt Fela was a professional marriage broker. She was very passionate about this profession, even though she did not have to do it for financial reasons, because she lived with my grandparents who supported her. As mentioned, my grandparents were quite wealthy people with a prosperous iron business. At that time—and even during the war—the business was managed by their son-in-law, Wolf, the husband of my other aunt, Andzia. According to the agreement, Wolf paid my grandfather and grandmother a living wage.

Aunt Fela was keen on me becoming her secretary, and since she maintained a lively correspondence with numerous clients—prospective marriage candidates—she often came to our home equipped with writing materials and set me to work. Whether I wanted to or not, I first had to sit through what was usually a lengthy presentation of the personal qualities and financial situation of the person she was proposing as a spouse. Then, everything she said had to be written down in the form of a distinguished, yet somewhat pathetic-sounding, marriage proposal. My aunt would then have each such epistle read to her, usually accepting the text I had written with satisfaction.

When someone in my family signaled that Aunt Fela was coming, I usually escaped to the farthest room and lay down on the couch, feigning a headache. But it didn't help, because my aunt was well aware of my evasions and tricks, and would pester me with her requests for so long that I finally had to capitulate and start writing. She usually updated me about the results of our joint matrimonial endeavors, praising the effectiveness of my letters; however, she always remained completely silent about the fee she received. Aunt Fela—with her blonde wig, haughty stature, and very distinguished manner—was a well-known figure in our town and one of the originals of that lost era. She was a typical matchmaker from the Jewish shtetl.

No less unique was my Uncle Szyja, my father's brother. He was a rich man in the 1920s, having made quite the fortune trading in machinery, successfully continuing the family tradition started by Grandfather Benjamin. Uncle Szyja traded large sums of money and willingly accepted money that people had saved, paying them high interest. People put in their money, collected the interest, and whenever they demanded a return, they would receive their money without delay. Business was going well, and this uncle—who was better at wielding a billiard cue than a pen—employed a secretary to accompany him in all his business dealings. The secretary was a man named Biber, and he had a slight stutter. They both wore elegant, black bowler hats.

Uncle Szyja was usually in a good mood, and he liked to tell jokes and play pranks, always keeping a serious face when people burst out laughing. For example, he had an inkwell of his own invention that looked like it was filled with black ink. He also had a fake "stain" made of synthetic material. He would surreptitiously place the inkwell and the "stain" on the bed or tablecloth of the people he was staying with, making it look like an inkwell had spilled on the bedding or napkin, creating a black stain. When a member of the household—usually the lady of the house—would cry out in horror at this sight, my uncle would calmly and solemnly pick up the inkwell along with the fake stain and put it in his pocket, signalling that everything was actually fine. Everyone would laugh, and Uncle would be pleased with his joke. He would then go off in search of his next dupe.

One day, at dinner time, he knocked on the kitchen door of his client, the wealthy stick and cufflink manufacturer Bromberg. When his maid opened the door, he put on a miserable face and, as a poor man would, held out his hand asking for alms. The servant ran into the dining room and received fifty pennies from her employer for the rather decent-looking man who had knocked on the door. She handed the money to the supposed beggar. Then, Uncle Szyja suddenly became animated, waving his hands menacingly and yelling out loud, "What, such a rich man and he gives only fifty pennies! Isn't he ashamed? What can I get for this amount!" Lured into the kitchen by the sounds of shouting, Bromberg rushed in, saw Szyja standing at the door holding a fifty-penny coin next to the terrified maid, and burst out laughing. He invited the supposedly poor man inside.

Another time, a train that was about to leave for Warsaw was full of commotion. All the seats were occupied, and it was so crowded that you couldn't have stuck a pin in it. Uncle Szyja entered the second-class carriage, leaning on Biber's arm. Uncle's face was contorted, while he held his stomach with his free hand and groaned. Biber looked worriedly at the passengers in the tightly packed compartment and announced that he was taking a typhoid patient to the hospital in Piotrków. The passengers got up hastily from their seats, each grabbing his belongings and coat. Within a few moments, the compartment was empty, and both new passengers could now sit down comfortably.

There was also the ticket prank. My uncle, together with Biber and another merchant, got on a train going in the direction of Sosnowiec. All three were going to Łazy, which was halfway to Sosnowiec. Of course, all but Szyja had purchased their tickets at the ticket office. Before boarding the train, Uncle Szyja took the ticket from Biber and wrote his own name and surname on the back of it before handing it back to his sidekick, who was somewhat surprised by this action. All three took their seats comfortably, and my uncle quietly read a newspaper. After some time, the conductor came into the compartment to check the tickets. Biber and the merchant gave their tickets to the inspector. Seeing that the travelers were going to Łazy—a railway terminal without connecting traffic, so tickets were not collected from arriving passengers—he put the tickets in his pocket.

The conductor then turned to Uncle Szyja and asked him to produce his ticket. Uncle Szyja put down his newspaper, looked at the conductor with astonishment, and said that the conductor had already taken the ticket from him and put it in his pocket, because he, too, was going to Łazy. A little bewildered, the conductor denied this, saying that he had not taken the ticket from him. It looked like there was going to be a fight, and Uncle Szyja's companions were clearly upset by the situation. Only Uncle Szyja remained calm. He said that the conductor was obviously mistaken, and to prove it, he took out his identity card, handed it to the conductor, and said that he had the habit of always writing his name on the back of his train ticket. If the conductor searched among the tickets collected from passengers, he would surely find his ticket marked by his name that had been taken from him earlier. The conductor pulled out a handful of tickets from his pocket, turned them over, and, of course, found the one with Szyja's name—identical to the one on the identity card my uncle had shown him. The conductor apologized to my triumphant uncle and, saluting, left the compartment. When the three of them arrived in Łazy, Biber, who cared greatly about the honesty of all his boss's transactions, pulled him aside. Stammering and blinking, as was his custom, he said to my uncle, "A good piece of work, but morally unacceptable, you have committed fraud!"

When Uncle Szyja's wife, Mania, was pregnant, she went to see Dr. Finkelsztajn, a gynecologist known among the Jewish population of our town. He was commonly called the *Fishele docter*. My Aunt Mania would go for her pregnancy check-ups, paying rather high fees, because *Fishele docter* was a commercially aware doctor and loved to make good money. When the delivery date arrived, Dr. Finkelsztajn was summoned as the critical moment approached. He came quickly holding his small medical bag, and since it was freezing cold that day, the doctor was wearing an expensive fur coat. He hung it up in the hallway and immediately got down to work. Everything went well, and a son was born.

My uncle invited the doctor to sit down and have a drink. The doctor accepted, drank, ate, thanked Uncle Szyja, and demanded his fee. Uncle held out his hands helplessly and said that he did not have the money on him but would send the payment later. The doctor was very upset and told Uncle that if he did not have any money to pay him, he should pawn his fur coat, because the fee was sacred and had to be paid immediately. Uncle agreed and said that the money was on the way. He then arose from his seat, took the fur coat hanging in the hallway, pawned it in a nearby pawnshop, and returned home to pay Finkelsztajn. When the doctor went to leave, he was horrified to find his fur coat missing.

"Where is my coat?" shouted the anxious disciple of Asclepios, the Greek god of medicine. In a cool voice, my uncle answered, "Mr. Doctor ordered me to pawn the coat, so I obeyed. Your coat, because I don't have my own fur coat."

People kept retelling my uncle's funny story, laughing every time, because the doctor's greed and exorbitant fees were well known. During the war, when there was an epidemic of spotted fever that decimated the population of the Jewish ghetto in Częstochowa, Uncle Szyja and his wife died on the same day in the ghetto hospital for infectious diseases.

The years 1926 and 1927 were not particularly successful for me academically. I attended several local gymnasiums, but somehow could not settle down in any of them. Finally, I joined the Stanisław-Niemiec Gymnasium in Radomsko,[21] where I managed to pass the seventh grade exams. It was very difficult as I had to commute every day from Częstochowa to Radomsko and back. I would get up at dawn, because the train left at five o'clock, and I would only return home after classes at around six o'clock in the evening. Autumn was the most challenging time of the year for this journey—it was still dark outside when I went to the train station in the morning, and evening was already falling when I returned from school.

21 Radomsko is located some 40 kilometers northeast of Częstochowa. The Stanisław Niemiec Male Gymnasium (1915–1933) was in a building on Bugaj Street. It opened on October 20, 1915, with two classes. Stanisław Niemiec was its founder and principal. See the blog "Gimnazjum Męskie Stanisława Niemca w Radomsku," http://radomsk.pl/gimnazjum-meskie-stanislawa-niemca-w-radomsku/ (accessed August 18, 2025).

The journey from Częstochowa to Radomsko took an hour. However, a large group of my peers living in Częstochowa, forced by various life circumstances to attend schools in Radomsko, accompanied me on my daily journeys to the Stanisław-Niemiec Gymnasium, and many of them attended the same school. I made friends with Leon Rozensztajn and David (Dudek) Giszykter, who were my classmates. The main reason why I had to continue my studies in Radomsko was that there were only six grades in the Integrated Grammar School, which I had completed. The opening of the seventh grade depended on a minimum number of students. Only three students were promoted to the seventh grade, so the school management decided not to open a seventh grade class in the new school year. The three of us thus began our wanderings around Częstochowa's schools, but never managed to acclimate to any of them. As a result, two of us—Dudek Giszykter and myself—ended up in Radomsko.

During the 1930–1931 school year, I passed my final high school exams, received the baccalaureate, also known as a maturity certificate, and enrolled in the Faculty of Law at the University of Warsaw, which, at that time, was named after Józef Piłsudski. My studies went very well, and I passed my exams without any difficulty. I mastered the very extensive material of legal sciences with ease and never failed an exam. However, during my third year of studies, a great tragedy befell our family. Following a long illness, my beloved sister, Zosia, died on February 6, 1934. Zosia suffered from arthritis, and the doctors prescribed her large amounts of salicylic acid to help her. However, this drug pampers the joints but bites the heart, and as a result of the intensive treatment with salicylic acid, Zosia developed heart disease and died when she was only twenty-three years old.

Our family suffered greatly, and we were distraught. Zosia was a tall and very pretty girl. She loved life and was well aware that her disease was incurable. We tried to save her as much as we could, sparing no money or efforts. However, the doctors offered no hope. Her poor heart beat desperately in her chest, and she was kept alive with strong doses of digitalis. Finally, the doctors decided to take Zosia to a hospital in Warsaw, where there were many outstanding cardiologists, but it was too late. On her way back from the hospital, Zosia died in the ambulance, in the presence of my father and Aunt Frydman. We buried our Zosia in the Jewish cemetery in Częstochowa, and her grave became a place of constant pilgrimage for my parents, who spent a lot of time there, unable to part from the resting place of their beloved daughter.

In the summer of 1935, a year after Zosia's death, I graduated from law school with a Master of Law degree. At the same time, Józef Piłsudski died, and with his death, elements of the extreme right—led by the National Party—began to gain a foothold in Poland. Piłsudski's party, the BBWR, was replaced by the OZN,[22] which had fascist and antisemitic tendencies. This movement was headed by Edward Śmigły Rydz, the new marshal of Poland and Piłsudski's successor, who differed from his mentor in both personal qualities and political views.

Nazi dignitaries soon began to visit Poland. Himmler was received with honors,[23] and Herman Göring was given a lavish hunting party in the Białowieża Forest,[24] famous for its wisents (European bison). We did not have to wait long for the effects of this friendship. Openly anti-Jewish riots began at Polish universities. During lectures, Jewish students were ordered to sit on the left side of the room on specially designated benches (ghetto benches),[25] so Jews would stand in silent protest during lectures. When Jews were leaving the lecture halls, militiamen from the fascist OZN,[26] Endecja, and the radical national groups attacked them and beat them with sticks and clubs until they bled. University courtyards became arenas of

22 OZN (Obóz Zjednoczenia Narodowego, Camp of National Unity) was a Polish right-wing political party founded in 1937 by sections of the leadership in the Sanacja movement.

23 Heinrich Himmler visited Poland in February 1939 and was hosted by General Józef Zamorski, the chief of the Polish State Police. Photos of this visit can be found in the Narodowe Archiwum Cyfrowe (National Digital Archives), Wizyta szefa policji niemieckiej Reichsführera SS Heinricha Himmlera w Warszawie [photos of the visit of the German police chief *Reichsführer SS* Heinrich Himmler in Warsaw], https://www.szukajwarchiwach.gov.pl/en/jednostka/-/jednostka/5987876/obiekty/438898 (accessed February 3, 2025).

24 As President Ignacy Mościcki's guest, Field Marshal Hermann Göring hunted in the Białowieża Forest in February 1938, and on his way back to Berlin, he was in Warsaw for a few hours. See *The New York Times*, February 26, 1938.

25 The ghetto benches were a form of institutionalized segregation in Polish universities from 1934 to 1939, where Jewish students were required to sit on specific benches. Initially implemented at institutions such as Warsaw University, Lwów Polytechnic, and Vilna University, this system was part of a broader wave of discriminatory practices against Jews during that period. Jewish students protested silently and were often subjected to attacks by nationalist groups. See Zofia Trębacz, "'Ghetto Benches,' at Polish Universities: Ideology and Practice," in Regina Fritz, Grzegorz Rossoliński-Liebe, and Jana Starek, eds., *Alma Mater Antisemitica akademisches Milieu, Juden und Antisemitismus an den Universitäten Europas zwischen 1918 und 1939* (Vienna: New Academic Press, 2016), pp. 113–135.

26 On OZN, see earlier.

incessant bloody brawls, the only victims of which were Jewish students, whom the militiamen infallibly recognized. Sometimes, however, mistakes were made, and Polish students, who had the misfortune to look like Jews, were also beaten on their heads.

The plenary sessions of the Sejm began discussing legislative proposals that were clearly directed against Jews. The wife of a radical right-wing OZN party dignitary, MP Prystor, submitted a bill banning the ritual slaughter of cattle, justifying her position by saying that the use of a special sharp knife used for Jewish ritual slaughter, as prescribed by religious tradition, was inhumane.[27] A bill was filed to prohibit Jews from engaging in trade with religious ceremonial items. People in government circles began speaking and writing about the need for compulsory mass emigration of Jews from Poland, and Madagascar was mentioned as a possible destination for such forced exile.[28] The government officially praised the boycott of Jewish trade and industry, with the then prime minister, General Sławoj-Składkowski,[29] succinctly expressing this

27 Kromołowski refers to the bill proposed by MP Janina Prystorowa, wife of former Prime Minister Aleksander Prystor, in February 1936. After much discussion in April the same year a law on the slaughter of livestock was passed, which did not ban ritual slaughter, but limited its scale to strictly defined needs of the Jewish, Muslim, and Karaite communities. A total ban on ritual slaughter was proposed in 1937 by MP Juliusz Dudziński and was approved by the subsequent Sejm to take effect at the end of 1942. However, before it could be considered by the Senate, the war had already broken out, and it was never passed. See Jerzy Tomaszewski, *Żydzi w II Rzeczypospolitej* (Warsaw: Instytut Historyczny Uniwersytetu Warszawskiego and, Wydawnictwo Neriton, 2016), pp. 213–214.

28 In 1937, the Polish government sent a three-man commission to Madagascar to explore the possibilities of deporting Jews there. The idea was played with by British and Dutch antisemites as well. It was also considered by the Nazis in early 1938, when Adolf Eichmann was asked to prepare a report on the subject. The idea was considered in a more serious manner by the Nazi regime two years later following the occupation of Poland with its large Jewish population. Yet Germany lost the Battle of Britain and had no control of sea routes through which these mass deportations were supposed to be conducted. Therefore, other "solutions" were sought after. For the attempts to speed up forced emigration of Jews from Poland to locations other than Mandatory Palestine, which was limited by the British Authorities to 1,000 immigrants a month from August 1937, see Polonsky, *The Jews in Poland and Russia: 1914 to 2008*, vol. 3, pp. 90–91.

29 General Felicjan Sławoj-Składkowski was the prime minister of Poland between May 1936 and September 1939 before and at the outbreak of World War II.

sentiment, which the Polish press used as a slogan and defining imperative of that period: Yes to the economic boycott of Jewish merchandise!

At the same time, Hitler was expelling all Jews of Polish origin from Germany and sending them back to their homeland via the border post in Zbąszyń.[30] He burned books by Jewish authors—including those of Heinrich Heine—smashed windows in Jewish stores with the help of his assault battalions, and beat Jews in the streets of German cities.[31] Following this example, it seemed that the Polish government openly supported anti-Jewish heckling, and the newly sown seeds of anti-Jewish slogans fell on fertile ground. Spontaneously, without any coercion or agitation, many Poles joined antisemitic movements, believing that the persecution of Jews would be a solution to all the economic difficulties, unemployment, and poor social and living conditions.

It was in this political atmosphere that I had hardly any opportunity to continue my legal career in Poland. To practice as an attorney, one had to complete a five-year legal internship in the office of a practicing attorney. To qualify for the internship, one had to be approved by the Board of Attorneys, which was mostly controlled by the National Democrats, who strongly opposed the admission of Jews into such positions. Moreover, the lawyers usually demanded a fee for accepting a trainee, and I had no money.

For my parents, it was a trying period financially. At that time, while my father's soap factory employed three workers, he was confronted with many difficulties, and although my father was ill, he nevertheless had to do the physical work of boiling the soap himself. When my parents separated from their business partner, they had to pay him his share and assume responsibility for his debts. During my studies, my cousin named Lejzerowicz who owned a legal practice in Warsaw, and his brother, the

30 See earlier for more information on this.

31 On May 10, 1933, some 20,000 books by Jewish authors were publicly burned opposite the University of Berlin. Ceremonial, public book burnings took place throughout Germany. As Kromołowski says, many books were burned solely because their authors were Jewish. On April 1, 1933, a general boycott against German Jews was declared. SA (Sturmabteilung, Storm Troopers) members stood outside Jewish-owned stores and businesses to prevent customers from entering. On the night of November 9–10, 1938, the "Kristallnacht" pogrom (Crystal Night or the Night of the Broken Glass) was carried out. In just two days, hundreds of synagogues were burned, thousands of Jews were arrested, and some ninety Jews were killed. See Saul Friedländer, *Nazi Germany and the Jews: The Years of Persecution, 1933–1939* (New York: Harper Collins, 1997), pp. 270–278.

physician Dr. Leon Lejzerowicz, helped me financially. For some reason, however, disciplinary proceedings were instituted against my cousin, and so he could not nominate a trainee in his legal practice.

My only remaining alternative was to try to be appointed to a court service apprenticeship. This option would make it possible, after serving in the court for two years, either to continue in the court service—provided I passed the judicial exam—or to leave the court service and, after completing the court apprenticeship ex officio, apply for an advocate's apprenticeship, and continue training in an advocate's office for an additional three years. This, after passing the advocate's exam, would give me the right to open my own office. This somewhat complex, dual-track path applied to lawyers who wished to devote themselves to a judicial or attorney career.

I therefore began trying to obtain a nomination as a court trainee—an unpaid position. I had to submit my diploma, an application form, and numerous other documents to the president of the Court of Appeals in Warsaw, Kazimierz Rudnicki, who was directly subordinated to the minister of justice in administrative and judicial matters, Witold Jerzy Grabowski,[32] a well-known antisemite who did not hide his hostile attitude toward Jews. Time went by, and after waiting in vain, I began making personal appeals. I paid repeated visits to Rudnicki but received no concrete information. At first, he dismissed me, declaring that the main reason for the rejection was lack of vacancies in the courts, but when my interventions became too frequent and insistent, he told me directly that the real reason he could not appoint me as an unpaid applicant was because I was Jewish. The refusal was categorical, and all my hopes were dashed. With Poland under General Felicjan Sławoj-Składkowski as prime minister and Grabowski as minister of justice, it was clear that a Jewish–Polish citizen was denied the right to a legal career. I had to come to terms with this fact and look for some other kind of gainful employment.

After countless efforts, my father—with the help of my mother's nephew, Joachim Dawidowicz, a very wealthy man with considerable influence in merchant circles—succeeded in securing me the position of assistant legal advisor at the Association of Jewish Industrialists and Merchants in Częstochowa. This very respectable institution in our city was located on Wolności Avenue and was very active among the local Jewish merchants. At that time, the legal advisor there was Jan Glikson's trainee lawyer, Marian Hassenfeld. I began working there as a secretary

32 Witold Jerzy Grabowski (1898–1966) was a Polish lawyer, minister of justice, and chief prosecutor (1936–September 30, 1939).

and as his assistant—or, as they called it, a "Man Friday"[33]—with a salary of seventy złoty a month. There was a lot of work, mainly in the field of tax advice, but also in civil law. We had to participate in arbitration court sessions in the roles of documentation clerk and legal expert, which included duties such as typing, organizing vocational training for trade workers, and managing the association's income and expenses.

In addition to the modest salary, there were also opportunities for additional—and completely legal—sources of income. Jewish merchants, burdened by excessive taxes at that time, came to our office seeking advice and assistance. While advice was free of charge, other activities relating to legal defense were not part of my official duties. At the request of a client, I would go to the tax office, examine the basis of a tax assessment, and write appeals to higher authorities or intervene on the spot with the appropriate clerk. I quickly became familiar with the peculiarities of tax law, and the merchants gained confidence in me, especially because I always tried to do my best. I settled many matters to the benefit of my merchant clients, so I made quite a bit of money. I developed good relationships with the treasury officials, most of whom already had legal education at that time. Meanwhile, my boss, Hassenfeld, had passed the bar exam and started his own legal practice, and so he rarely came to the office. I therefore became the legal advisor, as well as being the secretary, at the age of twenty-three, which greatly boosted my self-esteem—not to mention the material benefits of the job.

During my second year working at the Association of Jewish Industrialists and Merchants, I went to a dance party organized by the Parents' Committee of the newly constructed building of the Jewish junior high school on Jasnogórska Street, dressed in formal clothes and slightly too tight but elegant Delka shoes. That is where I met Stella. We were introduced by my schoolmate Leonek Lewinson, who was dating Stella's schoolmate, Miss Przyrowska—or perhaps Przedborska, I don't remember her last name anymore. I danced with Stella in the main hall once or twice, but then my friend Lewinson dragged us to an open but unlit school classroom close to the gymnasium where the party was taking place. The sound of the dance music still reached us there, and we continued dancing in pairs in that dim classroom. Stella and I clung to each other as we danced

33 Man Friday is the companion and servant of the protagonist Robinson Crusoe in Daniel Defoe's famous novel. Crusoe rescued him from a group of cannibals on a Friday, which gave him his name. It refers to a trusted assistant who handles many tasks.

and kissed passionately. Stella was a short brunette, with big, very pretty black eyes, curly hair, and passionate lips. From that day on, I met Stella almost every night. Sometimes we walked through the city's streets, which were deserted at that late hour. We were regular visitors of a fashionable café called Café Europa on the corner of Śląska Street and Second Avenue, frequented by young people at that time. We became inseparable, bound together by deep mutual compassion and affection.

I was not an outwardly attractive young man, so until I met Stella, I had relied mostly on paid love from street girls. Stella was the first girl in my life who gave herself to me with genuine affection. I fell in love with her truly and warmly, and our relationship developed and grew. We were both sexually and emotionally compatible, and we became—informally, but de facto—a married couple. I was, however, well aware that Stella's parents had reservations about me. Her mother in particular, who came from a wealthy Jewish family (the Bem family), did not like me and was unwilling to accept me as her daughter's husband. At the time, we did not care about her parents' approval, and we were together day after day without thinking about the future. We were still young, and anyway, the future looked very dark and dim—for us and for all Polish Jewry. The anti-Jewish campaign was becoming increasingly harsh, malicious, and dangerous, not only in Hitler's Germany but also more and more violently in Poland.

On Saturday, June 19, 1937, a completely unexpected anti-Jewish pogrom occurred in Częstochowa.[34] That morning, the son of the Jewish merchant Zelwer chased away some young thieves who were ransacking an old ironware store that belonged to his father, located in the square by the synagogue on Garibaldi Street. During the pursuit of the thieves, young

34 The period between 1935 and 1937 saw a wave of anti-Jewish violence. A few weeks prior to the described pogrom, another pogrom broke out in Brześć nad Bugiem on May 13, 1937. Following the Częstochowa pogrom, a wave of pogroms spread to a number of towns around Częstochowa: Kamińsk, Mstów, Żarki, Cykarzew, Radomsko, Koniecpol, Kleszczew, Przedbórz, Działoszyn, and others. See Tatiana Berenstein, "KPP w walce z pogromami antyżydowskimi w latach 1935–1937," *Biuletyn Żydowskiego Instytutu Historycznego*, 15–16 (July–December, 1955), pp. 3–74, specifically pp. 24–25. For a specific study of the Częstochowa pogrom on June 19–21, 1937, see Michał Trębacz, "Pod murami Jasnej Góry: Pogrom w Częstochowie 19–21 czerwca 1937 r.," in Kamil Kijek, Artur Markowski, and Konrad Zieliński, eds., *Pogromy Żydów na ziemiach polskich w XIX i XX wieku*, vol. 2, *Studia przypadków* (*do 1939 roku*) (Warsaw: Instytut Historii im. Tadeusza Manteuffla Polskiej Akademii Nauk, 2019), pp. 409–428.

Zelwer was beaten by Polish thugs on the adjacent Wały Dwernickiego Street. Josek Pendrak, a Jewish porter passing by, came to the defense of the beaten Zelwer, whereas Stefan Baran, a notorious brawler and drunkard in Częstochowa, who had committed several crimes and had served multiple prison sentences, took the side of the Polish hooligans harassing Zelwer. Baran started pushing Pendrak, and then he picked up a large cobblestone and attacked him while simultaneously demanding money for vodka. During this argument, Pendrak, feeling seriously threatened, drew a revolver from his pocket and warned Baran that he would use it if he did not stop his attack. In spite of the warnings, Baran continued throwing stones at Pendrak, shouting obscene curses. Pendrak pulled the trigger and killed Baran on the spot.[35] Baran's body was brought to the hospital, and Pendrak was arrested by the police.

However, the events of the day did not end there—on the contrary, they were just beginning. A rumor spread at lightening speed throughout the city that Jews were murdering Christians, and in response, National Democracy circles began to methodically organize a pogrom. Special Endecja emissaries on motorcycles circled the surrounding villages and suburbs, and crowds of hooligans began streaming onto the city's streets in the afternoon. They stormed Jewish stores located in the city and along the avenues where the elegant and expensive Jewish shops were situated. They smashed the display windows and front doors using the benches placed along the entire length of this stylish boulevard. In an instant, the street was filled with shards of glass from the shop windows and remnants of broken shutters. Goods were looted on a massive scale, Jewish passersby were beaten, Jewish apartments were broken into, furniture was destroyed, and bedding looted from Jewish homes was torn to pieces.

The pogrom continued through Sunday and Monday with the absolute indifference of the local police. Village women would come to town barefoot and leave dressed in shoes looted from Jewish stores. Whole sacks were stuffed with stolen goods. Jewish wood stores were set on fire, and any goods that could not be taken away were demolished in the stores. Almost all the stands of the Jewish market stallholders were destroyed, and their goods were plundered. The cigarette kiosk of the Jewish war invalid Kawa was set on fire. The pogrom lasted four days, during which seventy-five Jewish citizens were severely beaten, N. Lipowski was killed, and

35 The exact details and sequence of events are hard to verify. Trębacz writes that Baran was most likely encouraged by two Polish teenagers, who urged him to continue fighting even when he saw the gun. See Trębacz, "Pod murami Jasnej Góry," p. 416.

more than 150 Jewish stores and market stalls were smashed and robbed by the violent mob.

It was not until the fifth day that the mounted police from Golędzinów arrived in Częstochowa—the result of alarming telegrams sent from the Jewish community to the central authorities in Warsaw, as well as telegrams sent by Jews abroad who had heard about the pogrom in Częstochowa via the foreign press. The prosecutor of the attorney general's office arrived too. The police began to disperse the mob, and Governor Dziadosz of Kielce, who had also come to Częstochowa, began personally directing efforts to calm the unrest.

The local clergy did not react at all during the pogrom, and the bishop of Częstochowa, Dr. Teodor Kubina, posted his proclamation to the people on the walls of the city. He wrote that the anger of the Polish people was just, since a Jew had killed a Christian. There was also a rather vague phrase in the proclamation that called for calm and to leave the matter of punishing the murderer to the authorities.[36] The prosecutor demanded the death penalty for Pendrak. However, the defense, headed by the Jewish lawyer Ludwig Honigwil, and the appeal by the lawyer Leon Berenson, managed to reduce the sentence to six years in prison.[37] In the first days after the outbreak of World War II, Pendrak was released.

Following the pogrom in Częstochowa, another anti-Jewish pogrom took a devastating toll in Przytyk.[38] All anti-Jewish elements united in a common fight against Polish Jews and organized themselves within the National Democratic Party, the National Radical Camp, and in the openly pogrom-supporting National Unity Camp. In Warsaw, a league was formed to forcibly remove the Jews from Poland to either Madagascar or

36 The bishop's appeal was ambivalent, expressing understanding of the drive for revenge yet also calling for restraint against further outbursts of violence. Ibid., p. 423.

37 According to other sources, the sentence was thirteen years. See Trębacz, "Pod murami Jasnej Góry," p. 427. Some 300 people involved in the pogrom were arrested. Sixty received light sentences, while the others were released. See "The Third Pogrom," in Mahler, *The Jews of Czestochowa* (Częstochowa, Poland), pp. 177–183. According to Trębacz, anti-Jewish violence in the late 1930s can be seen as a recurring element of political struggle, rather than isolated events. The example of Częstochowa in 1937 highlights how antisemitism became a daily reality and part and parcel of the political culture of the time. See Trębacz, "Pod murami Jasnej Góry," p. 427.

38 The Przytyk pogrom was a riot that broke out in Przytyk, Poland, on March 9, 1936, in which two Jews and one Pole were killed, several dozen Jewish apartments and shops were destroyed, and more than twenty people were severely beaten.

Mandatory Palestine, as mentioned earlier. The demand to purify Poland of its Jewish presence seemed to become one of the chief slogans in the government's policy program, and any actions aimed at destroying Jewish industry, commerce, and crafts were a prelude to the realization of this program: first, to deprive the Jews of the means of their existence, and then to banish them from the country.

This was happily adopted by the antisemitic ONR (Obóz Narodowo-Radykalny, the National Radical Camp), a faction of the National Democratic Party. Actions against Jewish economic entities throughout Poland, carried out by this organization, took place with the knowledge of government authorities and the police—perhaps even with their tacit approval and satisfaction. Posters inciting the Polish population against Jewish merchants began to appear in the streets, showing, for example, the image of a Jew with a hooked nose, long beard, and whiskers, who poisoned foodstuffs and allowed vermin into drinks intended for sale. An assortment of caricatures of Jews performing various criminal activities against the health and safety of the Polish population were placed on colorful placards and posted in the busy commercial districts of Polish cities.

ONR distributors sold anti-Jewish newspapers full of criminal invective and slogans calling on the Polish population to boycott Jewish stores and stop buying Jewish goods. Picketers organized by antisemitic hoodlums stood in front of Jewish stores, especially on market days, directly preventing Polish customers from entering. Whole groups of nationalist thugs roamed the Jewish commercial districts, shouting anti-Jewish slogans and chants and chasing away potential Polish customers. "Don't buy from the Jew, take this good advice, he who buys from the Jew, steals from himself twice" was a rhyme chanted all day long by ONR hoodlums in front of Jewish stores in Częstochowa.

In the presence of the Polish police and justice authorities, crowds of picketers and strike groups in compact columns entered the Jewish trading district on the morning of an ordinary market day as the stores were opening. Sons from some of the best Polish families participated. Wearing King Chrobry swords pinned to their lapels, armed with wooden clubs, and led by students and antisemitic provocateurs, the column of Polish storm battalions would stop in front of each Jewish store, and two picketers would step forward and take up guard duty. The column then moved on to do the same in front of the next Jewish store. The picketers' duty was to physically push away Polish customers—especially peasants—and prevent them from entering the store. Fights frequently broke out. Those who resisted—stubborn customers who had been buying from Jewish stores for years and refused to submit to the terror—were beaten with clubs or, at the very least, insulted with offensive language.

It is not difficult to imagine the panic that gripped the Jewish merchants in the face of this unpunished and steadily intensifying boycott campaign. Trade in the Jewish districts almost came to a standstill; it could only take place secretly and under the cover of darkness, when the picketers had gone home and some peasant would quietly slip into a Jewish store and demand an appropriately low price.

Polish merchants, who had run small stores on the outskirts until now, sensed an opportunity, and, using the support of the authorities and low-interest bank loans, they began to push into the Jewish district, opening stores and wholesale businesses. This posed dangerous competition, because the Polish merchants used picketers to violently drag shoppers away from the Jewish stores and lead them to the newly opened Polish stores.

The specter of economic extermination hung over the heads of the Jewish merchants. Bankruptcies and the closure of small businesses—and even industrial enterprises—were commonplace. My father's soap factory also declined considerably, with profits falling catastrophically. Our customers, who were mainly small Polish provincial shopkeepers from surrounding villages, abandoned us and took their business to Polish soap factories that emphasized their Catholic affiliation by placing appropriate inscriptions on their products: Christian Soap Factory—Stanisław Lewandowski, or Christian Soap Factory—Dobosz, for example, was stamped on each piece of soap to make it clear that their product was not Jewish. A certain Mrs. Obrączkowa, the owner of the Dobosz Christian Soap Factory, would buy raw soap from my father, then cut the lumps of soap into bars and stamp them with her company's name.

My father began working for the Jewish-owned oil company Galicja. He purchased a special cart to distribute kerosene and, with a couple of sturdy horses, distributed petroleum in the surrounding towns and villages. An added attraction for buyers who bought from my father was special equipment for storing and measuring petroleum, which were given out free of charge to our customers provided that they would only buy kerosene from the Galicja company. This fairly expensive equipment was supplied to us by the oil company and served as an important tool in the competitive struggle among the many oil companies.

My brother Henio worked for my father and, along with our coachman, handled the delivery of the goods, as well as selling soap, which was delivered directly to the store and was generally bought by local shopkeepers. In this way, my father was able to stay afloat and successfully counter the unfair competition fiercely pursued by the local Polish soap factories. Things got worse, however, when my brother was called up for active military duty and was conscripted into the 23rd Grodno Lancer Regiment in Postawy, near the Soviet border. A worker named Stefan Maksymek was hired to replace him distributing petroleum and selling soap, but he stole from my father and more often than not returned from his deliveries drunk. A year before the outbreak of the war, my brother returned home after completing his military service, and to my parents' delight, he set to work with renewed energy. My father's finances improved immediately, despite the constant and unabated boycott campaign led by anti-Jewish elements with the seemingly tacit approval of the government.

The protests in the Sejm by Jewish deputies and senators, united in the so-called Jewish Circle, brought no change in the anti-Jewish sentiments of government officials. On the contrary, they provoked demonstrations and loud calls for pogroms from Christian deputies and senators, delivered from the Sejm tribune. With increased vigor, the nationalist and clerical press continued to publish extremely hostile articles against Jews and distributed pamphlets filled with fallacious information about the Jews and the Mosaic religion, such as *The Protocols of the Elders of Zion*[39] or the publication of the notorious antisemite, Father Trzeciak.[40] In this way, members of the intelligentsia, the clergy, and the ruling National Unity Camp (OZN) appeared to help foster this atmosphere in Poland.[41]

39 *The Protocols of the Elders of Zion* was a document commissioned and forged by the foreign office of the Russian secret police that claimed to reveal a Jewish plot to take over the world. The work originated among circles of the Russian secret police, based on materials borrowed from earlier conspiratorial anti-Jewish writings and theories. The protocols were disseminated, and eventually became one of the most widely distributed antisemitic publications of modern times. The conspiratorial content presented in the publication serves to explain its attractiveness to antisemitic ideologues, parties, and movements. On the impact of the protocols' forgery, see Esther Webman, ed., *Global Impact of the Protocols of the Elders of Zion* (Routledge Jewish Studies Series) (London and New York: Routledge, 2018); Yohanan Petrovsky-Shtern, "Contextualizing the Mystery: Three Approaches to the Protocols of the Elders of Zion," *Kritika: Explorations in Russian and Eurasian History*, 4:2 (2003), pp. 395–409.

40 Stanisław Trzeciak (1877–1944) was a Polish Catholic priest, theologian, and professor who wrote many antisemitic publications, basing his conspiratorial view of the Jews on *The Protocols of the Elders of Zion*.

41 Kromolowski's emotional indignation at the stark manifestations of antisemitism during this prewar period is understandable, considering the time and circumstances of writing.

On the streets of Polish cities, and in our city as well, assaults by National-Socialist hooligans and militiamen on passersby with Jewish appearance continued unabated. On his way home one evening, a Jewish lawyer named Natan Rozensztajn was attacked by National Democrats who stabbed him in the back. Bleeding and unconscious, he was taken to the hospital, where he fought for his life for a long time. Jewish passersby were beaten and kicked, and hardly anyone dared to go out after dark. I was personally a victim of such an attack. As I was returning home from work one evening, I was suddenly struck with a fist armed with brass knuckles by a passing thug. I lost consciousness and fell to the ground; but fortunately, apart from a bleeding wound and a large bump, I did not suffer any serious injuries.

As I have already mentioned, the Nazis deported Jews with Polish citizenship who were living in Germany back to Poland. This caused a new wave of attacks by Polish antisemites, who complained about the increasing number of Jews in Poland, estimated at 3.5 million. These people, displaced from Germany with only the bags they could carry, found themselves in a desperate situation. The Jewish community did all they could to help them. Committees supporting Jewish refugees and committees to fight Hitlerism were formed spontaneously, including in Częstochowa. I volunteered as secretary of one of these committees, helping many refugees find housing and employment. Collections of money, linen, and clothing were organized for the benefit of these people, among whom was my uncle, Bernard Górski. His bookshop in Berlin had been confiscated, along with much of his life's work, and he had been taken to the Polish-German border in Zbąszyń with only two suitcases.

It is a striking fact to note that the waves of antisemitism swept through Poland not only among the educated and bourgeois classes, but also across wide swaths of the Polish proletariat, including those organized in the ranks of the PPS. There were no Jewish workers in any of the factories in Częstochowa—such as Częstochowianka, Pelcery, Motte (these were large textile factories funded by French capital), in the Belgian hat factory, or in Hantke's steelworks—which employed thousands of people. The trade unions, who pressured the management of the factoriess, were strongly opposed to the employment of Jews. Even in factories belonging to Jewish industrialists, Polish workers fought against the recruitment of Jewish personnel. Only in places where Polish workers were in the minority could Jews only hope to get work, which was the case in small Jewish enterprises. This struggle to find employment occurred despite the fact that the Jewish proletariat made up a significant portion of the population in Poland's industrial cities. Jewish poverty in the cities was immediately evident when walking along the streets of the Old Town—such as Nadrzeczna, Garncarska, Kozia, Targowa, or Senatorska—or seeing the poor living in old hovels. Carters, porters, stallholders, peddlers, and numerous others were deprived of the necessary means of subsistence and lived on alms or occasional work.

The same miserable scene was also evident to passersby in Lódź's Bałuty District or on Warsaw's Nalewki, Gęsia, Mila, or Gnojna Streets. A small group of very wealthy Jewish industrialists and financiers in Poland was often identified by Polish antisemites with the entire Jewish community. Some of the Jewish intelligentsia, property owners, and merchants engaged in larger-scale trade were prosperous; however, this was a relatively small group—often completely assimilated—who catered to Polish society and were reluctant to admit their Jewish origin.

Such assimilationists were the most eager to break with their Jewishness or even convert to Catholicism to have a career in public service or science, and sometimes such people were, in fact, themselves antisemitic hardliners; for example, Bohdan Wasiutyński, a professor at the University of Warsaw, descended from the old Jewish Buchbinder family, or Stroński. Both were among the foremost leaders of the Polish National Democracy in the prewar period. The Arct family of the famous Warsaw publishers was of Jewish origin. The great Polish poet Antoni Słonimski had a Jewish grandfather, the well-known mathematician Zelig Słonimski. The brilliant Polish poet Julian Tuwim—one of the greatest Poland ever had—as well as Lechoń and Brandys, a well-known novelist, had little to do with the Jewish community, although they were of Jewish origin.

However, the assimilationists and converts did not enjoy much benefit from their attempt to escape their Jewishness, because the Polish antisemites reminded them of their Jewish origin at every opportunity, and when the Jews were beaten on the streets of Polish cities, they also sometimes took a blow to the head. Despite being baptized and declaring themselves native Poles, their Jewish noses would betray them, and they could not rid themselves of it.

It is no wonder that a considerable part of Jewish society—especially the youth—not only in Poland but also in other parts of the Diaspora, sought a solution to this Jewish Gordian knot of constant existence among enemies and in an atmosphere of hatred. For some, Zionism offered a way out, aspiring to create a Jewish state on lands historically connected with the Jewish nation and the cradle of its religion in Mandatory Palestine. Others saw the solution to the so-called Jewish question in communism, which was supposedly going to eliminate national and religious differences and establish equality of all before the law by creating a classless society. Lured by such humanist slogans, young Jewish men and women joined the then-illegal Communist Party or were active in MOPR (International Organization for the Assistance to Workers) circles. In Częstochowa in the interwar period, there were many communists among the Jewish youth, as well as among high school students. High-profile court trials were commonplace in Częstochowa for membership to the so-called communist *yacheykas* (Bolshevik cells), which were fiercely pursued by police, secret agents, and confidants.

Among others, there were trials of students of the Częstochowa gymnasiums—including M. Peretz, M. Prusicki, Grejniec, and many more—which resulted in prison sentences and the expulsion of these Jewish students from their schools, just before their matriculation exams. Many young Jews ended up in the dock, with many sent to prison, while others had their lives shattered because of their communist beliefs.

The future showed how wrong all those young people were, those who so steadfastly believed that communism was the only right and just solution to the ills afflicting humanity as well as to resolving the Jewish question. It turned out that in all communist countries—with the Soviet Union at the forefront, even up to the time of writing these words in the 1980s—the persecution of the Jewish people has not ceased for even a moment. On the contrary, it has intensified. Being a Jew in such countries results in a loss of trust by the authorities, which is necessary in order to get a job, obtain a higher position, or be admitted into a university. Jews are considered a hostile element there, seen as as traitors and conspirators. They are outlawed. The only salvation and escape from rampant antisemitism is complete and comprehensive assimilation— and even that is not secure in the long run.

In the spring of 1939, I received a decree from the president of the Court of Appeals in Warsaw stating that my application to be appointed a court trainee was rejected. No grounds for the refusal were given. The authorities of pre-September Poland thus ruled out my continued legal career, and I understood then that a Polish Jew could not devote himself to a career as an attorney or judge in their country. In my case, it seemed that the opinion of the Ministry of Justice was consistent with the general situation of Polish Jews at that time, who, as mentioned earlier, were often considered parasites and enemies of the Polish nation. I swallowed this bitter pill, and to sweeten the taste, I went on vacation with my friend Antek Weinberg—also a lawyer, who later died in Treblinka extermination camp—to Yaremche, on the Prut River.[42] The atmosphere in the country was tense with talk of a possible attack on Poland by Nazi Germany.

Hitler categorically demanded that Poland return Danzig and Pomerania, claiming that these were historically German territories. The Polish foreign minister at the time was trying to negotiate with his German colleague Joachim von Ribbentrop over the so-called Pomeranian corridor while Nazi storm troopers were already operating in Danzig and beginning to feel at home there. It seemed that such persecution of the Jews did not help Poland's cause, as the Germans were preparing to invade Poland, loudly proclaiming—so all of Europe could hear—that not only Danzig but also Kraków were essentially German cities (*Urdeutsche Stadt Krakau*).

Despite this, that summer was beautiful. On the Prut River, Antek and I lounged in the sun, swimming in the cool, clear river that flowed swiftly between the boulders deposited abundantly by the glacier. We stayed in an elegant guesthouse with very good food and polite staff. We enjoyed a well-deserved vacation, fresh air, and the beauty of the mountainous landscape of this corner of the southern Beskids. On our return to Częstochowa via Lwów, the situation had already become dangerous, and there was talk of war with Germany.

42 Yaremche is a city in Nadvirna Raion, Ivano-Frankivsk Oblast (province) of west Ukraine. It was part of Poland until the invasion of Poland by the Soviet Union in September 1939 and its subsequent annexation. The Prut is a 953-kilometer-long river in Eastern Europe and a tributary of the Danube.

CHAPTER FIVE

WORLD WAR II BEGINS

On September 1, 1939, Germany declared war on Poland and invaded Polish territory.[1] An indescribable panic arose in our city. The Polish-German border was a dozen or so kilometers away from Częstochowa, and the German army was soon expected to occupy the city. Whoever could do so fled eastward, as far away from the Nazis as possible. The Jewish population fled en masse, hoping to reach the Soviet Union, where no physical extermination seemed to be imminent. In fact, the flight from these border areas had already been taking place for several days, ever since the German demands toward Poland had become uncompromising. Husbands abandoned their wives and children, and children fled without their elderly parents, who were left to the mercies of fate.

We, too, decided to run away, all of us together. My brother Henio and my father harnessed our pair of horses to a carriage, on which we hurriedly loaded some provisions, bedding, and underwear, and on Friday evening, we traveled toward Warsaw, leaving the apartment and all our belongings to the mercy of fate. The road leading to Warsaw was jammed with people and all kinds of makeshift vehicles. Everyone was fleeing in

1 On August 31, 1939, Nazi Germany staged a false-flag attack on the German radio station in Gleiwitz (today Gliwice, Poland), blaming Polish saboteurs for the assault. The incident was orchestrated by the SS as part of Operation Himmler and served as a pretext for Germany's invasion of Poland on September 1, 1939, marking the outbreak of World War II.

terror from the Germans. We progressed slowly, passing villages and small towns, until we reached the vicinity of Radomsko, 40 kilometers northeast of Częstochowa. Here, we stopped in a small forest to eat, feed the horses some hay, let them rest, and wait for daybreak.

The night was warm. We lay down wherever we could, and fell asleep covered by our coats. At dawn, we moved on. Izydor Częstochowski, an acquaintance of my father, joined us on foot, and we continued our journey. After a few kilometers, we saw low-flying planes with black crosses on their wings firing at people walking along the road. We left our horses and carriage on the roadside and hid in a ditch. Soon after the planes had flown away, we heard the whir of engines. Cars, motorcycles, and transports filled with soldiers were approaching us, along with the shrill rattle of huge tanks making their way along the road. We quickly pulled over to the side of the road and watched them.

The army advanced, fully motorized and armed to the teeth, equipped with modern military equipment such as cannons towed by tractors. According to my father, Izydor Częstochowski—the man who was accompanying us—was an educated man, knowledgable about several European countries. Suddenly, he started waving his hands, clapping and shouting.

"Vive la France! Gentlemen," he assured us, "this is the French army. I can tell by their uniforms and the emblems on their helmets. They came to Poland to help! They will defend us from the Germans."

My father and brother, caught up in the enthusiasm of our so-called globetrotter, also started to cheer and shout joyfully. There was a village grocery store nearby, and I noticed that soldiers were jumping out of their vehicles and going inside. I approached the store and watched them buy cigarettes, cold drinks, and whatever food was still on the shelves. To my horror, I realized that they were speaking German. One of the soldiers was paying in German Marks and explained that 1 Mark would be worth 2 złoty, arguing that "Polen ist kaputt und Deutschland siegt" (Poland is finished, and Germany wins).

Horror-stricken and stupefied, I quickly turned around and ran to my father, who was still waving his handkerchief enthusiastically, which apparently pleased the Germans very much as they smiled and waved, taking the cheering people for *Volksdeutsche* (ethnic Germans). In preparation for war with the Germans, my father had taken his old Belgian revolver, which he carried in a leather pouch visibly attached to his belt. I told my family that these were German soldiers, that I had heard them speaking German, and that they were by no means French. Frowning, we all began retreating toward our carriage, which was near the roadside trees. I told my father to unfasten the pistol, and I threw it—along with the magazine and holster—into the manure.

After some consideration, we decided to return to Częstochowa, as the German army had already outpaced us and further escape seemed pointless. We found ourselves in an area completely under Nazi control. It was Saturday, September 2, when we turned back, sneaking through side streets to the town we had recently left. On our way, we passed the burning town of Kłomnice[2] and witnessed the first casualties of war: burnt human and animal corpses. No one extinguished the burning houses; there was not a living soul around.

We reached the Warsaw turnpike so we could get back on the highway. However, there were already a lot of German soldiers here, and we could hear shouted commands and loud conversations spoken in guttural German. At the entrance to the turnpike, German military police stood guard, their chests covered with metal plates, and they subjected anyone entering the town to a strict search, scrupulously checking their pockets, sleeves, and trouser legs. They also searched our carriage. I wondered what would have happened to us if they had found my father's gun. No doubt, we would have been shot. We were ordered to move on and hurriedly got into our carriage. Częstochowski, our companion in this fruitless escape from the Germans, was no longer with us, so we continued alone along the road leading to Warsaw. At no point did we encounter the Polish army, which had either been crushed by the Germans at the border or had retreated east.

The resistance shown by the Polish army was weak and completely insufficient.[3] There were many dead and wounded Polish soldiers, and thousands were taken as prisoners of war. There was no sign of the Polish air force in the sky, and a great number of panic-stricken Polish soldiers had run away, abandoning their weapons and uniforms. Among the Polish prisoners of war was a large number of soldiers dressed in civilian clothes; however, they were captured by the Germans during their escape.

2 Kłomnice is located about 22 kilometers northeast of Częstochowa.

3 The Polish army was overpowered both numerically and technologically by the Wehrmacht, whose superiority in air power, armor, and mobility proved decisive. Nevertheless, Polish forces fought with great determination and courage, resisting the invasion for over five weeks. To make matters worse, on September 17, 1939, the Soviet Union invaded from the east, and within weeks Germany and the USSR completed the occupation of the country.

It was only after this defeat that it became clear how poorly armed and unprepared for modern warfare the Polish army had been. It is unclear to what extent the assurances from the Polish command about the army's strength and modern weaponry were mere lies. In the face of German tanks and mechanized weaponry, the Polish cavalry charged with sabers and lances. The boast of the Polish commander in chief Rydz Śmigły that "we will not give up even a button"[4] turned out to be a deceitful pipe dream. Right at the beginning of the war, the Polish command posts vanished, and no mobilization could be carried out. My brother Henio, a reservist who wanted to join his 27th Infantry Regiment, stationed in Częstochowa, found only empty barracks just a few days before the war broke out.[5]

Despite trying to defend itself, the German air force bombarded Warsaw with no resistance from the virtually nonexistent Polish air force. The Polish army command and some troops were interned in Romania. The entire country was left to the mercy of Nazi terror. In the border battles near Częstochowa and Kłobuck, Polish units were crushed by German tanks. The same happened on the northern coast, at Westerplatte,[6] where, after a short resistance, the Polish army surrendered to the Germans.

Attempts at Polish resistance resulted in disproportionately heavy losses in personnel and military equipment, with the Polish armed forces unable to withstand the might of the German attack. The panic that prevailed among the population as they sought to escape the Germans—thus blocking roads and preventing the army from moving—further increased the defeat. German planes, diving low, fired on people fleeing along the roads, resulting in a high number of civilian casualties. The defeat was tremendous and terrifying in its scope.

4 Marshal Edward Śmigły-Rydz, commander in chief of the Polish armed forces at the outbreak of World War II said the following in 1935: "Not only will we not give up the entire dress, but we won't even give up a button." See *Kurjer Bydgoski*, 182 (August 8, 1935), p. 2.

5 Częstochowa was protected by units of the 7th Infantry Division. Technically outpowered by the German forces that were part of the 10th Army, the Polish troops were forced to withdraw behind the Warta River. The Wehrmacht entered Częstochowa on September 3, 1939. See Jan Pietrzykowski, *Hitlerowcy w Częstochowie w latach 1939–1945* (Poznań: Instytut Zachodni, 1959), p. 9.

6 The Westerplatte Battle was the first battle of World War II in Europe. It occurred on the Westerplatte peninsula, an enclave of the Republic of Poland, in the harbor of the Free City of Danzig (Gdansk). Approximately 205–225 Polish soldiers stood their ground for seven days against the German army.

Returning to Częstochowa, we realized that we were falling into the hands of the Nazi murderers, who made no secret of the fact that their goal was the total extermination of the Jews.[7] I had already realized that our escape from the motorized German army in a horse-drawn carriage was doomed to fail. But, my brother and I did not want to leave our elderly, sick parents and decided not to escape by train, as some of our friends and acquaintances had already done a few days before the outbreak of war. Those who did so usually reached the eastern territories and, after these were conquered as well, made their way deep into Russia and managed to save their lives.

With my parents in the carriage, we traveled along the completely deserted streets of the suburbs of Częstochowa. From time to time, we saw German motorized units driving toward Warsaw. German patrols were stationed densely behind the Three Crosses, next to the entrance to Warszawska Street, but we were not stopped and were allowed to continue on our way. However, when we approached New Market Square, Nowy Rynek,[8] a German soldier ordered my brother and me to get off the wagon and continue walking with our hands raised. My parents were allowed to remain in the wagon. I passed by Stella's parents' house and couldn't resist the urge to see her. So, I jumped over the open gate and ran up the stairs. The apartment was locked. After looking around for a while, I discovered that the inhabitants of the building had hidden in the cellars, since the Germans had ordered all men—under penalty of death—to gather at an assembly point. I was advised to go there as well.

Reassured that Stella was safe under her parents' care, I again went out to the empty street and walked toward New Market Square with my hands raised. A soldier with a rifle at the ready directed me to St. Zygmunt's Church. In front of the church stood a group of German soldiers. Several heavy machine guns were placed nearby, their barrels pointing toward the entrance of the church. Another German soldier opened the heavy door and pushed me inside.

Crowds of men were assembled in the dim interior of St. Zygmunt's Church. Most of them were Jews, as the entire district was inhabited by

7 Writing in the 1980s, Kromołowski could, in hindsight, anticipate the future mass annihilation of the Jews that was to unfold in occupied Poland. However, a possible reason why he and other Jews of Częstochowa could have had this conviction at the outset of the war is due to the massacre carried out by the Germans against Jews and Poles in Częstochowa on September 4, 1939, known as Bloody Monday.

8 Today Plac Daszyńskiego (Daszyński Square).

the Jewish population. Hasidim in long black kapotes with beards and sidecurls stood in groups talking vividly. Some wore their traditional round fur hats, as if they had been taken directly from the yeshiva. Others sat on church pews staring dully ahead. They lay against the walls, on the altar, and on its steps. Traces of blood were visible on the floor, which was wet from spilled water. Many Jews were wounded, and they had bloody rags on their heads, hands, and legs. The stench was terrible.

Some terrified young Hasid with a wounded hand told me what had happened.[9] A few hours earlier, the Germans opened the church doors wide and started shooting into the crowd with machine guns. They ordered that the dead and the seriously wounded be taken outside. Everyone was frightened and anxiously awaited what would happen next. All the surrounding churches in the old city were overflowing with civilians gathered inside. The sound of machine-gun fire could also be heard coming from the nearby Holy Family Cathedral. A rabbi with a long beard, wearing a satin robe and white stockings, was sitting on the altar under the feet of the crucified Christ, wringing his hands nervously and whispering words of prayer with his pale lips. Other pious Jews stood facing the eastern wall, swaying intensely in prayer. The moans of the wounded, the sound of conversations, and the screams of people arguing for a sip of water drawn from a well in the sacristy could be heard.

It was a terrible, horrifying sight. On that infamous September day, the Catholic church was filled with tortured Jews—most of them dressed in a *tallit* (prayer shawl) and a yarmulka as worn by the Orthodox—who the German fascists had gathered at the feet of the crucified Jew, Jesus, the God of the Christians.

That September was unusually warm. It was hot and stuffy in the church where the Germans had gathered several thousand people, despite the broken church windows that let in some air. My brother and I sat on the

9 The massacre related by Kromołowski became known as Bloody Monday in Częstochowa. According to historians Jürgen Matthäus, Jochen Böhler, and Klaus-Michael Mallmann, on September 4, 1939, both Wehrmacht and Einsatzgruppe II soldiers killed sporadically, executing hundreds of civilians. See Jürgen Matthäus, Jochen Böhler, and Klaus-Michael Mallmann, *War, Pacification, and Mass Murder, 1939: The Einsatzgruppen in Poland* (Lanham: Rowman & Littlefield, 2014), p. 43. Jan Pietrzykowski's reconstruction of events emphasizes the large-scale nature of the atrocities and other persecutions committed during the first stage of occupation by the German Wehrmacht, saying that the Wehrmacht played the role later played by the SD and Gestapo. See Pietrzykowski, *Hitlerowcy w Częstochowie*, pp. 9–15.

floor by the wall. It was difficult to breathe in there. In the late afternoon, we noticed some movement by the church door. Suddenly, the door was opened wide, and the German command "*Alle Juden raus*!" (All Jews out) echoed loudly around us. People surged toward the exit. Soldiers stood in front of the church and, with rifle butts, hurried those who were leaving, saying, "*Schnell, schnell, schnell!*" (Quickly, quickly, quickly) and "*Hände hoch!*" (Hands up). We were running with our hands raised over our heads—thousands of men—through the deserted avenue, the longest street in the city, about 2 kilometers long, surrounded by German soldiers on motorcycles. Out of breath and half-conscious with fear, we finally reached the Zawada military barracks on Dąbrowski Street. The yard of the vast barracks was already filled with men who had been similarly dragged from other churches and assembly points in our city.

Between the crowds were German troops armed to the teeth, and several machine guns were positioned on the street of the barracks, manned by watchful soldiers ready to shoot. These were soldiers in the regular German army, the Wehrmacht. After a few hours, some German civilians appeared and announced in Polish that the merchants, industrialists, clerks, and professional intelligentsia would be released first. They were all to report to the sports yard—a basketball court surrounded by wire mesh.

At first timidly, and then more boldly and in greater numbers, people began to enter this fenced area. I recognized a few merchants, some high school teachers, a few tax and court officials, and also Leon Rozensztajn, a trainee attorney with whom I had been friends for years. He was already inside the fenced-off area and convinced me to try and take the opportunity to apply for early release as a qualified lawyer. We talked through the wire fence—I was still standing on the other side, debating what to do. The probability that the Germans would keep their promise was supported by the fact that the wicket leading to the basketball court was open and unguarded. It seemed that anyone could enter and leave freely.

However, I was not yet familiar with German cunning and perversity, so I allowed myself to be persuaded to enter the fenced area, expecting to be released. When a large number of "volunteers"—those of us who believed we were eligible for early release—were already behind the fence, armed soldiers appeared, closed the gate, and placed a guard in front of it. At the same time, the Germans started hurrying the crowds of people gathered in the barracks yard toward the exit, leaving the barracks yard deserted. We were the only ones left—hostages from Częstochowa who had been tricked.

The gate to the *Sportsplatz* was opened, and several Germans in civilian clothes, wearing swastika armbands, arrived. They ordered us to go outside and line up in two rows. A German with a disgusting, criminal-looking face spoke, and a civilian standing next to him translated what he was saying from German into Polish.

"You are a gang of Polish murderers, and you attacked peaceful German citizens living in Poland. You murdered many of them. You were the ones who mocked and ridiculed our leader Adolf Hitler, and you published his caricatures in your newspapers. From now on you are hostages of the German army. If even one single German soldier is killed in this entire area by your Polish bandits, all of you will be shot."

The German finished his speech and slammed his horsewhip against the shaft of his high boots. We stood there terrified, as if paralyzed. My heart jumped into my throat; I went pale and was close to fainting. Several actually fainted and fell to the ground upon hearing our fate.

We were taken to three rather large rooms on the first floor of the barracks. All the windows had iron bars, and the rooms were bare, except for long wooden tables along the walls. We lay down on them, barely alive after such a fright. The doors closed and the locks rattled: We were imprisoned. There were fifty of us in total, all men, Poles and Jews alike. The majority were Jewish merchants and industrialists. Only Leon Rozensztajn and I were lawyers. Among the Poles, I recognized two of my previous high school teachers: Franciszek Golenhoffer and the botanist Kostecki, who was nicknamed by the pupils Cyclops because he had a leucoma in one of his eyes. There was also the tax office assessor Kierasiński, the rich factory owner Lewandowski, the court secretary Krupski, and several other officials unknown to me.

The Poles quickly separated themselves from the Jews in the third and farthest room. Among the Jews were many acquaintances: the pharmacist Praszkiewicz, the industrialists Gerszon Preger and Juda Engel, along with his son, the tinsmith foreman Szpic, and many others whose names I no longer remember. We were held in primitive conditions, sleeping on tables or on the floor, and washing ourselves under the tap in the toilet. The Germans did not give us any food or drink.

Once a day, family members were allowed to come and bring us food. Sometimes my father came, and Stella often visited me. They brought food, tea in a flask, and some cigarettes. Father brought me an overcoat to keep me warm, as the nights were already cold. We were under constant guard by armed soldiers. We were not allowed to have any sharp objects on us, not even razor blades. We therefore could not shave, and we were all dirty and whiskery. Once, a German soldier conducted a personal search and found a razor blade in the pocket of my old teacher

Golenhoffer. He punched the old man in the face so hard that he fell to the ground, covered in blood.

At night, the Germans carried out selections and executions among the Polish prisoners of war, who were also being kept hostage. Terrifying screams and rifle shots could be heard. After such nights, the Germans would often order us to remove the corpses of the Polish prisoners lying in the square and dig graves for them. One night we were woken by the light of the Germans' electric flashlights shining into our eyes. They selected a dozen young men, including me. They ordered us to get up and get dressed. We were each given a shovel at the barracks gate. They lined us up in rows of four and told us to start moving. We were escorted by four German soldiers armed with rifles.

We walked quickly in the direction of St. Roch Cemetery, trembling with fear. It was the middle of the night, and we had been roused from our sleep and ordered to go toward the cemetery with shovels. It felt dangerous, particularly as we were always at risk of being shot if a German soldier was attacked, which was not improbable at that time. I was convinced that we were being led to our deaths, and that they would make us dig our own graves before shooting us. With hindsight, we know this happened very often.

Our horror increased when we realized that we were, indeed, being led into the cemetery and ordered to dig graves in an area previously measured for this purpose. It seemed that these graves could hold twelve people. Death was staring me in the eye. Fear paralyzed my movements, and I struggled to move the shovel. The Germans stood over us, rushing us and shouting "*Schnell, schnell!*" It was dawn when we finally finished, and two sizable graves awaited their "occupants."

Then we heard the whir of engines in the distance. Several trucks were driving along the road and stopped in front of the cemetery. Soldiers started unloading coffins from the trucks. Fortunately for us, they were not empty: Inside were bodies of German soldiers killed during the attack on Poland. This is what we guessed from the scraps of conversation we overheard among the Germans and from the metal signs on each coffin.

We were driven out of the cemetery, and the Germans began burying the coffins. Breathing a sigh of relief, we were suddenly invigorated and began talking loudly to each other. We were coming back to life. Shortly thereafter, the soldiers escorted us back to our prison in the barracks, and our comrades in misery were happy to see us healthy and in one piece. They had assumed something bad had happened to us.

One day in early October, after being held captive by the Germans for nearly six weeks, a group of military orderlies came to see us. They examined us quite superficially, asked if we were alright, and then left. The next day, we were told by one of the guards that by order of the town's German commander, Major Bartel, we would soon be released. Indeed, after a few days, we were told to leave. That morning, the barracks gate—with the Nazi eagle and swastika above it—was opened. I marched out into freedom.

However, in reality, my situation did not change much when I returned home. The German persecution of the Jewish population of Częstochowa took on increasingly dangerous proportions each day, and the Jewish quarter—the old town—was the terrain of their manhunt. My parents and I had lived in this area for a few years, after my father had converted our soap factory on Nadrzeczna Street into office space and part of the factory premises into housing. Every day, the Germans would come and chase men and women out of their apartments, taking them away for forced labor that often lasted until late at night. In fact, it wasn't real work, but merciless torment and abuse of people. They were ordered to dig out the stones lying at the bottom of the Warta River that flowed through the city. The river was shallow, so people could walk into the water with their trouser legs rolled up. They piled the stones from the river into huge heaps on the riverbank. Hundreds of Jewish men and women were ordered to do this obviously pointless work.

The Germans also mistreated the workers by beating them with clubs and rifle butts. One day, they dragged a large group of Jews to the river and told them to retrieve beams and planks of wood from the water—remnants of a wooden bridge that had been destroyed during the invasion. Despite the cold, the Jews were ordered to go into the water fully clothed, extract the heavy parts of the bridge, and then pull out the nails with their teeth. One of the workers, Judka Granek, refused to carry out this inhumane command and was shot on the spot. This innocent victim was one of the first fatalities of German bestiality in our town. The soldiers of the 72nd Gendarmerie Battalion[10] stationed at the Narutowicza elementary school on Krakowska (Żabia) Street stood out for their particular cruelty and torment of the Jewish population while performing this kind of work.

One winter night, the gendarmes chased several hundred men and women out of their apartments and into the market square, where they had to stand at attention for several hours in the freezing cold. Many

10 Reserve Police Battalion 72 was assigned to the Radom Police Regiment in the General Government in 1939. The first company of the Police Battalion 72 stood out for its particularly brutal conduct toward Jews. See Pietrzykowski, *Hitlerowcy w Częstochowie*, p. 167.

were beaten, and several dozen people were herded into the barracks in the school building. There, they were ordered to strip naked and were searched for weapons allegedly hidden under their clothes. The Germans performed gynecological exams on women and beat them until they bled. It was not until late in the morning that these exhausted and battered Jews were released.

Roundups of people to shovel snow in the streets and squares, as well as to perform various services within the German soldiers' quarters, were the order of the day. And it goes without saying that this work was done without pay. Not a day went by without German soldiers and Gestapo (the German secret police) appearing on Jewish streets, catching passersby with a barrage of insults and beatings using clubs and rifle butts. The most dangerous of these oppressors was the Gestapo officer Szabelski—a man of Polish origin, a former member of the Sanacja movement, and a policeman who crossed over to serve in the Gestapo. Szabelski cruelly beat every Jew he met on the street, taking them to shovel snow or clean the Gestapo's quarters, with no time to rest or eat.

Bands of Polish hooligans led by German soldiers completely destroyed the Old Synagogue on Mirowska Street. Later, the same gangs of Polish criminals led by the Germans burned down the New Synagogue on Wilson Street.[11] The Germans threw incendiary grenades inside the synagogue, creating a huge column of fire, until all that was left of this beautiful building were stumps of scorched, blackened walls.

The German hypocrisy became glaringly apparent when the local *Stadthauptmann* (city commissioner), the Nazi Dr. Wendler,[12] drew up a report on the burning of the Częstochowa synagogue. In the report to his superiors—the head of the Radom district—Wendler lied, saying that

11 Jews built the New Synagogue on Aleksandrowska Street (today Wilson Street), reflecting *Haskala* ideals by blending secular knowledge with religion. Led by scholars like historian Mayer Bałaban, it housed a renowned cantorial school founded by Abraham Birnbaum, whose graduates gained international acclaim. The synagogue stood for forty-six years before being looted and burned by German forces and Volksdeutsche on Christmas Day 1939. Its Judaic library was destroyed. See Jerzy Mizgalski, "The Jews of Częstochowa—A Short History," The World Society of Częstochowa Jews and Their Descendants, https://www.czestochowajews.org/ (accessed August 18, 2025). The Old Synagogue was located at the intersection of 32 Nadrzeczna and Mirowska Street. It was ransacked by the Germans in September 1939 and destroyed in July 1943.

12 This is referring to *SS-Brigadeführer* Dr. Richard Wendler.

the synagogue was burned down by Polish hooligans and students, who went out in hordes to desecrate and destroy the synagogue on Christmas Day after the service at Jasna Góra. Indeed, the synagogue was torched on Christmas Day, but this was organized by the Germans who recruited Polish hooligans with criminal backgrounds for exactly this purpose. The organizers and executors were gendarmes from the 72nd Battalion of the German police under the command of *SS-Hauptscharführer* Ditmann.[13] To prove that the fire was started by Poles, the Germans arrested twenty Polish students and criminals, accusing them of looting and burning down the synagogue. However, ten of them were released the following day, and only one sixteen-year-old Pole, Stanisław Deręgowski, was kept in custody and handed over to the judicial authorities.

Meanwhile, the Germans began to forcibly evict Jews from their apartments in the city center to make room for the steady influx of the families of German officials serving in the police and administration. The German gendarmes entered the selected apartment, threw its inhabitants out onto the street—without the right to take any belongings with them—before bringing in the new German family to live there instead. No Jew living in the city center or in the so-called better-off districts was certain whether they might one day be thrown out onto the street and left without a roof over their head.

Apart from the German gendarmerie, the Jewish Council of Elders (Judenrat)[14]—created by the Germans—was also involved in clearing out the apartments. The Germans demanded that the Council of Elders provide them with valuable and stylish furniture, bedding, kitchen utensils, and tableware. The Judenrat therefore established a special department known as Quartieramt, aimed at requisitioning Jewish furniture and household goods. It dealt exclusively with items from wealthy Jewish families, and huge amounts of valuable furniture were stored in *Möbellager* (furniture storehouses)—specially created by the Judenrat—at 22 Wilson Street. The manager of these warehouses was Machel Birencwajg, the son of a wealthy upholsterer's family, whereas the manager of the Quartieramt was the infamous Bernard Kohlenbrener, a Jew who had come to Częstochowa

13 See Liber Brener, *Resistance and Destruction in the Częstochowa Ghetto*, (Wrocław, Poland, <1952), translation of *Viderstand un Umkum in Czenstochower Ghetto*, pp. 5–11, https://www.czestochowajews.org/history/yizkor-books/liber-brener/ (accessed August 18, 2025).

14 On the establishment of the Jewish Council in Częstochowa, see Kromołowski's account later in this volume.

from Silesia and spoke good German. Kohlenbrener was ruthless in his requisitioning and more than faithfully served the Germans.

The Germans established the Judenrat in the first days after they took control of the city. It was a rather controversial institution, and it is difficult to assess its activities. On the one hand, it was the only official Jewish body permitted to communicate with the Nazi authorities, and it therefore dealt with provisioning and providing services for the Jewish population, organizing the health service, hospital supply, and assistance for the displaced and the poor—that is, constructive activities. On the other hand, it had to carry out the orders of the Germans and enforce them against the Jewish population, which was usually to their detriment.[15]

The Judenrat was responsible for organizing trade and commerce, as well as protecting order and security—especially after the establishment of the ghetto, where it was the only public administrative body. It set up a department to supply the Germans with the forced laborers they demanded, thus putting an end—of course, only partially—to the manhunts arranged by the Germans in the Jewish streets. It was now possible to buy one's way out of performing forced labor, which in principle was the duty of all Jews. Those who could afford to do so paid the appropriate monthly sum to the Judenrat through its forced labor department, which then recruited workers from among the poor and unemployed. Abuses by Judenrat officials were the order of the day in this regard. The Germans demanded ever-increasing numbers of forced laborers, especially when sending Jewish workers to labor camps outside the city, where terror prevailed and the Jews were mistreated. Evading this fate was extremely difficult, as no one—even for a high price—was willing to risk their life and health in these camps.

15 As Kromołowski describes, Jewish councils (pl. Judenräte) were set up within the Jewish communities of Nazi-occupied Europe on German orders. The Judenräte were given the responsibility to implement the Nazis' policies regarding the Jews. They were torn between the desire to help their fellow Jews and the burden to carry out German orders forced upon them. The role of the Jewish Councils is one of the most controversial subjects in the history of the Holocaust. See Dan Michman, "On the History of the Historiography of the Jewish Councils: Past Understandings and the Need for a Fresh Approach," *The Journal of Holocaust Research*, 39:2 (2025), pp. 1–27; "Reevaluating the Emergence, Function, and Form of the Jewish Councils Phenomenon," in *Ghettos, 1939–1954: New Research and Perspectives on Definition, Daily Life, and Survival, Symposium Presentations* (Washington, DC: Center for Advanced Holocaust Studies, United States Holocaust Memorial Museum, 2005), pp. 67–84; Isaiah Trunk, *Judenrat: The Jewish Councils in Eastern Europe under Nazi Occupation* (New York: Macmillan, 1972).

Even during this early period, the Judenrat's activities were already extremely detrimental and harmful. The Jewish police (Ordnungsdienst), who were subordinate to the Judenrat, carried out raids and nightly roundups against Jews who did not want to voluntarily report for work in these camps and places known for German torture and abuse of Jewish workers.[16] A particular scourge was the mass forced recruitment of Jewish laborers for water clearing and roadworks in places far from the city. The workers had to stay there for a long time: They were quartered in damp barracks with poor sanitary conditions, and they received very poor-quality food. They were beaten and forced to work beyond their strength. The camp in Przyrów[17] in Częstochowa County was one of the worst.

Shortly before the establishment of the ghetto in Częstochowa, members of the Judenrat were summoned to *Stadthauptmann* Wendler, who announced that a "contribution" of 1 million złoty had been imposed on the Jewish inhabitants to be paid within ten days. When it transpired that collecting such a sum was impossible and that the deadline had passed, the Germans arrested half of the Judenrat's members—along with their wives—and held them in prison as hostages until the amount was paid. After much toil and effort, the remaining members of the Judenrat succeeded in bribing Wendler with valuable jewelry, and the *Stadthauptmann* reduced the contribution to 400,000 złoty. This sum was paid, and the arrested members were released.[18]

16 The negative role of the Ordnungsdienst in Częstochowa is described in M. Kuszner, "The Activity of the Jewish Ordnungsdienst," in Mahler, *The Jews of Czestochowa* (Częstochowa, Poland), pp. 223–226. The Jewish Ordnungsdienst was established to enforce German orders, including collecting taxes, maintaining order, and gathering Jews for forced labor and sometimes for deportations. The Ordnungsdienst was often resented by the Jewish community. Many faced moral dilemmas, with some resigning from their job and others complying until the end. The Jewish police often acted with the motive to save themselves and their families from death. Nonetheless, Jewish police and their families were either deported to their deaths in October 1942 or murdered on July 20, 1943, at the Jewish cemetery along with other Jews.

17 Jews performed drainage work at Przyrów camp, Radomsko County. See Geoffrey P. Megargee, ed., and Martin Dean, vol. ed., *United States Holocaust Memorial Museum Encyclopedia of Camps and Ghettos, 1933–1945*, vol. 2, part A (Bloomington: Indiana University Press, in association with the United States Holocaust Memorial Museum, 2009), p. 293. About harsh conditions at the camp, including food shortages, working up to the knees in swampy waters, and being beaten, see Jakow Jachimowicz testimony, Yad Vashem Archives (YVA), O.3/3180, p. 5.

18 See Mahler, *The Jews of Czestochowa* (Częstochowa, Poland), p. 188.

After the establishment of the ghetto, the role and tasks of the Judenrat increased significantly. The council grew to enormous proportions, employing hundreds of people in its offices and departments. It must be admitted that the Jewish intelligentsia volunteered to work there, seeing it as an infallible means of rescue and protection from mandatory and dangerous work for the Germans. However, they avoided working in departments where violence was required or where the work risked harming the Jewish population.

Especially harmful for the community was the aforementioned Jewish police, whose officers wore caps with a navy-blue base and an orange brim, and were equipped with rubber truncheons. Also unique was the previously mentioned department of lodging and requisitioning—the Quartieramt—and the department of employment, the Arbeitsamt, which often engaged in trafficking individuals for labor. Bribery and corruption were widespread among officials in this department. It is understandable that the prison-like living conditions in the ghetto, the endless violence, the specter of extermination, and the constant hunger provided fertile ground for depravity, and sometimes even the most honest people broke down morally in this ruthless struggle for survival.

The Council of Elders was set up by order of the Gestapo.[19] It must be stressed that its members did not volunteer or choose to join; they were forcibly appointed to the position. Following the German occupation of the city, the Gestapo took over the building of the Commercial Bank on

19 The establishment of the Jewish Council in Częstochowa as elsewhere was not a decision of local Nazi authorities. Local Nazi authorities carried out a general Nazi policy formulated in Heydrich's so-called Express Letter sent to Einsatzgruppen commanders on September 21, 1939. The letter speaks of an "Endziel" (final goal) and outlines plans to concentrate Jews near railway hubs and to establish Judenräte, some of which had already been appointed as early as September 6, according to Dan Michman, indicating prewar planning. The official letter followed Heydrich's meeting with Einsatzgruppen, SS, and SD commanders, which means that they were already familiar with its contents and it is possible that the letter had been written even earlier. See Dan Michman, "Why Did Heydrich Write the 'Schnellbrief'? A Remark on the Reason and on Its Significance," *Yad Vashem Studies*, 32 (2004), pp. 433–447. For details on the establishment of the Judenrat in Częstochowa as reported by eyewitnesses, see Brener, "Resistance and Destruction in the Częstochowa Ghetto," pp. 11–20. Brener describes how, at first, a council of six was established on September 16. On October 1, it was transformed into a Council of Elders that consisted of twenty-four members, as was common for many larger cities or towns, while twelve was a typical number of Judenrat members for smaller communities.

Piłsudski Street, and soon summoned a representative of the rabbinate, Moshe Asz—son of the late chief rabbi, Nachum Asz—and demanded that he provide the names of known Jewish social activists and leaders. Asz provided the names of six such individuals, who were immediately summoned by the Gestapo and, under duress and despite their protests, were made members of the Judenrat, whose task was to govern the local Jews and represent them before the Germans. This council was composed of Mosze Asz, Lajb Bromberg (an affluent wealthy manufacturer of pins, as well as a Zionist activist), Nusen Dawid Berliner (a wealthy merchant), Aron Josek Krauze (a textile merchant), Leon (Lajb) Kopiński (a manufacturer of wood products and a member of the board of the Jewish Social Gymnasium), and Dawid Koniecpoler (a master carpenter). Leon Kopiński was elected chairman of the Judenrat.

However, with the growing number of agendas, more and more members were appointed, including Dawid Borzykowski. In addition, Lajb Bromberg died, and several other members stepped down due to ill health. The Judenrat in its final form, appointed by the Gestapo, included: Leon Kopiński, Nusen Dawid Berliner, Dawid Koniecpoler, Wolf Anisfeld (Zionist, Jewish high school principal, and professor of physics), Dawid Borzykowski (chemical merchant, merchant-association activist), Maurycy Galster (expeditor, merchant-association activist, and board member of many social institutions), Jeremiasz Gitler (Zionist lawyer, former president of Hashomer Hatzair), Samuel Kac (women's tailor and craft-association activist), Zelig Rotbard (merchant and social activist), Maurycy Kacinel (attorney), Maurycy Kopiński (factory owner and social activist), Bernard Kurland (commercial agent), Szymon Pohorille (attorney), Maurycy Praport (merchant-association activist), Hilary Zandsztajn (landowner), and Samuel Wajnryb (Gestapo trustee, co-opted on Gestapo orders).

The Judenrat thus consisted of people of great merit to local society—people of proven integrity, righteousness, intelligence, and high moral standards. However, people are made of very brittle stuff and are sensitive to any changes in circumstances and living conditions. It turned out that these people—with very few exceptions—were mainly concerned with saving their own skins and carried out the Germans' orders to the detriment of the population. One such person, a very rich textile merchant named Jakób Lewit, managed to obtain a Turkish passport for a large sum of money, left for Turkey, and from there traveled to Mandatory Palestine, where he settled and thereby saved his own life.

The Judenrat collected funds intended as gifts for various Nazi dignitaries, who constantly had to be bribed to mitigate their excesses against the Jews, ensuring that the orders of the higher authorities—always unfavorable to the Jewish population—were not executed too scrupulously. It was also often possible for the chairman of the Judenrat to get someone out of prison or to rescue someone from the hands of the Gestapo. To do so, however, the wealthier people had to be taxed—sometimes heavily—and often the funds collected in this way were used to provide food for the poor as well as refugees from small towns who had been displaced by the Germans and stripped of their property.

The money was also used to serve free meals in soup kitchens. There were cases when people refused to pay these taxes outright, and they were arrested by the Jewish police and held in custody until payment was made or, in more drastic cases, reported to the Germans. The Nazis were very eager to keep such wealthy Jews in the city's jail, releasing them only upon orders from the Judenrat. Such imprisonment was dangerous—especially for Jews—because the Gestapo or the military police often had to empty the prisons, and those arrested were then shot without trial in the nearby forest or sent to a concentration camp. The use of such a method when someone refused to pay these taxes had grave consequences, and there were numerous deaths. As a result, the Judenrat was generally hated and regarded as a tool of the Nazis for the destruction of the Jewish population.

Although trade and skilled work in the town prospered almost normally until April 1940, the Jewish population grew poorer with each passing day. Jewish stores sold out of their goods, with no possibility of restocking them, and craftsmen mostly dealt with small-scale services.[20] The authorities ordered that Jewish stores had to be marked with a Star of David, and the Jewish population had to wear armbands with the Star of David too. Anyone over the age of fourteen was prohibited from being on the street without this armband and was subject to a fine or arrest. Later, after the establishment of the ghetto, the punishment for this was death. The Jewish population was also not permitted to use trains or any other means of public transportation. Yet, until the establishment of the ghetto, Poles were allowed to live on the Jewish streets, which meant that trade with Poles continued. Peasants brought food in exchange for manufactured goods. Jewish butchers secretly conducted ritual slaughter, and at that stage, there was no shortage of food in the area populated by the Jews.

The Jewish population in the city began to grow rapidly, as Jews who had been expelled from other Polish towns that had been annexed to the

20 In many places, Jews were banned from running businesses from the very beginning of the Nazi occupation of Poland.

Reich (Warthegau)[21] were forced to move to Częstochowa. Large numbers of Jews from small towns and villages—those who had been forcibly resettled as well as those who had left of their own free will—also arrived in Częstochowa's large Jewish community. Many of these Jewish men and women came from Płock, Bodzentyn, Gdańsk, Poznań, Łódź, and even Warsaw, together with their parents. Shortly before the establishment of the ghetto, the Jewish population of Częstochowa numbered over 40,000.[22] While the wealthy still found housing, masses of poor, displaced people were allocated places to live in public housing, schools, orphanages, houses of prayer, or asylums, which soon became a breeding ground for epidemics—especially spotted fever—that was already rampant shortly before the closed ghetto was established.

This was the situation in the city when I returned home following my six-week captivity as a hostage in the Zawada barracks. Although my father was already quite seriously ill, he had managed to stay active. Using leftover raw materials and cattle tallow, which could still be bought from butchers, my father—with the help of my brother—set up a washing powder factory. This product, packed in boxes, was in great demand because there was a general shortage of soap and laundry detergents. My family's financial situation was not bad, and we therefore felt no deprivation during this period. My parents were still able to put aside savings for harder times, which everyone expected. After my return from prison, Stella and I were together constantly. Our relationship, which before the war was already close and intimate, was now even stronger. In spite of the overall precarious situation and depressing atmosphere, we began to contemplate marriage.

21 After its occupation in 1939, Poland was divided into three parts: the western and northern provinces of the former Polish state were annexed directly to the Reich; the eastern districts and Lithuania were annexed to the Soviet Union; and the central area was organized as the Generalgouvernement (General Government)—an area whose political future was undefined during the initial phase of the occupation. Approximately 1.8 million Jews were trapped in the German-occupied zone of Poland, and some 1.2 million Polish Jews were in the eastern areas of Poland under Soviet rule. Częstochowa was part of the Radom District within the General Government. The Warthegau (Wartheland) region annexed to the Reich was meant to be completely Germanized.

22 Approximately 20,000 Jews from Łódz, Płock, Kraków, Łęczyca, and other places were sent to the Częstochowa ghetto, which eventually held over 48,000 people, according to Dean, *USHMM Encyclopedia of Camps and Ghettos, 1933–1945*, vol. 2, part A, p. 216.

A few weeks after my release, my former superiors on the board of the Association of Jewish Industrialists and Merchants asked me to report for work. The former association's activities had now been taken over by the Department of Trade and Commerce under the Judenrat. Stella and I began to consider the offer. A serious issue was the fact that this department was part of the organizational framework of the Judenrat—an institution with a terrible reputation among the Jews of Częstochowa. However, the work performed in this department was mainly related to providing much-needed services to the population, and it would therefore be possible to help ease people's situation in various ways. The work specifically concerned one sector of the population: the merchants and craftsmen.

Many former board members of the association were on the council and knew me well; I was sure that the initiative to employ me—a lawyer and long-time professional—in the commercial department came from them. I went to the council's general department, headed by the lawyer Dr. Pohorille[23] who was both the mind and soul of this institution, which, in practice, performed all the functions of a Jewish magistrate. I was directed to the chairman of the Judenrat, Kopiński, who offered me a job organizing the commercial department, and later a managerial salaried position. I accepted the offer and asked that Stella also be employed in the same department. She was a proficient typist with a lot of experience in administrative work as former secretary of the Property Owners' Association, where she had worked until the outbreak of war under the legal guidance of my colleague, the trainee lawyer Natan Rodał.

We quickly organized the newly created commercial department, and the department was swamped with work right from the start. The Germans issued a decree requiring every active trade, craft, or industrial establishment to purchase tax and treasury registration cards, entitling them to engage in professional activity. The duty of mediating the distribution was imposed on the Judenrat, which, in turn, was imposed on our department. We had to do all this work ourselves, as the Germans did not want the Jewish population going directly to the local treasury department, the Steueramt.

Large numbers of people would come each day to our department—located at that time on the premises of the former Cooperative Bank at

23 Szymon Pohorille (1886–1943) was a lawyer, Częstochowa city councillor, social activist, and member of the Jewish Council (Judenrat) from October 1939. He was shot by the Germans on March 20, 1943, at the Częstochowa Jewish Cemetery. See Sętkowski, *Częstochowa Jews: A Biographical Dictionary*, pp. 362–363.

9 First Avenue—to fulfill their obligation to acquire these cards. It was necessary for us to complete an official tax form, make a proper tax act qualification in accordance with the specific category of enterprises, and collect a tax fee. Then the documents had to be taken to the tax office, where they were checked to ensure that the qualification was in accordance with the regulations, and that treasury office fees were collected. The office would issue an official written and stamped tax card, which we then transferred to the Jewish taxpayers.

At the beginning, I did all this work with Stella's help, and actually acted as temporary manager. My workload was full at that time, because I personally had to audit the legal classification of each individual enterprise, fill out all the forms, collect the money, and arrange to redeem the tax cards at the tax office. Our department also offered counseling for tax and fiscal matters, intervening when necessary at the tax office if an unjust tax assessment had been made and conducting appeal proceedings on behalf of Jewish taxpayers.

Our tasks also included paying taxes and stamp duties for taxpayers, as individual Jewish taxpayers were forbidden to enter the tax office. After the establishment of the closed residential area for Jews, the inhabitants were prohibited to leave the ghetto[24] under penalty of death, so our department was the only link between the economic activities in the ghetto and the tax office, and we could leave the ghetto thanks to a special pass issued by the *Stadthauptmann*. Most of the treasury officials were Poles and Ukrainians, and only a few managerial positions remained in German hands: Among others, the chief treasury inspector was Counselor Krum, a uniformed Nazi who was exceptionally antisemitic. For the purpose of our department's activities, petitioners were required to pay a special fee to the Judenrat. This was usually collected in the form of a stamp affixed to the back of the registration card or tax receipt. These stamps were specially printed for the Judenrat and bore the Latin inscription *utilitati et saluti*.[25]

Talk of a closed residential area, which the Germans were about to establish in the area inhabited by the Jewish population, became increasingly louder and more frequent. It was said that the ghetto would be guarded and not accessible to Poles. We would eventually learn that

24 The ghetto was established on April 9, 1941, by order of the *Stadthauptmann* (city commissioner), *SS-Brigadeführer* Dr. Richard Wendler. It was located in the eastern, old part of the city. See Brener, "Resistance and Destruction in the Częstochowa Ghetto," pp. 20–24.

25 This is translated from the Latin as "For benefit and well-being."

the next stage after the creation of the ghetto would be its liquidation and the annihilation of its more than 40,000 Jewish inhabitants. Those better informed claimed that this would be done by deporting the Jews of the ghetto to the extermination camps in Auschwitz or Majdanek, or to the death camp under construction at Treblinka in the eastern part of the General Government.[26]

Some people did not believe this news and maintained that the Germans would not dare such an inhuman act as annihilating innocent men, women, and children, and that the world would not permit such unheard-of savagery. The Judenrat zealously fought against these macabre rumors, referencing conversations with German dignitaries who maintained that if there were to be a resettlement from Częstochowa, it would only be to labor camps. While our future under German rule looked gloomy, there were few who foresaw the possibility of saving their lives from this Nazi hell. People lived for today and tried to push away any bad and gloomy thoughts.

In the meantime, Stella and I decided to get married. Our wedding took place on March 21, 1940, and was hosted by my in-laws, Gitla (Gustawa) Bem and Henoch (Henryk) Szmulewicz, in their apartment at 21 Warszawska Street. They lived in a two-room, one-kitchen apartment on the second floor of the front tenement house. Both our families were gathered there in their entirety. The wedding was conducted strictly in accordance with Jewish tradition, in the presence of the rabbi and his assistants, and there was a canopy under which Stella and I stood during the wedding ceremony. We drank wine from a shared goblet, and I broke a glass as part of the traditional Jewish wedding ceremony.

My father stood next to me, already very ill at the time. He made an extraordinary effort to attend my wedding, coming straight from his bed. My mother stood on my other side, visibly moved. Stella and I were also

26 The systematic annihilation of Jews at Auschwitz-Birkenau had begun by March 1942. The construction of the death camp Treblinka was completed in July 1942 as one of the Operation Reinhard death camps. The first transports reached Treblinka on July 23, 1942, including Jews from the Warsaw ghetto. Majdanek was a multipurpose camp that combined forced labor and annihilation of Jews. In the winter of 1941–1942, Zyklon B gas was used for the first time to murder those prisoners who were too weak to work. Mass murder using poison gas began at Majdanek in October 1942 and continued until the end of 1943. See the Yad Vashem website, wwv.yadvashem.org, and the United States Holocaust Memorial Museum website, https://encyclopedia.ushmm.org/.

emotional, deeply moved that we were getting married at such a difficult time, when the immediate future looked so tragic. However, the wedding ceremony proceeded according to custom and after saying the sacramental *Harei at mekudeshet li*[27] and placing the rings on our fingers, we were joined in marriage. There was a festive wedding feast and the wedding speech was given by the lawyer Szymon Pohorille. Before the clock struck curfew, all our guests left for their homes. Stella and I spent our wedding night on the family couch at my in-laws' house. My mother-in-law, who came from a once-prosperous Jewish merchant's home and had dreamed of a better match for her only daughter, clearly showed her displeasure toward me, but the die had already been cast. We soon moved into a sublet room in the home of a family we knew.

Wedding picture of Alfred Kromołowski and Stella Estera Kromołowska née Szmulewicz, March 1940.

Less than three months after our marriage, on May 17, 1940, my good father, Jakub Kromołowski, died at the age of only fifty-nine. We loved our father very much, and his death was extremely hard on all of us. Sadness and mourning engulfed our home. My mother was in despair, and I was also

27 This is translated as: "You are hereby betrothed [literally 'sanctified'] unto me."

very much affected by his death. I felt ill due to some heart palpitations, and had to seek medical help. Although I wasn't feeling well, I went with my younger brother to the synagogue to recite *kaddish*[28] for my dead father every day. For seven days after my father's death we sat *shiva*;[29] I neither shaved nor wore shoes, and we sat on low stools, as is customary. My father was a wise, noble, and good man, brave and enterprising. He always worked hard and was devoted to our family. My mother, who loved my father very much and kept saying that God took away her best companion in life, felt his death most painfully. We erected a memorial to my father, who was buried in the Jewish cemetery on Olsztyńska Street, where our sister Zosia was already buried. Life went on. I returned to work and to my everyday duties.

One day, a female manager was assigned to our department. Upon presenting a written nomination signed by the all-powerful head of the Judenrat general department, the lawyer Szymon Pohorille, she immediately took over the reins. She was no longer young and was unmarried, a local lawyer, and full of energy. The new "headmistress" reorganized the division of labor. She took over the department of issuing registration cards, and I was entrusted with all fiscal matters, including counseling and appeals, and Stella remained with my typewriter.

We soon noticed that the new manager had a very formal approach to performing her duties and placed various obstacles in the path of those seeking permission to carry out their professional activities. These obstacles always suddenly vanished after our manager received a bribe—either in the form of a gift or money. This took place quite openly, and having learned from experience, the clients would give the manager a *bakshish*[30] in advance, and then things would go smoothly. However, news of our manager's work methods spread, causing a public outcry. Members of the advisory committee, composed of representatives of merchants and craftsmen who worked in our department, also became aware of the situation. Our outrage at having to work under a person who used corrupt methods was all the greater because the entire Department of Commerce was considered corrupt—so the negative perception extended to us as well.

One day, when it went too far, Stella and I confronted our manager with the truth, calling her out on her actions. At first, stunned by our

28 The prayer traditionally recited for the dead.

29 In Judaism, *shiva* (meaning seven) is the week-long mourning period for first-degree relatives.

30 *Bakshish* is a word of Persian origin, which means bribe.

courage, she couldn't say a word, but after a while, she got up and ran to the Judenrat to complain. We did not have to wait long for the outcome of our manager's complaint. Disciplinary proceedings were brought against us for insulting the manager and accusing her of bribery and corruption. Stella and I soon found ourselves before a disciplinary tribunal composed of three Judenrat leaders: the lawyers Hassenfeld and Lampel, and the aforementioned trainee lawyer Natan Rodał. The lawyer Maurycy Kacinel prosecuted on behalf of the Judenrat.

I defended myself, whereas Stella was given a lawyer ex officio called M. Goldberg. A number of witnesses from among the local merchants and craftsmen, as well as from members of the trade advisory committee, appeared before the disciplinary tribunal. Every witness unanimously confirmed our allegations of bribery and acting to the detriment of clients, which the manager had committed against them by demanding money and gifts for activities that were part of her official duties and for which she received a salary.

The manager's guilt was proven beyond reasonable doubt. However, the disciplinary tribunal took the view that it was we ourselves—and not she—who were on trial. Consequently, Stella and I were found guilty of insulting the head of the department while on duty, and we were given a warning—an extremely mild and rather formal sentence. In fact, it was deemed an expression of condemnation of the conduct of our head of department. It was the end of the case, and no one brought disciplinary action against our manager for proven bribery; however, no one questioned our continued work in the department either. Ultimately, we had achieved one thing: Our supervisor completely changed her conduct at work. The atmosphere in the trade department was better, and the offering of bribes and gifts to the manager was definitely over.

The Germans kept issuing orders that made life increasingly difficult for the Jewish community, including the decree to disclose Jewish real and movable property. This also applied to converts and those in mixed marriages, where one spouse was of Jewish origin. Until mid-March 1940, the Germans closed and sealed all Jewish stores and commercial establishments, with the exception of stores selling basic food items.[31] The decree prohibited Jews from having more than 2,000 złoty per person, which was subsequently reduced to 500 złoty. Larger sums were to be deposited in a communal savings bank, where each person could withdraw no more than 100 złoty per week for the upkeep of each person.

31 Similar limitations were imposed on Jews throughout German-occupied Poland.

Of course, the Jews did not care much for this decree, and hardly anyone obeyed it. Before the order was issued, money was hidden from the Germans, and goods were removed from the stores and warehouses and hidden by Jewish merchants, who were well informed about what was about to happen. Trade continued surreptitiously; however, this illegal trade was uncovered by the German police—especially by the Gestapo—giving them a new reason to persecute the Jews. There were constant searches and denunciations by Jewish informers, who, regrettably, were not in short supply on the Jewish streets.

The list of goods that were strictly prohibited for trade and subject to the most stringent rationing included all types of leather goods, textiles, and cattle trading. However, people continued to trade covertly in these rationed goods, because they yielded the highest profits. People were prepared to take risks. At night, despite the curfew, cattle were herded from surrounding villages to the city. These cattle traders bribed the Polish police patrols—the so-called Blue Police[32]—so they would not intervene. The Germans rarely appeared on the city streets at night for fear of the resistance movement.

One day in June, as I was sitting at my desk in the commerce department busy with work as usual, a Polish policeman with a rifle on his shoulder suddenly came in and called my name. Surprised, I asked what was going on. He declared that he had been ordered to take me to the German District Office (Stadthauptmannsamt) on Sobieskiego Street. There was general commotion, and to Stella's horror, I got up from my seat and followed the policeman. I was anxious—being called to the *Stadthauptmann* rarely heralded anything good. I was fearful even though I had done nothing wrong. However, anything could happen with Germans, and I knew that many innocent people had already been sent to prison, and even sometimes to their death in the Olsztyn Forests.

I was brought before a tall Nazi dressed in civilian clothes, who turned out to be the *Stadthauptmann*'s deputy, Kadner. His lapel was adorned with the swastika—the symbol of the Nazi party—he wore glasses, and his gaze conveyed nothing good. He gave me a penetrating look and, speaking in German, stated my name, and said I traded in leather, which was prohibited,

32 In the fall of 1939, the Germans created the Blue Police (Policja Granatowa) consisting mainly of Polish police officers. This police force was soon made responsible for enforcing many anti-Jewish regulations issued by the Nazis. On the Blue Police, see Jan Grabowski, *On Duty: The Polish Blue and Criminal Police in the Holocaust* (Jerusalem: Yad Vashem, 2024).

and that they knew everything about me! I was dumbstruck. What does this German want from me? What do I have to do with leather, what does it all mean? I started to explain that I was a lawyer, that I didn't trade in leather, that I worked for the Judenrat, that all this must be a horrible mistake. The German continued, saying that I was lying before signaling to a nearby policeman to take me away.

I walked through the entire town with the policeman by my side, who told me that he was leading me to the prison in Zawodzie.[33] My terrified wife walked beside me, unable to understand what the Germans wanted from me. I recounted my conversation with the German, and we concluded that we didn't understand what was going on; but this did not improve my tragic situation at all. Upon arrival at the prison, my name was recorded in the prisoners' register, and my belt and shoelaces were confiscated. Then, a Polish prison guard led me to a cell on the second floor, opened the iron door, and pushed me inside. I found myself in a small room with a barred window, surrounded by a dozen or so people staring at me intently. They asked me what I was in for, what was happening outside, what was being written in the newspapers, whether I listened to the radio. Questions poured in from all sides.

After satisfying the curiosity of my companions in misery, I learned that we were in the Jewish cell, where people were imprisoned on charges of economic crimes. Among them were also a few political suspects, one of whom was a man called Rozen, the son of a wealthy merchant and owner of a house on 9 First Avenue, who had been imprisoned for illegal possession of a radio receiver and listening to foreign broadcasts. Another one named Gutman, a Jew from Będzin, was caught on the train without a Jewish armband. There was also a baptized Jew named Grosman, married to a Polish woman, who was arrested by the Gestapo for walking around without the Star of David armband, which also had to be worn by baptized Jews.[34]

33 Zawodzie-Dąbie is a district in Częstochowa, located on the right bank of the Warta River. The prison or detention facility still exists today at 22 Mirowska Street.

34 Since Nazi ideology was based on race theory, one's conversion to another faith did not change their race from the Nazi point of view. Grosman was therefore still required to wear the armband marking him as a Jew. In this respect Nazi persecution of Jews differed from other former religious persecutions of Jews in Europe, during which Jews could resort to conversion to avoid persecution. Nonetheless, conversions did save Jewish lives during the Holocaust. See Yaakov Ariel, "From Faith to Faith: Conversions and De-conversions during the Holocaust," *Simon Dubnow Institute Yearbook*, 12 (2013), pp. 37–66.

The living conditions in our Jewish cell were terrible. It was unbearably stuffy, and the heat worsened in the evening, when we spread the mattresses—filled with rotten straw—on the floor. During the day, these were piled in the corner of the cell, which measured about 12 square meters and held thirteen people. The mattresses spread out in the evening on the floor produced clouds of dust, making it impossible to breathe. In the middle of the cell was a tin bucket covered with a flap—the common potty. Every time someone opened the lid, a nausea-inducing stench emanated from this vessel.

After each sleepless night, I rose from my mattress to the sounds of banging on the cell door and the guard's calls to get up. All the mattresses were picked up from the floor and piled against one of the walls in the corner of the cell, amidst a cloud of dust. With the sounds of general grunting and coughing and amidst curses, the prisoner on duty removed the stinking bucket. Some invigorating air entered through a window set high near the ceiling of the cell.

When it was time for roll call, we stood up. A prison guard entered the cell and read out each prisoner's name. Then, another guard armed with a rifle escorted prisoners one by one to the toilet so that we could quickly satisfy our physiological needs and wash our faces with cold water under the tap. After this, the prisoners on duty brought in a container filled with a darkly dyed liquid meant to resemble coffee, and we received a piece of dark, hard bread. Once a day, we were given soup that tasted like slop; for a long time, I couldn't bring myself to swallow it. We were not allowed to walk outside in the fresh air, and we were taken to the prison bathhouse to stand under a hot shower only once a week. Later, we learned that there was another Jewish cell holding another dozen or so prisoners. After a few days, a guard gave me a food parcel sent from home, consisting of two chops and bread with butter. After having endured the prison rations, this food tasted simply heavenly, and it cheered me up a lot.

The worst thing about prison were the nights. You could often hear the whir of engines in the prison yard, heavy footsteps in the prison hallways, the rattling of locks on doors, the sound of loud conversations, and sometimes moans. These sounds would accompany those prisoners being taken to concentration camps or to their deaths in the Olsztyn Forests.[35] In most cases, these transports were carried out on the orders of

35 The execution site for prisoners from Częstochowa and Radomsko was the forests near Olsztyn, close to Częstochowa, where security police shot approximately 400 people in June, July, and October 1940. Among the victims were teachers, officials,

the Gestapo or the German military police, without a court sentence. Our breath would freeze in our chests, our hearts would throb in our throats, as we waited fearfully for the door to our cell to open. Amidst the sepulchral silence, we heard those heavy soldiers' footsteps in the prison hallways—the harbingers of death.

It was horrifying and inhumane what the German people—considered to be one of the most civilized nations in the world—were capable of. These German *Kulturträgers*[36] murdered completely innocent people, persecuting and torturing them in death camps. After all, among those of us imprisoned by the German executioners, not a single person had committed an actual crime—no act that violated universally accepted moral standards or could be deemed punishable under customary legal norms. The people imprisoned here had simply performed normal activities: listening to the radio, walking the streets peacefully, practicing the religion they believed in, buying and selling commonly traded goods or foodstuffs necessary for human life and survival. According to German legal standards, however, they were criminals, because they listened to the radio and used public transport, and, like our fellow prisoner Icek Czarny, traded in cattle.

It was possible that during any one of those sleepless nights, we could easily become part of a convoy to a death camp or execution yard. There was something disturbing about the fact that these crimes against humanity were committed by the nation that had given birth to Goethe, Schiller, Wagner, and Luther,[37] the nation that had claimed to be the mainstay of world culture and civilization—and it committed these crimes openly with the complete passivity and silence of global public opinion. However, at that time, I had not yet experienced or witnessed the many terrible deeds and crimes committed

lawyers, doctors, merchants, and students. See Maria Wardzyńska, *Był rok 1939: Operacja niemieckiej policji bezpieczeństwa w Polsce: Intelligenzaktion* (Warsaw: Instytut Pamieci Narodowej, 2009), pp. 266–267.

36 This is translated from the German as "bearers or transmitters of culture."

37 These historical figures, of course, were by no means innocent of anti-Jewish historical influence. The founder of the Reformation movement in Europe, for one, produced an infamous, mendacious anti-Jewish treatise *Von den Juden und ihren Lügen* (On the Jews and Their Lies) utilized later by Nazi propaganda. Wagner did not hide his antisemitism and antisemitic views of Jewish influence in music. In spite of their positive contributions to human civilization, there was a darker side to their role in history. As Kromołowski mentioned earlier, many Jews opted to stay in Nazi-occupied Poland based on their positive experience of the German occupation during World War I, which shows the gigantic leap antisemitic ideology made in Germany under the Nazis.

by the Germans against helpless victims; I was not aware of the annihilation of an entire nation—of millions of people—because they were Jews.

Nightmarish, sleepless nights passed, followed by hopeless tiring days, with nothing happening. I had already been held in this infernal German prison—entirely innocent, and subjected to neither investigation nor interrogation—for nearly fourteen days. I got to know all my comrades in the cell quite well. Gutman, who pretended to be a Christian Pole even in front of us in prison, could not hide his Jewish nose, his sad black Jewish eyes, or his dark beard, which he scrupulously scratched off every day with a razor, smuggled in and hidden despite the searches. He covered his head with a peasant blue *Maciejówka* with a leather peak,[38] and every now and then, he tried to convince us anew that he was a Christian Pole—he could show his baptism certificate—and that he had absolutely nothing in common with Jews.

Grosman also tried to convince us of his Polish origin, referring to his supposedly Sarmatian ancestors. He did not have a razor and therefore grew a large red beard. This pathetic, red-haired Jew with a Jewish name, desperately trying to escape from his origins, was both funny and tragic at the same time. These people were possessed by a pathological mania for Polishness, seeking in it a form of salvation from the looming catastrophe they already sensed approaching. Rozen, on the other hand, listened and observed, smiling ironically: He knew that he would not get out of that prison alive. And indeed, the Germans soon dragged him from our cell and shot him in the Olsztyn Forests—just for listening to a foreign radio broadcast.

One afternoon, I was sitting on the floor, weak and resigned, with my back against the heap of stinking mattresses, when all of a sudden, the cell door briskly opened, and the prison guard called my name. He ordered me to take my things and follow him. This meant freedom! I picked myself up off the floor and ran toward the door. In the prison office, my belt, shoelaces, documents, and money were handed back to me. The heavy prison gate opened, and I found myself on the street, where people were walking and cars were speeding by, their engines whirring. I approached a kiosk and bought a pack of German Juno cigarettes, inhaling the smoke with relish.

38 A *Maciejówka* cap was commonly worn during World War I by Polish soldiers and, among others, by Józef Piłsudski. In this case, it was used to emphasize one's Polishness rather than Jewishness.

I arrived home, and after I had washed and eaten, I sat down at the table feeling calmer and listened as my wife, Stella, filled me in on the events surrounding this disastrous affair. A few days after my imprisonment, Stella managed to arrange a meeting with the chairman of the Judenrat, Leon Kopiński, who, it turned out, had heard about my story and knew that I was not involved in the leather trade. I was, as the chairman explained, simply the victim of a misunderstanding. A man named Krymołowski, a leather merchant with a store in the Old Market Square, had been the one who had traded leather illegally. The coincidental similarity of our names—or the deliberate use of this similarity—resulted in my arrest by the Germans instead of Krymołowski from the Old Square, who was quietly sitting at home while an innocent man was being tortured in prison.

Luckily for me, a certain Borzykowski, Krymołowski's accomplice, was also arrested with me. Borzykowski's wife—supposedly together with Krymołowski—donated a large sum of money and valuable jewelry, and thanks to Kopiński's arrangement with the *Stadthauptmann*, Borzykowski was released from prison, and the whole affair was covered up. As a result, I was also released.

No one knew how much money was involved in this transaction, but the Judenrat must have paid a considerable sum as part of the negotiations with Kadner, the *Stadthauptmann*'s deputy who was in charge of the matter. It was common knowledge that German officials eagerly accepted bribes, providing them with a significant source of income drawn from Jewish misfortunes related to trade settlements and the prohibition of commerce in many strictly rationed items. In such cases, the Judenrat often managed to save the lives—and the freedom—of many Jewish merchants, who, despite the imposed prohibitions, continued their trade. A great deal of money and often valuable jewelry changed hands as the Nazi officials stuffed their pockets. And the members of the Judenrat—almost all of whom had some high Nazi official tamed in this way—sometimes succeeded by using bribery to soften the sharpness of German restrictions against the Jewish population, creating better living conditions for them.

However, there were many—especially among the intelligentsia—who strongly condemned these methods used by members of the Judenrat. The underground newspaper *Rasta*,[39] which was printed using a hectograph,

39 *Rasta* was an illustrated publication. The name "Rasta" is an acronym of Rada Starszych (Polish: Council of the Elders). The newspaper reported the life of the Jews under occupation including cruelties of the Nazi rule as well as criticism of

denounced the bribery and close comradeship with the Nazis practiced by Judenrat members, considering it a betrayal of Jewish national interests. *Rasta* was full of satirical poems and critical remarks against the chairman of the council and its members. Copies of this newspaper were mailed out, addressed to all the important figures in the Jewish community. Many hundreds of copies were distributed among the population as well.

The newspaper also contained drawings, caricatures of the criticized members of the council, and photomontages with appropriate satirical remarks and poems. The chairman of the council, Kopiński, was referred to as King Leon the First,[40] while his main aid, the lawyer Pohorille, was called Pocholere, alluding to cholera. The head of the administrative department, the lawyer Marian Hassenfeld, was known for praising and glorifying the activities of the Judenrat, so he was shown sitting on a barrel of Vaseline, accompanied by a caption describing Marian "Hałasenfeld" (meaning field full of noise) as an enthusiastic supporter of the Judenrat.[41] Other members of the council were also targeted by *Rasta*, such as the Jewish quartermaster Kohlenbrener,[42] known for his punctual and scrupulous execution of German requisition orders, along with Wajnryb, a merchant in dental goods who was a trusted man of the Gestapo.

Despite the announcement that the Jewish ghetto would soon become a closed-off area, and in the face of constant persecution, arrests, and increasing restrictions, life in the Jewish quarter went on almost as normal, proving stronger than German regulations. There was no shortage of food, and people traded and earned money—despite the fact that the Germans had closed and sealed most of the Jewish stores along with their goods inside. These merchants therefore "stole" their own goods from the sealed stores and sold them to Polish customers, allowing them to support their families.

the Judenrat and Jewish police. See Brener, "Resistance and Destruction in the Częstochowa Ghetto," pp. 55–56.

40 Leon Yehuda (Lejb) Kopinski (1885–1943), chairman of the Jewish Council, was murdered on March 20, 1943, at the Jewish cemetery. See Sętkowski, *Częstochowa Jews: A Biographical Dictionary*, p. 267.

41 Marian Mordechaj Hassenfeld (1901–1993), lawyer, legal advisor, academic teacher, and sport and social activist. Between January and August, he managed the Jewish Council's Registration and Statistics Department. See Sętkowski, *Częstochowa Jews: A Biographical Dictionary*, pp. 202–204.

42 Bernard Kohlenbrener (1911–1943), manager of the Jewish Council's Requisitions Department and Housing Department. He was murdered with his wife in March 1943. See Sętkowski, *Częstochowa Jews: A Biographical Dictionary*, pp. 239–240.

It was a simple plan but very cleverly thought out. The Jewish merchants, whose stores—along with the goods inside—had been closed and sealed, were given the opportunity to "ventilate" the goods. With the help of the Judenrat, bribes, and clever arguments, they managed to convince Linderman, the head of the Economic Department in the *Stadthauptman*'s office, that the goods in these Jewish stores needed to be aired out from time to time to prevent spoilage, mold, or damage by moths and other vermin.

For this purpose, the store was opened in the presence of a Judenrat representative and a Jewish policeman, the seals were removed, and the store owner and his family began cleaning the store. Windows were opened, and goods were removed from the store shelves, which were then cleaned, swept, and aired. While the representatives of the authorities were invited to partake in a treat, the best and most expensive goods were swiftly removed and hidden in a safe place prepared in advance. After some time, when the store had been sufficiently "aired out," the officials returned, the store was resealed, and the keys were taken back to the economic department of the *Stadthauptmann*'s office.

Such methods and numerous tricks—often stealing their own goods from the stores under the cover of darkness and replacing them with less valuable or damaged goods—allowed the Jewish merchants to circumvent the draconian German regulations and gain financial resources. All this came at great risk, because the Germans often detected such economic crimes and punished the perpetrators severely—usually with imprisonment or heavy monetary fines.

My recent experiences in a German prison slowly faded from memory, and I returned to work in the Commercial Department of the Judenrat. Both Stella and I earned modest wages in our jobs, which were sufficient to live on. Although my mother was still mourning my father's death, she and my brother Henio ran the very modest business that my father had started—producing washing powders using the leftover raw materials and semi-finished products from our soap factory. They lived in our small, one-story house on Nadrzeczna Street, where the washing powder factory—and our former soap factory—was located. The house was situated in a large open area, where my mother also planted a vegetable garden. It was in the center of the oldest quarter of the city, which was almost exclusively inhabited by Jews, and the Warta River ran alongside Nadrzeczna Street, separating it from Zawodzie.

According to the Nazis' plans, which were already partly known at that time, this area was supposed to be part of the future closed ghetto. Thus, we were fortunately spared the threat of resettlement, something that was a real nightmare for the majority of the Jewish population in our city. With increasing frequency, entire streets and city quarters were now subject to evacuation and "purification" of its Jewish inhabitants. This was a catastrophe for the displaced families: Not only were their most valuable furniture and household appliances seized but the displacement also entailed the looting of Jewish property—including paintings, sculptures, chinaware, silverware, and even clothing, underwear, and shoes.

Adding to this feeling of disaster was the fact that these displaced families were directed to the old quarter of the city, which was already overcrowded. The apartments were small, with several families squeezed into just a dozen square meters, where even finding a vacant spot to sleep was difficult. These apartments were also usually devoid of sanitary facilities and were damp and moldy. Suffice it to say that within a short period of time, the Jews were expelled from the 400 streets where they had lived before the German occupation of Częstochowa. They were forcibly resettled, initially within the boundaries of eighty-four streets, before finally being crowded into twenty-eight streets, which, with few exceptions, later constituted the closed ghetto and officially named the Jewish residential district.

It should be emphasized that the population density in the old quarters of the future ghetto, as described above, was further increased by the constant influx of Jews from surrounding villages and towns that had been systematically purged of Jewish residents by the Germans, as well as by the arrival of displaced persons from towns that had been incorporated into the German Reich.[43] The Jewish quarter, overcrowded to the point of impossibility, became a hotbed of misery and numerous epidemics, of which typhoid, spotted fever, and bloody diarrhea were the most dangerous.

At that time, my mother took in the wife of my cousin, a dentist, after her deportation from First Avenue. Her husband fled to the eastern territories when the war broke out. My wife's parents did not feel threatened by the displacement either, because they lived in their own property on Warszawska Street, which was part of the old town and, according to the German plan, was to be incorporated into the future ghetto. Although Stella and I were still living in our rented room, we had both my mother's apartment and that of my in-laws at our disposal in case of expulsion. We

43 During the course of the ghetto's existence, about 20,000 Jews from other cities, such as Łódz, Płock, and Kraków, and towns, such as Łęczyca, were sent to the Częstochowa ghetto. Its population reached over 48,000 people. See Dean, *USHMM Encyclopedia of Camps and Ghettos, 1933–1945*, vol. 2, part A, p. 216.

regularly stayed with my mother in her apartment, where we often ate dinner and where I kept my clothing and personal linen.

The situation regarding forced labor soon began to deteriorate dramatically. The Germans constantly demanded a large supply of unpaid labor in the ever-increasing number of German and Polish workplaces or outposts. Every day, between 5,000 and 6,000 men and women were taken to perform forced labor for the Nazis. This number grew daily, and the Judenrat—through its Department of Forced Labor (Arbeitseinsatz)[44]—had to supply the workers. In light of this, the Judenrat issued a decree by which all men between the ages of twelve and sixty were obligated to perform unpaid forced labor for the Germans at least once a week. Those who wished to free themselves from this obligation had to pay 4 złoty, an amount that was later increased to 6 złoty per day. In this way, a fund was established that could secure payment for these workers, amounting to 24 złoty for six days of work.

At first, there was no lack of volunteers for such work, because in the Jewish quarter, unemployment, poverty, and misery were the rule. Workers in these places received at least some payment, and the work was performed in the city itself or in the suburbs. These laborers worked only between eight and ten hours a day, and beatings and mistreatment of those who were directed to work according to German orders and who reported directly to the labor department were moderate. There were about 120 such workplaces, the largest of which demanded the most workers. These included the German Police (Schutzpolizei), a swimming pool under construction, a sports ground, the German district administration (Stadthauptmannschaft), German army (Wehrmacht) facilities, a German school, the railroad, the magistrate, delousing stations, the airport, and the post office. Shortly before the deportation *Aktion*, 7,595 Jewish workers were employed at these sites.

In contrast, the situation in the external forced labor camps—for which the Labor Department of the Judenrat was also obliged to supply workers—was desperate. Although these were paid jobs, laborers had to work from morning to night, live in dirty and cold barracks, and, worst of all, endure cruel beatings and abuse at the hands of German overseers. These were essentially penal camps, marked by the same harsh conditions as concentration camps, with food that was inadequate.

There were three such camps: in Przyrów, near Częstochowa; in Cieszanów; and in Wereszyn in the Lublin region. I have already mentioned some of these camps in short, but it seems appropriate to describe this issue

44 On the rise of quotas of Jews drafted into forced labor, see ibid.

of forced labor in more detail, giving a brief account of these camps to illuminate the forced labor that the Jewish workers had to render to the Germans. The camp in Przyrów was organized by the German water and drainage authority. The work consisted of regulating the Warta River and draining the riverside agricultural areas, which, for the most part, were flooded with water. The order was to send 300 Jewish workers to Przyrów, who had to stay there for two months. They were to be paid a meager wage by the Council of Elders for ten hours of work and received a meager food allocation, consisting of 300 grams of bread and a coffee-like substance, which, in fact, was a slop unfit for drinking. During the day, the workers received a thin watery soup, but this was at least hot and cooked.[45]

Initially, the *Werkschutz* (factory protection force) beat and kicked them at every opportunity, administering corporal punishment for even the slightest infraction. Later, however, money was able to "soften" their behavior a little, and conditions became somewhat better. As a result of the extreme poverty in the city, many of these workers voluntarily remained there for a second term following the initial two months. The next camp, which also consisted of 300 workers, met a far better fate, as not only the conduct of the workers had improved, but also the food. The farmers of Przyrów had contributed to this improvement in no small measure, as they supplied the labor camp with food and created better housing conditions.

On the other hand, a real tragedy took place in both Cieszanów[46] and

45 In October 1940, the labor office in Częstochowa sent workers to a forced labor camp in Przyrów. See Dean, *USHMM Encyclopedia of Camps and Ghettos, 1933–1945*, vol. 2, part A, p. 349.

46 In May 1940, the Germans established a forced labor camp in Cieszanów. Officially, it was a subcamp of the Bełżec forced labor camp complex, some 30 kilometers northeast of Cieszanów. On August 20, 1940, about 3,000 additional Jews from Radom, Częstochowa, and Warsaw arrived in Cieszanów. According to a report on the activity of the Central Camps Council in Bełżec from June 13 to December 5, 1940, there was no accommodation for these deportees. They stayed in two synagogues, the rabbi's house, and a few other dwellings. When the forced labor camp was closed the first time (in November 1940), an unknown number of forced laborers were allowed to leave Cieszanów for their hometowns. Some Jews were sent to the Bełżec forced labor camp. It is not known how many Jews remained in Cieszanów throughout 1940 and 1941. See the report in Archiwum Państwowe w Łodzi (APŁ), RŻL-47, 25. For more details on this, see "Wave of Deportation from Cieszanow, Poland, to Wierzbica, Poland, on May 1, 1943," Yad Vashem, The International Institute for Holocaust Research, https://collections.yadvashem.org/en/deportations/15044373 (accessed August 18, 2025).

Wereszyn. The Judenrat was forced to send 450 workers to each of these two camps, where they were housed in barracks and guarded by SS men. These were veritable concentration camps, because immediately after their arrival in the railroad cattle cars, the Jewish laborers were greeted with a hail of blows from clubs and rifle butts inflicted on them by the SS men. There were already thousands of Jewish workers concentrated in these camps who were forced by the Germans to perform completely illogical and purposeless tasks, such as extracting sand and stones from the bottom of the shallow river with their bare hands, while standing up to their waists in water, or transferring stones from one pile to another. They were forced to run up and down hills with heavy stones in their hands and to repeat these actions many times under the blows of rifle butts and SS whips.

In a completely aimless manner, the Germans chased crowds of Jews from the camp in Cieszanów to another camp in nearby Bełżec,[47] where there were also hundreds of similarly tortured Jewish workers. Then, the still beaten and tortured workers were chased under a hail of blows and completely aimlessly from Bełżec back to Cieszanów. Many Jews paid with their lives during this constant torture, either as a result of wounds received during these cruel chases or from the typhoid and spotted fever epidemics that pervaded both camps.

Many Jewish workers managed to escape from these German slaughterhouses. After returning to Częstochowa, Mordka Lewkowski recounted that many Jews were shot by SS men during these forced runs from one camp to another. It was enough for one of the pursued to fall or stop for a rest to receive a rifle bullet to the back of his head. We heard that in the village of Ruskie Piaski, the tormented and chased Jews were led into a peasant barnyard, where numerous corpses of Jewish workers, who had been shot by the Germans, were already lying on the ground.

In the camp in Cieszanów, the SS Major Dolf roamed among the working Jews on horseback, beating every Jew he met on his way with a whip and firing a pistol at anyone who took a moment's rest while straightening his

47 Bełżec functioned as a forced labor camp in 1940 before being shut down in the fall of that year. The construction of the Bełżec death camp began in November 1941. See Yitzhak Arad, *The Operation Reinhard Death Camps, Revised and Expanded Edition: Bełżec, Sobibor, Treblinka* (Bloomington: Indiana University Press and Yad Vashem, 2018), pp. 43–44. Officially Cieszanów was a subcamp of the Bełżec forced labor complex. See Alina Skibińska, "Powiat biłgorajski," in Barbara Engelking and Jan Grabowski, *Dalej jest noc: losy Żydów w wybranych powiatach okupowanej Polski* (Warsaw: Centrum Badań nad Zagładą Żydów, 2018), p. 230.

back. At night, the barracks were guarded by SS men, and no one was allowed to leave, even to relieve themself. According to Lewkowski, a Jewish worker called Kon asked one of the SS men to let him leave the barracks to go to the toilet one night. The guard gave Kon permission, but when he reached the courtyard, the guard shot him in the hand. Kon hid in the barrack with a bleeding hand, but the SS guard continued to search for him. When he found him, he firmly grasped his injured hand and led him outside. Upon seeing this, people with tears in their eyes begged the German to spare Kon's life. However, weeping and begging did not help. The German took Kon out into the yard and shot him there in cold blood.

That same night, the Germans shot three other Jews. Later, Jewish workers began performing extremely harsh labor in these camps, as well as in the camp in Hrubieszów, building the highway, draining swamps, and regulating the river. Whenever a German guard noticed one of the workers weakening or standing idly by, he would beat him with a whip or hit him with a rifle butt. Lewkowski went on to say that, on one occasion, a man named Lipszyc, who was standing next to him, was shot in such circumstances, and he was ordered by the SS gendarme to bury his corpse.

These and similar accounts by escapees or returning camp workers shocked us and convinced us that the German threat about the extermination of Polish Jews was not just idle propaganda or a means of keeping the population in the occupied territories calm and blindly obedient. It turned out that the Germans were systematically and deliberately aiming to fulfill Hitler's predictions written in *Mein Kampf*: to murder 6 million European Jews—of whom 3.5 million lived in Poland. Moreover, they were preparing to carry out this extermination in specially equipped and designated camps, while the alleged labor camps, such as Cieszanów, Wereszyn, Bełżec, or Hrubieszów, seemed to be temporary training and schooling camps for the SS personnel to adapt to their future tasks.[48] This was the enormity of the

48 Historical discussion of the origins of the Holocaust has been dominated by the so-called intentionalist–functionalist debate since the 1980s. The intentionalists argue that the Holocaust is a result of a long-standing plan by Adolf Hitler and top Nazi leaders, rooted in Nazi antisemitic ideology with a clear intention to annihilate all the Jews. Functionalists, on the other hand, argue that the Holocaust evolved more gradually due to various wartime circumstances, and with bureaucracy and low- and mid-level Nazi functionaries playing an important role and often driven by pragmatic motives and responses to unfolding events. Many historians now adopt a more middle-ground approach with varying emphases. It seems that Kromołowski was an adherent of the intentionalist approach.

tragedy that awaited us, and the concentration of large numbers of Jews in a few centers—which were to be closed ghettos—was a prelude to the planned liquidation as part of the German *Endlösung*, the Final Solution.

Part of this genocide—which was to be carried out on a scale never before seen—also aimed to seize Jewish property to help offset the enormous costs of the German war effort. At the same time, the plunder of Jewish property was a good opportunity for individual German officials to line their own pockets. For this reason, many Jews took the risk of fleeing from German-occupied Polish territories to the Soviet-occupied Polish territories. Soon after the Germans entered Poland, the Soviet army annexed the lands east of the Bug and San Rivers, as expected following the Molotov–Ribbentrop Pact.[49]

My friends encouraged me and Stella to escape. At that time, as preparations were underway to seal the ghetto, we had a real chance of success. Many fled, but we decided to stay—primarily because of our parents and siblings. After my father's death, my mother was very depressed; she was simply devastated. My conscience did not allow me to leave her and my brother to their fate. Stella also did not want to leave her parents and brother. We decided to stay and share the fate of our loved ones. We hoped that something might change. We naively thought that maybe the world would shake off its numbness, somehow break the chain of German crimes, and prevent the genocide. Should we then harden our hearts, cast off our scruples, and do as so many others did—flee into the world, escaping the hell the Germans had prepared for us? Many Jews were saved in the Russian territories, although there were many others who perished in the Siberian steppes and even in the *katorga* of the Soviet camps.[50]

See discussion in Yehuda Bauer, *Rethinking the Holocaust* (New Haven: Yale University Press, 2002), pp. 14–38.

49 This was the agreement made between Nazi Germany and the Soviet Union just before the outbreak of World War II. It was signed by the German foreign minister, Ribbentrop, and the Soviet foreign minister, Molotov—therefore known as the Molotov–Ribbentrop Pact. The pact included two agreements: the first dealt with economic relations, while the second was a non-aggression pact. The economic agreement was signed on August 19, 1939, and the non-aggression pact was signed on August 23, 1939, in Moscow. The pact had a secret attachment dealing with the division of the spheres of influence between USSR and Germany. The Soviet Union and Germany agreed to divide Poland. This pact enabled Germany to invade Poland on September 1, 1939, without concern for Soviet intervention. The Soviet Union in turn invaded Poland on September 17.

50 In the Soviet-occupied zone of Poland, there were 1.2 million local Jews and

On December 24, 1941, heavy snow fell, and a sharp frost took hold. Stella went into town to get some groceries, dressed in her fur coat to keep warm. However, she quickly returned, weeping and freezing—and without her fur coat. It turned out that a German policemen had torn off her coat in the street, leaving her out in the cold in just her dress. That day, German civilian officials stormed the Jewish streets, tearing furs off people and confiscating them—even if it was only a fur collar—beating and kicking men and women as they went.[51] News about the confiscation of furs spread through the city with lightning speed, so the Jews hastily began to hide all their fur garments in cellars and attics. Fur collars were torn off and replaced with collars made from cloth or velvet. Many burned their furs, gave them to Poles for safekeeping, or sold them.

The next day, the Judenrat announced that, by order of the *Stadthauptmann*, the Jews had to immediately hand over all fur coats in their possession for the needs of the German army. German gendarmes, policemen, and Gestapo officers searched every inch of the Jewish apartments for hidden furs, as well as in basements and attics. Inhumane beatings and even murders were carried out against those found in possession of even the smallest scrap of fur. This action was led by Police Lieutenant Frankowski, an unparalleled bandit of Polish origin from Poznań. The furs were collected and taken to three spacious rooms, specially designated for this purpose, on the premises of the Council of Elders, which now occupied the front of the house at 11 First Avenue. There, three furriers sorted them. Many of these furs were of great value. Senior German officers and officials came to the warehouses with their wives and mistresses, guarded by Jewish policemen, and took the most valuable and magnificent ones. Those that remained were taken by truck to German warehouses.

approximately 300,000 to 350,000 refugees from the western parts of Poland. See Saul Friedländer, *Nazi Germany and the Jews, 1933–1945* (New York: Harper Perennial, 2009), p. 163. After the invasion of the Soviet Union, the majority of Jews who remained in the invaded territory shared the bitter fate of the rest of Polish Jewry, murdered during the various stages of the Holocaust. Yet the majority of those who were deported to more remote regions of the Soviet Union survived. See Eliyana R. Adler, *Survival on the Margins: Polish Jewish Refugees in the Wartime Soviet Union* (Cambridge: Harvard University Press, 2020).

51 See Brener, "Resistance and Destruction in the Częstochowa Ghetto," p. 25; Kiel, *The Jews of Częstochowa*, p. 130.

The fur campaign, carried out on the orders of the governor, Dr. Lasch,[52] simultaneously took place in other cities and towns in the Radom District, to which Częstochowa belonged. In fact, furs were requisitioned across the entire General Government. This was part of the Germans' systematic and planned plunder of Jewish property, with the express goal to economically ruin the Jewish community, strip them of all their personal belongings, and then take their lives. To carry out this plan, the Germans expropriated Jewish factories, industrial plants, and even some larger craft workshops and offices. They first removed the owners of these businesses and then reopened them under German—and, often, Polish—administrators, the so-called *Treuhänders* (trustees).

In this way, Jewish owners and directors were expelled from such establishments, including the Gnaszyńska Manufaktura, the wallpaper factory, and the brickyard in Gnaszyn, near Częstochowa; the Zawodzie Paint Factory, which belonged to Dr. Aleksander Wolberg; the Angels Chemical Factory, owned by Dr. W. Sachs; the Warta textile factory; the Altman screw and nail factory; the Horowicz & Co. tool factory; the Landau Brothers metal factory; the Bromberg pin factory; the metallurgy foundry and enameling plant; along with dozens of other major manufacturing plants that were taken from their Jewish owners without any compensation.

The more valuable machinery and tools from Jewish factories were exported to the Third Reich, along with valuable paintings and other artworks seized from Jewish owners. Of course, this looting was carried out systematically throughout German-occupied Poland. These valuables had been collected by many Jewish families over generations and were worth billions. These priceless works of art, factory machinery and equipment, and property that the Germans took from the Jews in Poland are still in the possession of Germans today—both in the German Federal Republic and the German Democratic Republic.[53]

Jews were allowed to earn a living only through selling food or performing small-scale service work. However, even this meager economic activity was heavily taxed and constantly controlled. From morning until

52 Karl Lasch (1904–1942) was a Nazi official who served as governor of the Radom District (1939–1941) to which Częstochowa belonged, and later as governor of the Galicia District (1941–1942).

53 This memoir was written before the reunification of Germany. For an extensive study of the plunder of Jewish possessions, see Martin Dean, *Robbing the Jews: The Confiscation of Jewish Property in the Holocaust, 1933–1945* (Cambridge: Cambridge University Press, 2010).

evening, treasury officials, auditors, sequestrators, and bailiffs—mostly Poles—roamed through the Jewish apartments, mercilessly collecting current and overdue taxes and fees, and even prewar tax arrears. Jewish paupers were robbed of their last pieces of furniture and any objects of value—even those kept under their pillows for safekeeping—and personal body searches were performed to extract money from people's pockets.

The Polish tax officials often committed abuses during enforcement, seizing movable property for taxes that had already been paid. Many such cases came to my attention in the Commercial Department of the Judenrat. It was sometimes possible to successfully intervene with the treasury authorities and secure the return of wrongfully seized movable property or goods. There were also numerous occasions when I was able to reduce the tax assessments, which the officials deliberately exaggerated in the case of Jewish shopkeepers and craftsmen in order to destroy their already meager existence.

Among other things, these exorbitant tax assessments were imposed, by order of the German authorities, on all former owners of confiscated industrial plants placed under German trusteeship. The Germans knew full well that these people—having had their enterprises, along with any raw materials and finished products, taken from them, and their bank accounts confiscated—had no means of supporting themselves or their families. Nevertheless, they ordered the tax authorities to assess taxes for the same business year in which the takeover occurred, with the clear intent of destroying them completely. In this way, they forced them to sell off the last of their remaining property.

I must admit that in this part of my work, which was sometimes dangerous, I found understanding and favor from a handful of honest Polish senior treasury officials, who did everything they could to assist me in my appeals and interventions, even though they were directly accountable for their decisions to the German treasury counselor, Krum. Most notably among them were Czesław Rzepka, who was the chief of the treasury office in Częstochowa; Jan Motłoch, the head of the treasury execution and, in fact, a *Volksdeutscher*; and the Ukrainian Skomoroch, vice-counselor and Krum's deputy. Although it was sometimes necessary to bribe them, it paid off because, thanks to my many successful interventions, I managed to recover hundreds of thousands of złoty from the Germans' pockets. Additionally, some goods were returned to their Jewish owners, enabling them to survive the harsh conditions of daily life.

One time, a woman named Cymerman came to our office, weeping and wringing her hands. She told me that a tax collector had come to her home, demanding that she pay taxes on a hardware store that the Germans had taken over long before. While the sequestrator was searching the pockets of her husband's clothes, she removed her last 30,000 złoty from the drawer and hid it under a pillow on the bed, where her husband lay seriously ill. However, the sequestrator noticed that she was hiding something. He found the money and took it to cover the apparent tax arrears.

This was their last remaing money from their trading days, and it was all they had to support their family. Now they were penniless. The woman was distraught and begged for help. I went to the tax office the next day and told the whole story to the chief of execution, Jan Motłoch, asking him to do something to help these people, who were now completely ruined, not excluding the fact that Mr. Cymerman was bedridden. There was only one way to retrieve the money: The Cymermans' tax debts had to be written off retroactively.

I wrote an application on the spot and took it to the head of the tax office, Rzepka, who noted on it that his decision had been made a month earlier, remitting the entire tax arrears—an amount significantly exceeding the confiscated money. The rationale for this decision was that all property had been confiscated by the current authorities, so there were no funds to pay the taxes. There was such a provision in the tax law, and I referred to it in my application. Motłoch made a note under Rzepka's decision that the execution was therefore canceled, before stamping and signing it.

With this letter, I went to the head of the accountancy office, who ordered the arrears to be crossed out in the tax books, and demanded a return of the unjustly taken money. The demand was legally and factually justified, since the cancellation of execution was made a month ago, and the tax collector seized the money only yesterday. Consequently, the head of the execution decided to pay out the illegally seized money, and after I presented the appropriate order, the cashier of the account paid me the 30,000 złoty belonging to the Cymermans. One can imagine the joy of Mrs. Cymerman, who could not believe her eyes when I handed her the money that she had already considered lost.

Mrs. Cymerman was an acquaintance of mine from the prewar days, when she and her husband owned a prosperous hardware store on New Market Square. Later, in a labor camp after the liquidation of the ghetto, she took care of her mentally ill daughter. The German police, who supervised the labor camp, discovered this fact and both the woman and her daughter were shot. According to the camp authorities, mentally ill Jews and people who did not work—leading a parasitic life—must be shot.

CHAPTER SIX

THE CZĘSTOCHOWA GHETTO

On April 9, 1941, thirty yellow posts were hammered into the ground at thirty border points, which were intended to separate the Jewish residential quarter from the "Aryan" part of town, where only Germans and Poles were allowed to live. Attached to these posts were yellow plaques with inscriptions written in German and Polish, stating that the Jewish residential area was a restricted zone due to an epidemic of spotted fever, and that Jews were prohibited from leaving, under penalty of death.

By April 23, a Jewish policeman wielding a rubber truncheon stood in front of each of these signs at the thirty border points, ensuring that no unauthorized person left the Jewish ghetto.[1] The only way one could

1 The Big Ghetto, which functioned from April 1941 to October 1942, was approximately "400 by 400 meters, bordered roughly by the railway line and Wilsona on the west side, the Warta River and Nadrzeczna on the east, northeast was Kawia street, Kierdrzyńska and Jaskrowska streets, and on the south, Fabryczna, Narutowicza, and Strażacka streets." See Kiel, *The Jews of Częstochowa*, p. 137. According to Paszkowski, the deadline for Jews to move into the ghetto and for non-Jews to vacate the designated area was April 17, 1941. See Wiesław Paszkowski, "The State of the Research on the Holocaust in Częstochowa," 2004 Conference "Days of

leave the ghetto was to present a special pass issued by the German *Stadthauptmann*, bearing the Nazi seal with a German eagle clutching a swastika in its talons. Even the Judenrat members—including its chairman Leon Kopiński—had to show their passes when leaving the ghetto area. Jews with these passes were required to wear special white armbands with a blue Star of David, specifically designated for Jews.

At first, Poles were allowed to enter the ghetto, but at their own risk; shortly thereafter, the Polish population was prohibited from being in the Jewish quarter. However, uniformed Germans and civilians, as well as the Polish Blue Police and other Polish officials, were allowed to enter the area on official business. The Germans often came to watch the Jews crammed into the narrow streets of the ghetto and photograph them for fun—like watching wild animals in the zoo, deprived of their freedom. Sometimes, however, they took people to do odd jobs, before beating, kicking, and abusing random passersby who had not yet managed to find a safe place to shelter. People walking on the sidewalk had to get out of the way, step down from the pavement onto the road, and take off their hat whenever a German approached. Woe betides those who did not comply. They were punched in the face and then kicked when they fell to the ground.

Apartments and stores were frequently robbed by German soldiers, and there were also incidents of murder. Unsurprisingly, no one felt safe on the ghetto streets, and passersby slipped along the walls of the houses, looking around carefully. At the mere sight of a German walking down the street, people ran away and hid in the gateways or in nearby apartments and stores. There were often sudden commotions in the street when the Germans arrived, beating people and trying to catch them for forced labor. People sought shelter wherever possible, leaving the streets empty. In search of victims, the Germans swept through apartments—even cellars and attics—beating, torturing, and robbing Jews. They knew exactly where to look for Jews, and they always found their victims.

The streets of the ghetto, even on a sunny summer day, presented a picture of sadness, gloom, and desperation. The few pedestrians out on the street always hurried along, everyone wearing their obligatory Star of David on his armband, which had to be worn on the right sleeve of their coats, glancing around to see if any Germans were prowling nearby. Especially humiliating was the constant photographing of Jews

Remembrance," The World Society of Czestochowa Jews and Their Descendents, https://www.czestochowajews.org/conference-papers/2004-conference/ (accessed November 12, 2025), p. 6.

Street peddlers in the Częstochowa ghetto, Poland, c. 1942.
Yad Vashem Archives (YVA), 503/4721.

by German soldiers, who stopped both men and women and made them pose, putting them in various positions to take a whole series of pictures. Those who were reluctant or not sufficiently obedient were beaten, often to the point of bleeding.

The Jewish paupers in the ghetto suffered increasing poverty. Particularly tragic were the living conditions of the refugees from Łódź, who had managed to arrive here in quite considerable numbers shortly before the establishment of the Częstochowa Jewish residential quarter, fleeing hunger and the cruel conditions that prevailed in the Łódź ghetto. As a result of this poverty, epidemics and lice spread among these refugees. A delousing facility was set up in the building of the former *mikva* (ritual bath) in Garibaldi Street, but it did not help much.

To combat poverty and improve living conditions, a number of charitable institutions were set up in the ghetto. The Social Assistance Department of the Judenrat was particularly active. The director of this department was the trainee lawyer Natan Rodał (Bolesław Marcinkiewicz), and his deputy was Cesia Kozak. This committee provided wholesome and nourishing lunches for the Jewish population each day at six locations.

These lunches were either free or available for a minimal fee of 10 groszy. A soup kitchen was also set up for the extremely poor intelligentsia—especially those who had come from other cities. Here, lunches were served at a charge of 55 groszy, and later at an increased price of 1.10 złoty.

The Social Assistance Department was also responsible for distributing clothing, underwear, and shoes. The department received funds for these purposes either from voluntary fees and donations provided by the wealthier population or from indirect taxes and the previously mentioned sale of tax stamps, specially printed by the Judenrat. These stamps had to be affixed to requests for services provided to the Jewish population in connection with the council's activities. These tax stamps had a face value of 2 złoty.

These stamps were used in various different ways, but they were mainly used to collect the administrative fee that people had to pay when receiving food ration cards for bread, potatoes, coal, and other items in short supply. Food in the ghetto was rationed and was distributed only using ration cards. Food and heating supplies for the ghetto were brought in and distributed by a special department created for this purpose, headed by Stanisław Prusicki, the former director of the Jewish bank.

According to data from the statistical department—also created by the Judenrat—published in the yearbook compiled by the Department of Administration and Statistics, 14,960 people benefited from social assistance offered by the Judenrat in 1941, which corresponds to the 4,058 Jewish families living in the ghetto. In addition to benefits in kind, the Social Welfare Department also provided those in need with monetary aid. There was also a kitchen for the Department of Forced Labor, which provided free meals to workers employed in various German factories.

The local TOZ (Society for the Protection of Health)[2] in the ghetto carried out extensive charitable activities. It was highly effective in providing medical treatment, but it also offered social aid, mainly to Jewish children. The TOZ organized a network of daycare centers, where children were cared for by unaffiliated nurses, fed, and given clothing, underwear, and shoes. This was a long-established and meritorious Jewish charitable

2 Towarzystwo Ochrony Zdrowia Ludności Żydowskiej w Polsce (Society for the Protection of the Health of the Jewish Population in Poland, TOZ) was founded in 1920 and was dedicated to the prevention of social diseases, the promotion of hygiene, childcare, diagnostics, and basic medical treatment among the Jewish population in Poland. It operated until 1950, except for the years between 1942 and 1945.

institution in Poland, managed by numerous doctors and social workers who provided free medical aid and preventive treatment to the poverty-stricken Jewish population.

In Nazi-occupied Częstochowa, the TOZ was constantly active, taking advantage of financial subsidies sent both from the central board and the Joint (Joint Distribution Committee, JDC). Self-taxation among wealthier Jews and loans from the rich—intended to be returned after the war—also constituted a significant source of TOZ funds. Almost all Jewish doctors in the Częstochowa ghetto as well as nurses and orderlies worked voluntarily for the TOZ—and at great personal sacrifice. The organization was headed and resiliently managed by Dr. Adam Wolberg,[3] a former physician in the Polish army, captain of the 27th Infantry Regiment, which was stationed in Częstochowa. Mieczysław Konarski and Jakub Rozyne also managed the TOZ alongside Wolberg.

There was only one main hospital in the Częstochowa ghetto, located in the front section of a residential building on Przemysłowa Street. The hospital was primitively furnished, having been adapted from former living quarters. Unfortunately, the beautiful and modern Jewish hospital in Zawodzie—with all its equipment, beds, and furnishings—had been confiscated by the Germans and transformed into a military hospital. The director of the ghetto hospital was Dr. Jerzy Dobrzyński, a local surgeon. There was, however, another small and very basic infectious disease hospital with a few beds, but it was completely overwhelmed and ineffectual, given the constant overcrowding from patients suffering from the prevailing epidemics of spotted fever and typhoid fever.

While there was an overwhelming number of extremely poor Jews in the ghetto, there were those who were prosperous too. A few very wealthy people—mostly former merchants and industrialists—amassed considerable funds through the unofficial trade of hidden luxury goods or raw materials. Some ghetto inhabitants traded with peasants and Poles living on the Aryan side; although, this was dangerous, as they risked being caught by German patrols or betrayed to the police by informers. They smuggled goods—mainly foodstuffs and even cattle—into the ghetto from

3 Dr. Adam "Ajzyk" Wolberg (1894–1943) was a Polish army officer and a physician. He served as vice-chairman of the Society for the Protection of the Health of the Jewish Population (TOZ) and headed its Sanitary Department. Dr. Wolberg perished in the Small Ghetto of Częstochowa in 1943. He is buried in a mass grave in the local Jewish cemetery. See Sętkowski, *Częstochowa Jews: A Biographical Dictionary*, pp. 482–483.

the Aryan side or the neighboring villages. Smuggling mainly took place via the Warta River, which separated the Jewish quarter from the Aryan Zawodzie district.

Craftsmen were also considered prosperous, as they produced small-scale industrial goods that were smuggled to the Aryan sector and sold to the Polish population. Local bakers and grocery owners who dealt in smuggled goods also grew rich. It was possible to buy from them, at very high prices, various fats—butter, margarine, lard, and oils—and even luxury goods, such as sardines, sprats, cheese, canned meat, sausages, and ham.

Both legal and illegal rye-milling workshops were set up—small, homemade mills where milling was done using quern stones. Like mushrooms after the rain, numerous private cafés, eateries, and restaurants sprang up where one could eat and drink well. There were even ghetto gardens, where flowers and vegetables were grown, often in ghetto greenhouses and vegetable gardens, and where ice cream and cool drinks were sold in the summer. Children, who made a living from trading on the streets to support their families, were a frequent sight in the ghetto. Anyone who had the knowledge, cunning, and courage engaged in trade or ran some kind of business, because under the harsh and merciless conditions of life in the closed ghetto, money played an enormous role. In the ghetto, money could get you anything, and with a lot of it, you could live a prosperous, comfortable, and even luxurious life.

That is why people risked their health, freedom, and lives like never before to get as much money as possible. Life in the ghetto was like living under battle conditions, fraught with danger from everywhere. People lived for the moment and did not think about the future, which looked dark and hopeless. Moral boundaries were breaking down, and people were turning into traitors. There was a merciless struggle for one's very existence, and money meant power, strength, and more opportunities to survive. Various types of *nouveau riches* emerged, mostly from the margins of society—criminal elements such as informers, thieves, swindlers, bribers, and blackmailers. Professional informers to the German authorities—especially to the Gestapo and the Devisenstelle (money department)—did very well, offering information about wealthy Jews who possessed foreign currency, gold, or hidden rationed goods.

The most dangerous among these informers was Eliasz Szeftel—who, as a reward for denouncing others, was permitted to run a restaurant for the Germans—and Jehuda Majer Besser, a Jew from Zawiercie. An equally dangerous informer was a Jew from Łódź named Jakub Rozenberg.

There were many more of them, though not all were known by name. They made a lot of money, enjoyed great freedom, and had the privilege of leaving the ghetto without wearing the Jewish armband, as well as being on the Aryan side and moving around without any restrictions. They were the scum of society; the general ghetto population despised them. Despite their invaluable services to the Germans, they were not spared when the ghetto was later liquidated. On the contrary, they were the first to be sent to the cattle cars used by the Germans to transport the Jewish population to the extermination camps, or they were shot on the spot by German Schutzpolizei (Schupo) policemen.

Despite the persecution and constant danger in which we lived in the ghetto, and despite the death sentence constantly hanging over our heads, we possessed tremendous vitality. It manifested itself primarily in cultural and educational activities conducted, of course, in strict secrecy from the authorities. Secret schools were established, as well as education centers for youth run by former teachers of the local Jewish schools, primarily professors of the Jewish gymnasium. Examinations required by the Polish school regulations (including matriculation exams) were held, and school and matriculation certificates were issued, all of which were fully honored after the war.

Artistic groups were also active, mainly as part of the TOZ's social activities. It featured an amateur actor with an extraordinary *vis comica*, Jeszua Borensztajn, known as the "Dzigan of Częstochowa," after the Polish-Jewish comedian and actor. New young talent also emerged. The Jakubowicz brothers composed satirical pieces on current ghetto issues and wrote songs that were performed at secret shows and were often hummed by the ghetto's youth. There were choirs with well-known amateur singers such as Henryk Edelist and his son Ludwik, the amateur bass Grabiner, Roma Nadelberg from Łódź, Poznańska, and the granddaughter of Częstochowa's chief rabbi Nachum Asz, Sławka Zytenfeld. An impressive symphony orchestra, conducted by violinist Adolf Goldszajder, also gave concerts. Children's choirs were organized in the community centers, and performances for children and young people were also staged. In addition, readings and lectures on history and science were delivered by local professors such as the principal of the Jewish high school Professor Anisfeld, the historian Professor Mehring, Szefer, and many others. The Judenrat tried to legalize the activities of these groups, motivated by the need to find a source of income for the musicians, singers, and actors confined to the ghetto, but the *Stadthauptmann* categorically rejected this request.

As part of the ghetto's cultural activity, the previously mentioned underground newspaper *Rasta* was published. Written in Polish, this satirical publication spoke out against the Judenrat and contained humorous, often rhyming, pieces condemning the attitude of the prominent members of the Judenrat and their servility to the Germans, often at the expense of the Jewish population. The newspaper appeared sporadically and was edited by a clandestine group, which, as was later revealed, was headed by Dr. Adam Wolberg, one of the TOZ's leaders. The newspaper was in constant battle with the Judenrat, and it criticized many of their harmful and socially damaging actions. This fight did not end well for the TOZ: The Germans ordered its liquidation, and all its organs, posts, and assets were taken over by the Judenrat, which continued the TOZ's activities under radically changed leadership.

In analyzing the activity of the Judenrat as the ghetto's leading force, appointed by the German occupiers, it must be emphasized that aside from a number of negative aspects and often condemnable actions, there were also many positive elements of its actions and work. While this institution did not enjoy broad recognition among the Jewish masses—on the contrary, it was usually condemned—it is important to remember that many of its decisions were made under orders from the German authorities, and that, despite everything, it often helped the Jews in the ghetto survive. The Judenrat tried to ease German persecution and spare the Jews as much suffering as possible. Through its vigorous efforts to fight hunger, epidemics, and poverty in the ghetto, it helped alleviate the misery of the ghetto population and maintain relatively tolerable living conditions. Suffice it to say, in the entire General Government, the Częstochowa Judenrat was one of the most liberal, and it managed to create bearable living conditions.

In contrast, the Jewish police in the ghetto was universally hated. Its officers and leadership acted mercilessly. They often used physical coercion, beat people, and handed them over to the Germans—even though they knew that those handed over risked imprisonment or death. This infamous organ, created by the Germans to torment Jewish society, was under the leadership of the following people: Dr. Maurycy Kacinel, a lawyer who had arrived in Częstochowa after forced displacement;[4]

4 Maurycy Kacinel (1888–1942) was a lawyer, head of the Jewish police, and a member of the Judenrat. He died during the liquidation of the Częstochowa ghetto on October 28, 1942. See Sętkowski, *Częstochowa Jews: A Biographical Dictionary*, pp. 232–233.

the Częstochowa expeditor Maurycy Galster[5]—known in the ghetto as Knalster; Herman Parasol, who later became commander of the Jewish police in the forced labor camp for Jews in the Small Ghetto; Moniek Pławner from Radomsko, who was in the service of the Gestapo; and Rozenberg from Łódź, the right hand and informer of the German police officer Rhon.

The Germans established a number of large ghettos during this period to be used as concentration points for the Jewish population in the General Government. This was all part of the Nazis' preparation for the next stage of their criminal, genocidal action *Endlösung*—the deportations to extermination camps. The largest ghettos were set up in Warsaw, Kraków, Białystok, as well as Łódź, which was purely Polish even though it was formally annexed to the German Reich. In these ghettos, hunger, epidemics, disease, and the oppression of the persecuted and destroyed population were rampant to a greater degree than in Częstochowa. Hunger decimated the populations in these ghettos, and epidemics spread the destruction further. People died in the streets, and Jewish corpses lined the sidewalks and squares. The burial society could not keep up with the number of dead and had to adopt an accelerated system: The dead were buried in common mass graves, into which the human corpses—naked and swollen from starvation—were slid down special ramps.

Thousands of people starved to death, and many were also shot by German and Polish policemen on the ghetto streets or while trying to escape under the ghetto's walls—as seen in the Warsaw ghetto, which was surrounded by brick walls that separated it from the districts inhabited by Poles. The Częstochowa ghetto did not witness such tragic street incidents as in the Warsaw and Łódź ghettos. Perhaps this was also due to its Judenrat and its chairman.

In addition to the aforementioned large Jewish concentration points, the Germans also created a ghetto in every larger city and town, organized in a manner similar to ours and also headed by a Judenrat and the Jewish police. As events unfolded and the deadline set by Hitler and his closest circle of helpers for "the Final Solution of the Jewish Question," the *Endlösnung*—the complete annihilation of the Jewish population in Poland and other European countries under German control—approached, Jews

5 Maurycy Galster (1887–1943) was a merchant and mercantile activist and commander of the Jewish police. Together with his wife, he was murdered on March 20, 1943, in the mass executions at the Jewish cemetery. See ibid., p. 143.

were deported on a huge scale from these ghettos to the death camps, where they were poisoned to death in gas chambers.

In the immediate vicinity of our city, similar ghettos were located in Radomsko, Piotrków, and Kielce. From Kielce and its environs, the Germans carried out massive transports of Jews to the labor camp—actually a concentration camp—in Skarżysko-Kamienna,[6] where huge numbers of people died while working in the armaments factory, particularly from picric acid poisoning during gunpowder production. Several thousand Jews were held there under the supervision of the SS and the police commander of the Radom District. A similar camp also existed on the grounds of the chemical plant in Pionki. In Piotrków, Jewish prisoners were employed in military plants, glassworks, and a wood processing factory.

In the Radom District—of which Częstochowa was part—there were labor camps for Jews in Staszów, Sandomierz, Jędrzejów, Włoszczowa (near Częstochowa), Sędziszów, Jedlińsk, and Bodzechów.[7] There was also a ghetto in Radom itself, the capital of the district, from which Jews were taken to the above-mentioned labor camps, and later to the camp in Bliżyn, a camp which was set up to replace the former Stalag (German POW camp) for Soviet prisoners of war. In this camp, 4,000 people worked—including more than 1,000 women—initially in the quarries and later in large carpentry, clothing, and other workshops that had been established. Prisoners from Częstochowa were also transported here later on. The Bliżyn camp was under the command of the SS and district police district commander, so essentially making it a concentration camp, where Jewish workers were brought for forced labor, receiving insufficient food rations.

In the Lublin District—with the exception of Lublin itself—there were eight ghettos, which were ultimately liquidated in the following

6 Skarżysko-Kamienna (Kamienna in German sources) was a forced labor camp for Jews in Poland, operated by the German HASAG concern. Established in August 1942 and liquidated on August 1, 1944, it held a total of 25,000–30,000 Jews, with 18,000–23,000 perishing. See "Skarzysko-Kamienna," in Robert Rozett and Shmuel Spector, eds., *Encyclopedia of the Holocaust* (Jerusalem: H.H. The Jerusalem Publishing House and Yad Vashem, 2009), pp. 409–410. For a monographic study of the camp, see Felicja Karay, *Death Comes in Yellow: Skarzysko-Kamienna Slave Labor Camp* (Amsterdam: Harwood Academic, 1996).

7 On forced labor camps in the Radom District, see Józef Andrzej Młynarczyk, *Judenmord in Zentralpolen: Der Distrikt Radom im Generalgouvernement* 1939–1945, Veröffentlichungen der Forschungsstelle Ludwigsburg der Universität Stuttgart, 9 (Darmstadt: Wissenschaftliche Buchgesellschaft, 2007), pp. 277–285.

years.[8] In April 1941, about 250,000 Jews still lived in this district, but by the end of 1942, only 20,000 people remained. They were housed in so-called secondary ghettos in Międzyrzecze, Lukow, Parczew, Włodawa, Izbica, Piaski, and Zaklikowie. In Lublin, a forced labor camp for women was established at the airport in February 1942.[9] There, the SS authorities organized a large sorting operation for the clothes left behind by the murdered Jews. The 4,000 women selected from Majdanek were also housed here. A men's camp was also established at the airport, where Dutch and Belgian Jews were sent.

From 1941, there was a camp for Jews in Trawniki,[10] to which the Germans directed transports of Jews from Germany, Czechoslovakia, and Austria. Jews from nearby Opole Lubelskie were deported to the camp

8 There's discussion among historians about the term ghetto and which situations it applied to. Historian David Silberklang lists four ghettos in the Lublin district that fit the name in the first half of 1941: Lublin, Opole-Lubelski, Piaski, and Zamość. These ghettos housed barely 20 percent of the Jews in the district. Others were subsequently established, as Kromołowski says. See David Silberklang, *Gates of Tears: The Holocaust in the Lublin District* (Jerusalem: Yad Vashem, 2013), p. 159. For a detailed picture of various types of Jewish quarters and ghettos, see Dan Michman, *The Emergence of Jewish Ghettos during the Holocaust* (Cambridge: Cambridge University Press, 2011). Among reference books on specific ghettos, the most prominent publications are: Guy Miron and Shlomit Shulhani, eds., *The Yad Vashem Encyclopedia of the Ghettos during the Holocaust* (Jerusalem: Yad Vashem, 2009); Dean, *USHMM Encyclopedia of Camps and Ghettos*, 1933–1945, vol. 2, part A.

9 This was the Flugplatz camp. The camp mainly operated between 1942 and 1943. Already from fall 1941, Polish women were sent to the airfield to weave straw shoes at the airfield. From the beginning of 1942, men were imprisoned there too. From spring 1942, men from incoming transports fit for work were selected and sent to labor camps and to KL Lublin (Majdanek), while women, children, the elderly, and disabled were deported to transit ghettos or directly to death camps. See Jakub Chmielewski, "The Flugplatz Labour Camp," in *Lexicon: History of Lublin and the Lublin Region*, Ośrodek, Brama Grodzka—Teatr NN, https://teatrnn.pl/lexicon/articles/the-flugplatz-labour-camp (accessed February 4, 2025); Wojciech Lenarczyk, "Obóz pracy na Flugplatzu w Lublinie: Historia, funkcjonowanie, więźniowie," *Zeszyty Majdanka*, 26 (2014), pp. 66–69.

10 The Trawniki camp, located some 40 kilometers southeast of Lublin, operated in the years 1941–1944 and fulfilled several functions. It had an SS training facility for auxiliary forces of several nationalities, among whom the Ukrainian force was most prominent. These so-called Trawniki men played an important role in carrying out the Holocaust in the Lublin District. See more in Silberklang, *Gates of Tears*,

in Poniatowa. In the summer of 1941, the Germans started building a huge concentration camp in Majdanek, near Lublin. This was the largest extermination camp after Auschwitz—it could hold about 50,000 people. It was built under the personal supervision of Odilo Globocnik, commander of the SS and police in Lublin. In this camp's gas chambers, the Germans murdered hundreds of thousands of Jews from the Lublin District and other parts of the General Government, as well as Jews from Nazi-occupied countries across Europe.[11]

There were also ghettos in the Dąbrowa Basin and Upper Silesia—in Sosnowiec, Zawiercie, Będzin, and others. Jews from these places were usually sent to Auschwitz extermination camp, where they were annihilated.[12] In addition, there were more than 40,000 Jews in the Białystok ghetto, and around 20,000 Jews in the surrounding areas. The entire Jewish population—both from Białystok itself and from the transit points in Kiełbasin, Bogusze, Zambrów, and Wołkowysk—were sent by the Germans to the death camp of Auschwitz and Treblinka. The entire Jewish population in this district—and in the Białystok ghetto itself, which held out the longest—was brutally liquidated in mid-August 1943.[13]

pp. 241–247. As Kromołowski states, there was also a Jewish labor camp through which thousands of Jews passed. The labor camp existed until November 1943, at which point there were some 8,000–10,000 Jews. On November 3, 1943, they were taken to the SS auxiliary training camp, where they were shot naked in a trench. See Yitzhak Arad, *The Operation Reinhard Death Camps: Belzec, Sobibor, Treblinka* (Bloomington: Indiana University Press, 1987), pp. 422–423.

11 Construction of Majdanek (KL Lublin) began in the early summer of 1941, carried out by Jewish forced laborers and Soviet prisoners of war. Its size and function were modified several times thereafter. It variably functioned as a forced-labor camp, a concentration camp, a POW camp, and a death camp. See Silberklang, *Gates of Tears*, pp. 250–251. Historians estimate that the numbers of Jews who perished in Majdanek ranges from tens of thousands to 200,000. We can definitively estimate that tens of thousands either died as a result of harsh laboring in brutal, inhumane conditions, were murdered in the gas chambers, or were shot. See Tomasz Kranz, "Das Konzentrationslager Majdanek und die 'Aktion Reinhardt,'" in Bogdan Musial, ed., *"Aktion Reinhardt": Der Völkermord an den Juden im Generalgouvernement 1941–1944* (Osnabrück: Fibre Verlag, 2004), pp. 233–255.

12 Detailed information on transports to death camps and other murder sites can be found on the Yad Vashem website. See "The Deportations of Jews Research Project and Digital Database (Transports to Extinction)," https://collections.yadvashem.org/en/deportations (accessed August 18, 2025).

13 Deportations from the Białystok ghetto began on August 18 and lasted three days.

In the Kraków District, the Kraków ghetto had the largest concentration of Jews after Tarnów (32,000 Jews). In the middle of 1942, there were 17,000 inhabitants. In October 1942, 6,000 Jews were deported to the camp in Bełżec. The remaining Jews in the Kraków ghetto as well as those in other ghettos in the district were sent to the newly established camp in Płaszów, near Kraków. This was a labor camp for Jews (*Judenarbeitslager*), which was under the administration of SS and police commander of the Kraków District, Scherner. Jews had to live in barracks and worked in brush-making, locksmithing, tailoring, and glass workshops. They were escorted daily to various workplaces outside the camp.[14] In time, the Płaszów camp was reclassified as an SS forced labor camp (*Zwangarbeitslager SS*), and in January 1944, it was declared a concentration camp (KL).

The Jewish population was also deported to camps in Pustków, Mielec, and Sędziszów. Later, the population was concentrated in Pustków, and finally, together with Jews from Stalowa Wola, Rożnów, and other towns in the Kraków district—including those from Płaszów, Kraków, and Tarnów—they were deported to the death camp in Auschwitz. A significant portion of this district's Jewish population had already perished during the ongoing selections, murdered on the spot by SS men and German policemen.

The Jewish communities of the Warsaw District were gradually annihilated, and after selections, during which many people were murdered, any remaining Jews still alive were sent to the Warsaw ghetto. In this way, the Warsaw District—except for Warsaw itself and a few other towns—became *Judenrein*. Of the approximately 600,000 Jews living there in mid-1940, about 50,000 remained at the end of 1942 (according to official figures). In the Warsaw ghetto, the Germans gathered over half a million Jews, who almost from the very beginning were deported to various extermination camps or else killed on the spot. The Jewish population in the ghetto died of hunger and disease by the thousands. The worst conditions in the Governorate prevailed in this district, and the population suffered

Most of the Jews of the ghetto were deported to Treblinka, some were sent to Majdanek, Poniatowa, Bliżyn, and Auschwitz, while 1,200 children were deported to Theresienstadt, and later to Auschwitz. About 150 fighters from Białystok joined the partisans. Only 2,000 Jews were left in the ghetto, but they were deported to Majdanek three weeks later. See entries for Białystok and other ghettos in Miron and Shulhani, *The Yad Vashem Encyclopedia of the Ghettos in the Holocaust*; Dean, *USHMM Encyclopedia of Camps and Ghettos, 1933–1945*, vol. 2, part A.

14 On the Kraków ghetto, see *USHMM Encyclopedia of Camps and Ghettos, 1933–1945*, vol. 2, part A, pp. 527–530.

terribly. Deportations of groups rounded up by the Jewish police took place almost daily. Initially, people were sent to labor camps in the Lublin District and later to Majdanek and Treblinka, the main execution sites for the Jewish population of the Warsaw and Radom Districts.

The Jewish population in the General Government in the second half of 1940 was estimated at around 1.9 million people. After the Galicia District was incorporated into the General Government, the number increased by roughly 600,000 people. In all five districts of the General Government, there were thus about 2 million Jews. Korherr's paper "Die Endlösung der europäischen Judenfrage" (The Final Solution of the European Jewish Question) shows that 1,274,166 Jews had been deported from the General Government to camps by the end of 1942, and at the beginning of 1943, there were still 300,000 Jews living in the Governorate.[15] In the Warthegau—the land areas adjacent to the Warta River in Poland that was incorporated into the German Reich—the liquidation of Jewish centers took place much earlier.

During the summer of 1942, tens of thousands of Jews from the districts of Łódź, Łęczyca, Łaski, Sieradz, Wieluń, and others were deported to the camp in Chełmno, on the Ner River. A selected part of the population was sent to Łódź. In the fall of 1942, during the period of mass murder of the Jews in the occupied Polish territories, and after the September *Grosse Sperre* action had already taken its toll, there were around 90,000 Jews in the Łódź ghetto.[16] After the Warsaw

15 Dr. Richard Korherr (1903–1989) was a Nazi German statistician and chief inspector of the SS statistical bureau, holding the rank of *SS-Sturmbannführer*. On January 18, 1943, Heinrich Himmler ordered Richard Korherr to report on "the Final Solution of the Jewish Question in Europe" (*Die Endlösung der europäischen Judenfrage*) until December 31, 1942. Korherr completed the report under this title and sent it to SS officer Rudolf Brandt on March 23, 1943. The German document can be found online: Richard Korherr, "Der Inspekteur für Statistik beim Reichsführer SS (1943), 'Die Endlösung der europäischen Judenfrage,'" Berlin, NS-Archiv, Dokumente zum Nationalsozialismus: Korherr-Bericht, lange Fassung, facsimile of the extant text typed in German on seventeen letter-sized pages, retrieved February 2, 2025. For a summary of the report in English, see "The Richard Korherr Report," Holocaust Education & Archive Research Team, http://www.holocaustresearchproject.org/holoprelude/korherr.html (accessed August 18, 2025).

16 The deportations took place between September 5 and 12, 1942. On Saturday (Shabbat), September 5, at 5:00 PM, chairman of the Jewish Council in the Łódż ghetto Chaim Mordechai Rumkowski announced a week-long general curfew—(*Gehsperre*, often referred to simply as *Sperre*)—until September 12.

ghetto, this was the place where the Jewish population lived in the worst conditions. Famine, epidemics, hard labor, and insufficient food decimated the population. Just as in the Warsaw ghetto, here too, people died in the streets. The head of the Jewish Council, Chaim Mordechai Rumkowski, his administration, and the Jewish police not only servilely carried out all the orders of the occupation authorities but also fought all the opposition elements and helped with the deportations of people to the death camps.[17] There were constant selections during which the elderly, the weak, the sick, and those unable to work were sent on transports.

In addition, the Łódź *Gauleiter* Arthur Greiser[18] saw to it that the Jewish labor force was brutally exploited at the numerous German work sites. The guarded, hermetically sealed Łódź ghetto was essentially a huge labor camp, central to the entire province, which brought enormous profits to German companies. According to confidential German information, it seems that the ghetto yielded a monthly income of about 37 million Reichsmark. Of a total of 89,059 Jews living there in mid-October 1942, 75,000 were employed in various industrial plants.

These workers worked across various industries, such as the construction, clothing, metal, electrical supply, foundries, wood processing, leather, and textiles industries. The Łódź ghetto cheaply produced various products or semi-finished products for the major German companies, drawing enormous profit from it.

All workshops, offices, and stores were ordered to close. During this week, some 15,000 children, elderly, and ill Jews were deported to the Chełmno death camp. See transports from Łódź for the relevant dates in "Yad Vashem: The Deportations of Jews Research Project and Digital Database (Transports to Extinction)," https://collections.yadvashem.org/en/deportations (accessed August 18, 2025).

17 Chaim Mordechai Rumkowski (1877–1944), chairman of the Judenrat of the Łódź ghetto, is a very controversial figure both among historians and the broader public. He is viewed by some as a traitor and by others as a figure who made an attempt to preserve the ghetto as a whole while being forced to comply with Nazi deportation orders. Rumkowski and his family were deported to Auschwitz and murdered at the end of August 1944.

18 Arthur Greiser served as *Gauleiter* (governor) of Warthegau, the western part of occupied Poland that was formally annexed to the Nazi Reich. Greiser was tried by a Polish court in 1946. He was hanged in front of the Warthegau governor's mansion. See "Greiser, Arthur" Shoah Resource Center, The International School for Holocaust Studies, Yad Vashem, https://wwv.yadvashem.org/odot_pdf/Microsoft%20Word%20-%206314.pdf (accessed August 18, 2025).

In occupied Poland, the Germans organized "death factories" for the planned physical annihilation of the Jewish population. These macabre centers of extermination[19]—especially the gas chambers of Auschwitz where so many perished—were not only for Polish Jews but also for Jews from all over Europe.

No wonder that in the face of such danger, people looked for rescue in various ways. Whoever had acquaintances or friends among Poles, and, above all, had money, fled to the Polish town quarters or tried to build a hiding place—or, as it was called then, a bunker—either within the ghetto or on the Aryan side. Underground and well-concealed bunkers were also constructed in villages, forests, and other less populated settlements. This was done with the help of Poles, who were willing to risk their lives for large sums of money that they received from these Jews in exchange for providing them with food. While this was not done often, many of these bunker builders—often with their families—managed to miraculously survive the period of the worst merciless extermination of the Jewish community, which the Germans began in the fall of 1942 and lasted over two years, until the Soviet army entered Poland.[20]

Jews with what were considered to be "good looks"—without decidedly Semitic features—fled the ghetto and tried to live among the Polish population, mostly in Warsaw. They had false baptism certificates and personal identification cards and pretended to be Christians. They lived there under false names and surnames and strolled freely in the streets—even engaging in work or commercial activities. People who didn't have such "good looks" sometimes rented a room in an apartment belonging to Poles, paying exorbitant prices for the rent. They had to hide and did not

19 Other killing centers or "death factories" were Chełmno, Bełżec, Sobibór, and Treblinka death camps.

20 Partial deportations of the Jewish communities from many places in Poland to their deaths had already begun in the spring of 1942 within Operation Reinhard. In the fall, the deportations reached their most destructive stage, and many towns were declared *Judenrein* (purged of Jews). See "The Deportations of Jews Research Project and Digital Database (Transports to Extinction)," Yad Vashem, https://collections.yadvashem.org/en/deportations (accessed August 18, 2025). The Mass murder operations against Jews had already begun in the USSR after the German invasion of the Soviet Union in June 1941, including in Soviet-occupied Polish territories. Among the most brutal mass murder operations were the Babi Yar massacre on the outskirts of Kiev, on September 29–30, 1941, and the Ponary Massacres near Vilna starting in June 1941 and lasting till July 1944.

dare to go out, so their hosts, or other family members, who were able to move around freely and communicate with Poles without raising suspicion of their Jewish origin, took care of their food supply. However, all these undertakings were extremely dangerous and, more often than not, had tragic outcomes for those in hiding.

A new profession was born during these tragic times, which provided an easy source of income. People tracked down hiding Jews, blackmailed them, and threatened to turn them over to the Germans. These denouncers—known as *szmalcowniks*[21]—did this for as long as the victims had cash or jewelry, after which they handed over the Jews to the German police or Gestapo, who murdered them mercilessly. Next to the Germans—who anyway constantly searched the apartments in the Polish districts in their hunt for Jews in hiding—they were the greatest enemies of those who had escaped from the ghetto. Many Jews also hid in the Polish district of Częstochowa, as well as in dugouts in nearby villages or outlying areas. Not a few Jews died as a result of denunciation or after having been accidentally discovered by neighbors, who informed the Germans—either out of fear for their lives or overzealousness. There were many dangers for those in hiding, and many of them died largely as a result of being handed over to the Germans by unfriendly Poles. On such occasions, the Poles who had given shelter to Jews in their homes were also executed; or sometimes, they were sent to concentration camps or shot on the spot.[22]

"Good-looking" Jewish youths with the "right" looks tried to save themselves by going together with Poles to Germany to work on a farm or in factories, and they often managed to survive. However, the overwhelming majority of the Jewish population saw no prospect of rescue for themselves and were prepared for the worst. Often, people who tried to save themselves by escaping or hiding among Poles, returned to the ghetto, either because they could no longer endure the constant tension and fear of being discovered by blackmailers, or they had lost their shelter after running out of money. Although persecution and pogroms had reoccurred from time to time—not only on Polish soil but also in other European countries and in Russia, which was free from anti-Jewish extremes—the situation of the Jews under Nazi occupation was tragic and unprecedented in their history.

21 From the German word *Schmalz* (literally meaning lard), used metaphorically to allude to the mercantile or self-interested motives of the denouncers.

22 Here, Kromołowski addresses the severity of punishments that Poles in occupied Poland faced if they were caught or denounced for sheltering Jews.

But even during the most ruthless persecutions—in the times of the Spanish Inquisition, during the massacres organized by Chmielnicki's Cossacks,[23] or in the pogroms in tsarist Russia—there was some way out, some form of rescue. Spanish Jews could be saved by being baptized, often only fictitiously. It was possible to escape Chmielnicki's hordes in the western parts of Poland or to find a good hiding place at a Polish neighbor's. Pogroms were short-lived, passing like a storm, taking with them a certain number of victims, but most survived the catastrophe.

Under the Germans, however, there was no possibility of rescue. This well-organized and trained army of persecutors—armed to the teeth and with the aim of morally, mentally, and physically destroying the entire Jewish population—encircled the Jews from all sides. They created a number of special formations to exterminate the Jews. Through terror and constant murder, the Nazis created an atmosphere of fear around the Jewish people, paralyzing all organized resistance to the annihilation. The Germans maintained the illusion that they were not aiming to exterminate the Jews, but were merely seeking to force them to change their lifestyle and take up useful manual labor.

Before each extermination *Aktion* operation that ended with shipments of deportees to the death camps, the senior officers of the Schutzpolizei in charge stressed that the Jews were being sent to work—and not to their deaths. This was an unprecedented perfidy, as the Germans deliberately stoked Jewish hopes for survival in the camps, instilling the conviction that all fears were groundless, and that resistance would result in inevitable repression. And the Germans succeeded. All these methods resulted in the complete passivity of Jewish society, a servile attitude toward the enemy, and a state of mental and physical numbness.[24] Such was the obedience

23 The Chmielnicki Massacres (1648–1657), carried out by Bohdan Chmielnicki's Cossacks and their allied Tatar forces, were a series of brutal pogroms against Jews and Poles during the Chmielnicki Uprising against the Polish–Lithuanian Commonwealth. A critical assessment of the Jewish losses, which reevaluates previous assessments, can be found in Shaul Stampfer, "What Actually Happened to the Jews of Ukraine in 1648?" *Jewish History*, 17:2 (2003), pp. 207–227. Stampfer estimates the Jewish casualties at approximately 18,000–20,000, whereas previous estimates had been significantly higher.

24 In spite of the pervasive helplessness of the Jews facing systematic annihilation by the Nazis and their collaborators, as emphatically conveyed by Kromołowski, Jews nonetheless found multifaceted ways of putting up resistance. The most obvious were armed forms, such as the Warsaw Ghetto Uprising or the Sobibor Uprising

that masses of people—driven by the Germans—went to railroad sidings and, without resistance, boarded cattle cars that would take them to their deaths. Some, and these were the majority, did not believe that the Germans intended to murder the entire Jewish nation, while those who did not believe the German lies and understood that they were going on their last journey could not muster enough strength in themselves to oppose the executioners, to resist them, and to defend themselves from extermination.[25]

There was yet another category of people among this calamitous nation imprisoned in ghettos—all sorts of prominent people who were at the service of the Germans: the Jewish police and its leadership, the Jewish Councils with their high-ranking functionaries, and all kinds of informers, confidants, and henchmen who were in direct contact with the German authorities. They believed that they would be spared and would not share the fate of the Jewish people. They believed that they would be rewarded for their services in this way—with their lives being saved as that reward. The Germans perpetuated this belief, giving evidence of it. At a time when all Jewish children were being torn from their mothers and fathers and sent to the gas chambers, the children of Jewish policemen, members of the Judenrat, and doctors were spared. They remained with their parents, even when the deportations were followed by concentrating the few remaining workers. The families of these prominent people were not separated by the Germans and lived together, even when the ghettos were liquidated, which can explain the often asocial and dishonest behavior of this group of prominent functionaries. They believed that by blindly carrying out the orders of the Germans, they could save their own lives and the lives of their closest family members.

It also often happened that people previously known for their honesty and high morals—nonprofit social activists—turned out to be inhumane

in 1943 or the formation of Jewish partisan units and numerous underground organizations. The scope of resistance also included cultural and spiritual forms, such as running Jewish newspapers, schools, theaters, maintaining Jewish holidays, keeping the Sabbath, and others.

25 At different stages of the implementation of the Nazis' anti-Jewish policies, Jews held different perceptions of what was in store for them. Many were hoping to survive as forced laborers either in the short term or the long term. As deliberate, systematic, mass-scale murder unfolded, the Germans' intention to completely eliminate all the Jews became more manifest and more difficult to conceal. Yet the choices available to the Jews, who were undernourished, exhausted, and burdened by care for their family members, were limited.

and ruthless in their actions. Honesty and morality proved to be just a thin, superficial layer that cracked and disintegrated when the struggle for physical survival came to the fore. This was not the case with everyone; not all prominent people were heartless egotists during these years. There were many noble figures who chose to lose their lives rather than save themselves at the expense of their fellow human beings. Even during the period of the ghettos, with the enormous concentration of Jews, there were many people who organized resistance and fought, opposing the destructive plans of the Germans with guns in their hands. Among those who tried to organize a political underground in the ghetto were prewar party activists from numerous Jewish groups, ranging from right-wing Zionists to left-wing extremists, communists, and Bundists. There were occasional clandestine meetings—often at the cemetery on the occasion of the funeral of a party activist—but the discussions were fruitless, and no concrete decisions were made.

The Gestapo's political department in Częstochowa had a list of prewar political activists who were frequently detained. Izak Rząsiński,[26] a left-wing activist and former textile merchant, Wilek Krakauer,[27] a lawyer trainee, Żarnowiecki, a socialist activist and former magistrate and juror, were arrested and taken to concentration camps. Berkensztad, together with his wife, and Motek Kusznir—Bund activists—were beaten and tortured by the Gestapo. Their companions managed to bribe two Gestapo officers and as a result, Motek Kusznir and Rajzla Berkensztad were released.

Prominent individuals who sought to impress the Germans also included the more skilled Jewish craftsmen. The Germans allocated to them an entire and quite impressive building at 14 First Avenue—the Franke House—to serve as their residence and workshops. Quite a few Jewish professionals lived there, including tailors, shoemakers, furriers, seamstresses, and corsetters, among others. They could live with their families in comfortable, furnished apartments with several rooms each. For this privilege, they had to provide craft services for the Germans, especially for police officers, the Gestapo, and senior Nazi officials, along with their wives and families. This artisanal elite—*nutzliche Juden* or useful Jews—were protected in various ways. They were often paid

26 Izaak Izrael Rząsiński (1887–1942) was a merchant and local government activist. He perished in Auschwitz on June 4, 1942. See Sętowski, *Częstochowa Jews: A Biographical Dictionary*, p. 395.

27 Wolf Aron Krakauer (c. 1912–1942) perished in Treblinka. See ibid., p. 269.

for services rendered, received good food, were exempt from compulsory labor, and did not have to pay tributes and taxes—both fiscal and to the Judenrat. Among this elite group of craftsmen who survived Nazi persecution, together with their wives and children, were the women's tailor Samuel Katz, the men's tailor and specialist in sewing uniforms Bernard Baum, and the shoemaker Dorfsman.

During this time, I continued to deal with tax matters, and the scope of my duties increased considerably. I was essentially the only link between the ghetto and the tax authorities, as when the Nazis sealed off the Jewish residential area, Jews were not allowed to leave the ghetto. Almost every day, equipped with a pass and wearing a Jewish armband with a Star of David, I walked through the streets on the Aryan side of town toward the tax office on Śląska Street. I would be there for a few hours in the morning, performing my duties—making current tax payments, filing appeals on behalf of Jewish merchants and craftsmen, and trying to prevent unjust tax assessments and thus erroneous executions. I applied for tax payments in installments and, as a representative of the ghetto economic sphere, I participated in the complex tax procedure, defending the Jewish taxpayer's interests. Only in a few exceptional cases did the tax office summon Jews in person to present to the official. In such cases, the invitation to the tax office replaced a pass, but people did not want to go to the office alone and almost always asked me to accompany them.

As mentioned earlier, in the course of my regular tours of duty, I met many Polish tax officials and became acquainted with them. I also talked with them about the future of the ghetto and its inhabitants. Almost all of them said that the day of the ghetto liquidation was near, and that the Germans were hastily building an extermination camp for Jews in Treblinka, east of Małkinia.[28] They advised me to escape from the ghetto, because the Jews would soon be deported from there. They told me about the terrible conditions in which the Jews lived in the Warsaw and Łódź ghettos and about the transports of Jews to the extermination camps, which were already taking place elsewhere in Poland.[29]

28 Treblinka death camp was located in the General Government 4 kilometers from the train station of Małkinia on the main line running from Warsaw to Białystok. Some 870,000 Jews were murdered in this death factory. See Silberklang, *Gates of Tears*, p. 252.

29 While Kromołowski likely did not know this at the time, it is an example of how he weaves hindsight into his recounting of events on the ground. See the Foreword of this volume.

Following the German army's victories in Western Europe and the Balkans, they then set out to conquer the Soviet Union on June 22, 1941. To our great horror, masses of troops, tanks, armored vehicles filled with soldiers, and cannons pulled by tractors moved day and night along Warszawska Street, one of the main streets in the ghetto leading to the East. At the beginning of the war with the Soviet Union, the German armed forces numbered about 7 million soldiers, grouped in 214 divisions, including 21 armored and 14 motorized divisions, and they had 5,649 tanks and over 10,000 motor vehicles.[30] With such a powerful strike force, they were once again successful, and their newspapers were filled with reports about new victories. The Soviet army was in retreat, and soon, endless columns of Russian prisoners of war—shabby, starving, and weak—and hundreds of carts filled with the corpses of prisoners began to pass through the ghetto's streets. The horrible stench of decomposing corpses spread through the streets where this horrible cavalcade of people and dead bodies dragged on. Grief and sorrow could be seen on the faces of the witnesses of this horrible spectacle. We lost all hope, realizing that we were a plaything in the hands of the German military machine, which was rushing the shattered Soviet army to POW camps and transporting the bodies of Soviet soldiers to the cemetery.

The communiqués of the German command constantly reported victories on the Russian front, the retreat of the crushed Soviet army, and the capture of hundreds of thousands of military prisoners. It seemed that the Germans wanted to conduct a *Blitzkrieg* (a lightning war) to capture Moscow and Leningrad before the onset of the autumn frosts and crush the Soviet army completely.

The war with Russia—conducted at such enormous expense and with huge numbers of personnel and military equipment—did not stop the Germans from preparing the liquidation of our ghetto in Częstochowa. In 1942, signs of this became evident. A meeting of German administrative dignitaries took place in Radom, the district capital, chaired by the SS and police general Böttcher, head of the district, with the participation of the Gestapo.[31] After this meeting, rumors of an imminent deportation

30 On the German military forces, see Rolf-Dieter Müller, *Hitler's Wehrmacht, 1935–1945* (Lexington: University Press of Kentucky, 2016).

31 Herbert Böttcher (1907–1952 or 1950) was *SS-Standartenführer* and police chief who oversaw the implementation of Operation Reinhard in the Radom District. After the war, Böttcher was extradited to Poland, sentenced to death by the Radom District Court, and executed. See Młynarczyk, *Judenmord in Zentralpolen*, pp. 75, 91–92.

spread through the ghetto. The administrative authorities, such as the *Stadthauptmann* and his clerks, became less and less concerned with ghetto affairs, and one could see an increase of German police and Gestapo men on the Jewish streets. There were more incidents of beating and mistreating passersby, as well as robbing Jewish stores and apartments—the Schupo and Gestapo men did not even spare the Jewish policemen guarding the ghetto's borders.

One day, Schupo guards burst into the Jewish hospital on Przemysłowa Street, looted all the valuables there, and beat the hospital staff. The ghetto was increasingly shaken by disturbing news. One Jew managed to escape from a "resettlement action"[32] in one of the nearby towns, where some Jews still remained. He recounted that the Germans came to the town and took away the remaining Jewish population—not even allowing them to take any clothing and underwear. They locked everyone in airtight cars into which an exhaust pipe led, filling it with exhaust fumes. The cars were driven along the road, and after several kilometers, the Germans opened the cars and ordered the local residents to remove the corpses of the gassed men, women, and children, and bury them in a common grave.[33]

According to Polish railway men, the Germans had been carrying out a large-scale, systematic deportation of the Jews in the Warsaw ghetto, directing them to sealed cattle cars, which took them to a death camp built in the woods near Treblinka.[34] There, under the pretext of bathing, they ordered people to strip naked. Men—and women and children separately—were herded and beaten with rifle butts and led to gas chambers, which were then hermetically sealed and filled with poisonous gas. Then, a group of Jewish prisoners—the Sonderkommando—pushed the corpses into pits that had been dug with shovels, which were later filled in with earth.[35]

32 Kromołowski is referring to the German term *Aussiedlungaktion*, which was Nazi code for deportation.

33 Kromołowski describes the special gas vans for mass killings, constructed and tested in the fall of 1941 in Berlin under Heydrich's auspices, and used shortly afterward at Chełmno. See Christopher Browning, *The Origins of the Final Solution: The Evolution of Nazi Jewish Policy, September 1939–March 1942* (Jerusalem and Lincoln: Yad Vashem and University of Nebraska Press, 2004), p. 356.

34 The deportations from the Warsaw ghetto to Treblinka began in July 1942.

35 The reference is to the Sonderkommando—groups of Jewish prisoners in the Nazi death camps who, among other things, had to clean the gas chambers, dispose of the bodies, and remove any valuables found on them. After a few months of such work, they themselves were usually murdered and replaced by

The Jews brought with them whatever belongings they could carry, because the Germans assured them that they would be sent to labor camps, where they would perform labor for the German army fighting in the Soviet Union. The belongings of the murdered Jews were then sorted, and any gold, jewelry, foreign currency, or money were sent to Germany.

These reports and similar news circulated in the ghetto with increasing frequency and seemed to confirm the widespread belief that the end was near—and that the same fate awaited us, just as was happening in the larger Jewish population centers being deported to extermination camps. The Germans prowled the ghetto in groups robbing, beating, and mistreating people. Among the most dangerous persecutors was the aforementioned Gestapo officer Szabelski. After the war, he was identified by a group of Jews, and the special court in Częstochowa sentenced him to death by hanging.

Schupo members Frankowski and Dzierżon used a huge wolfhound that was specially trained to attack and bite Jews, to viciously hunt them down, while Laszynski and Köster—also from the Schutzpolizei—robbed and murdered Jews in our ghetto. After the war, Heinrich Köster was captured by Jewish prisoners when he tried to escape disguised in civilian

Alfred Kromołowski testifying at the trial of Heinrich Köster, Częstochowa Court, 1946. Köster is in the background. Photograph taken by L. Kusznir. Courtesy of the Kromołowski family.

new prisoners. On the Sonderkommando, see Gideon Greif, *We Wept Without Tears: Testimonies of the Jewish Sonderkommando from Auschwitz* (New Haven: Yale University Press, 2005).

clothes. I stood before the special court in Częstochowa, and was a witness in his trial. The court sentenced Köster to death, and he was hanged in the prison courtyard in Zawodzie in Częstochowa.[36]

Notorious for their cruelty to the Jewish population of our ghetto were the Schupo policemen Handke—known as White Head—Opitz, and Schott, who in March 1942 shot the Jew Jesionowicz for leaving the Jewish quarter without permission and without wearing an armband. Jesionowicz was shot on Wilson Street near the Kacapski Bridge—a railroad overpass with a pedestrian crossing under the tracks. Szmitt, Kirsch, Klipsch, Schloser, Leutenant Werner, Willy Onkelbach, the driver of *Hauptmann* Paul Degenhardt, who was the chief overseer of the Jewish population who directed the selection and liquidation of the Jews—these are just some of the names of the cruelest German executioners, whose job was to execute death sentences on the inhabitants of the Jewish ghetto of Częstochowa.

After the war, Paul Degenhardt was identified by Jewish survivors and was tried as a war criminal by a German court in the German Federal Republic. He was imprisoned for some time, but was later held in a prison hospital due to ill health. He was a prolific mass murderer of Jews and deserved the death penalty a hundred times over.[37] However, the Germans spared the Nazi dignitaries as much as they could and handed down mild punishments to them. And this is why many German murderers from the SS, Gestapo, and Schutzpolizei, responsible for the genocide of the Jewish population in Poland, enjoyed freedom and even—to the great shame of the German judicial system—occupied high positions in the administration of West Germany.

36 Köster was sentenced to death on February 19, 1946. Köster played a leading role in the liquidation of the Small Ghetto in June 1943. See Jan Pietrzykowski, *Hitlerowcy przed sądem w Częstochowie* (Katowice: Wydawnictwo Śląsk, 1964), pp. 64–75.

37 Paul Degenhardt was the commanding officer of the Częstochowa Schutzpolizei in 1942–1943. Among other crimes committed, he oversaw the deportations of the Jews, starting with the first transport of some 7,000–8,000 Jews deported to Treblinka on September 22, 1942. In May 1966, Paul Degenhardt was sentenced in Lüneburg, Germany, to life imprisonment. He served seven years in prison and was released on health grounds. For more on this, see Binyamin Orenstein, "The Nazi Murderer Degenhardt," in *Tshenstokhover landsmanshaft in Montreal*, translated from the Yiddish by Gloria Berkenstat Freund (Czenstochover Society in Montreal, 1966), pp. 165–173; "Hauptmann Paul Degenhardt 'The Lord of Life and Death' in Częstochowa," https://www.Częstochowajews.org/history/degenhardt/ (accessed October 27, 2025).

At the end of March 1942, my mother became seriously ill. She had pains in her lower abdomen and was literally fading away before our eyes. I accompanied her to a gynecologist who, to my horror, diagnosed uterine cancer—a diagnosis that was unfortunately confirmed by other doctors. She needed an operation urgently. Dr. Achmatowicz, a surgeon of great fame from Vilna, was in the Aryan quarter, and we were advised to entrust him with the operation. I went to visit this surgeon using my pass, and he agreed to my request. The surgery was to take place in the Jewish hospital on Przemysłowa Street, where Dr. Achmatowicz and his assistant, the gynecologist Dr. Stróżewska, were expected to arrive.

Over the course of her disease, a Jewish doctor called Dr. Broniatowski took care of my mother. She agreed to undergo surgery, so we collected the appropriate funds, and our poor mother went into the operating room alone. To our great despair, the operation was unsuccessful as the disease had already spread to her intestines. Day and night, my brother and I sat at my mother's bedside. She died in my arms on the morning of May 23, 1942. It was just after the Jewish holiday of Shavuot, when I accompanied my mother's body from the hospital to her home.

My mother, a good and noble person, was buried in the Jewish cemetery on Olsztyńska Street in Częstochowa, next to my father's grave. Mother lived to be sixty-one years old. It was spring, the sun was getting stronger, the trees were starting to turn green. Of our entire family, only my brother Heniek and myself were left. After this painful loss, great grief and sorrow overshadowed our world.

The harbinger of the approaching tragedy—the liquidation of our ghetto—was the sudden demand by the German tax authorities that the Judenrat immediately pay all outstanding Jewish tax arrears, calculated at several million złoty. This sum was mentioned by Counselor Krum, the German treasury inspector, to Judenrat chairman Kopiński, who had been summoned for this purpose. Krum set a two-week deadline for payment, threatening sharp reprisals against the ghetto's inhabitants and the Judenrat, whose members would be imprisoned and charged with sabotage of German ordinances.

However, it was simply impossible to implement this order, as the Council of Elders had recently experienced great difficulty collecting a large sum of money for another contribution demanded by the *Stadthauptmann* Franke, Wendler's successor. The only way to meet the German demand would be to collect a high tax from almost every ghetto inhabitant. However, taxing the population again—already completely depleted of money—was beyond the capabilities of the Judenrat. Nevertheless, something had to be done to try, at least, to postpone the due date, reduce the amount demanded, and divide it into installments. The chairman of the Judenrat, Kopiński, called me into his office and instructed me to try to do something with the help of my Polish acquaintances—the heads of the tax offices—to obtain a milder decision.

The next day, I went to Śląska Street and reported the whole matter to Czesław Rzepka—a truly decent man from whom I anticipated advice and help. Rzepka, who was then the head of the 2nd Tax Office, advised me to go to Skomoroch—the deputy and assistant of Counselor Krum, the head of the tax offices—to explain the whole matter and ask for help. He was a Ukrainian nationalist, and a close associate and trustee of the local Nazi dignitaries.

I requested a meeting with Skomoroch, whom I knew well from before the war, when he was an ordinary tax assessor's clerk. Even now, I had managed to settle many Jewish taxpayers' cases with him, with favorable results. Skomoroch, of course, knew why I had come, and told me outright that he could try to ease Krum's demands and negotiate repayment terms with him—but there would be a cost: He demanded that the Judenrat furnish his apartment with stylish furniture and nicely equip his office.

Pleased with this news, I informed Kopiński, who immediately gave the appropriate order to the head of the furniture storehouse, Machl Birencwajg. Very soon a set of stylish furniture was brought to Skomoroch's apartment, and his dining room, bedroom, living room, and study were furnished to a high gloss, with new curtains and a crystal chandelier hanging from the ceiling. Even the kitchen was fitted with new modern furniture. The electricians switched on the electricity, and Skomoroch's apartment shone brightly with all these lamps.

Skomoroch also kept his word. The Judenrat soon received the Nazis' amended demand: The amount to be paid was now 250,000 złoty, divided into ten monthly installments. The demand was received in writing, stamped with the German eagle, and signed by Krum himself. The first installment was to be paid immediately, with the next installment due on October 1, 1942. Kopiński, pleased with the successful intervention, muttered a few words of praise for me and personally went to the tax office to pay the first installment. This was August 1942. However, payment of the second installment never came to pass, because on October 1, the Jewish residential district of Częstochowa no longer existed, and all the property left behind by the 40,000 slain Jews was looted by their German murderers.[38]

38 Five deportations took place on September 22, September 25–26, September

The New Synagogue (*Daitche Shul*) before its destruction.

September 21, 1942, was the Jewish Day of Atonement, Yom Kippur. Jews crowded into prayer houses and into the basement of the burnt synagogue on Wilson Street—the *Daitche Shul*—where a makeshift altar and benches had been set up, and services were held. According to the religious laws and traditions observed on this day, Jews fast and pray zealously, asking God for good health and life for themselves and their

29–30, October 4, and October 7. Between 33,000 and 40,000 Jews were sent to their deaths at Treblinka, and some 2,000 were killed during the roundups. See Pietrzykowski, *Hitlerowcy w Częstochowie*, p. 186; Kiel, *The Jews of Częstochowa*, pp. 145–147; Dean, *USHMM Encyclopedia of Camps and Ghettos*, vol. 2, part A, p. 216. A few survived the selection and later took part in the Treblinka Uprising in August 1943. See, for example, Szmul Willenberg testimony in "Revolt in Treblinka," in Schutzman, *Sefer Czenstochow*, vol. 2, pp. 169–174.

families, as well as for the prosperity of the entire house of Israel. Divine help was very much needed by the Jews at this time, because dark clouds were gathering over the ghetto, and only a miracle could save them from extermination. There was a pervasive sense of dread.

Two weeks earlier, by order of the Schutzpolizei, all adult Jewish men were ordered to appear for inspection in the town's two markets. The Jewish police ensured that this was carried out scrupulously. The masses flooded both the New and Old Markets in the center of the Jewish quarter and were lined up in two rows. These men were frozen in fearful anticipation, expecting the worst. Then, Schutzpolizei officers—headed by *Hauptmann* Paul Degenhardt and surrounded by an armed detachment of German policemen—appeared. Degenhardt walked among the silently standing ranks of Jews, stopping every now and then to look at their faces and, in his slightly stuttering voice, asked, "*Was bist du von Beruf?*" (What is your profession?). After receiving answers from tailors, shoemakers, carpenters, or laborers, he nodded and said, "*Ja, wir brauchen*" (That is what we need).

Everyone remained silent throughout the inspection, which went on for hours. To our great amazement, all members of the Judenrat—including clerks and employees—were also required to participate. When Judge Arnold Geisler, a converted Jew, was ordered to step forward, everyone thought he was going to be arrested—or worse. Degenhardt asked about his occupation, and when he learned that he was facing a Polish judge, he said calmly, "*Wir brauchen nicht*" (We don't need), and on he went.

After a few hours, the roll call was over, and everyone was ordered to disperse. It was widely rumored that this was a visible sign of the impending liquidation of the ghetto and a test to show the Germans how the Jewish population—especially the men—would behave and react to an order to report to the assembly points, and whether there would be armed resistance.

In the afternoon of Yom Kippur, while the Jews were still praying in the numerous synagogues, news suddenly began to circulate through the ghetto like an electric spark that the Germans were preparing something serious. Some said that a special unit, trained in organizing massive transfers of Jews, had been brought to the city. It was known as the Sonderkommando. These were units composed of Ukrainians, Latvians, and Lithuanians, who were experienced in murdering Jews. The Germans used them as auxiliary forces in all destructive actions against the Jewish population.[39]

39 The SS auxiliaries trained at the Trawniki camp played a key executive function in the ensuing actions, together with the local Schupo, Reservepolizeikompanie Köln,

Others confirmed that, at the railway siding of the Warta station in Zawodzie,[40] there were freight trains with cattle wagons. Their narrow windows were barred, and the interiors of the wagons were strewn with lime. These were the wagons used by the Germans to transport Jews from the ghettos to the death camps. In addition, reinforced patrols of Schupo and Polish Blue Police were searching for Jews in hiding in the Aryan quarter of the city. A Jewish girl who was hiding with Polish acquaintances was captured. She was the daughter of the well-known socialist activist Dudek Szlezynger. The girl was brought to her parents' apartment on Garibaldi Street, where the Schupo men shot her and her father in front of her mother.[41] These were the first victims of the impending liquidation of the Częstochowa ghetto.

The news caused an unprecedented panic in the ghetto. Everyone was overwhelmed with fear. The Yom Kippur prayer services were stopped, and masses of people left their places of prayer and returned home. They ran in panic through the streets, asking friends and relatives if the terrible news circulating in the ghetto was true. Jewish workers employed outside the ghetto had been exempted from work that day; however, they returned to their workplaces—despite the holiday—accompanied by Jewish policemen, only to get themselves outside the ghetto.

Those who worked in the clothing workshops inside the ghetto—newly established by the Germans, known as the sheds, in the former Metalurgia factory on Krótka Street—also went to work. The sheds were generally considered a place that protected their workers from deportation, due to their production of clothing for the German army. Considerable sums of money were paid to secure work in the sheds and to obtain an ID card confirming employment there, and many departments were already active and operating in the sheds.

and more than 200 Polish (Blue) Police. Dr. Herbert Böttcher's leading role and responsibility for the deportations as the SS and police leader (SSPF) in Radom should be emphasized. Böttcher was sentenced to death and executed by the Polish authorities after the war. See Dean, *USHMM Encyclopedia of Camps and Ghettos*, vol. 2, part A, p. 216; Pietrzykowski, *Hitlerowcy w Częstochowie*, p. 186. For an additional description of how different units carried out the *Aktionen*, see Abram Iżbicki testimony, in *Tshenstokhover yidn*, pp. 209–210.

40 This was situated on the right bank of the Warta River.

41 Michał Dawid Szlezynger (1894–1942), worker activist and city councilor, was also murdered by the Germans on September 21 in the Częstochowa ghetto. Sętowski, *Częstochowa Jews: A Biographical Dictionary*, p. 417.

Meanwhile, Jewish policemen appeared on the ghetto streets, dispersing the crowds while also assuring them that all rumors were false and unfounded. The policemen referred to the assurances of the Schutzpolizei in this regard; nevertheless, the panic did not stop. People wandered from one street to another. Streets that seemed dangerous were abandoned, as people moved as far from the center of the ghetto as possible. Whoever had prepared a hiding place or a bunker hid there with their family. People who had prepared hiding places with Poles left the ghetto under the cover of darkness, using secret, prearranged routes. There were also daredevils who risked their lives by jumping over the walls separating the ghetto houses from those on Aryan side. The ghetto was engulfed in falling darkness, and silence slowly followed.

My wife's parents also decided to leave their apartment on Warszawska Street, which they believed was unsafe due to its central location and large number of inhabitants. They and their sixteen-year-old son Tadzio moved into our small house on Nadrzeczna Street. This was a small, one-story building located deep within a wide square, set back from the street and separated by a high wooden fence. We lived alone in a three-room apartment with adjoining factory rooms. My wife's father had recently suffered a minor stroke. He was weak, unsteady on his feet, and had difficulty speaking.

We realized that we would not last long in our apartment if we wanted to evade the impending deportation. There was an attic above the apartment, which could be walled up with a dozen or so bricks. It was accessed by a ladder that could be pulled up afterward, thus concealing the entry point and making it a good place to hide. Unfortunately, we had no food supplies except for a quarter sack of flour, which was of little use, since we needed an oven to make even flatbreads—a primitive type of bread made only of flour and water, without yeast. And using the electric stove would be a problem, as we anticipated that the Germans would cut off the electricity. We also did not have any fat or vegetables. In short, hiding was impossible, and we had to prepare for the worst.

It was still nighttime when I decided to go out onto the streets. Along the wall of the neighboring two-story building adjacent to our square, I sneaked toward the exit leading directly to the street. I carefully turned the key in the lock, opened the gate, and looked outside. The street was brightly lit. All the streetlights were on—something that had never happened before. Usually, the street was dimly lit, with two or three lamps burning along the entire length of Nadrzeczna Street.

I cautiously poked my head out and looked to the left, where the street ended at the crossroads of Strażacka Street, which led from the

Warta River to Piłsudski Street. Strażacka Street, which was a few steps from our house, was the border street of the ghetto, separating it from the Aryan side. There was a Jewish police station here, but no Jewish policeman were present. To my astonishment, I saw a soldier from the Ukrainian Sonderkommando.[42] He was standing with his back against the fence surrounding the property that belonged to the Brassów Palace on Strażacka Street.[43] He held a rifle in his hand and wore a black forage cap bearing the death's head emblem, along with a gray-green chinstrap associated with the Russian *Vlasovists*—a formation named after General Vlasov, who had betrayed the Soviet state and joined the Germans with his nationalist Ukrainians. Now, together with his Hajdamaks,[44] he was engaged in murdering Jews.[45]

The ghetto was surrounded. The liquidation of the Częstochowa ghetto and the deportation of its Jewish population to extermination camps was beginning. The worst predictions had, unfortunately, come true. After the Yom Kippur holiday, the first day of this terrible, unprecedented ghetto liquidation began—a bloody pogrom orchestrated by the Germans.

42 He is referring to a Trawniki guard.

43 10 Strażacka Street is close to the corner of Nadrzeczna Street.

44 Hajdamaks were irregular peasant and Cossack insurgents active in Right-Bank Ukraine during the eighteenth century, chiefly under Polish rule.

45 Andrey Vlasov (1901–1946) was a Soviet general who was captured by the Germans in July 1942 and subsequently defected to them. He promoted anti-Bolshevism and was mainly used by the Nazis for propaganda purposes during the first two years of his collaboration with them. A type of Russian Liberation Army headed by Vlasov was formed close to the end of 1944 and the beginning of 1945, mainly with Red Army prisoners. See Steven O'Connor and Martin Gutmann, "Under a Foreign Flag: Integrating Foreign Units and Personnel in the British and German Armed Forces, 1940–1945," *Journal of Modern European History*, 14:3 (2016), pp. 321–341, specifically pp. 335–336; Catherine Andreyev, *Vlasov and the Russian Liberation Movement: Soviet Reality and Emigré Theories* (*Cambridge Russian, Soviet, and Post-Soviet Studies*) (Cambridge: Cambridge University Press, 1987) p. 3. It is unknown whether soldiers recruited by Vlasov were involved in the deportations of Jews from Częstochowa in September 1942. The association with Vlasov recruits is probably due to the fact that Trawniki recruits were also largely recruited from Red Army POWs until the fall of 1942, when the SS and police started recruiting young men from among the civilian population, mainly from the districts of Lublin and Galicia. See Martin Cüppers, Anne Lepper, and Jürgen Matthäus, *From "Euthanasia" to Sobibor: An SS Officer's Photo Collection* (Bloomington: Indiana University Press, 2022), pp. 186–187.

From the early hours of September 22, 1942, heavily armed Schupo units, Ukrainians, and the Polish Blue Police entered Kawia, Krótka, Warszawska, Spadek, and Garibaldi Streets. Jews of all genders and ages were driven out of their houses and apartments. They were allowed to take with them a small bundle or muffler. The ghetto streets were filled with crowds of terrified men, women, children, and the elderly. They were rushed to Krótka Street, where, in front of the former Metalurgia factory—now housing the sheds—the selection took place.[46] People were driven forward with rifle butts, jabs, and kicks. The moans and screams of the beaten and abused Jews echoed from all directions, mingling with the curses and orders of the German and Ukrainian executioners.

Young children were forcefully torn from their mothers, and wives from their husbands. Children were crying and yelling loudly, and hundreds of abandoned children, who had been separated from their mothers, wandered alone in the streets, desperately trying to find them. Women who resisted having their infants and small children torn from them were shot on the spot. Any attempt to resist was ruthlessly followed by shooting the victim in the head. Jewish blood was spilled in abundance. The elderly, who were weak and could not keep up with the running crowds, were shot in the head or neck. Every now and then, shots rang out. Men, women, and children were murdered on a massive scale.

Degenhardt, the overseer of the Jewish ghetto, stood in front of the Metalurgia factory, surrounded by his police assistants, a whip in hand, as he carried out a selection. People marched past him one by one. Without exception, women with small children, as well as any men with children, were sent to their deaths. With a swipe of his whip and a muttered "*Links*" (to the left), Degenhardt directed anyone who looked too intelligent, wore glasses, had a high forehead, or were bald to their death. Those who were too old, too gray, too young, too small in stature, were also directed to the left. Ukrainians from the Sonderkommando surrounded the deportees and chased them toward the station, where they were loaded onto the waiting cattle cars.

Those who looked young and healthy and were deemed fit for physical work were sent to the right and pushed inside the Metalurgia factory. This was only a small number of people, while the number of those destined for

46 The Metalurgia grounds were located at 13 Krótka. See Radosław Butryński, "The Częstochowa Ghetto," The World Society of Częstochowa Jews and Their Descendants, https://www.czestochowajews.org/history/czestochowa-ghetto/ (accessed October 28, 2025).

deportation grew steadily. The crowd of deportees—with children in their arms or hanging on the sleeves of their clothes, lamenting, crazed with despair—were hurried along by the constant blows of rifle butts toward the railroad ramp.

Rooted to the spot was a handful of desperate people, looking around helplessly and mourning the brutal deaths of their children and wives, husbands and parents. While standing at the gate of the Metalurgia factory, Leon Rozensztajn, the trainee lawyer, saw his wife carrying their two-year-old daughter, Hanka. Seeing that they were among the deportees, he ran out into the street to try to intervene and approached Überscher, who had taken over from Degenhardt in carrying out the selection. He begged for his wife and darling baby daughter to remain with him, but he was pushed back. In despair, wringing his hands, he sat down on a rusty barrel. Tears of pain flowed from his eyes, tears of sorrow for his beloved wife and young daughter.

After a while, two Schupo policemen approached him, asking if he was the Jew who had tried to join his wife and daughter. Rozensztajn affirmed, and a glimmer of hope appeared on his face, distorted by pain and sorrow. Perhaps, perhaps he would succeed, perhaps his prayers and pleas had not gone unheard, and his wife and daughter would be returned to him. They escorted him onto the street, where Überscher approached him and, without uttering a word, shot him twice in the head. The roar of gunshots was mixed with groans of despair. Rozensztajn fell to the pavement, a trickle of red blood spilling around him. During the liquidation of the Częstochowa ghetto, *Wachmeister* Überscher was one of Degenhardt's many assistants and stood out for his cruelty and ruthlessness. On the orders of his boss, he shot a great many old, sick, and infirm Jews.

On Berka Joselewicza Street, an old Jew named Klajman—the owner of one of the houses—wearing a *tallit* (prayer shawl) and *tefillin* (phylacteries), recited morning prayers. In spite of the summons from the Jewish policemen who, together with the Schupo, went around the apartments to check whether all the Jews had come out for selection, Klajman remained at home. He did not want to go out onto the street; he was old and weak. He stood by the east wall of his apartment and prayed fervently. A Schupo policeman entered Klajman's apartment and saw the elderly, praying Jew who had disobeyed the German order. The German raised his rifle and took Klajman's life with a few shots. The innocent blood of the old Jewish man spread over his white *tallit*, crying out to heaven for vengeance.

The *Aktion* continued as planned. The Germans continued murdering the Jewish population and deporting them to extermination camps unimpeded.[47] The entire Jewish quarter was surrounded by German police and Ukrainian Sonderkommando. Machine guns were set up in the streets. The Polish Blue Police and the Jewish policemen had their hands full chasing the Jewish population out of their apartments into the street and checking whether anyone remained inside. Each day, the systematic liquidation spread to additional streets and blocks of buildings. German selection points were opened from the early hours—"*Links, rechts*." Some Jews were sent to the right, others to the left. One side meant deportation, the other side meant forced labor for the Germans and a temporary stay of the death sentence. At the infectious disease hospital on Krótka Street, the Germans expelled the patients in just their underwear. With a short, barked order, the Ukrainian soldiers opened fire on the sick Jews. Everyone died on the spot.

The selections continued unabated. Jews were constantly kept on the move. They were lined up in a long row for inspection, their red booklets in hand—registration cards attesting to their professional usefulness to the Germans. Tailors, shoemakers, brush makers, and skilled workers hoped that these certificates—issued by the Germans—would save them from deportation and extermination. They wanted to work for their German executioners without pay, for a spoonful of food, and at the price of sparing their life. But no! The red booklets did not help. The Germans tore them to shreds and trampled them underfoot, shouting, "*Wir brauchen nicht*! We do not need you. Die, because you are Jews."

Degenhardt stood there, waving his whip, "*Links, rechts*." And whoever hesitated, objected, disobeyed an order was treated with a blow to the face or a bullet to the head. "*Was bist du von Beruf?*" (What is your occupation?) he invariably asked every Jew who stood before him.

On the first day of the liquidation of the Częstochowa ghetto, the Germans murdered 300 men, women, and children on the spot, ordering a mass grave to be dug for them on Kawia Street, in a large square designated for this purpose.[48] As a result of the entire *Aktion,* several thousand Jews were shot and buried in this new cemetery.[49] During

47 Specifically to the death camp of Treblinka.

48 During the first *Aktion* on September 22, 1942, some 7,000 Jews were deported from Częstochowa to Treblinka, via the Zawodzie railway ramp. Hundreds were shot dead and buried in a mass grave, as Kromołowski states. See Miron and Shulhani, *The Yad Vashem Encyclopedia of the Ghettos in the Holocaust*, p. 140.

49 By the "entire *Aktion*," Kromołowski is referring to all five transports that took place between September 22 and October 7, during which at least 2,000 were shot dead, and 33,000–40,000 people were deported to Treblinka where they were gassed. A few were kept alive to work in Treblinka. See earlier and Dean, *USHMM*

the following days of this *Aktion*, the Germans shot the elderly and the disabled. Many children—separated from their parents, lost, crazed with despair, crying, caught among the Nazis while searching for their mothers and fathers—were shot too. The Germans did this methodically. The Schupo policemen hurried the children to the cemetery, where they ordered the children to undress, lay down in a row—one next to the other on the edge of a ditch that had been dug—and shot the children.

The Nazis then ordered local Poles living on neighboring streets to bury the dead in the mass graves, giving them the children's clothes as a reward. Jewish corpses, scattered in the streets of the ghetto, were brought to Kawia Street. These were mainly the corpses of the elderly, as the Germans believed it would not be profitable to deport them to camps. Also included were those who, despite being summoned, did not come out for selection, as well as many others whose hiding places were discovered during searches of Jewish apartments, attics, or cellars.

A funeral service was organized. Jewish cartmen transported the corpses of murdered Jews on carts to Kawia Street. There, the Germans extracted any gold teeth and removed gold rings and wedding rings from their fingers—and when these rings could not be removed from the stiff or swollen fingers, they cut off the fingers without a second thought. They diligently searched the clothes of their dead victims for money or jewelry, which the wealthier Jews had sewn into the lining of their jackets, dresses, or coats in anticipation of the imminent ghetto liquidation.

The Jewish funeral service was led by Szlama Miska, a former member of the Jewish burial society (*chevra kadisha*), who was obliged to bury Jewish corpses according to Jewish law. Degenhardt assured him that he would be granted life in exchange for this difficult and highly demanding task of burying his murdered brethren. Nevertheless, at the end of the liquidation, despite his promise, Degenhardt ordered Miska's son, who was a Jewish policeman, to bring his father and mother to the railroad siding and push them into a train car. Szlama Miska, along with other ghetto inhabitants, was murdered in Treblinka death camp.

Meanwhile, in the streets of the ghetto, already emptied of its inhabitants, groups of German police, Gestapo, and Polish police roamed the abandoned apartments, stealing the most valuable objects and hidden goods. A short time before the ghetto's liquidation, the Germans, with the

Encyclopedia of Camps and Ghettos, vol. 2, part A, p. 216; Mizgalski, "The Jews of Częstochowa: A Short History," The World Society of Częstochowa Jews and Their Descendants, https://www.czestochowajews.org/.

support of Linderman, the administrator of Jewish goods stored in officially sealed Jewish shops, sold everything for a trifle to Polish merchants. While the liquidation *Aktion* was still in full swing, hundreds of trucks and horse-drawn carts transported—under German supervision—movable property and furniture from Jewish apartments to special warehouses set up on Garibaldi Street. Everything found in the Jewish ghetto was amassed in these warehouses: bed linen, underwear and clothing of all kinds, footwear, household utensils and appliances, pots, plates, and tableware—anything of practical value.

In these warehouses, which were under the supervision of the Schutzpolizei and included all houses on Garibaldi Street, Jewish men and women had to sort, pack, and bring in more and more goods from the streets of the empty ghetto. A separate building was devoted to collecting paintings, sculptures, and other works of art, as well as goods of various kinds that had been found in the ghetto's bunkers. The sorted items were then sent to Germany; anything that was not deemed good enough was sold to the Poles. The Germans also sold second-rate furniture to the Poles for little money. Of course, there were always people willing to buy Jewish-owned goods.

The liquidation and emptying of the ghetto in Częstochowa took a few weeks. Whoever was not murdered on the spot was shoved into a lime-strewn cattle car headed for Treblinka. Every man, woman, and child who was deported from the Częstochowa ghetto during this *Aktion* was murdered in the gas chambers of Treblinka—a total of around 40,000 Jews. In a similar manner, they murdered 3.5 million Polish Jews from Warsaw, Kraków, Łódź, Lublin, Białystok, and other Polish cities, either in Treblinka or in the other death camps of Auschwitz, Majdanek, Bełżec, and Sobibor.[50] These *Aktionen* were not carried out by criminal mobs but rather by uniformed German soldiers—mainly the SS, German police, and Gestapo, assisted by Ukrainian nationalists and the Polish Blue Police. They acted under the command of high-ranking German officers, most of whom had a university education, and on the orders of the government of the Third Reich.[51]

50 Estimates of the total number of Jews murdered in all of the death camps vary. More than 3 million Jews are estimated to have been murdered in Chełmno, Bełżec, Sobibór, Treblinka, Auschwitz-Birkenau, and Majdanek.

51 We should recall here that thousands of Righteous Among the Nations—of whom Poland, the country with the largest Jewish population during the war, accounts for the highest number—have been recognized by Yad Vashem. However, there seems to be a stark contrast between the help that was extended to the Jews and

Memorial stone in memory of the Jews of Częstochowa in Treblinka, Poland. YVA, 9810/88.

For an entire week, we sat in our apartment while the ghetto liquidation unfolded around us. During this waiting period, we suffered from hunger and nervous tension, making it impossible for us to sleep. From a quarter sack of flour—the only food we had—the women baked a kind of scone, using only water and no fats. There were seven of us—four men and three women, who, to make matters worse, were despairing and crying over our fate, which only increased our anxiety. We had reached the limits of our

the widespread indifference—though, to some extent, understandable given the horrific conditions of the occupation—or lack of involvement shown by the broader population, which left a deep impression on him. One should remember that the Polish population suffered from Nazi terror with severe consequences for any form of resistance. Aiding Jews could be punishable by death for both the helper and their family. Most Poles lacked the power or resources to challenge the armed and organized German forces. Prewar antisemitism in Polish society, attested to earlier by Kromołowski, also played its role.

physical and mental endurance. One day, I crossed over the fence and ran into a neighboring house in search of some food. I managed to get a piece of meat from a freshly killed calf from one of our neighbors, and we finally had a proper meal.

Another time, an acquaintance of my brother who was a Jewish policeman came and filled us in about the events of the past week. He told us how wealthy Jews were giving away all their material possesions, including expensive jewelry, to save their lives and the lives of their loved ones—even though this did not help much. German and Jewish policemen grew rich by taking these possessions in exchange for rescue—but they rarely kept their promises. Even if they managed to smuggle one or two such Jewish families at night to the transit camp for essential workers in the Metalurgia factory, there would be another selection the next day—this time inside the factory—and those temporarily rescued were sent to the trains.

During the weeks of the ghetto liquidation *Aktion*, jewelry and valuables worth millions of złoty passed into the hands of German Schupo men, Jewish policemen, and also some members of the Judenrat. A wealthy Jew from Zagłębie Dąbrowskie,[52] a certain Majtlis, offered an antique gold belt with diamonds to the Judenrat in exchange for saving his life. At night, this Majtlis was transported, hidden under sacks of flour to the Metalurgia factory, but a few days later, a selection took place there, and Majtlis was sent to Treblinka.

Precious stones and jewelry worth billions, as well as valuable antiques and art, were taken to Germany following the liquidation of the Jews in Poland and all over Europe. This is best illustrated by the Menten Affair. Pieter Nicolaas Menten was a Gestapo officer who, after the war, was found in Holland in possession of a museum collection of highly valuable works of art, which, as he himself admitted, he had stolen from Jews during his time in Poland.[53]

52 Zagłębie Dąbrowskie (Dąbrowa Basin) is a historical and industrial region in southern Poland, located in the Silesian Voivodeship.

53 The Menten Affair involved Pieter Nicolaas Menten (1899–1987), a Dutch citizen and an *SS-Hauptscharführer* implicated in the massacre of Jews in Podhorodce and Urycz (Eastern Galicia) during the summer of 1941. Exposed by investigative reporting in the 1970s, Menten was also accused of looting valuable works of art during the Nazi occupation. His trial, beginning in 1977, uncovered extensive evidence of war crimes and art theft. Finally on July 9, 1980, the Criminal Court in Rotterdam sentenced Menten to ten years' imprisonment for his participation in the

Finally, one sunny and warm September day,[54] the Jewish police herded us to the selection point in the New Market Square. We left with clenched hearts, convinced that we were going on our last journey. We left the door of our apartment open, as instructed, and went out into the street dressed in overcoats and carrying small bundles of personal items. I took a couple of shirts and some underwear, as did Stella. Each of us hoped that maybe it would not be so bad, and that by some miracle we would avoid deportation, which meant death. We walked one after the other along the narrow sidewalk of Nadrzeczna Street. In the opposite direction, crowds of Jews—men, women, and children—who had already been selected were walking toward the ramp. They were silent, dumbfounded, helpless, resigned. The children were clutching their mothers' skirts. It was a procession of people going to their deaths. They were surrounded by Ukrainian fascists—the assistants of the Germans in exterminating the Jewish people.[55]

Led by Jewish policemen, we continued walking along the street. The crowd of people heading to the selection site was growing constantly, because people from neighboring houses and streets were joining us in an unbroken stream. We entered Prosta Street[56] and passed the brick wall surrounding St. Zygmunt's Church. The road led to the New Market Square, where the selections took place. The crowd walked in absolute silence—old, young, women, and children, terrified and pale, carrying bundles, packages, and suitcases. No one thought of resistance. Resignation and

massacre of between twenty and thirty Jews in Podhorodce. His complicity in the murder of 180 Jews on August 27, 1941, in Urycz remained unproven. He served two-thirds of his sentence and recovered part of the seized works of art whose looting remained unproven. See Nawojka Cieślińska-Lobkowicz, "Predator: The Looting Activity of Pieter Nicolaas Menten (1899–1987)," *Holocaust Studies and Materials*, 4 (2017), pp. 112–147.

54 The reference is likely to the period of September 25–30, prior to the deportation of the Jewish Ordnungdienst (the Jewish police) and Judenrat members on October 4. See Dean, *USHMM Encyclopedia of Camps and Ghettos*, vol. 2, part A, p. 216.

55 He is referring to the Trawniki auxiliaries. Ukrainians formed a prominent part among the Trawnikis but other nationalities formed a substantial part of the units as well, including Russians, Belarussians, Balts, and Poles—the latter were recruited toward the end of Operation Reinhard. For more information, see Cüppers, Lepper, and Matthäus, *From "Euthanasia" to Sobibor*, p. 188.

56 Prosta is part of Mirowska Street today. See Stary Rynek–rys historyczny, Częstochowa municipality, https://www.Częstochowa.pl/stary-rynek-rys-historyczny (accessed August 18, 2025).

despair showed on everyone's faces. Only here and there, a child carried by their mother wept, or an old man groaned with effort.

The market square in front of the church had long been covered with grass by the Germans. The ground along the edge of the lawn was compacted and covered in sand. We were now walking along this road in a row, one after the other. We were getting closer and closer to where a German Schutzpolizei officer was standing at the bend of the road. He was redheaded and redfaced, standing in heavy boots with his legs wide apart, conducting the selection. The silence around was occasionally broken by his guttural shouts. We were ordered to take out our red booklets, which stated our personal information and occupation. Holding these *Ausweis* (identification cards) with which every ghetto inhabitant was provided after a special registration, we moved closer and closer to the selection point. I saw terrified people peering out from their tightly closed windows in the houses around New Market Square, watching us and what was happening on the square. It was not yet their turn to go to the selection point.

Up ahead, with a flick of the wrist, the redheaded gendarme sent quite a lot of people to the left—to the road leading to the railroad ramp, to their death. To the right, he directed a small group of people, who were lined up on First Avenue. These were the lucky ones who could stay in the city and continue working for the Germans. They could continue deluding themselves with hope of surviving this cataclysm.

A short distance away from the selection point, a group of Schupo men in helmets and full combat gear were manning heavy machine guns with their barrels aimed at us. Standing next to the *Wachmeister*[57] was the brother of the chairman of the Judenrat and head of the Department of Forced Labor, Maurycy Kopiński, who my father-in-law worked under as an accountant. As we approached the German in charge of the selection, I noticed that Kopiński was explaining something to him. The inspector paused his work, thought for a moment, and then waved his hand in a gesture of approval. At that moment, Kopiński took my father-in-law by the hand and led him to the right. My mother-in-law followed, then Stella, along with my brother and our cousin, who had come with us to the selection point. They all walked slowly toward the group of those selected to remain in the city. I was the last one in our group to pass by the redheaded German. I had just handed him my ID card, which stated my occupation as a lawyer, when the German shouted, "*Wir brauchen nicht*" (We don't need).

57 *Wachmeister* is the Ordnungspolizei rank equivalent to sergeant.

He tore up my ID card and gestured with his hand to the left—to the ramp. Suddenly, Kopiński pushed me to the right side, ignoring the protests, and said to me, "Go where your family is going."

I did as he said, and the German—preoccupied with a new victim—didn't notice me. We were incredibly lucky. The Schupo policeman replacing Degenhardt, who was eating dinner, had been bribed by the Judenrat. Kopiński happened to be present at this selection by pure chance, as he had some business for Degenhardt and was awaiting his return. Kopiński saved whoever he could, and by some lucky coincidence, we were spared—if only temporarily. There was no doubt that we owed our rescue to Kopiński, who, with great courage, intervened when he recognized his acquaintance and loyal employee, my father-in-law, Henryk Szmulewicz.

Half unconscious from both fear and hunger, those of us who had managed to pass the selection stood in a small group. I looked around and noticed that we were in the commercial center of Częstochowa with its many stores and warehouses. It made an incredible impression on me. New Market Square and First Avenue, leading to the railroad bridge, were both deserted. All the stores were closed, the houses seemed abandoned, and the streets were empty. Only the lawn of New Market Square was lined with silent people laden with bundles. They would stop for a moment next to a German *Wachmeister* before continuing in a line along a road to the left, disappearing into the depths of Ogrodowa Street, which led to the Warta railway station.

First Avenue was completely deserted. A Polish policeman with a rifle slung over his shoulder was walking slowly down the avenue, which was lined with chestnut trees on both sides. We were standing in a small group of around fifty or sixty people—women and men—at the intersection of New Market Square and First Avenue.[58] People were dumbfounded, and many women were crying. My wife Stella was doing her best to support her father, who was weak and unsteady on his feet. My mother-in-law was wiping her tears with a handkerchief. Despair and resignation showed on every face. Many were mourning their loved ones, who had been sent to the trains for their final journey.

58 "Two large cloisters were encompassed within the area of Częstochowa's Aleje [avenues]—one in the Nowy Rynek [New Market] (in the heart of the former Jewish quarter) and the other being the world famous Jasna Góra." Zvi Rozenwajn, "The Aleje [Avenues] of Częstochowa (Reflections)," in M. Schutzman, ed., *The Book of Częstochowa* (translation of *Sefer Czenstochow*), vol. 2 (New York: Czenstochower Landsmanshaft of New York, 1958), pp. 799–802.

Next to me stood the son of the jeweler Hipszer, whom I knew. He was very upset and had tears in his eyes. He told me that a moment ago, during the selection, his father had been directed to the trains. He asked if I had a cigarette. My brother said that the policeman walking in the middle of the alley was his friend with whom he had completed his military service. Maybe he had a cigarette. Indeed, at my brother's urging, a policeman named Napieraj approached us, took out a packet of German Juno cigarettes from his pocket, and handed them to Hipszer, who said he wanted to buy them from him. Hipszer lit a cigarette, inhaling the smoke with visible pleasure. He then took a thick, gold signet ring with a green stone from his pocket and handed it to Napieraj as payment.

After some time, two Jewish policemen and a German policeman approached our group and told us we could leave. We walked toward Wilson Street, thinking we were being led to the Metalurgia factory—the transit camp where the Germans held Jewish workers assigned to clean up the abandoned ghetto apartments. The Judenrat was also based there, and there was a kitchen where meals were cooked. We were hungry and thirsty, and a spoonful of hot food would do us a lot of good.

We turned onto Krótka Street but passed the Metalurgia factory. Our group continued walking until we reached a square near the Metalurgia factory, which belonged to the factory of the Landau brothers, who used to run it under the company name Braland. We entered through the gates of Braland, which promptly closed behind us with a clatter. We found ourselves standing in a large factory square, where mostly young Jewish men and women were gathered. There were about 1,000 people who, as we found out later, had passed an earlier selection to be used by the Germans for forced labor. They had been there for several days under very difficult conditions and without warm food. Once a day, bread was delivered from the neighboring Metalurgia factory, which was their only nourishment. They slept on the bare floor of the large, open factory hall. Some children and elderly people were there too.

They recounted that civilian Germans had come to select young, strong men and women from among the people gathered there on several occasions. They said that these people would work at various German outposts, where they would live and receive hot lunches. There were many volunteers, but not everyone was accepted. Disturbing rumors circulated here that further selections would be made because too many Jews remained after the ghetto's liquidation, and moreover, not everyone met the requirements. The Germans needed healthy, young, and strong people, so anyone who was unfit for work joined the transports that departed every day for Treblinka.

The liquidation of the ghetto was still in progress, and more and more streets inhabited by Jews were included in the *Aktion*. Each day, people were herded to the inspection; a handful of them were chosen and sent to transit camps located on Krótka Street, while the rest were sent to the railroad cars that shuttled between our town and Treblinka. In addition to the transit camps in Metalurgia and Braland, a women's camp was also established in the former factory of Ickowicz and Guterman, also located on Krótka Street, which soon became known as the selection street. In spite of the war with Soviet Russia and the huge demand for railroad transports to carry weapons, people, and supplies for the German army fighting in the Russian territories, the Germans still found enough time and transportion to carry out Operation Reinhard—the code name for the liquidation of Polish Jewry.[59]

After arriving at Braland, people rushed to the water pump next to the factory buildings. We were thirsty and hungry. Water was drawn and drunk directly from the tap or from a bucket found nearby. Later, baskets of bread were brought from Metalurgia, and the distribution of rations—consisting of a quarter of a loaf per person—began. Ludwik Tempel, a former wealthy forwarding agent who had escaped from Łódź to Częstochowa, was in charge of bread distribution. He was a member of the wealthy and well-known Tempel family in Częstochowa. He chose a handful of people to assist him, and I was one of them.

I brought bread to my wife and in-laws, who were in the factory buildings and had found a convenient spot to rest. Such spots had to be carefully safeguarded, because this already small building was overcrowded, and people hastily occupied every free space. Most people

59 Operation Reinhard refers to the murder operation of Jews on the territories of the General Government in occupied Poland, as part of the "Final Solution." Between March 1942 and November 1943, more than 1.7 million Jews were murdered, according to Arad—the majority in the three Operation Reinhard death camps: Bełżec (600,000), Sobibór (250,000), and Treblinka (850,000). In addition, tens of thousands were murdered in Majdanek. As can be seen in the example of Częstochowa, the murder operation was accompanied by mass killings of Jews in their hometowns during the deportation *Aktionen*. *SS-Brigadeführer* Odilo Globocnik was the one responsible for conducting Operation Reinhard, which was named after Reinhard Heydrich, who was assassinated on May 2, 1942. See Yitzhak Arad, "'Operation Reinhard': Extermination Camps of Belzec, Sobibor and Treblinka," *Yad Vashem Studies*, 16 (1984), pp. 205–239.

lay on the ground beneath the open sky, but it was difficult to sleep in such conditions. It was already the end of September, and although the autumn was warm and pleasant, it turned cooler after sunset, and those without coats or warm clothes suffered from the night chill. Many were sick, but no one helped them—everyone was concerned only with their own survival. My father-in-law lay there moaning quietly. My mother-in-law, also very weak, was in a state of extreme exhaustion. Stella took care of her parents as much as she could, bringing them water to drink and urging them to eat the bread I had secured.

The mood in the camp was depressing. People told each other about the tragic events of the day and mourned the loss of their closest family members. Families had been torn apart, and many were completely alone. Hardly anyone could sleep at night. There was talk of further selections to be made in our camp. The atmosphere was one of anxiety and panic. Many people suffered from digestive disorders and diarrhea. Aside from the quarter loaf of bread per person per day, no hot drinks or hot food was available. People ate the bread, washing it down with cold tap water. This is how they managed to survive for several days. Fortunately, the days were bright and sunny, so people lay and basked in the sun. We washed ourselves under the pump, and men shaved off the stubble that had grown over several days. Since a new selection was expected every day, everyone wanted to appear young and attractive.

One day, a few civilian Germans came to the square, accompanied by rifle-armed factory guards—the *Werkschutz*—in search of people to perform forced labor. Many volunteered, and immediately, a small crowd began gathering around the prospective employers. Everyone wanted to leave the camp as soon as possible, since the explosive concentration of people put everyone at risk of further selections. Besides, hunger and disease was rampant, and these Germans promised there would be good food at their workplaces. My brother Henio and my wife's brother Tadzio were among those who applied and were accepted as workers for the Hagen company, which was building a new railroad for military purposes. Only men were accepted for this work. We said goodbye, and I thought that perhaps this might be the last time we would see each other.

This large group of young men—surrounded by the *Werkschutz*—left the square, the gate closing behind them. As for myself, I did not even think of going with them. I did not want to leave my wife and in-laws. What will be will be. I wasn't expecting anything good. We were at risk of death at any moment. It felt like we were on the front lines—the only difference being that a soldier at the front has a gun and can attack or defend himself, while we were defenseless and at the mercy of an armed and organized enemy. We were a plaything in the hands of the Germans. Another night passed.

Early in the morning, there was grim news: The Germans were preparing another selection. Jewish policemen brought in bread and claimed that freight trains for transporting Jews were standing at the Warta railway siding, where deportations usually took place. They said that this selection would be particularly harsh, because too many Jews remained from previous selections in transit camps such as this. The Germans did not need so many workers. In the ghetto, people were still being cleared from the streets and transported to the death camp.

In our camp, there was overwhelming nervousness and panic. Women were blushing their cheeks and putting on lipstick. Everyone wanted to look healthy and young—to impress the Germans as being fit for labor. Stella put makeup on her mother and tied a kerchief around her head to cover her graying hair. The men shaved as if for a party. The Germans were picky. They only needed young and healthy people. Everyone tried to adopt both the appearance and demeanor of a worker seasoned in hard physical labor. This was a struggle for survival. The instinct of self-preservation, inherent in the psyche of every human being, came to the fore against the impending doom. However, not everyone behaved this way. There were also the apathetic and resigned, who were psychologically and mentally devastated by the experiences of the previous tragic days.

Around noon, the Jewish policemen opened the entrance gate and lined us up one by one. Everyone—women and men, all miserable, helpless, indifferent, and terrified by the selection—stood with their bundles, staring at the open gate. Beyond it, one could see several armed German Schutzpolizei policemen in greenish uniforms and round peaked caps on Krótka Street. On their uniforms were insignia of a German eagle clutching a swastika in its talons, along with two lightening bolts symbolizing the SS. Next to them stood Ukrainians from the fascist auxiliary units, wearing black uniforms.

In the center stood *Hauptmann* Degenhardt, who was short, dark-haired, and holding a whip. He was ruthless and harsh. He would personally be carrying out today's selection. He knew best whom to send to the railway cars and whom to assign to labor. One look from his cold, steel-colored eyes, and the decision was final. *Links*, *rechts*!

We didn't say goodbye or talk. There was grave silence. Tears streamed from our eyes and ran down our pale cheeks. I stood in the selection line behind Stella and my in-laws. I saw my father-in-law, weak on his feet, supported by Stella. We were fast approaching the gate. The *Aktion* was calm, fast, and efficient. The motion of a uniformed hand, armed with a leather whip, indicated the direction and conveyed the decision. A signal to the left meant the railway cars. Without any objection, the victims obediently followed Degenhardt's order. The group gathering at the end of Krótka Street was continuously growing, the number of Jews—both male and female—destined for deportation increasing by the minute. No trace of protest or opposition, no attempt at resistance. People went where the German ordered them, as if hypnotized; yet they knew very well that they were going to their death.

My father-in-law was directed to the left, while Stella was sent to the right—to stay. My mother-in-law wanted to follow her. She gestured toward Stella and said, "This is my daughter, *meine Tochter*." Degenhardt raised his whip and struck her, leaving a reddish streak on her face. "*Links!* he shouted in German to her.

Now it was my turn. His cold eyes gave me a sharp, penetrating look before he hissed, "*Links*." I joined my in-laws and stood in the circle of prisoners, but I was calm, composed, conscious, thinking coldly, "So, this is the end? First, the ride in the wagon stinking of lime[60] and human excrement, then (as we would later find out) the gas chamber and the agony of dying. No! I must do something to defend myself!"

I looked in front of me. Degenhardt and his armed assistants were standing with their backs to me, busy with the ongoing selection. About ten or fifteen steps away from me, a group of people who had been selected for work stood facing Wilson Street, near the Metalurgia gate. Among them was my wife, Stella. Next to her, a Jewish policeman was standing on the left side of the sidewalk. I knew him. His name was Mitelman.

The decision was made in a flash. I broke away from the group of prisoners and slowly, steadily walked the distance separating me from the group of "lucky ones" destined for work. I stood calmly, as if I had been directed here by a German. I took out a cap from my rucksack and covered my head. Mitelman saw my escape, but said nothing. I saw Stella lying on the pavement, crying spasmodically. A women lifted her from the ground and said to her, "There is your husband, standing here with us."

Every now and then, someone new joined our group. Time went by, and the selection continued. It seemed that I had once again won the duel

60 The floors of the cars were often coated with lime and chlorine to mask the stench, but these chemicals caused further suffering for the deportees.

with the Angel of Death. When the selection was finally over, we were told to move forward. The gate of Metalurgia opened before us. It was a transit camp for men, while the women—including Stella—were taken to the former metal factory Ickowicz and Guterman. The rest of those destined for deportation were directed along Warszawska Street to the Warta railroad ramp and onto the railway cars. Among those unfortunates were my in-laws, Stella's parents, whom we never saw again. They both perished along with millions of other Jews in the gas chambers of Treblinka. Standing with those selected for labor, one thought kept haunting me: Why didn't anyone try to imitate me and escape in a similar way? People stood as if paralyzed, helpless. And yet, there were many young and healthy people among them, capable of resisting and even fighting.

That day, I had my first cooked meal in over a week. In Metalurgia, there was a field kitchen, where coffee and meals were prepared. I ate a bowl of hot soup with potatoes and a piece of bread, and satisfied my hunger. I started to look around the camp, which was said to be the only place in the liquidated ghetto where a Jew could feel safe. People were standing aound and talking in the crowded factory square, which was not very large, while others were lying on the bare ground taking a nap or walking around.

At the far end of the square stood a tall factory chimney with a hearth long extinguished, surrounded by one-story, blackened factory buildings whose halls were filled with people. One building was full of sewing machines placed close together in the entire middle of the dark hall, whose windows were covered tightly. A sanitary post and temporary hospital were set up there under the direction of a local surgeon called Dr. Ignacy Szperling, who was a member of the Jewish police. A few doctors were working there, tending to the sick and those who had been wounded during the *Aktion* or beaten by the Germans. The entire first floor of the front building was occupied by the Judenrat and their families, as well as some of the doctors' families. Guards were located on the ground floor, next to the entrance gate, and this is where the German Schupo policemen and *Leutnant* Zoppart[61] from the Schutzpolizei, who supervised the camp, resided.

I started to look around for a hiding place. I had learned from my painful experience and decided not to go out for any future selections on

61 Dawid Koniecpoler mentions Zoppart, along with Roon and Werner, as Degenhardt's officers involved in the selection on June 26, 1943, when hundreds of Jews were shot in the cemetery, See "Tearful Dates," in *Sefer Czenstochow*, pp. 37–46.

the streets, not to look the Germans in the eyes, and to practice passive resistance. I knew very well that I was not an appealing worker for the German torturers, and I had no chance of surviving the next selections, which I expected would take place as long as Jews were held in German labor camps. It was generally believed that such camps would be short-lived, and that liquidations would continue until the complete annihilation of the Jewish population had been achieved.

I spent the night in one of the factory rooms lying on the floor covered with my overcoat. The next day, I was in the kitchen fetching a drink of hot water dyed black in an attempt to mimic coffee. When I returned to my spot with a piece of bread in hand, I saw that my overcoat was gone. Someone had stolen it. Fortunately, I still had my jacket, as well as the rucksack containing a shirt and a pair of underpants, because I had taken the rucksack with me to the kitchen.

It was 10 o'clock in the morning when the Jewish policemen once again started chasing people out of Metalurgia and into the street. Soon, Degenhardt and his staff would arrive, and another selection would take place to sift out those unsuitable for work. In fact, because their aim was not to select the best physical workers for forced labor but rather to physically exterminate as many Jews as possible, they required numerous and constantly recurring selections. The railway cars again sat in the siding, waiting for Jewish victims. Treblinka was operating at full speed, expecting new transports all the time.

I quickly slipped into the factory hall with the sewing machines that I had discovered the previous day. I lay on the floor beside them and crawled under the machine pedals, moving deeper and deeper. Crawling on my stomach and pushing myself forward with my hands and feet, I finally reached the center of the clustered machines. There were probably over a hundred of them. The hall was dark, and it was even darker under the pedals of the machines. Lying motionless, pinned to the floor, I thought to myself that I should not be visible from the outside in case of an inspection—unless, of course, the Germans pulled apart the machines and looked underneath for people hiding. But this was unlikely.

I soon discovered that someone else was also hiding beneath the pedals of the machines, not far from me. I whispered to the other hidden person. I could not recognize him from where I was hidden because it was so dark, but it turned out that he was an acquaintance of mine from Częstochowa, Dawid Albert. He had also discovered this hiding place to escape selections. We listened anxiously for voices coming from outside. At first, we could hear the bustle coming from the yard—the sounds of conversations, shouts, the stamping of feet—but after a while, everything went quiet. The silence was deafening. Afterward, I discovered that all the men from Metalurgia had been driven out into the street, where a selection took place.

After about an hour, the silence was broken by heavy footsteps coming from the square. They seemed to approach and then recede again. It was obvious that the Germans were inspecting the whole premises, searching for hidden Jews. After a while, in the bright light of the open door, we saw the silhouettes of two Schupo policemen. We froze, completely motionless, and held our breath. The Germans shined their flashlights and walked around the large room, illuminating the machines, but apparently, they did not notice anything suspicious, and so they left. We heard the sound of distant footsteps, and once again, there was silence. We breathed a sigh of relief, and continued to lie completely still.

Then, we heard people speaking in Yiddish. The conversation was coming from behind the partition by the entrance to the room. Szlama Miska and his wife occupied this room. Miska, as I mentioned earlier, was the head of a group of gravediggers from the newly established cemetery on Kawia Street. I heard their son, the Jewish policeman, tell his parents that he had come for them on orders from Degenhardt himself, who had instructed him to lead his parents to the train departing for the extermination camp with the fresh victims of that day's selection. If he disobeyed this order, he himself would be sent on this transport to the place of execution. Apparently Miska's role as a gravedigger was over, he was no longer needed by the Germans, so they decided to get rid of the witness to their crimes, and as a "reward" for a job well done, they sent him to a place of no return. I heard moaning and crying, and then the sound of footsteps followed by silence again. Miska led his parents out and went with them to the loading area. I wondered to what depths of bestiality the Germans had driven some Jews. This tragic event demonstrates how all blood ties burst loose, how all human emotions and feelings froze. Here was a son leading his own parents to their death in cold blood to save his own life. The German perfidy and mockery of human sentiment exceeded all limits.

For a long time, Dawid Albert and I lay in silence in our hiding place. Finally, we heard the sounds of footsteps, conversations, and shouts. People were walking around the yard, clinking pots and pans, and somebody was laughing aloud. Life was returning to normal. The selection was over. Those who had survived it happily returned to their usual activities. Others—and there were many more than those who remained—were gone forever. After a moment's hesitation, I decided to leave my hiding place. I crawled out quickly, stood up, and stretched my aching bones. Once again, my tactic of passive resistance had proven effective, and I had survived.

Now I was overcome by fear and anxiety about my wife's fate. Had there also been a selection in the women's camp? Had Stella managed to survive today's selection? I was also worried about my brother and brother-in-law working for the German company Hagen. I began trying to find some way to communicate with my wife, as she was close by. Our field kitchen also supplied meals for the women's camp in the Ickowicz and Guterman factory, providing their evening coffee and bread. The field kitchen was managed by the previously mentioned Maurycy Galster, a member of the Judenrat and head of the Jewish police. I knew Galster from prewar times, when he was a cashier at the Association of Jewish Industrialists and Merchants, where I had worked as a legal advisor, and I had often contacted him on business matters. Now, Galster was one of the so-called strong men in the Judenrat, holding an important position that required ruthless and energetic inidividuals.

I found Galster in the kitchen and asked him for permission to help carry the cauldrons of coffee and baskets of bread to the women's camp, openly admitting that I wanted to do so in order to see my wife, who was there. Galster agreed, and that evening, I went with some of the kitchen workers to the women's camp, which was opposite the Metalurgia on the other side of Krótka Street. To my great joy, I found Stella. She was lying on the floor, sad and deeply depressed—but alive and healthy. She was overjoyed to see me alive. We embraced and kissed. She cried as she told me how worried she had been when she heard about the selection in my camp, and how much she was suffering from the loss of her parents. She agonized over the fate of her brother and mine. She told me that the selection had also included the women's camp, and that Degenhardt had specifically chosen the older women, ordering them to join the transport to the death camp of Treblinka. There was no time for a longer conversation, but I managed to give Stella the piece of bread that I had hidden inside my jacket for her. We hugged silently, uncertain whether we would see each other again—if tomorrow's selection would spare our lives.

After returning to Metalurgia, I ran into my wife's cousin, Daniel Kasman, who told me in detail about his experiences over the past few days. He and his wife had tried to hide with friends on the Aryan side, but they were both caught by the Germans. They were about to be shot—they were already standing by the fence with their hands up—but instead, the Germans sent them back to Metalurgia, where a selection was taking place. There, he saw how Degenhardt ordered a group of young people to march, make various turns, form into two ranks, then into four; praised them for their good attitude and knowledge of commands; and finally ordered them to march to the railroad ramp and board a transport to Treblinka. Degenhardt was an exceptionally perverse and perfidious German who mocked the Jews and murdered people in cold blood on a massive scale.

The next two days passed relatively peacefully. Fewer amd fewer people remained in Metalurgia—some went to work at the German outposts, where they were housed in barracks, while others were sent to extermination camps. It seemed that the worst period of mass selections and deportations was over. On the third day, however, something new hung in the air as people whispered among themselves and wandered restlessly around the square. There were rumors that new cattle wagons had been brought to the Warta railroad siding, and that the Jewish police had been ordered to prepare for a new selection, which was planned to begin at 10 o'clock in the morning. I went out to the yard, trying to decide what to do next. Should I find a hiding place again, or should I attempt to leave this hellish camp for a work assignment?

I knew that in the early hours of the morning, the German *Werkschutz* came to take people to perform various jobs in the city. Some stayed for an extended period, while others were brought back to Metalurgia in the evening. I decided to try my luck. If I could get out of there, even just for this dangerous day, I might avoid the selection, which could prove disastrous for me.

At about 7:00 AM, the Schutzpolizei supervisor, *Leutnant* Zoppart, appeared on the square and ordered people to report for work on the railroad. This outpost was called Ostbahn, and the work involved repairing railroad tracks. People rushed toward the exit gate and began lining up in rows of fours. I also hurried forward and joined one of the last groups. The gate opened, and our column of several dozen people emerged onto the street, surrounded by railway men. We were already on Wilson Street, walking along the railroad tracks, when a German railway man stopped our column. He must have been a senior officer, judging by his insignia. He counted us and declared that there were too many people in this column. He split the group in half and ordered the first rows to go to work, while the last ones—including myself—were turned back and ordered to march back to the camp. This is not good, I thought to myself. Turning back meant walking straight into the lion's den, as the selection was due to begin soon.

One of the *Werkschutz* led our group back to Metalurgia and reported to Zoppart, who was standing in front of the gate, that we were not needed for Ostbahn. Zoppart replied that it was fine—this group would be ready when others came to recruit workers. He ordered the gate of the nearby Kosmos factory[62] to be opened and told us to wait there for the next call for workers. The gate closed behind us. There was a dozen or so of us in this completely empty building—there was not another living soul. Krótka Street was on the other side of a wooden fence, through which we could see everything happening there. But from the street we could also be clearly seen through the loosely placed fencing. Behind the factory building where we were—set a dozen or so meters back from the street, deep within the lot—there was another small square located on the far side of the two-story structure. Either we would be called to work at another outpost or, much worse, we would be ordered to report for selection. The key was to wait patiently and avoid being seen by the Germans. Judging by the traffic and commotion on the street, the selection must have already begun. We hoped to avoid danger by staying hidden in the other factory yard—perhaps even forgotten. Time passed, and we sat in silence, tense and nervous, in constant fear of whether they would open the gate and order us out onto the street.

Meanwhile, the din in the street had quieted down. It was early autumn, and the day was coming to an end. We decided to leave our hiding place and move to the front yard. We stood by the fence and started to bang our boots on the railing to get their attention. Hearing this noise, the policemen brought over Zoppart, who, upon seeing us, opened his mouth wide, smacked his forehead, and admitted that he had completely forgotten about us. What the Kraut didn't know was that by forgetting us, he actually saved many of our lives. He personally took us to the kitchen and ordered that we be given a good meal.

Once again, Providence had protected me, and I evaded the next selection, which was reportedly particularly harsh and during which a great number of young and healthy people—mainly men—were sent to their deaths by Degenhardt. I was convinced once more that the tactic of hiding from the Germans and using passive resistance during the extermination *Aktionen* was the best way of defying German orders. When they ordered you to come out, you had to hide; and when they ordered you to hide, you had to flee. In any case, not following orders resulted in death and

62 The Kosmos factory, manufacturing toothbrushes, was owned before the war by B. Ajzner, Markowicz, Kaufman, and the Szajkiewicz brothers. See Jakób (Yaakov) Lewit, "Industry in Częstochowa—Its Creation and Development," in Schutzman, *Sefer Czenstochow*, vol. 1, pp. 401–412.

destruction. I was convinced that no one should believe a single word the Germans said—that their assurances and oaths are lies, and that they are a nation of heinous murderers and degenerates.

On that day, the Germans liquidated the rest of the Jewish population from the parts of the ghetto that had yet to be resettled. They carried out a series of selections among the Jews at the German work stations scattered throughout the city. From an acquantaince of mine who was a Jewish policeman, I inadvertantly learned that my wife had also escaped this transport, but as to the fate of my brother and my sixteen-year-old brother-in-law, Tadzio, I had no news. Depressed and troubled by dark thoughts, I threw myself on the bare floor and fell into a deep sleep.

CHAPTER SEVEN

THE SMALL GHETTO

By order of the chief of the Radom District—SS and police chief Dr. Herbert Böttcher[1]—work began on constructing a labor camp for the remaining Jews in Częstochowa following the ghetto's liquidation. This camp was intended for 5,000 men and women who, as unpaid laborers, were to remain on site to clean the Jewish apartments and sort the belongings stolen from their owners. In addition, Jewish workers were to be used as unpaid laborers at several German military and civilian outposts, and to form the workforce for an ammunition factory under construction on the premises of the Pelcery, Częstochowianka, and Warta textile factories, as well as at the Hantke ironworks in Raków, a suburb of Częstochowa.[2]

1 For more on Böttcher, see earlier, and also Wolfgang Curilla, *Der Judenmord in Polen und die deutsche Ordnungspolizei 1939–1945* (Paderborn: Verlag Ferdinand Schöningh GmbH & Co KG, 2011), p. 425.

2 After the deportations, about 5,000 able-bodied Jews remained in the Small Ghetto, located along Nadrzeczna, Kozia, Mostowa, Spadek, and Garncarska Streets, enclosed by barbed wire and with a single gate. Some sorted Jewish property, while others worked in HASAG. Many hiding Jews emerged afterward, reassured by the German-permitted activities such as daycare for 120 children. See Dean, *USHMM, Encyclopedia of Camps and Ghettos*, vol. 2, part A, p. 216; Kiel, *The Jews of Częstochowa*, pp. 147–148.

The Germans designated a dozen or so houses in the old district of the city as the labor camp. These were old, crumbling houses—mostly without sanitary facilities—that had been inhabited since time immemorial by the poorest members of the Jewish population and were located along narrow cobblestone streets. The houses by the Warta River were damp and moldy. This slum was part of the liquidated ghetto, carved out of the oldest and least habitable streets. The camp was to be surrounded by barbed wire, and guarded by German policemen and their Ukrainian collaborators. The forced laborers were to be kept in barracks, subject to prison-like conditions and strict discipline.

A camp construction brigade was formed from those staying at Metalurgia and was divided into two groups. One group repaired the concrete pillars and strung barbed wire between them, while the other built a large field kitchen to feed the 5,000 people in the camp. Working on the construction of the camp was considered a "privilege," so recruitment was kept secret. These workers left the camp early each morning and returned to Metalurgia late in the evening. This meant they were exempt from selections, which usually took place on Krótka Street and targeted the Jewish population at Metalurgia or those working at other German outposts.

In addition, these workers had access to Jewish apartments, where they found various objects, clothing, underwear, and even some valuables, which they sometimes took for their own use. They washed and bathed in warm water—something completely impossible in the primitive living conditions at Metalurgia. Unsurprisingly, the construction brigade was made up mostly of relatives of Judenrat members and Jewish policemen, or particularly privileged individuals. When I learned that such a work brigade was being formed, I went to Pohorille, who was still head of the secretariat in the severely depleted Judenrat—several members of which had not been spared by the Germans during the ghetto's liquidation.[3] I asked him to add me to this work unit. Pohorille, however, refused my request, stating that all the spots in this brigade had already been filled and that the list of those assigned had been submitted to the Germans. I knew that no such list existed and that protégés of the Judenrat were constantly being added to the ranks of the construction brigade.

I now had to find another way to avoid the selections, which, despite the liquidation of the former ghetto, were still being carried out at short intervals. Not getting caught or deported was my ultimate goal during this

3 The transport on October 4 included members of the Jewish police and the Judenrat.

period of unimaginable terror and the relentless hunt for Jews, for which the Germans used hundreds of trained and fully armed SS men, Schupo men, Ukrainians, Lithuanians, and Latvians from the *Vernichtungsbatalione* (extermination battalions). It was a dangerous mission, as failure meant death in the gas chambers of Treblinka. It was a cold October, and I was still being held at Metalurgia in extremely difficult conditions. We slept on the cold floor of the factory hall—I didn't even have anything to cover myself with, because my overcoat had been stolen. There was no way I could wash myself. I was dirty, unkempt, starving, living in constant tension. My only consolation was knowing that my wife had luckily passed the selections and was alive in the women's camp.

In the first days of October, a large group of Jewish policemen entered the camp and began chasing people out into the street. They wore round caps with navy blue tops and orange brims. The peaks of their caps were edged with shiny metal trim. They carried rubber truncheons, which they used to beat the reluctant, and they wore orange armbands bearing the letters J.O.D.—Jüdische Ordnungsdienst.[4] Once again, a dreaded selection was imminent. Instead of going out into the street, I walked in the opposite direction, deep into the factory yard, moving as far away as possible from the gate and the street. Suddenly, I found myself at the door of the camp kitchen. In front of the kitchen stood a one-horse platform, on which Arnold Rotbard, my acquaintance from Częstochowa, was loading cauldrons of soup that bubbled under the lids and spilled in narrow streams as they were carried. I grabbed the handle of the pot, and the two of us loaded it onto the platform. We carried five cauldrons in this way, placing them on the wagon in complete silence.

I soon understood that this food was for the brigade building the new labor camp, and Rotbard confirmed this. With a whip in hand, he started climbing onto the platform. Without a word, I grabbed a white rag lying on the platform, attached it to my belt so that it looked like an apron, jumped onto the platform, and, taking a large soup ladle in my hand, sat on the lid of the soup pot, pretending to be a cook. Although Rotbard knew exactly what I was trying to do, he never said a word. He urged his horse to start moving and off we rode.

4 A Jewish Ordnungdienst armband from Częstochowa can be found on the Jewish Historical Institute website, https://delet.jhi.pl/en/library/item/1322076 (accessed August 18, 2025). In this specific case, it also includes "żydowska służba porządkowa," the Polish translation of Jüdischer Ordnungsdienst (Jewish Order Service).

We rode out onto Krótka Street, where lines of people were forming ahead of the selection. Large numbers of German, Ukrainian, and Jewish policemen were running around with their rubber truncheons. We rode down the middle of the street, our cart's wheels rattling on the cobblestones. Every now and then, Rotbard swung his whip, shouting "Make way!"

He wore a navy-blue cap with a lacquered peak and a black leather strap—commonly worn by Polish villagers. It was supposed to give Rotbard a Polish appearance. Now he sat on the coach box, urging his horse, which was galloping with the last of its strength. Rotbard tried to leave the street as quickly as he could and get out of the Germans' sight, as one could only expect the worst from them. I sat on my soup pot, tense and nervous, clutching the ladle in my hand. I prayed we would soon reach a safer area, away from the Germans, because my ruse was entirely illegal, and an inspection could end tragically for me. But my face did not betray me, and I waved the ladle and sat with my legs spread on top of the pot. No one stopped us; on the contrary, the Germans and Ukrainians moved out of our way, and we hurried along to the sounds of clattering and the cracking of the whip. The soup would occasionally spill out from beneath the lids, leaving a white trail behind us.

Finally, this macabre ride was over, and we entered the Warsaw Market Square[5]—a spacious square once used for fairs but was now completely deserted. The square bordered on Garncarska and Jaskrowska Streets. This was the site of the future labor camp. There were already concrete pillars with coils of barbed wire attached. We could see wooden trestles with barbed wire nailed to them, and by pushing them aside, a space was created through which a cart could pass. Similar concrete posts with barbed wire were also found on the neighboring Nadrzeczna Street, which ran parallel to Gancarska Street—the street we had just entered with our cauldrons of soup. Farther away, we could see Senatorska Street fenced off with barbed-wire posts, near Warsaw Market Square.

We were surrounded by silence. Not a soul could be seen on the deserted streets. Before us stretched the narrow streets of the old town, dead, empty, uninhabited. As we continued along Gancarska Street, I decided to quickly slip off the platform and enter a house through a half-open gate. It was a one-story, red-brick building with a narrow courtyard. Through the closed windows, I saw the front rooms filled with bedding almost to the ceiling. I walked down the narrow hallway into the first room, which was completely filled with quilts and pillows without covers or pillowcases.

5 Today Plac Bohaterów Getta (Ghetto Heroes Square).

I looked around carefully. After a long moment, two human figures rose from beneath a heap of feathers.

Fortunately, these were Jews hiding here whom I knew. One of them, Szaja Dresler, was an electrician by profession who had owned a store with electrical appliances on First Avenue before the war. The other, Noah Edelist, was a Hasid and the wealthy owner of a metal products factory. They asked me for news, and we began talking. They told me about their well-camouflaged bunker in the adjoining house, where they and several other people had hidden before the ghetto liquidation had begun. They were fortunate because they had accidentally built this bunker in a part of the ghetto that the Germans had designated as the labor camp. For this reason, the houses abandoned by the inhabitants were not searched thoroughly, and movable belongings—even furniture—were often left completely intact in the apartments.

The food supplies in their bunker were already running low, so they had been forced to come out and search for some food. They were in this house trying to find something when they heard my footsteps. They thought I was a German and hid under the piles of bedding, which had been stored there for the workers of the labor camp under construction. I briefly told them about the tragic events of the past few weeks and the terrible fate that had befallen the deported inhabitants of our town. It had been four weeks since the beginning of the liquidation *Aktion*, and the selections and deportation of Jews continued. People from the more affluent ghetto areas had already been evicted—from First Avenue, New Market, and Katedralna Street; now, the remnants of the population—mostly those found in hiding places and bunkers—were being captured on the streets of the Aryan side and deported.

They both wept bitterly upon hearing my story: They had all left their families behind and now assumed their loved ones had shared the sad fate of the rest of Częstochowa's Jews. From them, I learned about the Germans' apparently well-known plan to establish a labor camp for the small number of Jews left behind after the ghetto's liquidation. Those who were well informed even knew in which part of the ghetto the camp would be established. Hence, quite a number of bunkers were created—often cleverly built and well supplied—in which many adults and children hid, hoping to be saved. These bunker inhabitants would leave their hiding places at night in search of food and water in abandoned apartments.

The labor camp under construction around the outlets of Kozia, Senatorska, Garncarska, Nadrzeczna, and Jaskrowska Streets was located near a small market square, not far from Warsaw Market Square. This was to serve as an assembly point for the labor camp workers and also as a gathering place for selections and deportations to the extermination centers. The eastern side of the camp would include parts of Kozia, Senatorska, Garncarska, Nadrzeczna, and Jaskrowska Streets, with part of Mostowa Street and Spadek Street on the western side. Only one side of Mostowa Street was to be included as part of the camp—also known as the Small Ghetto. The other side of the street belonged to the Aryan side but remained uninhabited for the duration of the camp's existence.

Entrance to the Small Ghetto, Częstochowa. YVA, 9810/21.

Later, the Germans climbed onto the roofs of the houses on the other side of Mostowa Street to hunt Jews, shooting at passersby and murdering many in this way. Among others, the physician, Dr. Gutman, who was peacefully walking along this street, was murdered during such a game.

For the time being, however, I was overjoyed with my lucky escape from the selections that were still taking place. I was so tired from my recent experiences, and I only wanted some rest. I lay down on a pile of soft bedding, covered myself with a quilt, and tried to fall asleep. However, sleep did not come for a long time. Before my eyes I kept seeing Krótka Street—the crowds of hurrying small children who had been torn from their parents, how they had called to them and stretched out their tiny, skinny arms to their distraught mothers. I heard heartrending screams and cries for rescue. This horrific image of human tragedy is something I will never be able to erase from my mind.

When I woke up, it was dark outside. I was alone in a stuffy room laden with bedding. Hunger was twisting my gut, and thirst was burning my throat. I decided to go out under the cover of night—just like the bunker inhabitants did—to look for some food. I sneaked out onto the street. The night was dark and moonless, as if the street and houses were drowning in darkness. Not a single lamp was lit. Apparently, the Germans had turned off the electricity in the city's Jewish quarter. The wind rattled the open windows, blowing the white curtains. No one was around. I moved slowly along the walls.

The gates of all the houses were wide open, so I slipped inside one of them and climbed the stairs to the first floor. Through an open door, I entered an apartment consisting of a room with a kitchen. Linens lay on a made bed; the furnishings remained untouched. On the table, a napkin covered plates of food. It looked as if the inhabitants had only briefly gone out and would return soon. I sat down at the table and ate the cold potatoes, nibbling on the bones of the leftover meat and chewing on the dried pieces of bread, which satisfied my hunger somewhat. I drank cold water from the tap.

Then, I found a piece of soap and washed myself in the cold water. Using a kind of brush, I scrubbed my feet, which were as dirty as the earth. I found a towel and dried myself thoroughly. I felt refreshed and lighter. I opened the closets and cabinets and pulled out the drawers. I found some clean men's underwear and several pairs of socks. I put on two pairs of clean underpants, two collared shirts, and fresh socks. I tucked the other pair of socks into the pockets of my pants. I found cigarettes in one of the drawers; matches were lying on the kitchen counter. I lit a cigarette, inhaling the smoke. Then I found a razor and shaved off several weeks' worth of stubble. After that, I went to bed and fell asleep.

I awoke to the sound of a loud conversation coming from the street. The conversation was in German. I heard heavy footsteps tapping steadily on the stone sidewalk. A German patrol was walking along the street. I climbed the stairs to the attic and hid behind some dusty equipment. The Germans passed by, so I left my hiding place and began wandering around the deserted house. Although the apartments were unlocked, they had not yet been touched. All the furnishings remained in place, and the closets were filled with linens and garments. In one of the apartments, I came across a spirit heater and a flask of alcohol to fuel it; in another, some potatoes and an onion. I placed the heater on the floor, covering it with a drawer taken from the closet so the flame wouldn't be visible, and cooked myself a potato soup, which I ate hungrily.

From this point on, I wandered around abandoned apartments every night, sneaking from house to house in search of food. During the day, I slept—usually hidden in an attic, for fear of being discovered by the Germans. During my nearly week-long wanderings through these apartments, I did not encounter any other human being. Sometimes, the silence of the night was broken by the sound of distant gunfire; during the day, I could hear the steady clatter of heavy footsteps of German patrols. By this point, the streets were already surrounded by concrete pillars with coils of barbed wire, which, according to my predictions, meant that the labor camp's construction was approaching its end. I found increasingly less food, and the garbage I came across was not fit to eat. I decided to try to reach the Jewish workers in the area—those building our new "headquarters"—thinking that they must have some food. My hunger was getting unbearable.

I finally reached a house that overlooked two streets. It had two gates, and that night, I slipped into Nadrzeczna Street through the second one. I lurked in an apartment, observing the street from the window. It was dawn on a cloudy and cool October day. After some time, I finally noticed a group of Jews leaving a house. They were wearing gloves and were pushing a cart of rolled-up barbed wire. Some of them carried scissors to cut the wire. There were about a dozen of them, walking alone without an escort. I went down to the gateway, and when the group passed by, I stepped out and joined them. Among them were people I knew—Kempner, Gąsiorowicz, and Kasman.

They told me that they were finishing the construction of a fence surrounding the entire area of the future camp, according to German orders. They said they had to hurry, because in a few days, Jews working at various German outposts were expected to arrive—in addition to those still concentrated in the transit camps on Krótka Street. Without a word of protest, they allowed me to stay with their group, and we worked on building the fence. No Germans or *Werkschutz* could be seen—they said they were working unsupervised.

Then we went to a newly built kitchen, located by the square on Nadrzeczna Street. The field kitchen was just starting to prepare food. Nobody asked me any questions, and no one was surprised by my presence. I explained to my comrades that I had managed to escape from Metalurgia almost a week ago and had been hiding in abandoned houses since then. I was given a portion of hot soup with potatoes and a large piece of bread.

After many days of forced fasting, the bowl of hot soup gave me strength and made me feel better. I also found out that this entire brigade of camp builders had been given special permission by the Germans to spend the night here after a day's work, not returning—as before—to Metalurgia. I remember that there were still selections and deportations of Jews in special transports every few days, because, according to the Germans, the number of Jews exceeded the planned workforce of 5,000 in the *Zwangsarbeitlager für Juden* (forced labor camp for Jews). A yellow plaque with this inscription had already been prepared by the builders' brigade to be placed at the camp's entrance on the side facing the Warsaw Market Square.

For a few days, I worked with others in the group to put up the barbed wire in the camp. We spent the nights in a house on Nadrzeczna Street. Now, more and more Schupo men as well as Jewish policemen could be seen on the streets of the camp. Members of the Judenrat began looking for somewhere for themselves and their families to live, as well as for a place to set up their offices. Jewish policemen and doctors did the same. They were to live in separate houses, closed off to outsiders. An appropriate building for a hospital was needed, as well as quarters for the management of the Jewish employment office. Life and traffic returned to the streets of the Small Ghetto, foreshadowing the camp's imminent opening and its planned use as living quarters for the assigned Jewish laborers.

One day, the entire camp was surrounded by Ukrainians from the Sonderkommando, armed with rifles. They were placed several dozen meters apart to keep watch, and received orders to shoot anyone trying to illegally escape from the camp area. A guard booth was set up in front of the exit, which was a kind of gate made of movable trestles covered with barbed wire, and a one-story building on Warsaw Market Square, outside the camp fence, was occupied by the Schupo. The *Wachen* (guards) guarding the camp and the German camp commandant's office were to be located here.

In the final days of October 1942, I stood hidden in a nearby gateway at the entrance to the camp and watched with a trembling heart as people from Krótka Street entered. Jewish men and women, led by Jewish policemen, walked slowly in step, looking around anxiously. They advanced in groups, men and women separately. In front of the camp gate, there were a few Schupo men headed by *Wachmeister* Überscher, who had been appointed camp commandant.[6] He was an exceptionally bloody thug

6 Otto Überscher was the commandant of the camp—also known as the Small Ghetto. He took an active part in the deportations of September/October 1942. See Miron and Shulhani, *The Yad Vashem Encyclopedia of the Ghettos*, pp. 141–142.

and had personally shot more than one Jew during the *Aktion*. Now he stood calmly, smiling at the sight of the emaciated remnants of the Częstochowa ghetto—what had once been over 40,000 inhabitants—entering the camp. My heart froze in my chest as the women entered the camp. Would I see Stella, about whose fate I had heard absolutely nothing for a long time?

There was a hubbub all around. Shouts of relief and welcome mingled with weeping, lamenting, and wailing. Some were reuniting after many days or weeks of separation and uncertainty, while others were learning of the loss of their loved ones. The tableau of human tragedy and joy that unfolded before me was heartbreaking. Some fell into each other's arms, kissing and shedding tears of joy; others stood in mute despair with tears of pain and suffering running down their faces.

Finally, I spotted Stella. She was walking slowly, looking around, the tension visible on her pale face. She was looking for me. I shouted her name in joy and ran toward her. She saw me. We fell into each other's arms, both of us crying. The terrible tension erupted in tears. She was mourning her parents, and together we worried about the fate of my brother and hers, about whom we had received no news. We had not yet given up hope of meeting them here, as people from various German outposts would soon be arriving. I knew that all the Jews from Częstochowa who were still alive would be quartered here and escorted out to work each morning.

However, we had to return to our less-than-joyful reality and find a roof over our heads, so I joined Stella to look for a place to live. We were informed that everyone had to find temporary housing until the Council of Elders were able to organize the allocation of apartments. On the street, we met a lawyer friend, Natan Rozensztajn, who had also just found his wife. They told us that they had their eye on a large room at 8 Jaskrowska Street and that we could live there together. We gladly accepted their offer, and the four of us began furnishing our new apartment. The room was large and bright, and was located on the second floor of a well-preserved house. We divided it with a makeshift partition sewn together from several curtains. There were two spacious beds with straw-filled mattresses, enough pillows, a blanket, and a quilt. We shared the bedding and set about tidying up our new abode. I brought dinner from the field kitchen, which consisted of a watery soup with bits of potatoes floating around and some bread. The November night fell quickly, and in the dark—the electricity had not yet been switched on—Stella and I recounted our experiences during those tragic days of forced separation.

Thus began our life in the camp, full of tension, anxiety, and replete with danger. Over the next few days, people from various outposts scattered around the city were brought to the camp. They were grouped together, and each one was placed in a separate house. If there were only a few people in a group, then several outposts were placed together. This was the moment our two long-awaited brothers also returned: my wife's brother Tadzio and my brother Heniek, who had been working for the German company Hagen building a railroad junction in Stradom, a suburb of Częstochowa. There, too, several selections had been carried out by German Schupo, but they had luckily managed to avoid deportation. The joy was completely mutual—they had also been very worried after hearing what havoc the Germans had wreaked on the Jewish population during the ongoing ghetto liquidation campaign. Both our brothers moved in with us. There was a spare room on the first floor with two beds and some bedding. Heniek and Tadzio continued working for Hagen, and every morning, the *Werkschutz* together with one of the German foremen came to collect the workers and took them out to work. At the end of the eight- to ten-hour work day, people from Hagen were escorted back to the camp.

From then on, our material situation improved significantly. Henio and Tadzio, like all other Jewish workers at Hagen, engaged in trading. Of course, this was illegal and severely punished by the Germans, but nobody cared. Life meant more than even the strictest German restrictions. In any case, the *Werkschutz* and the foremen from Hagen were easily bribed, pretending to be both deaf and blind to what was going on. It was not only the Hagen men who engaged in trading but also most of the Jewish workers who worked outside the camp. Although primitive, it was quite lucrative.

The German warehouses on Garibaldi Street stored Jewish property that had been gathered by the Germans, which, after sorting, was shipped to Germany. The warehouse workers stole whatever they could: men's and women's shirts, underpants, briefs, shoes, underwear, even buttons. Returning to the camp after their day's work, they brought these stolen items back with them, hiding them under their outer garments, or even wearing a few pairs of underwear each. Many smuggled large quantities of stolen goods on the carts used to bring food to the camp. In order to sell these stolen items, which often originated from their own homes, they needed intermediaries—people to take the goods out of the camp to find Polish buyers. Under German occupation, the Polish population learned to trade. "Only he who trades stays alive," sang the Polish traders, buying everything that the Jewish workers brought to them.

These commercial transactions were conducted on the street—more precisely, at the gates of houses along the roadside. The Polish merchants knew which streets the Jews took on their way to work. For example, the Jewish workers of Hagen passed through Ogrodowa Street, where the merchants—often regular customers—waited. The *Werkschutz* or foreman turned around, pretending not to see, and the whole outpost stopped for a moment. The merchants and sellers entered the gateways and the goods were quickly brought out, the price negotiated and then paid for in cash. Within a few minutes, the transaction was over. The outpost continued quietly on their way to work, while the Polish traders quickly disappeared with their newly purchased goods. These were dangerous transactions, but everything in those days was risky. There were times when the Germans caught workers from one of the outposts trading with Poles, while at other times, a personal search of the Jewish workers was conducted when leaving the camp. The guilty were beaten mercilessly or, worse, sent to other camps, while the Poles were imprisoned. However, no one cared, and after a few days, the tension eased and trading continued.

With the money they earned as middlemen in this street exchange, our brothers bought foodstuffs in Polish stores—fruit, sausage, meat, and other produce—and sold them in ad hoc market squares within the camp after work. In this way, they made a double profit—by acting as intermediaries selling personal items for others and also by trading in food. They had many "clients" in the camp, since everyone had grown sick of the unsavory camp food. My wife cooked tasty dinners, and we all ate together. Thanks to our brothers—and mainly thanks to Henio, who was a good merchant and organizer of this commercial enterprise—we all enjoyed relatively good food and were less dependent on the meager, sterile food from the camp kitchen. Soon, our health improved considerably, and we regained our strength after the tragic experiences of the past months.

The Germans soon set up a camp labor office to supply workers at the request of German foremen and companies, as well as to ensure that every inhabitant of the camp was engaged in some form of work. This would also expose those who evaded employment. The labor office, or *Arbeitseinsatzkommando*, was directly subordinate to the Judenrat and occupied premises just outside the exit gate, near the German *Wache*. Within a short time, all camp inhabitants were registered, and each was issued a work certificate to present in the event of inspection, which were carried out on the streets at every opportunity, usually by the Jewish police, and played a very important role in the camp. The Jewish police had a separate building for their administrative needs, which also included a prison. The Jewish police station was also located on Kozia Street, and the policemen, together with their families, occupied another house, also on the same street. Woe to anyone who failed to show proof of work. They were arrested and imprisoned until a job was found and a policeman escorted them to the designated post. Later, anyone who was not employed was handed over to the Germans by the Jewish police, and they were then deported either to extermination camps or to camps infamous for their harsh discipline, where people died of hunger and work exhaustion. Among such camps operated by Jewish forced labor were the gunpowder and ammunition factories in Skarżysko-Kamienna and Pionki, as well as the labor camp in Bliżyn.[7]

My wife was assigned to work in the camp sewing workshop, and I went to work in the housing allocation office—the Quartieramt—which was just being set up. The head of this office was a member of the Judenrat, the former principal of the Jewish secondary school in Częstochowa, Dr. Anisfeld, nicknamed Apollo. There was considerable malice in this nickname, as our Apollo was exceptionally ugly. He had a large amaranth-colored nose and, worse, a reddish, swollen face completely covered with pimples and warts. He also spoke through his nose and lisped. He was, however, a man of tremendous knowledge and great honesty, with a reputation for fairness.

Our office had plenty of housing at its disposal to allocate to applicants. In principle, there was no difficulty obtaining apartments, because many were vacant due to German orders to house several people together in one apartment. Thus, several men had to live together, as did the women, and two or even three married couples in a one or two-room apartment. In addition, those working on the larger work sites had to live together, so they could be escorted to work quickly and efficiently by the *Werkschutz*. Under threat of immediate execution, no Jew or group of Jewish workers was permitted outside the camp without being escorted by armed Germans or *Werkschutz*, who were often Ukrainians, Latvians, or Poles in the service of the Germans.

7 See earlier for more on Skarżysko-Kamienna. Pionki was a forced-labor camp in the Radom District, which housed approximately 1,000 prisoners who were forced to work in a munitions factory. See Czesław Pilichowski, *Obozy hitlerowskie na ziemiach polskich 1939–1945: informator encyklopedyczny*, vol. 1 (Warsaw: Państwowe Wydawnictwo Naukowe, 1979), p. 386. In Bliżyn, a forced labor camp for Jews was established on March 8, 1943, holding some 5,000–6,000 prisoners at its peak. It became a subcamp of Majdanek in February 1944. See Dean, *USHMM Encyclopedia of Camps and Ghettos*, vol. 2, part A, p. 201.

I did not have an important position in the Quartieramt; I was merely a sort of janitor or errand boy. I had to stand in front of the door to the room where Apollo worked, letting people in one by one, and only with permission. If there were no visitors, which was usually the case in the morning when people were working outside the camp, I ran around delivering various papers, according to the boss's orders, or I wrote out the housing assignments on special forms supplied to us by the Judenrat. Later, Jeremiasz Gitler, a lawyer, took Anisfeld's place, as Anisfeld—the mathematics and physics teacher—was ill and lay in bed, writing some kind of scientific treatise.

As a result of the Germans' order to assign separate streets to accommodate single women, bachelors, and married couples, the tasks of the camp Quartieramt increased. Resettling all the camp residents entailed a lot of work, and so the staff of the allocation office was significantly expanded. We were joined by Bosek Wołkowicz from Łódź, Abrasza Wilhelm, Roman Sztukl, and Rosenberg. During this period, while Anisfeld was still head of the office, I had little work, and it seemed that the work was fairly safe. I had no contact with the Germans, and this alone made me feel more at ease. However, I soon learned that working inside the camp—also known as the Small Ghetto—carried the risk of being transported either to a death camp or to labor camps designated for the rapid physical extermination of Jewish workers. Fortunately, our camp did not initially fall into this category.

The Schupo men assigned as camp supervisors regarded their positions as especially privileged: Not only did it protect them from being sent to the Russian front or to perform dangerous police work in the occupied Russian territories, where Germans were murdered in huge numbers by partisans, but it also gave them plenty of opportunities to plunder Jewish property. For this reason, they showed particular brutality and ruthlessness in their treatment of Jews and outdid themselves in abusing, beating, and murdering the inhabitants of the Small Ghetto in order to win the favor of their superiors and thus take refuge for as long as possible in this role. Earnings flowed into the pockets of the Schupo men not only from the routine looting of Jewish property stored in the warehouses under their supervision in the houses on Garibaldi Street, but also through their role in supplying the camp with food.

The Jewish workers received no pay for forced labor for the Germans; nevertheless, they still had to be fed. Moreover, the Nazis insisted that the camp be financially self-sufficient. As a result, the various establishments where Jews worked were required to pay an agreed-upon amount per laborer. These sums went straight into the pockets of the German camp administration, including the Schupo and German police. The money was used to purchase food through the Judenrat and to pay electricity and water bills to the city administration's cashier's office. This was how the Schupo men stole considerable sums of money, because instead of providing abundant and nutritious foodstuffs, they bought miserable scraps and the worst-quality and cheapest ingredients. The cooks in the camp kitchen also stole, taking the best and most valuable food for themselves. All of this was done at the expense of the camp's working population, who received food of the lowest possible quality: thin soup made from substitutes and offering no nutritional value, along with a quarter of a day's ration of black bread. The kitchen also served so-called coffee—hot water colored with chicory.

Those inhabitants of the camp who did not have the time, opportunity, or means to trade with the Polish population, or to trade in smuggled food within the camp, were dependent on such food. In addition, many were reluctant to risk engaging in trade, which was severely punished by the Germans. Those who traded and schemed—despite the risks—were well fed, even under camp conditions, while others suffered from hunger, their strength and health deteriorating day by day. The most important German facilities that used Jewish labor included: Luftwaffe—construction of a military airport; Hagen—construction of railroads; HASAG (Hugo Schneider Aktiengesellschaft)—construction of charcoal devices for powering trucks, so called gas-mobiles; HASAG Eisenhütte—ironworks and steelworks; *Möbellager*—furniture warehouses; Schutzpolizei warehouses—storerooms and a sorting office for all movable belongings stolen during the liquidation of the Częstochowa ghetto, where over a dozen houses on Garibaldi Street and Wilson Street were destined to be used; the municipality—waste and sewage disposal of the town; Ostbahn—repair, maintenance, and building of railroad lines; and many other such organizations.

The Germans paid special attention to the Schutzpolizei warehouses, where high-value objects and goods—meticulously collected by the Germans from the twenty-eight streets of the Częstochowa ghetto following the deportation of over 40,000 Jews from the city—were stored. All these material goods were carefully separated and systematically exported to Germany from our city and others. Among them were significant quantities of precious metals, gems, foreign currency, and various collections, such as works of art, antiques, and philatelic items worth billions of dollars. These were stolen from Jews murdered in the gas chambers of German death factories, who, before being deported, were ordered to leave behind all their belongings and enter the execution sites naked.

Not surprisingly, the opportunity to exploit Jews and their property gave rise to a significant number of German draft dodgers from various police forces—such as the Gestapo or Schutzpolizei—who secured long-term employment through this involvement.[8] Also, Germans from other military formations of the SS and SD, as well as civilian members of the NSDAP, were employed in the liquidation of Jews. Any Jew who was still alive became the object of conspiracies and bargaining, at times provoking sharp conflicts between the German civil administration and the secret and uniformed police.

The civil administration, represented in our city by *Stadthauptmann* Dr. Franke,[9] under the directives of the civil administrative authorities of the Radom Governorate and District, pressed for the complete physical annihilation of all Jews. However, the police military formations attached to the Schutzpolizei and the Gestapo, as well as the civilian German economic agents, fought acrimoniously to keep the Jewish labor force alive as long as possible. For this reason, the executioner of our town's Jews, *Hauptmann* Paul Degenhardt, together with his superiors in Radom, sought to keep the rest of the Jews in the labor camp. He had many accomplices in these endeavors, including Dr. Lüth,[10] director of a major ammunition factory being built on the site of the former Pelcery, Warta, and Częstochowianka textile factories—now part of the German armament concern HASAG.[11]

8 Kromołowski brings up important aspects about the Jewish persecuters, such as their personal enrichment and how they sought to find a relatively safe job away from the front line.

9 Dr. Eberhard Franke was the manager of the general administration department in Kraków's Main Division of Internal Affairs and *Stadthauptmann* in Częstochowa (August 1941–March 1943). He persecuted Polish and Jewish civilians, conducted Jewish selections, oversaw the theft of Jewish property, and issued death-penalty orders for those aiding Jews. See records of investigation and documentation of the Main Commission to Investigate Nazi Crimes in Poland, undated, United States Holocaust Memorial Museum (USHMM), RG-15.155M; Młynarczyk, *Judenmord in Zentralpolen*, p. 72.

10 Dr. Ernst Lüth was the commercial director of the HASAG factory from July 1942.

11 As Kromołowski describes, many companies became part of the armament industry, including HASAG, which had four factories in Częstochowa: Pelcery, Warta, Raków, and Częstochowianka. See Witold Medykowski, *Macht Arbeit Frei?: German Economic Policy and Forced Labor of Jews in the General Government*, 1939–1943 (Boston: Academic Studies Press, 2018), p. 290.

Lüth claimed that the Jews were indispensable to him as unpaid labor and, moreover, had a great advantage over other workers: They could perform the health-damaging and dangerous work of making gunpowder and ammunition, because, as forced laborers anyway condemned to death, their lives were considered expendable. Lüth then went on to argue that with this kind of work, the Jewish prisoners would die like flies, but this was precisely one of the German methods of finally resolving the Jewish question, a policy of exterminating the Jews through labor.

It must be understood that Nazi officials like Lüth fought to keep the Jews alive for a certain period of time not out of altruistic motives but for purely selfish reasons. As mentioned before, for them and their helpers, Jewish forced laborers were an excellent means of escape from the Russian front and an inexhaustible source of easy income under the guise of sacrificial and useful work for the *Vaterland* (Fatherland).

Fortunately for us surviving remnants of Polish Jewry, the battle over the fate of the Jews was won—if only briefly—by Germans like Lüth and Degenhardt. After the labor camp was created, a major inspection by General Böttcher himself resulted in the decision to leave no more than 5,000 Jewish men and women alive in the camp. Strict rigor and blind obedience were demanded: Whoever didn't work would be shot or deported to a death camp. The sick and those unfit for work would face the same fate. There was no room in the camp for the elderly, the disabled, or children.

The *Judenarbeitsansatz*, the Jewish labor department headed by Bernard Kurland,[12] had already registered and listed the camp's inhabitants. Square metal badges with numbers were then produced. They had a round hole and a Star of David. Every official camp inhabitant was required to wear this badge affixed to their outer clothing. On December 5, 1942, a total of 2,474 men and 358 women were legally registered and employed at twenty-seven external outposts. There were also some who were legally registered to stay in the camp and work for the camp's institutions.

However, a large number of people stayed in the camp illegally, including children hiding in various camouflaged rooms and bunkers.

12 Bernard Ber Kurland (1898–1943) was a clerk, commercial agent, and sports and social activist in Częstochowa. He used his position to save Jews during selections, support the resistance, and facilitate escapes. Despite his efforts, he was murdered by the Germans at the Jewish cemetery on July 20, 1943, and buried in a mass grave. See Sętkowski, *Częstochowa Jews: A Biographical Dictionary*, pp. 279–281.

At the beginning of April 1943, after many of the bunkers and people in hiding had been discovered by the German and Jewish police, there were officially 4,008 people—2,662 men and 1,346 women—in the camp. In addition, thirty-five children of policemen and doctors were permitted by the German authorities to stay in the camp. In reality, these numbers did not reflect the actual number of people: It was widely known that a significant number of men, women, and children were still in hiding in previously undiscovered or newly constructed bunkers, huts, and dugouts in the camp. The Germans were constantly on the lookout for these bunkers and the people illegally staying there. Those captured by the Germans were killed on the spot or sent to extermination camps. Hunting for Jews took place day and night. The Germans often used trained dogs for this purpose. *Wachmeister* Dzierżon was notorious for having an especially vicious dog that terrorized the Jews it was trained to stalk.

At five o'clock in the morning, a wake-up call was sounded by the camp trumpeter Majtlis in the camp's streets. Every morning, he took out his trumpet and invariably played the same melody, which became very well-known among the camp inhabitants and contained all the sadness and hopelessness of our tragic reality. It still rings in my ears to this day.

At the sound of the wake-up call, the whole camp would rise from their beds and leave their homes. Those who worked outside the camp gathered by the gate of Warsaw Market Square and were escorted by armed guards to their place of work. Those who worked in the camp had to report to their establishments and institutions. Anyone found at home during the day was taken to a German or Jewish police station, where their fate was decided: Many were shot on the spot by the Germans for evading work, while others were imprisoned and received only bread and water. They were then sent to the HASAG ammunitions factory under construction, where people were beaten and tortured, and many were killed by the merciless *Werkschutz*, who were mostly Ukrainians but often also Poles who declared themselves to be *Volksdeutsche*. The head of the *Werkschutz*, or *Werkschutzleiter* at HASAG was a cruel and merciless German executioner, Klemm, who was called Lumer Idel by the workers.[13] Shooting people was an ordinary pastime for him. He walked

13 Hermann Klemm was commander of the industrial guard (*Werkschutzleiter*) from 1942 to spring 1943. See Binyamin Orenstein, "Life in HASAG-Pelcery until November 1944, following the Selection on 24th July 1943," in *The Destruction of Częstochowa* (English translation of the Yiddish *Churban Czenstochow*)

around the factory grounds with a whip or revolver in hand striking or shooting anyone who rested while working, even for a moment. The son of a Polish gymnasium teacher, Kmicikiewicz, was also a terror to the HASAG workers; he shot people with a rifle or beat them with his rifle butt until they bled.

In the initial period, the work at HASAG was an inferno, especially when its workers were stationed there, as not only the *Werkschutz* but also the German foremen beat and killed them. For even the most trifling infraction, a worker was led to the guardhouse, or *Wache*, where they were punished by flogging. They beat both men and women with a rubber pipe on their bare buttocks. The Germans also shot many workers who went to the latrine at night under the pretext that the prisoners were trying to escape. It was not until the end of December 1942, when workers from all the outposts had already been living for a while in the camp, that about 1,000 HASAG workers were also brought in and assigned to several specially designated and guarded houses, and at the beginning of 1943, the HASAG workers took up residence on the camp's grounds.

After the establishment of the forced labor camp, not a single day passed without someone being shot by German bullets. Überscher, the camp commandant, was constantly on the prowl, accompanied by Schupo men, inspecting apartments and checking passersby. Many of those legally residing in the camp were shot without any justification; those who did not go to work were shot on the spot, as were those who were caught hiding in attics or cellars on the Aryan side. There were constant selections. Each morning, when the workers left for work, the Schupo men picked out the elderly, disabled, or those who appeared unwell from among the Jews in the camp, deeming them unfit for labor. These people were sent to death camps and never heard from again. *Aktionen* were also carried out against children. They were caught in various hiding places and bunkers and were either sent to extermination camps or killed on the spot. *Aktionen* of this kind began to intensify and took on a wider scope in 1943, when the German army's early victories on the Russian front gradually turned into a string of defeats. After the German offensive was

(Central Administration of the Częstochower Landsmannschaft in the American Zone in Germany, 1948), pp. 263–269, https://www.czestochowajews.org/wp-content/uploads/Churban-Orenstein-Life-until-November-1944-263-269.pdf (accessed October 27, 2025).

repulsed at Stalingrad, the fury of the Germans became more focused on the Jewish prisoners.[14]

On January 4, 1943, a cold winter day, our camp was surrounded on all sides by Schupo men, armed to the teeth and wearing combat helmets, together with Ukrainian fascists and the Polish police. A special unit of German police entered the camp. Anyone inside the camp at that time was driven out to Warsaw Market Square. Everyone—men and women—was ordered to line up in double rows. The Schupo and Jewish police entered houses, apartments, basements, and attics. Illegal camp inhabitants who were hidden away in the bunkers—women with children, the old and the sick—were forced to the assembly point. The Germans discovered a bunker in a house at 88 Nadrzeczna Street, where young resistance fighters who were part of the Zionist movement Kibbutz[15] were hiding.

Among them was Mendel Fiszlewicz, an escapee from Treblinka who, in the course of his escape, ended up in the Częstochowa camp. Here, along with the resistance movement, he decided to fight the Germans and seek vengeance for what he had seen and experienced during his time as one of the few selected for work in the death camp. Fiszlewicz witnessed the unbelievable slaughter committed against the innocent Jewish population by the Germans. In Treblinka, he saw how the Polish Jews, deported there by train, were stripped naked and thrown into the gas chambers, dying there in agony. The corpses of the murdered were doused with gasoline and burned. Then, the charred corpses were buried in mass graves dug by bulldozers.

Mendel Fiszlewicz led the young fighters and was determined to fight for his life and not allow himself to be murdered by the Germans without resistance. Among the fighters was Izydor Fajner (Faja) and several young girls, among them Jadzia Mas, who had been active in the underground movement for a long time. After being discovered, all the young fighters, along with others found hiding in bunkers or those deemed unfit for labor, were sent to the German guardhouse and locked in a room on the first floor.

14 Kromołowski refers to the first defeat of the Germans, marked by the Battle of Stalingrad (July 17, 1942–February 2, 1943), a pivotal Soviet victory during World War II that halted the German advance and marked a turning point in the war.

15 The Kibbutz group consisted mainly of Hechalutz members, initially led by Rywka Glanc, Yehuda Gliksztajn, and the *shomer* (member of Hashomer Hatzair) Avraham Zilbersztajn. See "The Resistance Movement in the Small Ghetto," in Brener, "Resistance and Destruction in the Częstochowa Ghetto," p. 115.

I found myself in a group with my Judenrat office colleagues. We stood in even ranks, facing the German guardhouse. Schutzpolizei Lieutenant Rhon was standing in front of the building, conducting the selection. Überscher, the camp commander, had banished us from our office to the assembly point. I was very nervous. Because everything had happened so quickly and unexpectedly, there was no time to escape and find a safe hiding place. I was angry with myself: I had allowed myself to get caught by a German and to be led to a selection, which, from experience, usually ended in disaster for me. Behind the people lined up in long rows were several young boys, including our messenger boy, Marianek Faktor. Marianek was a very sensible thirteen-year-old, and he realized that the selection could end badly for him, as the Germans had sentenced all children to death. The selection had already begun. Rhon walked through the ranks of frightened men and women, pulling out those who, in his opinion, were unfit for labor or whose appearance he simply did not like.

His cold, penetrating stare then turned to me. A movement of his hand, with his fingers pointed at me, meant that I was to step out of line. The next moment, Rhon told me to go to the guardhouse. Now it's over, I thought. I'm doomed. I climbed the stairs to the first floor, where there was already a large group of men, women, and children in two spacious rooms. People were in despair. They were crying, wringing their hands, and lamenting their fate. Any moment now, trucks were to arrive to take us to Radomsko—the assembly point for Jews headed for Treblinka extermination camp. In various towns of the Radom District, liquidation *Aktionen* of the Jewish population were still taking place. From our camp, the Germans used this opportunity to deport those unsuitable for work or those caught breaking camp rules to their deaths.

Deep inside the room, a group of the Zionist Kibbutzniks stood by the window. Among them was a tall, young, but gray-haired man calmly explaining something to the others. This was Mendel Fiszlewicz, their leader. I stood alone and forlorn. I didn't recognize anyone around me, nor did I know what to do in this unexpected, desperate situation. But I was not broken or resigned. All I could think about was how to save myself from deportation, which meant certain death.

Then, Polish policemen entered the guardhouse and, with the help of their rifle butts, pushed the resisting people onto the stairs. There was panic and wailing. Along with the others, I went out to the staircase without resisting. Someone pushed me forward, and the brightness of the day blinded me for a moment. I was in Warsaw Market Square. A few steps ahead of me stood Rhon, talking with a Jewish policeman. On the right side of Warszawska Street, trucks covered with tarpaulins were parked, and Schupo and Jewish policemen were pushing people onto them.

Suddenly, I made up my mind. I walked boldly up to Rhon and, in a loud voice and in my poor, broken German, said that I was an employee of the quartermaster's office and had with me, in writing, the entire plan for relocating the population of the camp, drawn up in accordance with *Hauptmann* Degenhardt's last order. From my jacket pocket, I took out a bundle of papers that I happened to have with me. I showed them to him and explained which streets were assigned to single men, which to single women, and which to married couples. I said I was an expert, explaining that the quick and efficient execution of the *Aktion* depended on these documents. Rhon listened to me without interrupting. Then, he turned to the policeman, Rozenberg, standing next to him and asked him if it was true, to which Rozenberg replied in the affirmative. Rhon nodded and said, "*Also weg in die Arbeit*" (So, go to work).

I quickly moved away and joined the ranks of the still-standing crowd. Meanwhile, the unfortunate victims of today's selection continued to come down the street from the guardhouse. They were loaded onto the waiting trucks, which were standing in a row. I had not yet properly calmed down after my recent encounter, and I stood dumbfounded among the crowd. Now, one by one, the fighters from Kibbutz were exiting the guardhouse. Fiszlewicz was the first to leave, followed by Fajner. However, instead of obediently entering the waiting trucks, Fiszlewicz suddenly ran forward and took out a revolver from his pocket. When he reached the Schupo lieutenant Zoppart, a no-longer-young German standing in the square, Fiszlewicz aimed the revolver at him and kept pulling the trigger, but the revolver did not fire. Instead, Fiszlewicz struck the German's hand with the butt of his revolver. Using his other hand, Zoppart drew his revolver from the holster and shot Fiszlewicz in the head. He fell to the ground, covered with blood.

Meanwhile, Fajner ran toward Warszawska Street, trying to get out of the square and as far away from the Germans as possible. One of the Schupo soldiers grabbed the rifle from his shoulder and fired several shots at Fajner. One of the bullets hit him. Fajner stumbled, ran a few more steps, and then fell to the ground. For a moment, the Germans just stood there stunned, surprised by this sudden attack, but they quickly came to their senses. With their rifle butts, they drove the people intended for transport forward, including the girls from the Kibbutz, and pushed them onto the trucks, which started up quickly and, after a moment, disappeared around a bend.

Now Rhon, who was in charge of the *Aktion*, was giving orders. The Schupos pointed the barrels of their rifles at the crowd. Everyone was told to put their hands up and stand back. They held us in check with their fingers on the triggers of their rifles. After a while, two cars filled with Schupo men arrived, under the command of Frankowski, an SS and police lieutenant known for his cruelty. The Schupos surrounded us from all sides, their rifles still aimed at us. We stood motionless with our hands raised. Members of the Judenrat, headed by Leon Kopiński, were summoned. The Schupos, led by Frankowski, ordered everyone to pass by them one by one. I retreated as far as possible, heading in the opposite direction. Frankowski was counting the people passing before him. He pulled aside every tenth one. The crowd was swaying restlessly. I managed to get under the wall of a two-story house bordering the market square and pressed myself against the wall of this house.

In the meantime, Frankowski and his Schupo men had finished their counting, and his assistants surrounded the twenty-five men selected from the crowd and led them away. Among this group, I noticed several elderly people. For the execution site, the Germans chose a square inside the camp, adjacent to one of the houses. I knew many of those selected personally. Among them was Maurycy Rodał, a confectioner, and Natan Rozensztajn, with whom we had lived together for some time on Jaskrowska Street. I also saw young Sielcer. He rushed to escape but was caught and brought to the execution site. One of the Judenrat members, a policeman named Maurycy Galster, was also led away. Frankowski ordered him to be shot as well. There was panic among the Judenrat. Kopiński intervened and spoke to Rhon, and Galster was released.

The firing squad was lined up. The lawyer Rozensztajn did not want to stand up. He knelt before Frankowski, hugging his knees and asking that his life be spared. Frankowski took out his revolver and shot Rozensztajn a number of times in the head. *Feuer* (Fire)!

Then the cry of one of the condemned: "Esti, I love you so much!" Shots rang out. Twenty-five bloodied corpses fell against the wall.[16] Afterward, we were ordered to enter the camp. Sadness and mourning

16 For another account of the *Aktion* on January 4, 1943, see Jerzy Einhorn, *The Maple Tree Behind the Barbed Wire: A Story of Survival from the Częstochowa Ghetto*, tr. Joan Tate (New York: JewishGen, 1996), pp. 155–156. See also Wiesław Paszkowski "The Jewish Fighting Organisation (ŻOB) Monument," The World Society of Częstochowa Jews and their Descendents, https://www.czestochowajews.org/czestochowa-today/czestochowa-jewish-cemetery/jewish-fighting-organisation/.

overwhelmed us. People returning to the camp after work listened with horror to the stories about this tragic day. My wife, who at that time was employed outside the camp in the warehouses on Garibaldi Street, had been at work that day. I told her about my experience and how close I had come to death. I felt sick; chills shook my entire body. I think I had a high fever. I went to bed, barely alive from exhaustion, and eventually fell asleep. I dreamed that a rifleman was smashing my head with his rifle butt.

On the evening of that tragic day, our camp commandant, *Wachmeister* Überscher, was invited to the Judenrat for refreshments to celebrate the wedding anniversary of the chairman of the Judenrat. All members of the Judenrat were present, including Galster, who had barely escaped death and had drunk himself into a stupor. Only Apollo, our former quartermaster, did not show up, hiding behind his illness.

The first attempt at resistance against the Germans in our camp had failed, resulting in the heroic death of the young fighters Fiszlewicz and Fajner, who fell in battle with the Nazis, killed in defense of life and honor. As a result of this, twenty-five innocent Jews were shot before the eyes of their fellow camp inmates. Over 300 Jews—men and women of various ages, including several children—were taken by the Germans to Radomsko and then to Treblinka. One of the young members of the fighting group, Jadzia Mas, committed suicide by hanging herself in a barrack in Radomsko.

This first incident of armed resistance heightened the vigilance of the Germans, who were convinced that there was an underground movement in the camp. This, in turn, led to the tightening of the camp's regime. Increasingly frequent searches were conducted among people returning from work to the camp. They searched for weapons and ammunition, as well as smuggled food. Executions also took place more frequently. A mentally disabled woman named Cymermanowa and her daughter, a young girl who was taking care of her sick mother, were captured. Both were executed in the area of the camp. Several tuberculosis patients, taken from the camp hospital, were also shot.

The increasing tyranny was the harbinger of the approaching end of the camp, and ultimately the physical liquidation of the rest of the Jewish population. This led many to attempt escape to the Aryan side or to elsewhere. Whoever had Polish friends or acquaintances established contact by various means and tried to organize their escape. This was very difficult and was extremely dangerous for both sides. Few Poles, even best friends, were willing to risk their lives to save Jews. However, there were some brave people who agreed to hide Jewish families or groups of Jews, either for ideological reasons, large material gains, or both. Of course, this required a lot of money and was only available to very wealthy people. Sophisticated bunkers were built, mostly in private homes located in deserted or rarely frequented neighborhoods, and they were mainly underground with well-camouflaged entrances.

Many Jews were lucky enough to survive the war hidden among Poles. I knew a dozen or so such people who lived for several months in these well-camouflaged hiding places. The entrance to one of them was through a dog kennel in which the owner kept an evil dog. Unsurprisingly, the Jews needed money to pay for this, and many found it by working in managerial positions in the Schupo's warehouses on Garibaldi Street. There, they would scrupulously search through the accumulated clothing or bedding, sometimes finding jewelry or foreign currency sewn into them, which allowed them to finance their escape and their stay in a bunker. One day, they would disappear from the camp, and all traces of them would be lost.

There were some noble Poles who rescued their Jewish friends selflessly, hiding them in their homes, and when it became dangerous, they looked for a hiding place for them with relatives or friends. I knew a Polish family in the working-class suburb of Raków who hid a Jewish family of three people, one of whom was a converted Jew and the son-in-law of the houseowner. This Jewish family survived the Holocaust.

Wróblewski,[17] the parish priest of the Holy Family parish, was known for his nobility. He saved many Jewish children, mostly girls, by placing them in Catholic orphanages or shelters for homeless children. If a Pole was caught hiding Jews, they were shot by the Germans along with those in hiding or sent to concentration camps. Stanisław Krakowiak of Raków, near Częstochowa, was sent to Auschwitz for hiding his Jewish wife and her brother, who had escaped from our camp. The Germans shot Krakowiak's wife and her brother, and sent her two young sons to a Catholic orphanage. Stanisław Krakowiak survived and was reunited with his sons after the war.

At the same time, many Poles handed over hiding Jews to the Germans or found a source of income from blackmailing Jews: They extracted all their money before denouncing them.[18] A well-known merchant from Częstochowa was hiding his Jewish acquaintance Abram Kaplan. After

17 Rev. Bolesław Wróblewski (1867–1951) was recognized by Yad Vashem as Righteous Among the Nations on June 18, 2024, for rescuing Miriam Rothschild (née Rubin), born in 1942. See Righteous Among the Nations Database, YVA, M.31.2/14052.

18 Jews faced constant danger from informants. Fear of denunciation discouraged Jews from seeking help and deterred compassionate Poles from offering assistance.

having extracted a large amount of foreign currency and jewelry from him, the host murdered Kaplan and looted the rest of his jewelry. He then buried the corpse of the murdered Jew. The murder was not known about until after the war. The culprit was sentenced to a long prison term; however, he was released a few years later as a result of an amnesty.[19]

In February 1943, a new misfortune befell our camp. The Germans began deporting people to Skarżysko-Kamienna, where there was an ammunition factory, and next to it a forced labor camp for Jews, which was a veritable extermination camp.[20] The Jewish workers there—poorly fed and manufacturing gunpowder under conditions of ruthless discipline—died in huge numbers from picric acid poisoning. The Germans mercilessly murdered those weakened and yellowed by picric acid, especially at the factory Werk C. A Jewish prisoner could survive only a few months there. The commandant of this *Lager* was Battenschläger, a German known for his cruelty.

One day, our camp was again surrounded by Schupo men and Ukrainians. This *Aktion* also involved Polish and Jewish policemen under the command of police officer Majznerowicz, who had accepted the *Volkslist* and joined the Nazi cause. At the very beginning of this *Aktion*, the Schupo men burst into our office and drove everyone out, including myself, to the guardhouse. This *Aktion* was clearly directed against people working in the camp's institutions and primarily included white-collar workers from among the professional intelligentsia. The Germans gathered about 200 mostly young people there and announced that all of us were being sent to the Skarżysko-Kamienna camp to work in ammunition production. The Jewish intelligentsia was apparently of no use to the Germans, and it seemed that the aim of this *Aktion* was to liquidate the remnants of the Jewish intelligentsia—first those with academic qualifications.

I was acquainted with some people imprisoned in the Skarżysko-Kamienna camp: Roman Sztukle, a lawyer; Lajb Fogel, a trainee lawyer, and his brother Abram; the Bocian brothers, journalists, and the sons of the publisher of the Yiddish-language newspaper *Chenstochower Tageblat*, who was well-known in our town; Hammerman, also a lawyer; Adolf Mokrauer, an accountant; and many others whom I did not know personally,

19 On this case, see Jarosław Kapsa, *Częstochowa: Inne opowieści* (Częstochowa: Częstochowskie Stowarzyszenie REGION, 2008), pp. 90–92. Some of the details differ.

20 According to Karay, HASAG transferred groups of workers from its plants in Częstochowa and Kielce to the Skarżysko factories in spring 1943. See Karay, *Death Comes in Yellow*, p. 49.

but who, according to my colleagues, had received higher education. As night fell, we sat on the floor, waiting resignedly for daybreak, when the Germans would load us onto trucks and escort us to Skarżysko.

I was lucky again this time, but my rescue came unexpectedly from the least likely source. I owed it neither to my own ingenuity nor courage, for I was completely depressed and did not expect to escape this hopeless situation. To my great surprise, in the morning, my name was suddenly called, and I was instructed to go to the exit door in the second room. Helenka Tenenbaum, my distant relative, was standing there. She handed me bread and cigarettes, and told me not to be afraid because I was going to be released and would return to the camp.

Helenka was employed as a housekeeper by Paul Degenhardt. As I have already mentioned often, he was the camp supervisor and the one who carried out almost all the selections and personally directed the deportation of the Jewish population of our town to the extermination camps. He was a ruthless murderer and executioner, who was responsible for the deaths of Częstochowa's Jews. During a selection in which he sent both her parents to Treblinka, Helenka was chosen to clean the German police offices, where several Jewish girls were employed. He then ordered her to be his housekeeper. Helenka was a beautiful young woman with an unusually captivating appearance. She had long blonde hair that she wore around her head like a crown, she was tall, and she had a shapely figure and the gait of a queen. She had light blue eyes, framed by long lashes, and small, voluptuous lips. Some malicious people whispered that she was Degenhardt's mistress, but she firmly denied these rumors.

Due to her position, she enjoyed a great deal of personal freedom: She had her own bicycle, which she used to ride around town—with neither a Jewish armband nor an escort. Every evening, she returned to the camp on her bicycle and spent the night in a single-room apartment on Kozia Street, where single women lived. Everyone in our camp knew of—and recounted—many kind and helpful actions she undertook for those in need, whether to save lives or to bring some relief and comfort by mitigating the harsh discipline through her interventions with Degenhardt. Even the Judenrat turned to Helenka for help in situations dangerous to the camp. She never refused anyone. She was called the Queen Esther of our camp and was compared to the biblical Esther, the slayer of Haman at the time of the Persian King Xerxes.

Soon after Helenka's visit to the guardhouse and the conversation that took place in the presence of *Wachmeister* Überscher, Degenhardt arrived, surrounded by several members of the Judenrat headed by its chairman,

Kopiński. Hammerman and I were released, whereas the rest were loaded onto trucks and taken to a camp near the ammunition factory in Skarżysko-Kamienna. Although Helenka also tried to secure the release of a few more people—including both Fogl and Bocian—her efforts were unfortunately unsuccessful.

Almost all of those taken to Skarżysko suffered a martyr's death there. After some time, news reached us that Lajb Fogel had been shot by a *Werkschutz* for trying to resist. I did not see anyone else from among my friends and colleagues deported as a result of this action. The fact that I survived that terrible ordeal is thanks to my wife, Stella, who, in tears, pleaded with Helenka to intervene on my behalf with Degenhardt. Stella was Helenka's schoolmate; they had been in the same class in the Jewish gymnasium.

As a result of these frequent deportations, the camp population decreased steadily—particularly the number of children, both legal and illegal inhabitants. The total number of children was estimated at between 100 and 120. One day, Degenhardt accidentally discovered where the children were being fed, and where they were living and playing under the care of volunteer caregivers. After this event, we all expected the worst possible restrictions and persecutions; but to everyone's astonishment, Degenhardt legalized this hitherto illegal and secret dayroom, which was located in a house occupied by physicians and their families. He even ordered a special food supply for these children, especially rations of milk and butter. There were those who were horrified by Degenhardt's unusual generosity, seeing it as a harbinger of further tragic events. Unfortunately, it turned out that those pessimists were right.

Some time after the dramatic transport to Skarżysko, another deportation took place, this time to the camp in Bliżyn, which was no less a horrific site of execution of the Jewish population. To our great horror, the Germans captured Tadzio, my wife's sixteen-year-old brother, as well as Jakub Mas, a man worn out by life and the father of Benclowiczowa, who lived with us in a shared apartment on Garncarska Street. We had been living there together—three couples in a room with a kitchen—since the resettlement plan that I mentioned earlier had been carried out.

All of those captured for this deportation—about 200 people—had already been taken from the camp area and placed in the custody of the Polish police on Piłsudskiego Street to await deportation. There was little time for rescue. I could only expect such help from Helenka Tenenbaum, as only she could ask Degenhardt to release my young brother-in-law. Mas's daughter also begged me to ask Helenka to save her father from deportation. He was a sick man and going to Bliżyn would inevitably kill him. I immediately went to Helenka's apartment on Kozia Street to ask her for help. To my surprise, she was very understanding and concerned about the fate of our Tadzio, promising to immediately appeal to Degenhardt for his release. If she succeeded, she said that she would also ask for the release of old Mas from the transport.

Thanks to Helena Tenenbaum's intercession, Tadzio Szmulewicz and Jakub Mas were excluded from the transport to Bliżyn almost at the last moment. Once again, she saved the lives of two people and truly deserved the title of the Queen Esther of the ghetto. Mas had been a wealthy man before the war—he was the owner of a bicycle-parts factory as well as a warehouse selling bicycles and toys on 7 First Avenue. When they both returned to our camp, Benclowiczowa, Mas's daughter, came to thank me and asked me to give Helenka a beautiful gold bracelet as a token of their immense gratitude. I immediately went to Helenka with this gift and handed her the precious jewelry; however, she categorically refused to accept it. Helenka said that she did not trade in human lives, and that if she managed to do something to alleviate the Jews' tragic fate, she derived moral satisfaction from it and did not want any reward. I returned the gold bracelet to Mas's daughter and repeated Helenka's words to her.

Learning from my painful experience, I decided to give up my work in the lodging department, and, more broadly, my work in the camp's institutions, whose workers were the first to fall victim to German persecution, deportations, and the tragic selections. For a long time, my brother had been working for the German company Hagen constructing railroad tracks, and he suggested that I try to find work there. The senior worker, or *Vorarbeiter*, was a man named Hase. He readily agreed to take me on and promised to get me a job from the German foreman, Szymanski, that wouldn't require too much physical effort. I thus started working at Hagen, which took me away from the camp and its many dangers for the entire day, returning only at dusk.

We left the camp early each morning. It was still dark as it was the cold season. We passed through the city under the watchful eye of the *Werkschutz*, heading toward the western suburb of Stradom. There was a railroad station bearing the same name, and our task was to build new railroad tracks under the direction of German engineers. Sometimes, when necessary, we had to unload wagons of sand and gravel needed for this construction. Hagen did not provide any meals for us, but we were given a lunch break; whoever had brought some food could eat it then. One could also, without fear, buy bread and a piece of sausage in one of the Polish stores located in the neighboring Piastowska and Stradomska Streets.

There was neither punishment nor persecution in this camp, as it was a civilian company, and we worked unsupervised. Each week, Hase collected money to bribe the foreman, who usually sat in the office, so that when he did supervise our work, he watched only superficially. Hase, on the other hand, made sure that the day's work was done, and that the right amount of track was properly laid. Sand and gravel had to be poured; sleepers and heavy rails were put in place and then bolted down. The work was quite difficult and required a good deal of physical exertion; however, it was done in a peaceful atmosphere and offered the opportunity to trade with Polish merchants on the way to work.

After a few days, Hase offered me an "extra *fein*"—as he said—position as a track switcher on the narrow-gauge railroad. Various materials, rails, sleepers, bolts, sand, and gravel were brought from the depot for the railroad work via the narrow-gauge railroad, which ran in both directions on a single track. It consisted of a locomotive and a dozen or so trolleys. The trains traveled one way full of materials and returned empty to take the next load. At a certain point, about halfway along the route, there was a passing loop—a sizable iron disc with a pair of parallel rails and a crank equipped with a system of gears.

When a train carrying materials was moving on one track and an empty train was coming from the opposite direction, the crossing barrier had to be quickly closed. Then, one had to run to the switch—the handle—turn the crank, and open the crossing. Only then could the trains pass each other without colliding. Next, one had to rush to the barrier and open it to allow the train heading into the depot to pick up a new supply of building materials to pass, before closing the crossing. This operation had to be repeated each time a new pair of trains appeared, announcing their approach with the sound of special horns. The locomotives were small and usually driven by German drivers, or *Lokführers*. Although the work was not too hard, it required constant attention, quick orientation, and was performed outdoors. In winter, the cold, snow, and wind were a nuisance; there was nowhere to hide from them. I was not especially happy with this job, but it was less physically taxing than the daily gritting of tracks, carrying sleepers and rails, or emptying the wagons of sand and gravel.

During my third week as a *Weichenwechsler* (track switcher), on a cold February day, I stood at my usual observation post under the fence, protecting myself from the gusty wind. Fine snow was falling, and visibility was not good. As usual, I was on the lookout for the arrival of the trains, which passed each other about every fifteen minutes. I saw them. The one traveling on the warehouse side was filled to the brim with materials; however, the other one on the opposite side was going a little faster, as its wagons had already been unloaded at the worksite. I ran quickly to close the barrier to thus stop possible pedestrian and vehicle traffic on Stradomska Street, and then I rushed over to the switch to turn the crank to open the passing loop to enable both oncoming locomotives—coming from opposite directions, each pulling a dozen or so trolleys—to pass.

Usually, a single strong, decisive movement of the hand was enough to turn the switch crank, but now I suddenly found that it wouldn't move—it couldn't be turned. I pulled with all my might, using both hands; but, to my horror, I saw that it was not working. I shouted and tried to signal to the drivers that they were in danger. I shouted "*Halt! Halt!*" at the top of my lungs, waving my arms like a madman. But nothing: Either it was the wind whistling or the clatter of the wheels that drowned out my shouts. In any case, the drivers did not notice my warning signals. Suddenly, the two locomotives collided with a great bang and a clatter. I noticed that moments before the collision, both drivers had managed to jump from the trains. The two railroad cars, together with the wagons and the materials—beams, rods, and rails—formed a disorderly, jumbled mass. The wheels of the locomotives continued to turn for a few moments, and then everything stood still. I was terrified. The Germans would think I had derailed the trains on purpose, that I had committed sabotage. Much lesser offenses had been punished by death, and here, two trains with building materials were lying derailed and twisted.

At first, the two engine drivers were as horrified as I was by the accident and watched the destruction. Then, one of them, a tall thug, caught up with me, picked up a stick from the ground, and started beating me all over. I fell to the ground, semi-conscious, silently saying goodbye to life. The second driver then snatched the stick from my tormentor's hand, and they were both shouting at each other. I got up from the ground and started to explain in my broken German that the switch did not work and that it must be broken. After a while, the engineer Franke—a tall, bulky German—arrived. He approached the switch, examining it carefully, and tried to move the crank. It wouldn't budge, even when the German pushed it forcefully and vigorously.

Franke ordered them to leave me alone and went to make a phone call. After a while, two Germans arrived, one of whom was a maintenance man for mechanical equipment. I knew him, because every now and then he came to check the mechanisms and oil the switch. They started examining and disassembling the switching gear. It turned out that due to wear and tear and the frost, some parts of the steering mechanism had broken. This caused the failure, which resulted in the crank becoming immobilized and the entire mechanism ceasing to function. The technical supervision was to blame. Meanwhile, our brigade arrived and stopped in horror, staring at the tangled mass of iron and derailed locomotives—and at me, standing helplessly, waiting for the verdict. Franke nodded at me and told me to go. In an instant, I was among our men and smiled at my brother, who was horrified at what had just happened.

Hase gave the signal to march out, and we walked briskly toward the camp. That was the end of my career as a track switcher for Hagen, whose technical management, it must be said, treated me humanely and fairly. Three days later, for a 50-złoty bribe that I gave to the *Vorarbeiter* in the quality control department, I was included among the ranks of workers at the notorious HASAG Apparatebau factory.

Over 1,000 people—men and women—left our labor camp every day for HASAG, which was located on the other side of the city, on 1-go Maja Street (May 1 Street), near the Stradom suburb. Some worked in the production of charcoal-powered apparatus for trucks. This was a German invention designed to save expensive gasoline. There was also an active plant for the reconditioning of shell casings—the *Rekalibrierung*. A large portion of the crew worked on constructing the ammunition factory and assembling automatic machines for manufacturing rifle bullets.

I worked in the *Prüferei* (inspection station), which tested the airtightness of the apparatus used to propel devices (*herd*) with compressed air. When such a device was leaking, the air would blow a soap bubble at the site of the hole. The soapy liquid had to be applied with a brush to the surface of the metal wheel before compressed air was pumped in. If any holes were found, the leaks were marked with chalk and the part welded again. It was checked repeatedly until it was completely leak-proof and deemed fit for use, and the word "*Gut*" (OK) was written on it in chalk. The cylinder was then taken away for further assembly.

Although the work was light and did not require much physical effort, one had to be careful not to get struck in the face by the foreman. One also had to avoid being sent to the *Werkschutz* guardroom, where corporal punishment was administered by whipping the victims on their bare buttocks, often until they lost consciousness. This happened when the foreman—or, even worse, the *Betriebsleiter* (factory manager)—checked the quality of our work. They would take the finished product with the word "*Gut*" written on them back to the testing table, lubricate them with soap, and let compressed air in. If some bubbles popped out, it meant that the job had not been done correctly, and they were slapped in the face and subjected to other punishments, after which the delinquent would return half-dead and covered in bruises on their burning, aching buttocks—an injury referred to as a map—which made it impossible to sit for quite some time.

The foreman at *Prüferei* was a German named Walter, a heavy-handed and brutal torturer with fists like loaves of bread. Each time he appeared in the factory hall, he beat and kicked people who, in his opinion, were not working diligently. No less dangerous were the production manager, engineer Spaltenholtz, otherwise known as "Pale Joseph," and the technical director Dr. Bretschneider. The *Werkschutz* were constantly roaming around the factory, and the less active workers were not spared their blows either. There was the previously mentioned *Werkschutz* supervisor, Klemm, the bloody executioner and torturer of Jews, and the political director, engineer Walter Fasold, who was dubbed "Boxer," as he would knock the toughest man off his feet with a single punch to the face.

There was a set piecework quota, and we were required to check a certain number of apparatus, so the work was done quickly and, as they say, with a lick and a promise. We would write "*Gut*" in chalk, make sure the parts were taken away as quickly as possible for assembly, and then we would take a nap. This was large-scale sabotage, carried out by all the Jewish workers, who performed their tasks with the least possible effort. There was always someone looking out for any approaching Germans. When this happened, the password "*zecks*" was uttered, which, in our secret language, meant imminent danger. Then the work burned in our hands, and everyone worked diligently so that, once the German was gone, we could return to resting and napping.

HASAG created an illusion of safety. It was widely believed that the Jewish workers there were truly needed by the military industry, and therefore the factory management would protect them from transports to the extermination camps. Also, as many Poles worked at HASAG, we could cash in some valuable items and buy food or even medicines through them. The Polish workers also acted as intermediaries, sending letters and messages or contacting Polish acquaintances who were often safeguarding Jewish money or valuables. The Polish workers at HASAG often acted as go-betweens, delivering items on the basis of a written authorization. Simply put, they did not do this for free: They had to be paid well for each step, for each item, for each piece of food, but they usually fulfilled their obligations reliably. These activities were risky and dangerous because any contact with Jews was forbidden and severely punished.

As I have already mentioned, the work at HASAG was extremely rigorous, and we were constantly exposed to danger, but no less dangerous were the *Werkschutz* during the march back to the camp after a day's work. Sometimes roll call lasted for hours in the factory yard, during which the workers were counted and punished for alleged offenses against discipline. The *Werkschutz* and their leader Lumer Idel ran around pulling people out of the ranks, beating them, kicking them, or leading them to the guardhouse where they were flogged. When we finally left the factory hungry and exhausted, we dragged ourselves through the streets, the wooden soles of our clogs tapping along the ground, unsure what surprises would be awaiting us at the entrance to the camp: selection, deportation, or, at the very least, a thorough search by the camp's Schupo unit.

One day—it was March 20, 1943, and the Jewish holiday of Purim—I had just returned from HASAG and was exhausted. Perhaps I had fever, because I could barely drag myself through the camp streets. All I wanted was to go to bed, fall asleep, and forget the tragic present and the hopeless tomorrow.

For a while, the Judenrat—on Degenhardt's orders—had been registering Jews with relatives in Mandatory Palestine. There were constant rumors that opportunities were opening to join relatives living there. Almost everyone wanted to register. Those who had no relatives in Mandatory Palestine submitted made-up names and addresses. There was talk of exchanging Jews for German citizens interned in the Middle East by the British and French. Many clung to this idea of going to Mandatory Palestine. The reliability of the registration was demonstrated by the fact that it was carried out on forms sent by the Germans, which contained many fields, including the name, degree of relationship, and address of the relative. If one had several relatives, they all had to be listed on the registration form. The Judenrat opened a veritable registration office where several people worked. The influx of registrants was enormous, and the whole affair thus had the appearance of authenticity.[21]

21 Such a psychological ruse also helped the Germans entice the Jews in hiding to come out of the bunkers and face the imminent *Aktion*. These forms were also designed to expose those with undesirable occupations or education, as seen in the persecution of the intelligentsia that followed. See Kiel, *The Jews of Częstochowa*, pp. 154–156.

I personally did not believe it to be true. I had seen many times how the Germans lied, cheated, and used the most despicable tricks to trap and murder Jews. Escapees from Treblinka related that the Germans ordered people to strip naked, telling them that a warm bath awaited them. In fact, the alleged baths were gas chambers, and nobody ever came out of this macabre bath alive. The Germans lied that the Jews being transported by trains would be sent to work camps or to autonomous Jewish republics, where they would be taught productive work. In reality, however, immediately after the arrival of each train, a merciless mass execution took place. These were perfidious German lies meant to suppress resistance and convince people of the promised work—especially since these assurances came from German police officers like Degenhardt, a captain of the SS and police, and thus an official responsible for his words. This was psychological propaganda, which led to the distressing fact that people were going to their deaths like sheep to the slaughter. When we entered the camp that day—March 20, 1943—with our HASAG outpost, we were struck by a strange silence. We could not see the Schupo who usually stood in front of the gate conducting random personal searches. The camp streets were deserted.

At the entrance to the house on Garncarska Street where my wife and I lived, I met Jakub Horowicz and his wife Franka Fiszpam coming out of the gate. Jakub—also a lawyer and a good friend of mine—was carrying a stuffed rucksack on his back. His wife was also laden with a similar bundle. Surprised, I asked them where they were moving to, thinking they were moving to a different building. Instead, I was astonished to hear that, by order of the police, anyone with academic diplomas and independent professionals had to appear immediately at the Warsaw Market Square together with their families. From there, they would be taken to the railroad station to board an international train bound for the port, before sailing to Mandatory Palestine. Jakub and his wife were thus going to the assembly point. He was serious about it, and I even saw a glint of joy in his eyes. His wife, too, expressed her happiness that they would finally be free. The Germans, they said, want to send people with higher education first. Then it would be the turn of others who had registered to go to Mandatory Palestine.

I wrung my hands in despair and tried to convince them that the Germans could not be trusted or believed, that being sent to Mandatory Palestine was all nonsense, and that they should not voluntarily place themselves in the hands of these German criminals. I did everything in my power to try to convince them of the German hypocrisy. However, Horowicz did not utter a word, took his wife's hand, and off they went.

My wife Stella was in the apartment. I told her I was tired and wasn't feeling well. I stripped off my clothes, slipped into bed, and fell asleep. I was woken by a jolt to my shoulder. Two Jewish policemen were standing by my bed. One of them, whose name was Oderberg, told me briefly that I had to get up, get dressed, and report immediately to the assembly point in the Warsaw Market Square, because I was on the list of people with higher education who had been selected to go to Mandatory Palestine. Since I had not reported so far, they had received an order from the Germans to find me and bring me there.

Looking carefully at the policemen, I saw that they were being completely serious. Apparently, they also believed these German fairy tales about Jews being sent to Mandatory Palestine. I told them I was sick and had a fever. They told me that now was not the time to be sick and that they would wait for me in the street to take me to the square. I nodded, but it took me a while to move from my bed. Finally, I got up, got dressed, and dashed to the basement, ordering Stella to stay put. I hid there for an hour or two before going out onto the street. There was a commotion all around. People were coming out of their homes, and they were standing and talking in groups on the streets. Some were wringing their hands and crying. There was both excitement and dejection in the air. A great misfortune had happened, a new Jewish tragedy deliberately plotted and prepared by the Germans with diabolical cunning and refined cruelty. It was on this day, the festival of Purim, which is celebrated as the anniversary of the miraculous rescue of the Jews, that the Germans chose to mock the Jewish workers and show them that nothing could save them from extermination at the hands of the Germans.

According to the list compiled by the Germans, all Jews with higher education and their families gathered in the Market Square to leave for Mandatory Palestine, as had been assured by the Schupo officers headed by Degenhardt. They had come voluntarily, convinced of the credibility of the German assurances: doctors with their wives and children, engineers and teachers, lawyers and law graduates. The Council of Elders, headed by chairman Leon Kopiński, together with their family members, were all present. Several hundred people gathered in anticipation of their departure to Mandatory Palestine.

However, armed German Schutzpolizei then emerged from the gates of Warszawska Street, surrounded the Jews gathered in the market square from all sides, and herded them into tarpaulin-covered trucks waiting on the street. Only now did the victims understand the horrible truth, but it was too late to turn back. They were struck with rifle butts. Those who resisted were chased away, and those who protested were beaten. Judenrat member Zelig Rotbard, who had persuaded his young daughter Fela to go with him to the market square, now begged the German officers to release her, but to no avail.

Instead of going to Mandatory Palestine, the loaded trucks turned onto the road leading to the Jewish cemetery on Olsztyńska Street. Near the cemetery, several people tried to escape. Bernard Kurland, head of the Labor Department, jumped down. He was followed by the chairman's brother, Maurycy Kopiński, and Władek Kopiński, the chairman's son. Anna Breslerowa née Nowak also jumped from the truck.[22] Shots were fired after the escapees, but the trucks did not stop and drove through the gates of the cemetery, which was filled with Schupo men, Ukrainians, and Polish policemen. The people crowded into the trucks were pushed out, and the body of the Judenrat chairman Leon Kopiński, who it was said committed suicide by taking potassium cyanide, was thrown from the truck. In the burial hall, everyone was ordered to take off their clothes. In pairs, the Schupo led the naked Jews to a common grave dug earlier.

The first to be led out was twenty-year-old Fela Rotbard. A shot rang out, and Fela Rotbard, with a bleeding skull, rolled to the bottom of the grave. The executions continued; shots were fired, Jewish blood was poured in abundance, human corpses now covered the inside of the common grave. The Germans murdered the elite of the Jewish intelligentsia without mercy.

Among the victims were also children. Until then, the children of Jewish doctors had been legally residing in the camp. Dr. Winer's beautiful daughter, Lili, had been celebrating her seventh birthday that day and had come to the market square with her parents straight from her birthday party. She wore a white bow in her raven-black hair. The child stood terrified, but she was so beautiful that it even intimidated the German executioners who were so accustomed to shedding innocent Jewish blood. In the end, *Wachmeister* Überscher approached Lila Winer, lifted her in his arms, and fired a shot at the child's head, shouting, "For the Führer and the Fatherland!" Now, in a common grave in the Jewish cemetery rested 127 new victims of German barbarism! When will the avenger appear?!

Bernard Kurland escaped and survived this unprecedentedly cruel murder. As a result of Helenka Tenenbaum's intervention, he was spared

22 See also the reconstruction of events by Paszkowski in Wiesław Paszkowski, "The Jewish Intelligencia Mass Grave," The World Society of Częstochowa Jews and Their Descendants, https://www.czestochowajews.org/czestochowa-today/czestochowa-jewish-cemetery/jewish-intelligencia-grave/ (accessed August 31, 2025).

and took over as head of the labor department, along with the dentist Anna Bresler, who was allowed to return to the camp. The remaining escapees were murdered by the Germans, including Maurycy Kopiński, to whom I owe my survival of the September selection. On the same day, in a bunker on Wilson Street, I heard that the Germans shot five fighters from the Jewish resistance movement who were in hiding.

The Schutzpolizei trucks brought the clothes and underwear of the Jews murdered in the cemetery back to the camp. This was the end of the Council of Elders and the pathetic fate of its members who served the Germans, obeyed all their orders, and believed that, as a reward, their own lives and those of their families would be spared. In fact, just the opposite happened. The labor camp still existed, several thousand Jews lived there, and the Judenrat members were cruelly murdered by the merciless German fascists. Apparently, at this stage of the final liquidation of any still-existing Jewish concentrations, the Judenrat was deemed unnecessary and potentially dangerous in the future, as it knew all about the rampant bribery and robbery of the German police officials. Like in all criminal organizations, inconvenient witnesses are liquidated. On this day—March 20, 1943—similar liquidations also took place in other Jewish camps, including in Radom, Piotrków, and Tomaszów Mazowiecki.

All these events heralded the approaching end of the still-existing Jewish communities in Poland, and the ongoing liquidation of the Warsaw ghetto—about which we received news—confirmed the full horror of the situation. As a result, the resistance movement in our camp, modeled after the Jewish Fighting Organization founded in the Warsaw ghetto, intensified its efforts. Jewish youngsters—both male and female—organized themselves into small groups of five and decided to defend themselves against the deportations to death and to never surrender without fighting back.[23]

The resistance movement was still led by the previously mentioned Dr. Adam Wolberg. The youthful communist activist Tencer was also among the leadership of this movement, but together with his wife, he escaped from the camp and hid among the Poles for some time. The rumor was that he was captured and shot by the Gestapo.

Most of these militants came from the Zionist youth movements, especially Hehalutz. They were very active and intensively prepared to

23 The first armed attempt at resisting the deportation in the Warsaw ghetto took place in January 1943. The uprising began on April 19, 1943, and lasted until its suppression on May 16. During these twenty-eight days of resistance, the Nazis lost several hundred soldiers.

defend the camp. They were armed with a number of grenades, flasks of gasoline, Molotov cocktails, and German Schutzpolizei uniforms. They built several bunkers and dug a few underground tunnels in the camp with concealed outlets leading outside the camp. These bunkers and tunnels were located at 66 and 68 Nadrzeczna Street. They collected money vigorously to buy weapons. Usually at night, the combatants visited the wealthier inhabitants of the camp—especially those who were known to have gained considerable funds by systematically robbing the Schutzpolizei warehouses—and collected money.

After the tragic incident involving Fiszlewicz and Fajner,[24] the second armed combat action took place on April 23, 1943. The combat group, called Nadrzeczna 66, organized an operation to dislodge the railroad tracks. The idea was to derail German trains carrying munitions, weapons, and reinforcements to the Russian front. In the morning, armed with pistols and tools to unscrew the rails, the fighters joined the workers' brigade at the Ostbahn railroad outpost. Unexpectedly, the entire brigade was suddenly stopped on its way to work by the Gestapo and Schutzpolizei. Three Jewish fighters were shot on the spot, after which every second laborer working at the Ostbahn outpost was shot as punishment.

By then, the Germans were well informed by their—unfortunately Jewish—spies about the activities of the resistance movement in the camp and had apparently been warned of the intended action. Once again, the camp regime tightened considerably, and tension and general nervousness increased. One spoke of the near liquidation of the camp. Heinrich Köster and Laszynski, experts on political matters at the Schutzpolizei, were the new commandants appointed to replace Überscher. They both spoke Polish well and were constantly circulating the camp, inquiring and spying. Their task was to detect bunkers and tunnels, as well as to capture members of the fighting organization. They recruited a few Jewish informers, whose identities were later revealed.

On the Aryan side, the Germans intensified their pursuit of hidden Jews. For this purpose, the Germans used their whole network of informants and squealers. Captured Jews were either shot on the spot or brought to the camp and executed in Warsaw Market Square. Many Jews on the Aryan side secretly returned to the camp, joining the work brigades coming back from work. Many returned to the camp with our HASAG brigade, unable to stand the nervous tension of being a perpetually hunted animal.

24 See the events of January 4, 1943, described earlier.

On May 1, 1943, all work brigades were stopped at the main gate in the morning and sent back to the camp. The Schutzpolizei commandant ordered everyone to return to their apartments to await further orders. Even the brigade of HASAG workers who were so important to the German armaments industry did not go to work that day. All of the *Werkschutz* who reported for their workers were ordered to leave the camp area and return to their work stations. Liquidation was imminent, and panic spread throughout the camp. Any moment now, the Germans were expected to move in and begin the slaughter.

Individuals tried to escape from the camp in garbage and waste containers that the Germans were allowing to leave. Some succeeded. Various speculations were made, but no one knew the real reason for closing the camp. This lasted for three days. Finally, some news arrived. Dr. Wolberg, who was staying outside the camp in the sanitary post on Garibaldi Street, cryptically informed us that there would be no liquidation of the camp, and that everyone would soon return to work. This news was confirmed by Machl Birencwajg, who was also outside the camp living on Wilson Street as the manager of the furniture warehouse (*Mőbellager*).

On the morning of May 4, at the usual time, the camp's streets once again rang with the sound of a wake-up call, and the camp's inhabitants went out to work in droves. Life was returning to normal, to the harsh forced labor for the Germans; but this was better than extermination in the gas chambers of the Nazi death camps. However, the liquidation of our camp and the extermination of its Jewish population was only postponed for one month.

The military situation in which the Germans found themselves on the Russian front was directly related to the fate of the remaining Polish and European Jews. The German offensive on the Eastern Front collapsed, and the Soviet successes were accompanied by a massive increase in resistance and partisan activity. These facts provoked a furious reaction from the German ruling circles, who only then began to realize that the military defeat of the German Reich was imminent. This was reflected in a harsher extermination policy against the Jews. By this time, in the early summer of 1943, more than 90 percent of the Jewish population in Poland and a very substantial proportion of the Jews in other European countries had already been exterminated by the Germans.[25] It seems that due to

25 In January 1942, according to the data prepared for the Wannsee Conference (January 20, 1942), there were some 2,284,000 Jews in the Generalgouvernement in Poland. One year later, according to the Nazi statistician Dr. Richard Korherr's

the uncertain military and political situation, the German authorities accelerated the process of further decimation of the Jewish population. The extermination of the Jewish remnants, physically and morally battered and isolated in labor camps, was the only victory achieved by the Germans at that time. Although they were preparing for a new offensive on the Russian front, the defeats suffered so far, especially at Stalingrad and Leningrad,[26] together with the collapse of the previous offensives, made the Germans so furious that they took revenge on the Jews within their grasp. The fact that the number of Jews in partisan units had risen contributed in no small measure to this fury, and even led to considerable consternation among the chief executioners of the Jews, such as Odilo Globocnik[27] and Adolf Eichmann.[28]

The uprising in the Warsaw ghetto was actually initiated by the first armed resistance of ghetto fighters on January 18–20, 1943, when German police authorities began deporting several thousand Warsaw Jews to Treblinka. The Germans decided to completely demolish the Warsaw ghetto after deporting the population unfit for work to the Treblinka extermination camp. The remaining Jewish professionals from the armaments industry and other factories working for the German war machine were deported to the Lublin region, along with all equipment and raw materials. In accordance with Himmler's order of February 16, 1943, and Krüger's order of April 18, 1943, the process of razing the Warsaw ghetto to the ground was to be carried out under Globocnik's personal responsibility and with the participation of plenipotentiaries from the boards of those armaments factories operating in the ghetto: Franz Konrad and Walter Többens.

report from March 23, 1943, cited earlier, fewer than 298,000 were still alive. Such were the grim effects of Operation Reinhard. See Silberklang, *Gates of Tears*, p. 15.

26 Regarding Stalingrad, see earlier. Leningrad (today St. Petersburg) was under siege from September 8, 1941–January 27, 1944, at the end of which the German forces were pushed away from the city. The siege had a devastating effect on the city and its civil population, and exacted a heavy price from the Wehrmacht, which had consequences for the outcome of the war.

27 See earlier for more on Globocnik.

28 Adolf Eichmann (1906–1962), SS officer and a key organizer of the Holocaust, played a crucial role in implementing the "Final Solution" after becoming head of the so-called Center for Jewish Emigration following the annexation of Austria by Nazi Germany in 1938. His 1961 trial in Israel further exposed the atrocities of the Holocaust to a global audience, increased Holocaust awareness, and interest in Holocaust research, and prompted further legal action against other Nazi criminals.

On April 19, German police surrounded the ghetto and entered it with the aim of forcefully evicting the remaining inhabitants. It was then that the uprising of the Jewish Combat Organization (Żydowska Organizacja Bojowa, ŻOB), under the leadership of Anielewicz, broke out. The SS and police commander of the district, von Sammern personally led the armed action against the ghetto fighters, later handing over command to General Jürgen Stroop, who was assigned to Warsaw by Krüger. Governor Fischer, the Warsaw commandant general, and chief of security police Hahn cooperated with Stroop. The ghetto put up fierce resistance, and the Germans suffered great losses, as the ŻOB attacked with a hail of bullets from regular guns and machine guns, grenades and bottles filled with incendiary liquid that set German tanks and armored cars on fire. High above the fighting ghetto flew the white-and-red Polish flag and the blue-and-white Zionist flag. Stroop, unable to break the ghetto resistance by armed struggle, gave the order to blow up the bunkers and houses where the fighters were hiding. With incendiary and demolition bombs, the entire ghetto area was turned into fire and ashes.

Nevertheless, the ghetto defended itself fiercely for many weeks. The fighters suffered enormous losses but managed to destroy and burn all the machinery, goods, and raw materials in the German Többens armaments plant. Fighting in the ghetto continued until around May 15, 1943, although afterward there was still sporadic firing by fighters still hiding in the ghetto ruins.

The Jewish Fighting Organization in the Warsaw ghetto, mostly composed of Zionist youth from Poalei Zion, Hashomer Hatzair, and others, hoped that their heroic struggle and uprising against the Germans would also lead to a similar uprising and armed struggle in the Aryan part of Warsaw, in other centers of the country, and in camps where organized groups of Jewish fighters were already active at that time. They hoped that their armed uprising would spread throughout the country and bring about a revolt of the entire Polish nation, hastening Germany's military defeat, which already seemed imminent as a result of its losses on the Russian and African fronts. Meanwhile, it seemed that the Poles remained deaf to the heroic uprising of the Jewish fighters, and although the Jewish struggle reverberated throughout Poland and the world, the Poles seemed to have nothing to say about the Jewish uprising apart from a terse statement in the Armia Krajowa (Polish resistance organization) organ, the Information Bulletin of April 24, 1943, which wrote, among other things, that the fighting citizens of the Polish State from behind the ghetto walls were closer, more comprehensible to the society in the capital than the passive victims letting themselves be dragged to death without resistance.

Instead of Polish armed assistance, only slogans about helping the Jewish fighters began to be proclaimed. This was limited to sporadic actions by the Polish resistance to extract the fleeing remnants of the ŻOB from the sewers instead of proclaiming fighting in the Polish territories. The struggle by the Jewish heroes of the ghetto was not an act of despair; it was initiated with the intention of inciting by example an armed struggle against the German executioners by the entire underground armed force that was already organized at the time and by the entire nation to counter German terror.

From almost the very beginning of the plan by Hitler and his accomplices for the merciless destruction of the Jews in Poland, Europe, and throughout the world, the Germans found ardent supporters and collaborators.[29] But needless to say, this was a German plot to destroy the Jews.[30]

Already in the prewar years, almost immediately after the death of Józef Piłsudski, deliberate and biased actions against the Jews were evident. Jews were always blamed for the plight of the bourgeoisie, economic stagnation, and cultural backwardness. For years, the Sanacja government had pursued a policy of economic and legal discrimination

29 There were Ukrainian, Estonian, Latvian, Polish, and Russian collaborators of the Nazis who operated in German-occupied Poland.

30 The German invasion of Poland in September 1939 marked a turning point in Nazi anti-Jewish policy. With over 2 million Polish Jews under German control, the previous strategy of forced emigration of Jews became unfeasible. The war and territorial expansion overwhelmed Germany as the number of Jews had now reached an unprecedented scale, prompting the Nazis to shift from a German-centered framework to a broader plan to "cleanse" all occupied territories of Jews. Poland had the largest Jewish population and was therefore logistically central for the execution of the Final Solution. It was away from the public eye of Central and Western Europe, thereby facilitating the Nazis' murderous plans. For a detailed explanation, see Browning, *The Origins of the Final Solution*, pp. 12–14. It was first and foremost the Nazis' intention and governmental decision to annihilate all Jews—men, women, and children. In fact, the mass killings of Jews had started before death camps in Nazi-occupied Poland began a technologically based mass annihilation of Jews. Systematic mass killings of hundreds of thousands of Jews in shooting pits, what is sometimes referred to as the Holocaust by bullets, was carried out by the Nazis in the summer of 1941 upon the invasion of the Soviet Union, which were territories densely populated by Jews.

against the Jewish population. Especially since the establishment of the OZN, anti-Jewish policy had played an increasingly important role. It was a platform for rapprochement between the extreme right-wing parties—the National Party (Endecja); the Radical National Front (ONR), which formed anti-Jewish militias with Chrobry's swords in their lapels; and OZN, the ruling party created in place of the former BBWR (Nonpartisan Bloc for Cooperation with Government).

The anti-Jewish campaigns—boycotts, picketing of Jewish stores, and pogroms against Jews—were organized on a permanent basis by the Endecja and ONR militias together with OZN, and found support from the highest state authorities. Prime Minister Felicjan Sławoj-Skladkowski's slogan, "Yes to economic warfare," launched in the Sejm in June 1936, found not only the support within the Polish nation, but also its implementation. The government appeared to support the actions of these militiamen against Jewish merchants, from whose stores they violently—and with the passive acquiescence of the police—chased away potential clients and also sustained the efforts of various trade unions, craft guilds, and associations of free professions to adopt a clause to disenfranchise the Jews in Poland. Simultaneously, demonstrations were organized at the universities and colleges, and an unofficial *numerus clausus* was introduced in schools.

Conditions were thus created in Poland in which anti-Jewish sentiment could grow, a perfect breeding ground for the pogroms that took place in Przytyk, Brest-on-the-Bug, Białystok, Częstochowa, and many other places in Poland. In the second half of 1938, Nazi influence increased in Poland in terms of racist legislation against Jews. On January 18, 1939, a few days before Ribbentrop's visit to Warsaw, MP Benedykt Kienć presented to the OZN parliamentary club a bill depriving Jews of Polish citizenship rights, which was widely reported in the *Kurier Warszawski* of January 19, 1939.

According to Kienć's bill, Jews would lose their active and passive electoral rights, the right to serve in the army and in the state administration, and the right to work in some factories and enterprises. They also could not attend public schools or secondary and higher-education institutions, they could not be teachers or workers in the media, cinemas, or theaters, and those working in free professions could not give advice to Polish citizens. Jews would not be allowed to buy property or run banks, they would not be allowed to open any enterprises, and in the already established ones they would be allowed to employ only Jewish personnel. The bill further provided that Jews should report to the treasury offices full information about their property and dispose of their property only with the permission of the treasury authorities. Property not declared within a month would be forfeited to the treasury. Jews were to pay a duty to the state, from 20 to 50 percent of the value of movable and immovable property. This compulsory contribution was to be used to establish an emigration fund for Jews.

Such projects were submitted for debate in the Polish Sejm at a time when the world was outraged and shocked by the persecution of Jews in Germany and by the course of the famous "Kristallnacht" pogrom, the real St. Bartholomew's Night, when Jews were murdered, their property looted, and Jewish stores, apartments, and synagogues burned throughout Germany.

Deputies Ratajczak, Konieczny, and Krengielski submitted a new bill to the Presidium of the Council of Ministers, in which they demanded that the government, without waiting for the adoption of the Kienć bill, immediately revoke the Polish citizenship of 600,000 Jews living in the eastern provinces.[31] Also, Wacław Łypacewicz, in his anti-Jewish propositions, suggested that the government should immediately issue a law on restricting civil rights of the Jewish population. Some Polish political commentators praised the system and legislation of the Third Reich and recommended that these models be adopted in Poland. Among them were primarily E. Fiedler and Father Pastuszka. The latter admitted that the Nazis were absolutely right about the Jewish question.

Another commentator, Kazimierz Kierski, went even further, accusing the Jews of aiming for economic supremacy in Poland and world domination. Kierski wrote in his book *Kwestia żydowska w Polsce* (The Jewish Question in Poland) in 1939 that the Polish nation, following the example of the Germans, should adopt such a solution that all Jews should be forcibly removed from the borders of the Polish state. The head of the OZN, General St. Skwarczyński, made an analogous statement already at the beginning of 1938 clearly emphasizing that the solution of the Jewish problem could be seen in a radical reduction of the number of Jews in Poland through mass emigration. When the Germans expelled 17,000 Jewish Polish citizens in October 1938 and forcibly delivered them to the Polish border at Zbąszyń, the Polish border guards refused to allow them to enter Polish territory. These Jews were kept outdoors in a camp under inhuman conditions for several months.

The Jewish MP Zomersztajn submitted a firm interpellation on this matter. Nevertheless, about 5,000 Jews remained in Zbąszyń for a long time, and the authorities did not allow them to leave the camp. The Polish

31 *Kurier Warszawski*, January 25, 1939.

government also negotiated with the French foreign minister Delbos during his visit to Warsaw in January 1938 regarding the idea of forced transfer of many Polish Jews to Madagascar. The press reported that an agreement had been concluded under which 30,000 Polish Jews were to be forcibly resettled on this island. The Polish government sent a special commission to Madagascar, headed by Lepecki, to examine the possibilities of Jewish settlement on the island—*Madagaskar: Kraj, ludzie, osadnictwo* (Madagascar: Country, People, Settlement). Jan Wagner (pseudonym Jan Zieminski) put forward the problem of emigration of Polish Jews as a political issue of international importance. Angola, Madagascar, and other tropical countries were considered as destinations for Jewish emigrants.

Discussions held at the Evian Conference in July 1938, regarding the problem of Jewish refugees from Germany, covered only a small part of the general problem of expelling Jews from Europe. MP Suszyński, a budget referent of the Ministry of Foreign Affairs, declared in the Sejm on January 19, 1939, that the ministry had already been conducting for some time a campaign concerning the emigration of Jews from Poland,[32] and that now there was still time for a quiet solution of the matter of the emigration of Jews on a pan-European plane.

Prime Minister Składkowski, answering interpellation 117 by OZN MPs on the measures aimed at mass Jewish emigration in order to radically reduce the number of Jews in Poland,[33] delivered an extensive statement to the effect that the Polish government had already made efforts to obtain immigration areas for Jews and was considering the matter of financing this emigration and liquidating Jewish property and capital. Łypacewicz's and Kierski's pronouncements revealed that the Polish government treated the matter of Jewish emigration from Poland in the context of the emigration of Jews from across Europe. "All these Jews should be forcibly resettled in these areas," Kierski wrote, "and forbidden to return. If at least some Jews remain among the Aryan peoples, the Jewish question will never be settled"[34]—no matter whether these areas were to be located in Madagascar or Rhodesia or Guyana. Kierski also wrote that all Jewish property was to be taken over by the state.

Łypacewicz stated the need for the immediate establishment of labor camps for Jews, in which initially 200,000 Polish Jews were to be removed

32 *Kurier Warszawski*, January 20, 1939.

33 *Kurier Warszawski*, January 24, 1939.

34 Kazimierz Kierski, *Kwestia żydowska w Polsce* (Poznán: Nakl. Zwiazku Popierania Polskiego Stanu Posiadania, 1939), p. 61.

from the country's economic life, including 10,000 Jews active in free professions. In these labor camps, they would perform work useful to the country, such as agricultural land reclamation, reforestation of wasteland, river regulation, draining of swamps, and road construction. According to Łypacewicz, the camp regime would be similar to that in military camps. The cost of living would be 1 złoty a day (60 groszy for food, 20 groszy for clothing, and 20 groszy for other expenses). These labor camps would be organized according to the model of labor camps in fascist countries. The above ideas suggested a complete elimination of Jews from economic, political, and cultural life, confiscation of property, and forced emigration. A committee for the colonization of Jews was formed in 1938, and a delegation was even sent to London.

Accordingly, Polish Jews, deprived of everything, of human dignity, of civil rights, and of all movable and immovable property, were to be turned into forced laborers. The opinion voiced about Polish national character by the poet Juliusz Słowacki was often invoked in later years as having proved prophetic. In *Grób Agamemnona* (Agamemnon's Tomb), he famously described Poles as the "peacock and parrot of nations," a harsh critique of what he saw as a tendency toward uncritical imitation of foreign models.[35]

The Nazis found an atmosphere saturated with antisemitism. Despite the fact that Polish soil was soaked with the blood of its Jewish defenders, soldiers, and freedom fighters of both the November and January insurgents, Berek Joselewicz's soldiers and Piłsudski's legionnaires. Despite the fact that Poland was soaked with the blood of the Jewish defenders of Warsaw, the soldiers of September who gave their lives for its freedom, the heroic defenders of the Warsaw ghetto, who died within its walls fighting under the Polish white-and-red banner. On Polish soil rest the ashes of dozens of generations of Jews who lived and worked for 1,000 years, giving their strength and abilities, their intellect and property to Poland. Those tens of Jewish generations entered "a Poland made of wood and left behind a Poland made of stone." The development of trade and industry, the expansion of cities and towns, and the considerable contributions to Polish culture were the work of Polish Jews.

35 Juliusz Słowacki composed *Grób Agamemnona* (Agamemnon's Tomb) in 1839 and published it in Paris in 1840, in response to his journey through Greece, during which he visited Mycenae and the so-called Treasury of Atreus or the Tomb of Agamemnon. Słowacki's tone is critical, accusatory, and sorrowful. He laments the servitude of Poland as it still remained partitioned and subjugated to Prussia, Austria, and Russia.

Another issue of not insignificant importance that emboldened the Germans to murder 6 million European Jews on Polish soil with impunity and to plunder their property was the silence of the world in the face of a genocide that had no precedent in human history. The world, and primarily the governments of the countries allied in the great anti-fascist coalition, led by the United States and Great Britain, were informed of the genocide against the Jews that the Germans were committing in Poland and Europe, as well as in Russia. This information was particularly alarming in 1942 and 1943, when the physical destruction of the Jewish population in the occupied Polish territories intensified.

The world was informed of this, and the world remained silent. The air forces of the United States and Great Britain, flying over the death camps with their fuming and smoking crematoria chimneys, did not drop even a single bomb to stop or delay the mass murder taking place in these death factories.[36]

On both January 6 and April 27, 1942, USSR Foreign Minister Molotov sent a note to all allied governments notifying them of the mass execution of the Jewish population and other peoples of the Soviet Union. The Jewish community in Zurich received news of the mass extermination of Jews being carried out by the Germans in occupied-Polish territories and passed this information on to the Swiss police director Rothmund. R. Kastner, a representative of the Relief and Rescue Committee in Budapest, stated in his reports that by the middle of 1942, many reports and eyewitness testimonies had been sent about the situation of the Jews in occupied Polish territory.[37] Apparently, the governments of the allied countries continued to pretend that they knew nothing about the Jewish blood being spilled and the genocide perpetrated by the Germans against Jewish children, women, and men.

On July 21, 1942, a massive public demonstration was held in New York City, followed by a rally at Madison Square Garden.[38] At that time,

36 The US Air Force flew over Auschwitz in 1944.

37 R. Kastner, *Der Bericht des jüdischen Rettungskomittets aus Budapest* (1942–1945).

38 On July 21, 1942, some 22,000 people gathered at Madison Square Garden for a rally sponsored by the American Jewish Congress, the Jewish Labor Committee, and B'nai B'rith to protest Nazi atrocities against European Jewry. President Roosevelt sent a message praising the Jewish people's determination to fight for victory over the Axis and promising that the Nazis would not succeed in annihilating the Jewish people and would be held accountable. In the following weeks,

Prime Minister Churchill sent a telegram to those gathered in New York in which he emphasized, among other things that the Jews were Hitler's first victim and at the forefront of the resistance to Nazi aggression. Despite this, it seems that neither the government of Great Britain nor the government of the United States took action to prevent the disaster.

The three-day closure of our camp and the uncertainty surrounding its future not only served as a shocking experience for the over 5,000 inhabitants but also as a warning. We realized that dramatic events were fast approaching, and that the Germans, concerned about the growing resistance movement, were preparing for the camp's liquidation. At this time, in the first days of 1943, the Germans were made aware by their informers about the existence of an organized armed movement within the camp, whose activity was now undoubtedly clear. It was known that there would be an armed uprising if the camp were liquidated, and that the fighters would not passively allow themselves to be dragged to their deaths without a fight.

Initially, there were two separate groups of fighters in the camp. The headquarters of one group was in the house at 66 Nadrzeczna Street and was formed by six young women: Różka Gutgold, Saba Rypsztajn, Pola Szczekacz, Dana Szczekacz, Sara Gutgold, and Lusia Gutgold. They began recruiting among the camp's youth, and after a short time, the group's numbers increased. Many young people who were determined to fight the Germans joined the group. Mendel Fiszlewicz, Icchak Windman (Lolo), Lolek Frankenberg (Francek), Mietek Weintraub (Marduch), Hipek Hajman, Awiw Rozyne, Marysia Rozencwajg, Pola Hirsz, Jadzia Mas, Władek Kopiński (son of the chairman of the Judenrat), Izydor Fajge (Faja), Harry Gerszonowicz, and many others belonged to this group. Mendel Fiszlewicz became the commander of this group, whose members were of a leftist political orientation that bordered on communist ideology and who were between the ages of seventeen and twenty. They were

expressions of sympathy and protest continued: the House of Representatives' chaplain offered a special prayer for Jewish victims, major church organizations issued condemnations of Nazi crimes, August 12 was observed as a national day of fasting and prayer, and demonstrations were held in several US cities. There was visible public activity and protest against Nazi horrors yet little actual action meant to rescue European Jewry. See Alex Grobman, "What Did They Know? The American Jewish Press and the Holocaust, 1 September 1939–17 December 1942," *American Jewish History*, 68:3 (1979), pp. 327–352, http://www.jstor.org/stable/23882020 (accessed November 6, 2025).

divided into small combat groups of five, armed with knives, homemade grenades, and petrol bottles. They owned a few pistols, though they were not very functional.

The second militia group operated under the name Kibbutz. These were Zionist-oriented, pioneer youth, and it was organized by Rywka Glanc, Jehuda Gliksztajn, and Abraham Zylbersztajn. In December 1942, these two groups held a meeting in an underground location and decided to merge and form the Jewish Fighting Organization (Żydowska Organizacja Bojowa, ŻOB). Mordechaj Zylberberg (Mojtek) became the commander of the ŻOB in Częstochowa. His deputy was Mietek Abramowicz. Within a short time, the ŻOB had over 300 members and carried out energetic preparatory activities. Several tunnels and bunkers were dug, weapons, explosives, and gasoline were purchased, grenades were fashioned, and food supplies were gathered. The ŻOB's military advisor was Dr. Adam Wolberg.

The ŻOB members in the camp formed one of the branches of the Warsaw headquarters of the ŻOB, and they were very active in May and June 1943, following the Warsaw Ghetto Uprising. At their disposal, they had large sums of money collected from within the camp to purchase weapons. Precautions during such purchases were mandatory, because Gestapo informants were often the weapons' dealers. Therefore, the fighters mainly concentrated on making homemade grenades, which they stored in underground bunkers. I have already written about the military action of Mendel Fiszlewicz and Fajner, their tragic death, and the execution of twenty-five Jews. As already mentioned, his unsuccessful effort cost the lives of many people and alerted the Germans to the existence of an organized resistance movement in the camp. Nonetheless, the organization continued its activities and was met with general support and sympathy.

Hundreds of workers were employed in constructing the previously mentioned tunnels and bunkers. Later, the underground set up permanent posts to guard the access to the tunnels where stockpiles of weapons and ammunition had been accumulated. One of the tunnels led out into an open field on Jaskrowska Street on the Aryan side; a second tunnel also led outside the camp, into the basement of a house at 17 Old Market Square. The fighters placed particular emphasis on their own manufacture of grenades, because these weapons were very effective, not very expensive, and, most importantly, their production was not associated with the high level of danger associated with purchasing pistols or rifles from unreliable people.

The grenades were made in a deserted, half-ruined old forge in a backstreet passage of the camp. At night, when the whole camp was asleep, combatants already seasoned in production would gather in the old forge to create the tops of grenades, which were filled with explosives and then taken elsewhere for final assembly. The group of chemists was headed by Kaufman—known as Mikrus—a very talented boy and chemist. A specially trained platoon of combatants, led by Leib Cukierman, Abramek Czarny, Harry Gerszonowicz, and a fighter nicknamed Jacek, took part in this dangerous production of weapons. These homemade grenades were tested by five fighters who joined one of the outposts in the suburbs of Częstochowa in order to reach the small town Mirów, where the grenades were tested deep in the Mirów Forests. It turned out that they worked well, possessed high explosive and destructive power, and could serve as a good offensive and defensive weapon.

The fighters also engaged in information and propaganda activities. They published a bulletin in which the ŻOB command urged Polish society to help the Jews and materially support the Jewish resistance. The fighters had a radio transmitter in a bunker outside the camp, located on the premises of the German outpost *Möbellager* on Wilson Street, where they hid with a group of elderly people and children. The radio broadcast political news, and this was how, in the second half of April 1943, we heard about the ongoing deportation of Jews from the Netherlands to extermination camps in Poland[39] and about the heroism of some Dutch women who took children from among the ranks of Jews destined for deportation, saving them from extermination. This is also how we received news of the Warsaw Ghetto Uprising and about the heroic death of one of its leaders, Michał Klepfisz.[40]

39 The first transport of Dutch Jews left for Auschwitz-Birkenau on July 15, 1942. Dutch transports to death camps continued regularly until September 1944. Some 107,000 Jews were deported, with only 5,000 surviving. More than 75 percent of Dutch Jews were murdered in the Holocaust. For details on these transports and others, see "The Deportations of Jews Research Project and Digital Database (Transports to Extinction)," Yad Vashem, https://collections.yadvashem.org/en/deportations (accessed August 18, 2025).

40 Michał Klepfisz (1913–1943) was born in Poland. Growing up, Michał was a member of Tsukunft, the youth branch of the Bund, as well as a leader in Morgenstern, the Bund's sports organization. He was a chemical engineer. During World War II he was a member of the ŻOB (the Jewish Fighting Organization). On April 20, during the Warsaw Ghetto Uprising, Michał sacrificed himself to shield his comrades from a German machine gun, allowing them to escape. After the Germans were driven away, his body was buried, and in 1944, the Polish government-in-exile

Meanwhile, a group of ŻOB members managed to escape from the camp to the Olsztyn Forests and to Złoty Potok, near Częstochowa, to join the Polish partisans, including Moniek Flamenbaum, Alek Herszenberg, Janek Krauze, Heniek Rychter, Jerzy Rozenblat, and Szlamek Szajna. However, after a short stay in the forest, the Polish partisans refused to allow Jews to join their ranks. They even persecuted these Jewish fighters, who then had to hide from this reactionary Polish partisan group who were part of the Armia Krajowa.[41] They had to flee from the forest and take refuge in the *Möbellager* bunker. However, this bunker was discovered by the Germans and surprised the combatants, who did not manage to use any of their weapons. All those found were shot in the Jewish cemetery.[42]

In April 1943, Hipek Hajman was arrested upon entering the camp. Anti-German literature was found on him, and he was placed in the custody of the Jewish police inside the camp. The ŻOB command, however, decided to break Hajman out. During the night, five fighters—Harry Gerszonowicz, Lolek Frankenberg, Awiw Rozyne, Mietek Wajntraub, and Kuba Rypsztajn—freed Hajman, who was immediately sent to Warsaw to purchase weapons together with another fighter called Windman. Both were

posthumously awarded him the Virtuti Militari medal (Michał Klepfish Collection, USHMM site https://collections.ushmm.org/search/catalog/irn548843).

41 The Armia Krajowa (AK) was a Polish resistance organization during World War II that sought to resist the German occupation and prepare for an uprising following Germany's defeat. Although there were not many Jews in the AK, the organization established a Jewish Affairs Section in 1942 to report on the situation of the Jews and facilitated cooperation between Polish and Jewish military groups. The AK also provided support during the Warsaw Ghetto Uprising and engaged in sabotage activities, including the 1944 Warsaw Uprising. See Rozett and Spector, *Encyclopedia of the Holocaust*, pp. 269–270. The attitude of the AK toward anti-Jewish policies is a very controversial topic in Polish-Jewish relations during the Holocaust. Extensive analysis of Holocaust survivor testimonies largely confirms the view echoed by Kromołowski that the AK exhibited hostility toward Jews, even though about 30 percent of testimonies describe instances of the AK rescuing and protecting Jews. See Joshua D. Zimmerman, "The Polish Underground Home Army (AK) and the Jews: What Postwar Jewish Testimonies and Wartime Documents Reveal," *East European Politics and Societies*, 34:1 (2020), pp. 194–220.

42 An account of this can be found in "The Resistance Movement in the Small Ghetto," in Brener, "Resistance and Destruction in the Częstochowa Ghetto," p. 124. The bunker was located at 34 Wilson Street. The Germans discovered the six young Jewish fighters on March 17, 1943, and murdered them at the Jewish cemetery on March 19.

recognized by Polish blackmailers, robbed of their money, and turned over to the Germans. Windman managed to escape and returned to the camp, while the Gestapo sent Hajman to Trawniki, where he was murdered.[43]

To make grenades, the ŻOB men used materials captured in German warehouses and at various outposts. Large quantities of metals and explosives were stolen from there and smuggled into the camp in carts carrying the vats of soup and coffee for Jewish laborers working outside the camp. The house at 14 First Avenue—Franke's house, which housed only useful Jews (*nützliche Juden*), such as tailors, shoemakers, and other craftsmen exclusively working for the Germans—was also used for smuggling. However, very soon, the ŻOB was forced to stop producing grenades because the Germans had been tipped off about the weapons factory.

Various criminal elements pretending to be part of a fighting organization extorted money from camp inhabitants. At the head of one such gang were the Szwimer brothers. The ŻOB sentenced them to death by shooting. Köster and Laszyński's trusted spy, who was also a Gestapo informant, was the baker Motel Herman, known as Kulibajka. For a long time, the ŻOB suspected him of spying on behalf of the German camp commandant, but they became certain of this when a letter from Herman to the Gestapo was intercepted in *Möbellager* by Machl Birencwajg, who was working with the ŻOB. The letter contained information and news about the resistance movement in our camp. The baker Herman was also sentenced to death by the ŻOB command, and he was executed. A bottle containing the text of the sentence, with full justification and execution details, was placed next to the traitor's corpse.[44] It was absolutely certain that the Germans would immediately learn about the punishment of the traitor by the ŻOB, and that reprisals against the resistance would begin.

Following the execution of the Judenrat and its chairman Leon Kopiński, the real power in the camp now belonged to the ŻOB, which operated clandestinely. Formally, however, the camp was now run by the the labor department, which was headed by Bernard Kurland and Dawid (Tadek) Zylbernac, who was married to Leon Kopiński's sister (Leon, as mentioned earlier, had committed suicide on his way to the cemetery). The *Judeneinsatz* was the camp authority approved by the Germans, but in reality, it was loyal to the ŻOB command.

On April 22, 1943, there was another unsuccessful ŻOB action that had an extremely tragic end. The aim of this action was to carry out acts

43 Ibid., pp. 124–125.

44 Ibid., pp. 125–126. The bottle is said to have been laid in the traitor's grave.

of sabotage by unscrewing railroad tracks and derailing transports with weapons, ammunition, and reinforcements on their way to the Eastern Front. These transports were coming from Germany through the village of Błeszno, heading east. The fighters were equipped with pistols and tools to unscrew the rails. They joined the group of Jewish laborers who were part of the Ostbahn outpost working on the railroad tracks. However, one of the *Werkschutz*, a Ukrainian named Karno, discovered that Dawid Altman did not belong to the personnel of this outpost. Together with another *Werkschutz*, who was a *Volksdeutscher*, they took Altman to a German guardhouse. In an attempt to free Altman, Harry Gerszonowicz took out his pistol and opened fire on the two *Werkshutzes*. One fell and was seriously wounded, and Altman managed to escape. However, the remaining fighters did not manage to escape and were surrounded by Schupo policemen. They tried to defend themselves by shooting at the policemen, but Gerszonowicz and Rozyne died on the spot, while Cwi Lustiger barricaded himself in a nearby barn and defended himself by shooting at the Germans until he ran out of ammunition. Wounded and soaked in blood, Lustiger was captured and handed over to the Gestapo, who tortured him in the Gestapo cellars at 10 Kilińskiego Street. He did not betray anyone from the ŻOB and was shot by the Gestapo in the Jewish cemetery. As revenge, the Germans shot twenty-five Jewish workers from the Ostbahn work group.[45]

At the same time, the Gestapo officers discovered Władek Kopiński, the aforementioned son of the Judenrat chairman who had been hiding since his escape from the cemetery on March 20. He was also a member of the ŻOB, and was shot dead by the Germans after actively resisting them until the very end.[46] A short time later, a group of about fifty fighters were killed in the surrounding forests in a fight with a Polish partisan group of the Armia Krajowa. They did not agree to cooperate with the Jews and began firing at them. All the Jewish fighters were killed by these Polish partisans who deliberately shot at them.[47]

45 See "The Resistance Movement in the Small Ghetto," in Brener, "Resistance and Destruction in the Częstochowa Ghetto," pp. 126–127; see also "Memorial Stones," in Schutzman, *Sefer Czenstochow*, vol. 2, pp. 285–326, https://www.jewishgen.org/yizkor/Czestochowa6/cze2_285.html (accessed August 18, 2025).

46 See "The Resistance Movement in the Small Ghetto," in Brener "Resistance and Destruction in the Częstochowa Ghetto," p. 127.

47 According to Brener, fifty men divided into ten groups took to the woods before, during, and after the liquidation of the Small Ghetto. Most of them perished while fighting. Ibid., p. 128.

At that time, the ŻOB command revealed the activities of two informants in the camp. One of them was the Jewish policeman Jakub Rozenberg, who was in the ghetto in the service of the Germans and moved freely on the Aryan side. The other was also a Jewish policeman, Moniek Pławner, who came from Radomsko. Rozenberg reported to the camp commandants Köster and Laszynski, while Pławner was in the service of the Gestapo.[48]

On June 8, 1943, a Schutzpolizei unit headed by Degenhardt unexpectedly raided the *Möbellager* at 22 Wilson Street. The Germans had apparently been informed by their spies that an arms depot was located there, that fighters, elderly people, and children were hiding there, and that the manager of the facility, Machel Birencwajg, was actually a member of the resistance movement and worked closely with the ŻOB. The Germans discovered the bunker, and during their search, they found a forged identity card (*Kennkarte*), shot several people on the spot, and Birencwajg's wife (née Szenfeld) was taken together with other prisoners and shot in the Jewish cemetery. Machel Birencwajg escaped and hid with Polish acquaintances. However, he was soon identified as a Jew by an unknown Polish woman and was shot by the Germans.[49]

A few days later, the German police arrested a whole group of Jewish women and one of the ŻOB fighters in the haberdashery warehouses on Garibaldi Street.[50] The ŻOB command attempted to rescue and free the detainees held in Polish police custody on Dworcowa (Piłsudskiego) Street. A daring assault was planned; however, the ŻOB members Herszlik Prozer and Lajb Cymerman who had been assigned to this task were captured, and all of them, together with those arrested, were shot by the Germans at the Jewish cemetery on June 23, 1943.

On that day, too, Dr. Adam Wolberg, the ŻOB military instructor and one of its leaders, was shot dead on Garibaldi Street. He had been summoned by the Germans to provide medical assistance to an allegedly sick Jewish worker in one of the warehouses. When Dr. Wolberg arrived there, he was murdered with several shots to the back of his head by two

48 See "The Resistance Movement in the Small Ghetto," in Brener, "Resistance and Destruction in the Częstochowa Ghetto," pp. 129, 132.

49 Machel Birencwajg was shot at the Jewish cemetery on June 28, 1943. Ibid., pp. 105–106, 129–131; "Birencwajg Machel Michał," in Sętkowski, *Częstochowa Jews: A Biographical Dictionary*, pp. 47–48.

50 Brener mentions only the first name Gedalia. Brener, "Resistance and Destruction in the Częstochowa Ghetto," p. 131.

Schupo policemen, Klipsz and Bulle. The body of Dr. Wolberg was buried in the Jewish cemetery, together with everyone held by the Polish police as well as the ŻOB fighters who had planned a raid intended to free their comrade Gedalia.

Added to this group of executed persons was an unknown Jewish couple who worked as caregivers in the house occupied by the German police at 75 Third Avenue. The couple had German documents and pretended to be native Germans. In fact, they were both members of the Polish resistance movement and had been informants for one of the partisan organizations, to which they rendered invaluable services. A Gestapo informant, a resident of Częstochowa who was also an active member of the Armia Krajowa, provided information about Dr. Wolberg's involvement in the resistance movement and the Jewish couple's partisan affiliation. The name of this traitor has never been uncovered.[51]

All these events, which electrified the camp almost daily and greatly heightened tension and anxiety among its inhabitants, clearly pointed to the approaching end. It was easy to predict that the Germans would first and foremost try to liquidate the ŻOB men and their weapons stores, of which they were well informed by their Jewish spies. The ŻOB and our entire camp expected that the Schutzpolizei, Gestapo, and their accomplices would enter the camp at any moment to initiate an armed liquidation action. The ŻOB command ordered the immediate assassination of the German spies. ŻOB fighters Abramek Czarny, Pinek Wasilewicz, and "Bastek," by virtue of a death sentence, shot a Schutzpolizei informant, the Jewish policeman named Rozenberg. The next sentence was carried out on the Jewish policeman Domb, a zealous servant and spy for the Germans. Gestapo informant Moniek Pławner was also sentenced to death, but the Germans themselves shot him when they no longer needed his services.

After the Jewish traitors were eliminated, the ŻOB command decided to hand over some of the weapons stored in the tunnels to Jewish fighters, some of whom were in the surrounding woods fighting the Germans and the reactionary AK groups. ŻOB members Pinek Samsonowicz, Harry Potasiewicz, and Lolek Blank were designated to transport the weapons. With the help of Lajb Tenenbaum, a ŻOB member who worked at the HASAG ammunition factory under construction, as well as two *Vorarbeiters* called Wojdzisławski and Winter, a truck was obtained. The driver was bribed, and the truck was used to transport weapons. On June 24, 1943, the three fighters departed in it, loaded with weapons.

51 See ibid., pp. 131–132.

On the way, they were surrounded by German police and the Gestapo. It turned out that the driver was a Gestapo informant and had reported the action. The fighters immediately opened fire with pistols. Pinek Samsonowicz was killed on the spot, Harry Potasiewicz was taken alive, and Lolek Blank managed to escape. The Gestapo men brought Potasiewicz to the camp, placed him in the window of the Jewish police station, and ordered the camp inhabitants to pass in front of him, one by one. He was then ordered to point out any ŻOB members. The Gestapo men tortured the already half-dead Potasiewicz; however, he betrayed no one. Water was poured over the fainting ŻOB man, and he was eventually dragged to the Jewish cemetery; but, due to his wounds and the torture, he died on the way to the place of his planned execution.

After Potasiewicz's death, the Gestapo, relying on the chauffeur's information, captured Wojdzisławski and Winter, who had been intermediaries in hiring the car and bribing the chauffeur. The two *Vorarbeiters*, who were brutally beaten and tortured in Gestapo cellars, handed over Tenenbaum, the organizer of the unfortunate expedition. Tenenbaum was dragged around the factory halls of HASAG and ordered to point out any ŻOB members working there. However, Tenenbaum did not identify anyone. Together with the *Vorarbeiters*, he was brought to the Jewish cemetery, where they were executed.[52]

52 The events recounted by Kromołowski are found in ibid., pp. 132–133.

CHAPTER EIGHT

THE LIQUIDATION OF THE SMALL GHETTO

Throughout the entire period of these shocking events, I continued working at HASAG. Every morning, I set out with a very large work group to May 1 Street, where the plants were located. I returned to the camp in the late afternoon. Stella and I shared a warm meal that she had prepared, and we usually went to bed early. Sometimes, my brother and my wife's brother, who was also working at HASAG at that time, visited us. As we ate dinner together, we discussed the dramatic events taking place in our camp almost daily.

Stella worked in the warehouses on Garibaldi Street. This was fairly quiet work and did not require much effort. However, I kept pushing her to move to HASAG, so we could be together. I believed that in these hard times spouses should stay together and avoid separation. My wife eventually gave in to my persistent requests and went to work with me one morning. She had secured a job in a department where the senior worker was a friend and would take care of her. But she returned weeping, tired, and determined to avoid HASAG. She could not endure the discipline there and the constant fear of the cruel *Werkschutz* and foremen. She returned to her previous job in the German warehouses on Garibaldi Street to sort linen and clothing.

Wooden barracks were hastily built on the HASAG factory site, and the site itself was surrounded by barbed-wire fences. Jewish workers were also employed in this construction, and they told us that the barracks were intended for Jews to be quartered there to be able to work day and night for the German war industry.

At dawn on June 25, 1943, the camp trumpet sounded the wake-up call—the signal to march out to work. I dressed quickly and looked at my wife. She was awake, lying with her eyes wide open and smiling slightly. I kissed her goodbye, as usual, and left the house. Assemblies, roll calls, and counting the workers before leaving the camp all took place beyond the camp boundaries, in the square adjacent to the Warsaw Market Square. On that day, everything was calm and normal. Nothing foretold the events that were to take place. No German policemen could be seen, and the outposts were leaving the camp, escorted by *Werkschutz.* As usual, a few Jewish policemen stood in front of the camp gate brandishing rubber batons.

There was the normal everyday traffic at HASAG, the clatter of machines mixed with the shouting of foremen, and in our testing department (*Prüferei*), the dazzling welding devices hissed, buzzed, and flashed. Work was carried out quietly, and there were no incidents that day. The foremen seldom came in to supervise the work, and the hours passed at a snail's pace. We waited for the end of the workday and our return to the camp. Finally, the moment arrived, and we stood in formation in the factory yard waiting for the iron gate to be opened wide so that we could exit and return to the camp. Suddenly, surrounded by foremen, production managers, and supervisors, the plant director, Dr. Lüth, stood before us and said, "Today you will not go anywhere. You will stay here and live in the barracks that we are building. You will work for German industry as prisoners of HASAG. Right now, a great selection of Jews is taking place in your camp and the unnecessary and unfit for work are being liquidated. The camp will be destroyed and razed to the ground."

I stood there, half-paralyzed from fright. Only one thought pierced my dazed brain: Stella. What would happen to my wife? She was left there alone. My brother was there too. I didn't know if the Germans had released his Hagen group for work. I had to wait a long time for an answer. The camp was engulfed in death and conflagration. Innocent Jewish blood was again being spilled.

That day, after the outposts employed outside the camp had left, there was complete calm in the narrow streets of the camp. The usual daily activities were taking place. The camp kitchen was steaming, the janitors were cleaning the courtyards and streets, and a few passersby were sneaking around the walls of the houses. Nothing resembled the bloody events of the previous day, no German uniforms were visible, and there was no sign of the Schutzpolizei or Gestapo.

The ŻOB still remained on alert. Some of the fighters went outside the camp in the morning with various outposts, but a significant number remained in the camp. The ŻOB command ordered an assembly in one of the larger tunnels. Marek Folman, one of the defenders of the Warsaw ghetto, spoke to those gathered there. He talked about the heroic resistance, fighting, and death of many ŻOB men, who died with arms in their hands, inflicting heavy losses on the Germans.

After the recent bloody events, the Częstochowa command expected further reprisals from the Germans, so the fighters were equipped with weapons, posts were set up, and defensive positions were taken. However, all was quiet. After a few more hours passed in silence, the command ordered most of the fighters to leave their posts, leaving only the guardians of the arms depot in the tunnels. Mojtek, the commander of the organization, was sick that day and thus also remained in the tunnel.[1]

Around four o'clock in the afternoon, shortly before the return of the outposts to the camp, loud noises were suddenly heard in various locations. Shots from machine guns and small arms rang out. In an instant, units of Schutzpolizei, Gestapo, Ukrainians, and Polish police burst into the camp in an unexpected attack. Blood was shed immediately. The Germans shot at every Jew they encountered on Nadrzeczna Street, near numbers 86, 88, and 90, which were the target of the concentrated German attack. These houses were surrounded. Apparently, the Germans knew that the most important tunnels and weapons concealed by the ŻOB were located there. The Germans threw grenades into these tunnels, and the sounds of detonations could be heard. The screams and moans of the dying and seriously wounded were mixed with the incessant roar of gunfire and the clatter of machine guns. The fighters, who hours ago had left their posts in the tunnels and bunkers, were running from all sides to get to the arms

1 The Germans deceived the partisans by sending small groups of workers back to simulate the usual return from the day shift. When the ŻOB leadership called off the alarm, the fighters left their hiding spots and returned their weapons to the arsenal. At that moment, the police broke into the camp grounds. See Brener, "Resistance and Destruction in the Częstochowa Ghetto," p. 135; Wiesław Paszkowski, "The ŻOB Bunker Victims' Grave," https://www.czestochowajews.org/czestochowa-today/czestochowa-jewish-cemetery/zob-bunker-victims-grave/ (accessed August 18, 2025).

depots to fight back, but their efforts were futile. The Germans shot at anyone who came near the surrounded tunnels.

The fighters Szyldhaus, Josek Kantor, and dozens of others were killed. They died without having the chance to fight back and while trying to get to the lost fortifications. Seeing the hopelessness of the situation, the sick ŻOB commander Mojtek Zylberberg committed suicide in the tunnel where the weapons warehouse was located. The Germans broke into the tunnels, hanged Mojtek's corpse with his head down, and took their loot, consisting of all the weapons that had been collected with such difficulty: thirty grenades, eighteen revolvers, two rifles, and two German police uniforms. In the remaining bunkers, the fighters' resistance was weak, unorganized, and without command. They died without a struggle, without even having the chance to use the pistols they possessed.

A short time after the Germans entered the camp, the only ones left alive among the fighters were those who found themselves in the tunnel at 40 Garncarska Street. The tunnel's exit was located outside the camp, in the basement of a house at 17 Old Market Square. Under the command of Marek Folman and Rywka Glanc, the fighters barricaded themselves in this tunnel. They decided to make their way to the nearby forests, where Jewish partisans were active. However, while leaving the tunnel, they were surrounded by Germans. A fight ensued, during which the fighters killed one Gestapo officer and wounded a German policeman called Lebel. All the ŻOB fighters fell in battle, with only two pistols and a grenade at their disposal.[2] Marek Folman fell into German hands and died a martyr's death.

Other outposts who were returning from work were no longer allowed into the camp. The ranks stood silently in the square in front of the camp. The Germans chased everyone out of their apartments. Everyone was ordered to leave their homes and report to the square. Many people came with their children, as they were scared to hide in bunkers because of the gunshots, as well as the detonations and fires that the Germans had set off in many houses using combustible grenades.

In the square, the Germans carried out a selection, mainly targeting men. Those who were older or had children with them were pushed onto trucks by the Germans, Ukrainians, and Polish policemen, which would leave and soon return, stained with blood, to take the next batch of people. The selection took place amidst screams of beaten people and heavy gunfire.

2 Compare this description of the events of June 25–26 to the one found in Brener, "Resistance and Destruction in the Częstochowa Ghetto," pp. 134–137.

The inhabitants of the houses where the ŻOB tunnels and bunkers were located were shot on the spot. Women were kept behind barbed wire inside the camp, away from the site of these bloody butcheries. Amidst spasmodic weeping and moaning, they watched these horrible scenes, waiting for their turn. The surviving men, mostly young, were taken to HASAG and the ironworks in Raków, where they were led into barracks. Now it was the women's turn. Every woman who was older or had a child was pushed onto the trucks heading for the cemetery. When the empty, blood-splattered trucks returned, they were loaded with new victims.

The camp was burning everywhere, and the suffocating smoke drove out anyone hiding in the bunkers. These people were immediately packed onto trucks and taken to the cemetery, where the execution of innocent Jews—men, women, and children—was in full force. The whole monstrous action was personally directed by *Hauptmann der Schutzpolizei* Paul Degenhardt, the executioner of the Jewish population of Częstochowa.

Off to the side stood a group of Jewish boys between the ages of ten and fifteen, whose fate was about to be determined. Degenhardt intended to send them to the cemetery and murder them, deeming them unfit for work. Suddenly, Bernard Kurland approached the director of HASAG, Lüth, who was also present, and proposed that these boys be taken to work in the factory. Lüth agreed and told Degenhardt that the boys could be used in his armament plant. Thanks to this intervention by Kurland and Lüth, a dozen Jewish boys avoided certain death. Lüth could not have imagined that, by this act of goodwill, he avoided the fate of other war criminals: He was tried after the war but was acquitted.

A small child, abandoned by their mother or forcibly separated from her, lay on the ground in the selection area. The child was crying desperately and calling out. Suddenly, a tall woman holding another child's hand approached the crying child, whom she picked up, took by the hand, and, together with her little son with his head held high, calmly walked toward the car that was soon to be filled with women and children before leaving for the cemetery. Degenhardt approached her and suggested that she put the children on the truck but that she should not get on. However, the woman did not respond. With a stony face, an expression of pain and contempt, she climbed onto the truck together with the children. After a moment, escorted by two German armed thugs, the truck disappeared around the bend. This noble woman was Dr. Horowiczowa, who went to her death unwilling to leave behind her own beloved son, as well as the abandoned child of a stranger.

Little eight-year-old Rafał stood in front of one of the German trucks and told his distraught mother not to come with him and to leave him to his fate, because she was young and could save herself. Weeping, the mother pressed the good child to her breast and together they climbed onto the truck that carried them, loving and inseparable, to their deaths. Such heartrending scenes abounded amidst the lamentations of innocent Jewish children and the searing pain of distraught mothers. But the German criminals continued to carry out their extermination, while the world watched and remained silent.

When the last victims of the bloody slaughter had left the square, and those who were still alive and destined for forced labor were herded into factories, the Germans began liquidating the sick Jews in the camp hospitals. From the hospital for contagious patients, as well as the hospital for seriously ill people, all the patients were taken out into the courtyards in their underwear and shot in the back of the head. One of the patients, a young man, threatened the Germans with a raised fist and shouted, "Our innocent blood will be avenged. Be cursed, you German bandits to the tenth generation!"

Then, the Germans rushed to the camp hospital for the less severely ill. However, they found no one there. The deputy *Werkschutzleiter*, the German Milhof—the only man, as it turned out, to show humaneness among this band of murderers—had saved them by transporting them to the ironworks in Raków. Milhof did this at the request and persuasion of the Jewish doctor, Dr. Glatter.[3]

The camp streets kept on burning. Although several days had passed since the bloody pogrom had begun, there were still people hiding in the smoking ruins and among the rubble. Every now and then a figure would emerge from the half-demolished houses, choking from smoke. The Germans shot these unfortunates like ducks. Degenhardt, bored with the prolonged hunt for Jews hiding in the wreckage, finally announced an amnesty: Whoever came out of hiding on a certain day would be kept alive.

The order was announced by Jewish policemen, who walked among the ruins and burning houses. Those in hiding believed it. They came out of their hiding places dirty, hungry, ragged, half-suffocated. About 100 people came out of their burrows and bunkers. The Germans gathered them in the hospital building—one of the few remaining whole structures in the camp. They kept them locked up for two days, after which they shot everyone in the Jewish cemetery. Such was the German amnesty!

3 On Milhof and Glatter, see Brener, "Resistance and Destruction in the Częstochowa Ghetto," p. 138.

The Germans placed the 3,000 Jews who survived the liquidation of the camp in the HASAG ammunition factories, in the former textile factories Pelcery, Częstochowianka, and Warta, and in the ironworks in Raków. A few Jewish workers were sent to work in the warehouses of the German police on Garibaldi Street, which were already in the process of liquidation. Others were imprisoned in the building of the former *mikva*. Jewish policemen, along with their commander H. Parasol, were also imprisoned there.

A few days after these bloody events, I received a long-awaited message from my wife. On a scrap of paper, she wrote that she was in good health, and that she was with others in the building of the former *mikva* on Garibaldi Street. She wrote that she was with Helena Tenenbaum and was working with her and her brother in the vegetable garden located next to the kitchen. The camp kitchen was still open and provided lunches for the warehouse workers from Garibaldi Street.

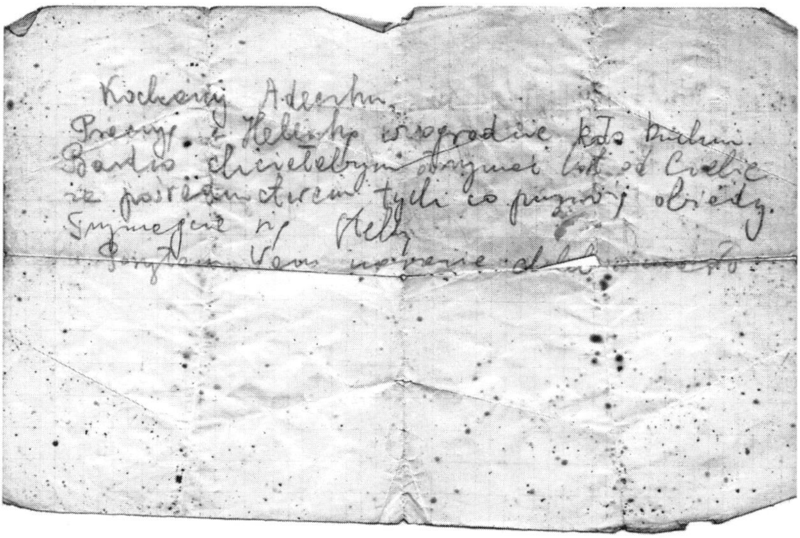

Note from Stella Estera Kromołowska to Alfred Kromołowski: "I am working with Helenka [Tenenbaum] in the garden next to the kitchen. I would very much like to receive a letter from you through those who deliver dinners. Stay well. Stella. In the meantime I am sending you some good butter."

I also received a message from my brother, who was now in the ironworks in Raków, where he worked and was barracked. Stella's brother was with me at HASAG-Pelcery and worked in the *Rekalibrierung* department. Thus, our family—so small and truncated by the dramatic events of recent years—had survived the hell of the pogrom. Reassured by this news, I immediately wrote a few lines to my wife and sent her news of myself and her brother. I sent the card with people from Garibaldi Street who came to our post with various orders before returning. To my wife I wrote that she should try to be sent to HASAG: By being together, we could support each other. Moreover, I believed that our outpost in a munitions factory would survive longer, and that the workers there would not be exterminated in the near future.

It soon became apparent that the Germans had also liquidated the useful Jewish craftsmen who were living in Franke's house at the corner of Wilson and 14 First Avenue. Some of these "useful Jews" and their families were murdered by the Germans on the spot, while the few remaining ones were taken to HASAG and placed in the so-called colony in houses inhabited by Polish and German administrative officials employed at HASAG. There, they continued performing services for the Germans.

The sounds of explosions and shooting could still be heard in the town. The Germans were now systematically demolishing house after house in every street in the Jewish camp. But first, they removed all movable property, which Jewish workers from Garibaldi Street transported to the warehouses. A few people were still hiding in the cellars of demolished houses as well as among the rubble and ruins. The Germans were constantly organizing expeditions to the area of the destroyed camp. Armed with pistols and rifles, they circulated the backstreets all day long, retrieving various objects from under the rubble and ruins, as well as people who were still alive, though semi-conscious from hunger and fear. They killed them on the spot, without mercy.

The Germans were insatiable in their search for valuable Jewish property. During the camp's bloody liquidation, they placed special baskets next to the trucks taking people to the execution sites, and Jews condemned to death were forced to throw their money, watches, jewelry, and wedding rings into them. The destruction was nearing its end. Property was looted. People were murdered, sometimes burned alive together with the houses in which they were hiding. Confiscated items and those objects found among the debris were taken to Germany. Some were also robbed for the executioners' own benefit. The hunt for Jews and the remnants of their possessions was also carried out by *Werkschutz* and civilian

Germans. *Werkschutzleiter* Klemm and his deputy Stieglitz, *Werkschutz* Kmicikiewicz, Schteininger, Doroshenko, and Pawelak were particularly active in the area. They also took part in the mass execution of Jews in the Jewish cemetery on the day of selection and the camp's liquidation.[4]

Living conditions in the HASAG factory area were terrible. After a whole day of harsh labor, in an atmosphere of fear for our very lives, hunger, and abuse by the German foremen, we had to sleep on the bare concrete floor in the factory halls. These were empty halls soon to be equipped with machines for producing rifle bullets. After some time, *holzwolle*, or wood shavings, was laid on the concrete floor, so we slept on that. At noon, we received some soup cooked in a field kitchen, consisting of a brownish stock made from beetroot leaves. We also received 200 grams of bread a day and some so-called coffee, which was a decoction of roasted acorns.

On the factory floor, the German foreman was the master of life and death. He maintained discipline by beating us, kicking us, and sending us to the *Wache*, where the *Werkschutz* beat us with a rubber hose on our bare buttocks. When we left the factory halls, we encountered the *Werkschutz*, who mistreated us for no reason whatsoever by beating, kicking, and shooting people under the pretext of thwarting escape attempts. The entire factory area was surrounded by barbed wire attached to concrete posts. Behind this fence, *Werkschutz* armed with rifles were on duty day and night. It was forbidden to be in the factory yard at night. Without warning, the *Werkschutz* fired at anyone who appeared in the square. Woe to those who fell ill with diarrhea. Their lives were in danger, especially when the illness intensified at night, and they had to run to the latrine located outside the factory buildings.

We all lay together in a swath on the floor, men and women in one room. At night, a drunken *Werkschutz* would come and take the first young woman he could find. After some time, she would return, having

4 Not only were the Germans insatiable in their search for valuable property, as Kromołowski describes, but by late 1942, a codified system of regulations regarding the hunt for Jews and their belongings had been established. The Germans mobilized the *Werkschutz*, Polish Blue Police, Sonderdienst, informers, and even the broader public to track down Jews who had evaded deportations and murder *Aktionen*. Confiscated Jewish property was cataloged in detailed lists, with a portion offered as a reward to those who assisted in capturing Jews in hiding. See Jan Grabowski, *Hunt for the Jews: Betrayal and Murder in German-Occupied Poland* (Bloomington: Indiana University Press, 2013), pp. 48–62, specifically pp. 58–59.

been raped, half-dead with fear. Often, such a victim did not return at all, because the *Werkschutz* also killed their victims.[5] They even shot Jewish workers during the day if they were caught baking a few potatoes over a fire. A woman named Wolska (née Wajnrajch) was shot by a *Werkschutz* while cooking some food. The bloodthirsty German foreman Oppel used to beat his Jewish workers with whatever he had at hand—a board, a piece of iron, or a hammer. Once, he broke a worker's rib in this manner, and beat another so severely that he could not walk or move for several days.

I received a few messages from Stella during this time. She wrote on scraps of paper, sometimes on cardboard torn from some box. She was healthy and wanted to help us somehow. I wrote to her repeatedly, using the same method, and urged her to try to get transferred to HASAG. Some people had been sent from the warehouses on Garibaldi Street to work in HASAG; however, Stella did not manage to do that, and we were still separated.

Not everyone in HASAG subsisted exclusively on factory food. Some had money or they managed to sell a ring or something gold—sewn into the nooks and crannies of their clothes—to the Polish HASAG workers in exchange for food to make up for the lack of calories. It often happened that someone, somewhere in a corner, would stuff himself with a fatty cutlet and eat a slice of buttered bread while hiding from both the Germans and his jealous comrades. Those who didn't have the funds could only gawk and swallow their saliva. I fell into this category. I didn't have a penny, and I decided to keep my dead mother's bracelet sewn into my jacket for even worse times—the so-called black hour—although the one I was living through wasn't any brighter. I was especially tormented by longing for my wife and brother and by fear for their fate, exposed as they were to constant danger.

Bernard Kurland became the Jewish camp manager. He was in direct contact with the factory director, Lüth, and tried to make our stay in this German hell easier. He managed to convince Lüth that better food would increase productivity and production. So, the HASAG management organized the sale of white, good-quality bread, and whoever had money

5 The phenomena of sexual violence and abuse against Jewish women during the Holocaust included rape, sexual slavery (in brothels for soldiers or as private slaves to officers), bartering sex for survival, sexual and psychological humiliation, and many other forms. See Sonja M. Hedgepeth and Rochelle G. Saidel, eds., *Sexual Violence against Jewish Women during the Holocaust* (Waltham: Brandeis University Press, 2010).

could buy this bread and eat their fill. Of course, this idyll did not last long, and when this bread trade came to the attention of the German police and the Gestapo, the sale was stopped and completely prohibited. However, Kurland managed to set up repair workshops for shoemaking and tailoring, as well as a room where every prisoner's hair could be cut and shaved free of charge. We were also allowed to use the factory bathhouse, where we could stand under the shower and wash ourselves with warm water from head to toe.

Three weeks and two days passed before July 19, 1943, arrived. From early in the morning, a strange restlessness came over the Jewish work crew in HASAG-Pelcery. People whispered in corners, spoke surreptitiously and in earshot, and exchanged knowing glances. Something dire was in the air. The German foremen paced the factory halls, carefully examining their Jewish workers, assessing their work and speed of movement. Foreman Oppel,[6] notorious for his cruelty and brutal treatment of Jewish workers, told someone that the boots one of the workers was wearing would be his property tomorrow. The entire factory was talking about this statement. Some maintained that civilian clothes and shoes were to be confiscated, and that all Jews would be given striped prison uniforms and clogs. Others said that there would be a ban on wearing pigskin shoes. From hour to hour, the atmosphere became increasingly tense. A general nervousness was growing.

Around noon, "Pale Joseph" Spaltenholz, one of the production managers of the *Apparatebau* department, entered the *Prüferei* hall and stood motionless in the middle of the factory, his long legs spread wide apart in his boots. Suddenly he looked at me. He stared at me silently for a long time, apparently assessing my physical condition, which was not the best. I trembled and turned pale. This scrutiny of my abilities as a physical worker did not bode well for me. I maneuvered as quickly as I could around my testing table, noisily blowing compressed air into and out of the casing, and smearing its metal surface with soap. All the while, my mind was racing. Something wasn't right. Why was he looking at me like that?

Somebody must have informed him that I wasn't really a manual laborer, and that, instead, I was a lawyer, an educated man—the kind of person the Germans liquidated at every opportunity. I suspected that this information was supplied to him by our *Vorarbeiter* Futerko, who

6 Oppel, a cruel HASAG manager nicknamed Hämmerl for his sadistic hammer attacks on victims, was put on trial in 1948 and sentenced to death. See Schutzman, "After the War," in *Sefer Czenstochow*, vol. 2, pp. 361–380.

was now hanging around Pale Joseph and bowing to him servilely. What should I do now? How could I hide here? The Germans were clearly preparing a new misfortune for us. This was evident from the foremen and *Werkschutz* running around and from the pale, fear-driven faces of the Jewish work crew.

After finishing work, I went in search of a hiding place. I wandered around the mostly empty factory halls, where machines had not yet been put in, and found nowhere suitable. It was dangerous to go out into the factory yard, as the *Werkschutz* chased people away, sparing no blows with rifle butts or kicks. Suddenly, I was overcome by feelings of negativity and despair. A strange depression and indifference possessed me. I had no strength left for this constant struggle against the deadly German machine that was targeting the murder of Jews. I felt cornered, alone, and lost in those half-empty factory halls. I was not the only one who felt this; it was shared by most of the Jews at HASAG. We were weak, defenseless, and at the mercy of the German satraps who were carrying out their elaborate plan of exterminating the Jews. Feeling weak, I collapsed onto the boards of the bench in our room and fell asleep.

I was woken by the din of distant conversations, the bark of orders, and the hum of activity. It was a dark night. The electric lamps of the factory square and on the winding streets were all lit. The *Werkschutz* were chasing the HASAG prisoners out of the factory rooms, which served as temporary accommodation. Everyone was rushed outside into the open factory square and ordered to line up according to their work units. We had to march forward in rows of four.

Our *Vorarbeiter* began lining up the *Prüferei* workers. In front of us, Jewish men and women were already marching in fours. We could hear the steady clatter of their wooden shoes on the cobblestones. We walked toward an alley that led to the entrance gate of one of the production halls and passed the revolving shed of the narrow-gauge factory railroad. Right next to it stood the HASAG foremen and engineers, saying, "Selection! They're going to murder the Jews again for misdeeds they haven't committed!"

The spotlight blazed a harsh, ominous yellow over the pale Jews. The Germans stood staring at us, eyeing their victims. They held curved canes stretched out in front of them and looked like dog catchers about to grab the animals by their haunches. With the sticks, they grabbed their prey by the neck or by the shoulder, pulled them out of the line, and placed them against the wall. They were all armed with pistols attached to their belts and rifles slung over their shoulders. Not one of these Germans was a member of the armed forces or the police, and not all of them were members of the Nazi party, but they all took part in the murder of the Jews with the same viciousness and merciless cruelty. These German bricklayers, carpenters, locksmiths, engineers, and doctors of chemistry were the symbols of the entire German nation, who, on that warm July night, participated in an unprecedented genocide.[7]

Also standing there were HASAG director Dr. Lüth; technical director Dr. Bretschneider; political manager Arnt; technical managers and engineers Joseph Spaltenholz, Francke, and Fasold; and the foremen Gintel, Oppel, Niziołek, Wirbatz, Keler, Walter, and many others. *Werkschutzleiter* Klemm and his assistants Stieglitz, Shevchenko, Doroshenko, the renegade Kmicikiewicz, the son of a Polish gymnasium teacher, Pawelak, and others whose names I did not know, all stood there together too. There were also representatives of the Schutzpolizei, making sure that the selection took place mercilessly under the commanders Laszynski and Handtke. *Werkschutz* with rifles stood ready to shoot.

We had already passed the railroad shed and were turning onto a street aptly named Selection Street. At this point, I felt the handle of the cane tightening around my neck. With a strong jerk, I was dragged out of line. I saw Spaltenholtz's cold, pale, merciless face. With a strong push, I found myself standing in a crowded group of unfortunates doomed to death. Behind me, in deadly silence and under blinding spotlights, the selection was taking place; ahead of me were the metal doors leading to the dark, empty factory hall, into which the *Werkschutz* were prodding us. In this hall, the vestibule of death, there were wails, cries, and screams of men—the victims of today's selection.

7 These remarks by Kromołowski echo the questions raised in the book by historian Christopher Browning, *Ordinary Men: Reserve Police Battalion 101 and the Final Solution in Poland* (New York: Harper Perennial, 1998). The book examines the role of ordinary German men—mostly middle-aged, working-class individuals—in the Holocaust. The book focuses on the German Reserve Police Battalion 101, which was tasked with carrying out mass shootings and deportations of Jews in Nazi-occupied Poland. Browning explores how these men, initially untrained and unprepared for such atrocities, became active participants in genocide. Through meticulous research, he highlights the psychological, social, and situational factors—such as obedience to authority, peer pressure, and desensitization—that transformed ordinary individuals into perpetrators of mass murder. Browning challenges simplistic views of evil and raises profound questions about human behavior and moral responsibility.

The hall's dark interior was filling up with new victims. My eyes became accustomed to the prevailing darkness, and I could already distinguish the silhouettes of people I knew. Gonzwa, a former policeman, the son of the owner of a paint store on New Market, was lying on the concrete floor. He was no longer young and wore glasses. This was reason enough for the Germans to deem him unfit for work and send him to his death. He was lying down and crying over his fate. A woman, his wife, approached him. "They sent you here too, you wretched thing," Gonzwa said, and they both began weeping.

A young, fair-haired, very pretty girl from the town Białobrzegi was standing next to me and crying. She was a victim of Spaltenholtz, who decided that she was too pretty to work in a German factory and sentenced her to death. The Germans were picky when it came to Jews: Some were too pretty for them, others too ugly; there were those who were lazy, and others too talented or too intelligent; some people were too young, and some were too old and therefore not suitable for work; this one was too handsome, and that one had a round back. A single harsh glance from a German could send an innocent man to hell. We were Jews, which was reason enough for the uncouth, brutal German foreman to deem someone expendable and send them to the cemetery, where the executioners were awaiting them. I was one of them, one of the condemned.

Standing next to me was Iziek (Ignacy) Wajnman, also a lawyer. He was balding even though he was only thirty years old. He looked old, so they took him out of the line and sentenced him. His foreman, Niciolek, was the one who did this. After a while, a new victim came in: Wajnman's wife, Tenia (Teresa), who had a master's degree in philology.

"Why did they send you here?" asked her terrified husband, wringing his hands.

"I asked to come. I want to be with you and share your fate. After all, I am your wife."

The dark factory hall was still filling up with new victims. The Germans had just pushed a young doctor, Jerzy Galster, inside. He had received a death sentence because he had issued a medical certificate releasing a Jewish worker from work who, according to the Germans, was perfectly healthy. In reality, the worker was suffering from bloody diarrhea. Galster's wife, who begged for his life to be spared, was also thrown into our death row. A similar fate befell Jarocinski, who begged for his wife to be spared. We were already over 200 people, both men and women, and mostly young. Some were lying motionless on the floor, seemingly taking a nap, while others were standing and looking straight ahead with mad eyes. There was a funereal atmosphere. People were crying. I was overwhelmed by a strange emptiness. I said goodbye to my loved ones in my mind. I became indifferent to everything.

Suddenly, the metal doors of the hall opened wide, and the *Werkschutz* started pushing us outside. Exiting one by one, we once again passed by the group of foremen and prominent HASAG officials, among them the director, Dr. Lüth. I also saw Bernard Kurland, the Jewish manager of our camp. We were told to walk toward the gate that led to the so-called colony, where the German foremen and officials in the factory administration lived. There were also cellars here—notorious bunkers, where prisoners sentenced to flogging or death were held. This was also the location of the *Werkschutz* guardhouse, the *Wache*—the execution chamber for Jewish workers.

Kurland suddenly noticed me and approached Lüth. He pointed at me, and explained something to the German. After a moment's reflection, Lüth nodded in agreement and gestured permissively. I was pulled aside, as if the decision about my fate was not yet final. Meanwhile, the procession of selection victims continued. Along a line of armed *Werkschutz*, men and women advanced slowly toward the gate leading to the colony.

What Kurland said to Lüth about me I will never know; he took it with him to his grave. I suppose he was referring to my relationship with Helenka Tenenbaum, whom Lüth knew personally. Kurland apparently wanted to save me from death, wanting to repay Helenka in some way. She was the one who had saved Kurland's life on March 20 when he jumped from the truck going to the cemetery, and as a result of her pleas, Degenhardt agreed that Kurland could return to the camp and become head of the *Judeneinsatz*.

I stood for a moment, unmoving and still uncertain of my fate. Old Krauze, father of a *Judeneinsatz* worker, was also pulled aside, probably also as a result of Kurland's intervention, whose opinion was valued by Lüth. After seeing that the Germans and the *Werkschutz* were busy herding the selected people and paying no attention to me, I slowly began walking backward and, once I had put some distance between us, suddenly ran deeper into the dark camp alley. No one noticed my escape. I reached the room with my flatbed, threw myself onto the mattress, and lay down, feeling half-dead and numb. A sob escaped from my tight throat. Tears were running down my face as I cried.

Meanwhile, all those who had been selected by the *Werkschutz* were led out through the factory gate and taken to the cellars, where they were to survive the night. Quite unexpectedly, toward the end of the selection, two policemen from the Schutzpolizei approached Lüth and, citing an order from Commandant Degenhardt's office, demanded that he hand over Bernard Kurland and his wife. They were both thrown into the cellars, condemned to death. The person who had been my savior a few hours earlier was now a victim himself of German hypocrisy and cruelty. Bernard Kurland was a wonderful man of extraordinary intelligence and with a good heart, sensitive to human misfortune.

In the early hours of July 20, 1943, there was unusual movement among the Jewish warehouse staff on Garibaldi Street. The commandant of the German police announced that everyone working there had the opportunity to reunite with his family at HASAG-Pelcery. They would be transported by car to May 1 Street, where the HASAG ammunition factory was located with its adjacent camp of Jewish workers. There were many volunteers—they had been waiting a long time to reunite with their loved ones after a lengthy separation. Over 100 people filled the police cars, their hearts filled with hope to see their loved ones, be with them, and share in their good or bad fortune.

The cars drove along familiar streets and actually entered through the main gate of HASAG, toward the former Pelcery factory. But instead of the factory gates opening, the doors of the cellars opened to the newcomers from Garibaldi Street instead. The Germans drove them all into the same prison rooms, where more than 160 people—victims of yesterday's selection—were being held and were awaiting extermination. Also arriving were cars filled with Jewish policemen, their commander Parasol, and their families. Everyone was driven into the cellars, everyone was sentenced to death!

Then, the Germans and the *Werkschutz* drove out the prisoners from the cellars and loaded them onto trucks. Some resisted, refusing to be pushed onto the truck. The most violent resistance came from the Jewish policeman Kornbrot. Schupo policemen, *Werkschutz*, and civilian foremen threw themselves at the prisoners, beating them on the head with rifle butts and striking their temples with hammers. The sadistic foreman Oppel did this job best. He used a bricklayer's hammer to hit his victims, stunning and incapacitating them. Other torturers tied the Jews' arms and legs together with wire and threw them into the trucks. They loaded people one on top of the other, and the cars, filled with stunned passengers, were driven to the cemetery, where the German torturers were already waiting. A series of machine-gun shots rang out, and blood flowed freely on the cemetery ground.[8]

8 According to Pietrzykowski, some 400 Jews were shot at the cemetery on July 20, 1943. See Pietrzykowski, *Hitlerowcy w Częstochowie*, p. 193.

On that terrible day, I waited for my wife Stella to come to HASAG; however, she did not come, and I never saw her again. Although a small group of Garibaldi workers—both men and women—arrived, my wife was not among them. Several kichen workers were part of the group that arrived. As the kitchen was located near the garden where, as my wife had informed me in her note, she worked alongside Helenka Tenenbaum and her brother. I asked the new arrivals from Garibaldi Street what had happened to my wife. My bleeding heart, however, told me the answer would be tragic.

Those I questioned hedged or evaded me with incomplete words, until finally one of them revealed the terrible truth: My wife had been shot, together with Helenka Tenenbaum and her brother by Schupo men in the garden where they all worked. They put an end to her young life. She fell at the hands of the German genocide criminals at the age of just twenty-six. I do not even know where her body was buried, and I never had the opportunity to mourn over her grave. On that terrible day, I was close to insanity. Despair and grief over the loss of my beloved wife filled my aching heart.

That day, a German from the Schutzpolizei was seen walking around the factory square looking for Helenka Tenenbaum's cousin. However, no one knew this cousin and could not point him out. He was also supposed to have shared the fate of the 500 Jews whose common grave had been freshly dug in the Jewish cemetery. That alleged cousin was me. The German looked for me, without success, as all day, I lay half-conscious from the pain of losing my wife, whom I loved so much.

CHAPTER NINE

HASAG FORCED LABOR CAMP

Construction of the wooden barracks was complete, and several rows of bunks were placed inside it. On them lay mattresses made of paper fibers and filled with paper as a substitute for straw. The entire crew was moved to the barracks in stages; there was a section for women, another one for men, and a separate area intended as a sick bay with a barrack surrounded by barbed wire for anyone infectious. Blankets were also distributed, but only a lucky few received one. Most prisoners slept in their clothes.

Machines for manufacturing rifle bullets were set into operation at an accelerated pace in the so-called *Infanterie*. The bullets were filled with gunpowder in the "laboratory," and the production of grenade launchers had already begun. The *Rekalibrierung* department was still active; however, the production of an apparatus for propelling trucks—the *Apparatebau*—was shut down.

Strict discipline was enforced both in the camp and on the factory grounds. It was absolutely forbidden to leave the workplace without permission from the foreman, even for a short while. Individual prisoners were also prohibited from leaving the camp's territory; only groups going to the factory area to work were allowed in. Work lasted twelve hours, and there were two continuous shifts, day and night. A short break was set aside for lunch. The meal—hot soup of indeterminate consistency—was brought from the kitchen in cauldrons by special workers and poured into bowls in the factory hall. The factory had its own railroad siding inside the factory buildings, as well as a transport and construction service called the *Baubetrieb*. A total of 3,000 Jewish men and women, whom the Germans referred to as *Häftlinge* (prisoners), were quartered at HASAG-Pelcery. Later, branches of the HASAG munitions factory were also set up on the premises of the former textile factories of Warta and Częstochowianka, where several hundred more Jewish prisoners who had been deported there were housed.

The HASAG-Pelcery labor camp, Częstochowa, Poland. YVA, 9810/30.

There were some initial escape attempts. At night, some sneaked into the wagons that were already partially loaded with boxes of shells. The next day, after the cargo had been fully loaded, the wagons sealed, and they had left the factory area, those hidden inside escaped, jumping out to freedom at the prearranged locations. Many managed to save themselves in this way. Others—and there were many more in this category—paid for these attempts with their lives. A young Jewish worker who tried to escape this way was shot by the Gestapo, and to deter others, six prisoners from his work group were captured, bound with barbed wire, and put on display in the barracks yard.

The death penalty was used more and more frequently. On one occasion, a *Werkschutz* shot a young prisoner for staying too long in the toilet. Another time, the deputy *Werkschutzleiter* Stieglitz mistreated a woman for a long time, beating her with a cane until she fainted before shooting her. Another *Werkschutz* shot a worker walking through the barracks yard for absolutely no reason. At night, the *Werkschutz* often shot at the women's barracks, severely wounding several women. Foreman Hausner once shot a woman on the charge that she was lazy and doing her job poorly. At night, the *Werkschutz* also often entered the women's section, selected young women, and raped them with complete impunity.

A foreman named Walter beat the workers savagely. Johannes Nikke, another foreman, took men and women to the *Wache* for the smallest infraction. There, the *Werkschutz* carried out flogging punishments of at least fifty lashes on their bare buttocks. After such a flogging, each victim would lose consciousness and had to be revived by being doused with cold water. Nikke also often entered the women's barracks at night, took out a dozen or so women, and led them to the factory hall to scrub the concrete floor with the gloves they used to refurbish shells. He once beat a worker named Wolman so severely that he had to be taken to the hospital.

The German *Meisters* Marianna Mietge and Frieda Redke, Klara Marchewka, and the so-called Pietrucha treated the Jewish workers no less bestially. Marianna Mietge took part in mass executions both in the area of the liquidated small ghetto and in the cemetery, shooting Jews with her revolver. These German women beat and tortured both male and female workers for the slightest offense and often for no reason at all. Every day, they drove people to the *Wache* and helped administer corporal punishment by holding the beaten person by the head or legs.

I was assigned to work under the notoriously cruel foreman Wirbatz in the acid-bath pipes section, the *Stossrohrs*—the part of the factory that produced grenade launchers, which was the latest German invention. Two tubs containing different types of stinking acid stood in a shed that was filled with cold water, with the gate and windows kept wide open whatever the weather. The other worker and I stood opposite each other on either side of the long tub of acid, on the constantly wet concrete floor. Each 20-kilogram iron pipe had to be gripped firmly and dipped into a tub of one type of acid, then tossed into another tub containing a different acid, dipped again, lifted, and set aside. We repeated this action over and over, handling pipes of the same weight, working all day and, every other week, all night as well.

The work was very hard, even for men accustomed to intense physical exertion. For me, it was extremely difficult and, given the state of malnutrition in the camp, downright deadly. To make matters worse, I had to do this work while standing in water and in the autumn chill, which intensified at that time of year. Kon, my workmate, was no longer a young man, but he was in far better physical shape and considerably taller than I was. This meant that he bore more of the iron pipe's weight while working, and our difference in height prevented any coordinated movements that could have made the work much easier.

I was not at all surprised when Kon complained about me to Wirbatz, who, in his customary manner, came into our wet, gloomy shed to inspect the efficiency of our work. Wirbatz gave me an angry look, muttered something under his breath, and immediately appointed another worker in my place who was the same height as Kon. He also ordered the *Vorarbeiter* to assign me to another department. To begin with, I was instructed to move a box of nails—weighing about 30 kilograms—from one end of the factory hall to the other. Wirbatz stood next to me, spread his legs wide, and watched my efforts mockingly. With great difficulty, I lifted the heavy box of nails, took a few steps on bent legs, and felt blood rush to my head. Trying again, I took a step and then fell to the ground, bringing the unfortunate box down with me, which broke apart, spilling nails all over the floor. The German had apparently been waiting for that. He started yelling and kicking me several times with his heavy shoe and pounding my head with his fists.

It is easy to imagine how the whole story would have ended had Wirbatz not been called to the phone and suddenly walked away. Taking advantage of this, I escaped from the factory building and went to the sanitary post, where one of the nurses dressed my wounds and bruises. Seeing my state of complete exhaustion, she asked the doctor to release me from my duties for that day. I dragged myself to the barracks, threw myself on my bunk, and tried in vain to fall asleep.

On that same day, for a small bribe—borrowed from a friend—I was given a new job through a *Vorarbeiter* from the rivets department. I was seated at a long table with a hammer and told to flatten one end of the rivet with a specific tool. This work suited my physical capabilities well. We worked in shifts—one week during the day and the following week at night. I recovered slowly.

I managed to bring my brother from the Raków ironworks to HASAG, and we reunited after being separated for so long. The aforementioned deputy *Werkschutzleiter* of the ironworks, Milhof—a German who stood out for his sympathy toward the Jewish prisoners—arranged such family reunions. In the end, for extending his assistance to the Jews, he was sent to the Russian front and was demoted to the rank of ordinary private. When I learned about such arrangements being made, I went to Zylberszac, who had taken charge of the labor department after Kurland's death, and he put my brother on the list of those chosen for exchange to come to HASAG. A few days later, my brother and some others arrived in a truck at the barracks square, and we were able to hug and talk to each other. My brother was happy to be out of the steel mill, where he had a very hard and exhausting job at the iron smelting furnace. His shoes and clothes were half-burned, and his health was impaired.

We managed to get him a job in the building department, the *Baubetrieb*, where a friend of mine named Birenholc was one of the foremen. Thanks to this, my brother was able to leave the factory buildings and had contact with Polish workers. Henio, brave and enterprising as usual, tried and sometimes succeeded to earn a few złoty by trading, so we were able to eat a little better, spread butter on our bread, or sometimes eat a potato soup, which I secretly managed to cook on the barracks stove. Almost every day after work, my late wife's brother Tadzio, Henio, and I would eat dinner together in a corner of the barracks and talk.

It must have been my third week of working in the rivets department when one night, during a shift, I felt sick. I had chills, a headache, and my legs were buckling beneath me. I had diarrhea, and it felt like I had a high fever. In the morning, after finishing work, I dragged myself to the sanitary post. The head of the camp health service was a Jewish doctor, a surgeon called Dr. I. Szperling. He examined me, asked me what was wrong, and finally stuck a thermometer under my arm. The thermometer showed 37.5 degrees Celsius, which, according to Szperling, did not excuse me from work. I spent the whole day lying on my bunk. I felt sick. My whole body shivered from fever, and I was plagued by ever-increasing diarrhea. Despite this, I had to go to work again, and I worked through the night with a debilitating headache and diarrhea, which weakened me. From time to time I had to run to the camp latrine or factory toilet, which was not at all safe.

I knew there was typhus going round the camp, and I fell victim to it. This was very dangerous because sick people were not tolerated in the camp routine, especially those with infectious diseases. The Germans would pull them from their beds and shoot them in the cemetery. For this reason, prisoners avoided being placed in isolation in the infectious disease *Revier* (camp infirmary), which was usually empty, and they tried to overcome typhus by showing up for work or lying in the barracks, which spread the disease more.

On the third day, my health deteriorated further, and I was so weak that I could hardly stand. This time, when I visited the sanitary post, I had a fever of 40 degrees Celsius, and Dr. Szperling diagnosed me with typhus. My brother took me, half-conscious and tottering on my feet, to the infectious disease hospital—essentially the mortuary. When I crossed the threshold of the hospital barracks, isolated and surrounded by thick coils of barbed wire, I was convinced that the end was approaching, and that I would not leave there alive.

Someone dragged me to a hospital bed, and I fell into an unhealthy, feverish sleep. The infectious disease hospital was visited twice a day by the camp doctors, Dr. Przyrowski from Częstochowa and Dr. Łuński from Łódź. The latter took an interest in me and prescribed me some yellowish tablets to take several times a day, which I drank with boiled water dyed dark to imitate coffee. There were several people in the barrack with typhus; however, the doctors did not report these incidents to the Germans, knowing the tragic consequences that would follow for the sick patients. In their reports, they invented cases of non-infectious diseases.

My fever did not subside completely, but it went down a little. I was still tormented by diarrhea, however. Opposite me, my schoolmate Benio Zylbersztajn lay completely unconscious. In addition to typhoid fever, he had contracted encephalitis, and his condition was serious. I lay on a bunk right next to the window and often saw my brother and brother-in-law, who did not abandon me during my illness. They tried to comfort me and brought me egg yolks mashed with sugar (*kogel mogel*), which the nurse gave me at their request. This strengthened my body that was so weakened by illness.

After a few days, my fever dropped significantly, and I felt a little better. One day, Dr. Szperling came to our room and saw that the floor was not very clean. He summoned an orderly, a certain Feldman, whom he started to hit with a broom in front of the patients and chased him around the barracks. After doing this, and after the screams of the beaten victim had fallen silent, Szperling suddenly ordered me to get off my bunk and go to a different one on the opposite wall. In turn, the feverish, sick person lying there was sent to my place. This was the end of Szperling's visit. Completely ignoring the sick patients and muttering something under his breath, he left the barracks. This Jewish doctor, the son of a local tinsmith, was disliked in our camp. Many patients condemned him for his excessive strictness, his aversion to his fellow Jews, and for sucking up to the Germans. In contrast, the three other doctors—Przyrowski, Luński, and Bresler—earned considerable goodwill. Thanks to them, the typhus epidemic was brought under control in a relatively short time, and the Germans never found out about it.

After some time, my fever subsided completely. I started to get up and walk around the hospital room. Dr. Luński decided that any further stay in the infectious diseases hospital was unnecessary and could even be dangerous, because the Germans might enter at any time as a result of someone revealing the outbreak of the epidemic. I left the hospital weakened and on trembling legs. It was the second day following the death of Benio Zylbersztajn, who never regained consciousness.

I had a voracious appetite and ate everything I could get my hands on. My brother bought more bread, and I also received a portion of a rather nutritious and tasty soup, which was cooked by order of the Judenarbeitseinsatz to feed convalescents. The money for this came from prisoner aid funds sent to the camp from the Aryan side. I also started looking around for work, because there were constant searches for those who refused to work, and anyone in the barracks or outside the factory buildings during the day was carefully watched.

Moreover, while in the barracks, one had to lie on a bunk pretending to be a sleeping night-shift worker, which was extremely annoying due to the swarms of fleas and bedbugs. The bedbugs, in particular, were a veritable plague, nesting in such numbers that they fell from the ceiling onto sleeping people and bit them painfully. We would sprinkle our mattresses with a layer of extremely sharp caustic soda, which the Germans used to clean the thimbles of artillery shells. However, this did not help much, and we usually left our beds not only bitten by the bugs but also burned and drugged by the extremely alkaline chemical. The only salvation was the bathhouse, which fortunately could be used daily and was visited by the masses. Bodies bitten by bedbugs and caustic soda combustions could be abundantly doused with warm water, which brought temporary relief and kept the body relatively clean.

However, the bathhouse was also the site of brutality on the part of the *Werkschutz*, who came there to abuse the Jewish prisoners. They would bring sharp rice brushes, which were used for scrubbing the floor; but instead, they scrubbed their victims until they bled, saying that they were helping remove the dirt. A not infrequent visitor to the bathhouse was the *Werkschutzleiter* assistant Stieglitz, who came especially when women were bathing. He would watch their naked bodies, making various crude gestures and vulgar remarks. He also used vulgar Jewish expressions taught to him by Abramek, a camp orphan depraved by the inhumane living conditions.

Right next to the bathhouse was the delousing room. It contained a large steam boiler in which Liber Brener, who operated the delousing room, was able to professionally vaporize any garment, even the shabbiest ones, freeing them from these dangerous parasites. Thanks to the work of the delousing unit, the camp avoided an epidemic of spotted fever. After bathing, it was obligatory to undergo a visual inspection by Horowicz, a specialist in the detection of pubic lice. He was armed with a powerful magnifying glass and a stick, with which he very skillfully maneuvered through the thickets of hair. When these very annoying and dangerous insects were detected, he carried out an immediate treatment in the form of shaving the infested lower abdomen and rubbing the area with a spatula dipped in a gray-colored ointment. Similar treatments were applied by a nurse to bathing women.

That year, winter began early, and the frosty air seeped through the barracks' cracks and numerous holes. We were cold in our almost unheated rooms, so people eagerly stayed in the warm factory halls, where work was performed in two shifts to mount and install automatic machines for the production of rifle bullets and cases. One factory hall after another was opened for production, filled with the constant hum of machines ejecting steel bullets impetuously into barrels. Men and women worked here under the supervision of German foremen, who ran through the factory halls making sure that production went without a hitch. Lazy or bad workers were hunted down, and when a machine stopped working as a result of some malfunction, the attendants were first beaten and kicked, and only later was the cause of the stoppage investigated.

One of the technical managers, the previously mentioned engineer Walter Fasold—also known as the Boxer—was particularly cruel in this department and beat both men and women. He did not hit with an open hand but with a curled fist, delivering boxing punches to the workers in the head, jaw, or temple that could knock even the toughest guy off his feet and often render him unconscious. One night, he entered the room so quietly that a boy named Tobias Niemiec, who was asleep at the machine, was not warned in time. Fasold caught up with the boy, dealt him several blows to the face before lifting the almost unconscious boy up and throwing him headfirst into a barrel half-filled with rifle casings. The boy, barely alive, was extracted from the barrel and taken to the hospital.

Other German foremen and engineers were no less brutal. Without distinguishing between sexes, Jewish workers were constantly beaten, kicked, and led to the guardhouse, where they were flogged for the slightest offense. There were times when Jewish workers were taken out of the factory halls and placed in one of the barracks, which were deserted during the day. From there they were taken to one of the extermination camps or to the munitions factory in Skarżysko-Kamienna or in Pionki, where the harsh labor and poisonous fumes decimated people.

After much effort, in which my brother played an important part, Zylberszac, as the current head of Judenarbeitseinsatz, assigned me to work in the unit responsible for cleanliness inside the camp—the *Reinigungskommando* (cleaning squad). A dozen or so people performed cleaning work under the direction of Jewish foremen, sweeping and cleaning the barracks area and keeping the latrine and washroom clean. The best aspects of this job were the irregular working hours and the complete peace and quiet from the Germans, who took no interest in this unit, while direct supervision was provided by three Jewish foremen: Szymek Gostyński, Kaufman, and Tadek Fisz. They were all very moderate in their demands and treated their subordinates decently, with understanding, and with the proverbial "wink of an eye." No discipline was administered here; shouting loud orders and rushing around could only be heard and seen when our bosses noticed an approaching German *Werkschutz* or—something that rarely happened—the German *Werkschutzleiter* himself.

The downside of this work placement was being constantly outdoors, which was especially troublesome on cold autumn and frigid winter days. It was necessary to thoroughly sweep the entire, very large yard, collect garbage and refuse into a tin wheelbarrow, and perform the same tasks in the latrine and washrooms. Afterward, the garbage—and often human excrement—was transported to the dump, where it was burned and the ashes buried in pits. These tasks had to be performed several times a day, and people were assigned shifts. Work in the *Reinigungskommando* was generally safe, not too hard, and belonged to a privileged order. That is why one had to invest a great deal of effort and use any protection to get into this cleaning unit.

We had a small room in the building that contained toilets and washrooms intended for storing equipment—brooms, shovels, wheelbarrows, and more. There was an iron stove there, which burned stolen coal, and one could warm up their stiff hands by the fire and drink some hot water, which replaced tea. Compared to the hard and dangerous work of munitions production, the *Reinigungskommando* was a peaceful haven amid the ever-churning waves of the camp's sea. With a broom in one hand and a shovel in the other, I walked around the barracks yard carrying out my duties, thanking blind fate and my patrons for this work assignment, which often stank of human excrement but at least did not stink of Germans.

In January 1944, a large number of Jews from the Łódź ghetto arrived at HASAG.[1] They were terribly emaciated and starving. Living in conditions of terror and abject poverty in the Łódź ghetto, these people looked around in disbelief at our camp, where, despite everything, each person received a daily ration of bread and beet soup, and did not die of starvation. Although the majority of HASAG prisoners were poorly fed and exhausted from the harsh labor and strict regime, there was also a group of people who did not lack bread and butter. These were primarily the *Vorarbeiters*—the foremen—who were able to gain the trust of the Germans supervisors and engineers by various, mostly by dishonest means. These people were the camp's "aristocracy." Together with their wives or mistresses, they lived in separate barracks, known as the official barracks, and they ate well.

Most of their money came from bribes, which they took from people in exchange for lighter work and protection from the terror of the foremen. Of course, they shared the bribes with their German superiors. Worse, they knew how to extort these bribes. If you didn't give them a bribe, they would report you to the foreman, make him think you were lazy, and the German would punch you in the face and beat you at every opportunity, turning each day—and sometimes even the night—into a living hell. Such a "dignitary" as Mr. *Vorarbeiter* walked slowly and with dignity, dressed in high, shiny boots, was well fed, and wore clean clothes. These people were recruited exclusively from the margins of society, most often from among the illiterate and manual laborers. The privileged ones also included people with money, as this meant one could buy better food, cigarettes, and even medicines and newspapers from the Polish workers. With money, one could also arrange for easier work—often doing almost nothing, with the knowledge and consent of the foreman and mediation by the powerful Jewish *Vorarbeiter*. However, this was very expensive, and only a few could enjoy such privileges.

There were also people who traded. They sold gold items, rings, and other jewelry to the Polish workers—things that the wealthier people had managed to hide in their clothing. They also sold various pieces of clothing, underwear, and other personal items. At HASAG, a very small group received

1 According to Pietrzykowski, Jews from the Łódź ghetto as well as prisoners from the Płaszów camp arrived in January 1944. Pietrzykowski, *Hitlerowcy w Częstochowie*, p. 195.

outside funds—channeled clandestinely from underground organizations, often in dollars—to carry out political activities. In reality, these so-called political dodgers used the money for their own needs and lived in relative abundance, by camp standards, without sharing it with anyone or engaging in any political work. After all, what kind of political activity was possible under conditions of iron discipline, pervasive despondency, and utter exhaustion from working all day beyond one's strength?

The only positive thing that can be said about these alleged political activists is that they allocated some of the money they received to running and maintaining a clandestine kitchen for the sick and those convalescing, which was open for some time and played a useful role in providing food and helping the sick recover. I remember that this kitchen was run by Zosia Weksztajn, the nurse Kolin, and Bosek Wołkowicz from Łódź. The act of feeding the sick was carried out in strict secrecy, hidden from the *Werkschutz* and their new manager, a German named Herman, who was supposedly a medic by profession. In contrast to the many good people who often risked their lives to help fellow prisoners, the head of the camp health service, the surgeon Dr. Szperling, behaved in a particularly antisocial manner. He often refused to prescribe medicine to the sick workers, but supplied them to German foremen and *Werkschutz* with exaggerated servility. The sanitary post had quite a large stock of medicines and medical supplies from the Jewish ghetto pharmacies, the labor camp's hospitals, and the JUS (Jüdische Unterstützungsstelle) welfare center in Kraków.[2]

However, there were not many people like this among the prisoners in HASAG. The overwhelming majority suffered from hunger, exhaustion, and cruel persecution by the German civilian superiors and *Werkschutz*. Numerous people fainted from exhaustion and died from untreated or poorly treated diseases. There were many *Muselmänner*,[3] who were

2 The Jüdische Unterstützungsstelle (Jewish Aid Center, JUS) was a Jewish humanitarian relief organization that initially operated under the name Jewish Social Self-Help (JSS; Polish: Żydowska Samopomoc Społeczna, ŻSS). Funded largely by the American Jewish Joint Distribution Committee (JDC), JSS supported branches across the General Government, running orphanages, hospitals, public kitchens, and ghetto welfare programs. After the 1942 mass deportations to death camps, JSS was dissolved and restructured as JUS, which continued limited humanitarian work until 1944.

3 The German term *Muselmann* (pl. *Muselmänner*) was widely used among concentration camp inmates to refer to prisoners who were near death due to exhaustion, starvation, or because they had given up hope.

extremely emaciated from hunger and exhaustion. When a child was born in the camp, it was immediately killed.[4]

Depression and resignation were widespread in the camp. There were also cases of suicide. I remember that the pharmacist Praszkiewicz, among others, took his own life as a result of depression. News coming from the Aryan side about the continuous and merciless extermination of hiding Jews by the Gestapo and the German police contributed greatly to this state of mind. Captured Jews were shot, along with the Poles who helped them. There were bands of *shmaltzovniks* (blackmailers), who tracked down and denounced hiding Jews. There were cases in which the Germans shot some of the captured Jews on the spot, while others were sent to HASAG, as was the case with the Rozencwajg family. This was a bad sign for us. It seemed that no prisoner would leave HASAG alive. However, in spite of the general gloom and desperation, there was a group of pious Jews in our camp, the Hassidim, who stuck together and held prayers on Saturday and holidays in one of the barracks, observed all the religious rituals, and paid their foremen not to work on those days.[5]

During this period, I tore out my mother's gold bracelet, which had been sewn into my jacket, and my brother and I sold it. With this money, we were occasionally able to buy an additional piece of bread and a bit of fat, potatoes, or onions. My late wife's brother, Tadzio Szmulewicz, ate with us, and thanks to these additional rations, our physical condition improved somewhat. I sometimes also managed to get a piece of horse

4 Births were indeed almost unknown in the camps. Babies were murdered by the Nazis or put to death by their mothers or other women. Pregnant women themselves were usually murdered in concentration camps upon arrival. Theresienstadt was an exception: Women who arrived pregnant were allowed to give birth. For more on this, see Helga Amesberger, "Reproduction under the Swastika: The Other Side of the Nazi Glorification of Motherhood," in Hedgepeth and Saidel, *Sexual Violence against Jewish Women*, pp. 168–209, specifically pp. 172–174. However, Kromołowski mentions later that some women still gave birth in the camp.

5 Despite the harsh conditions, and even after the devastating *Aktion* of July 20, 1943, religious Jews secretly maintained their religious life. They engaged in Torah discussions from memory. At one point, a small Torah scroll was smuggled into the camp, and from it they would read the Torah portion on Shabbat. Two pairs of tefillin were used by anyone who wanted during the day. High Holiday prayers and the sounding of a smuggled shofar brought moments of solace amid the despair. Hanukah was commemorated with makeshift Hanukah lamps crafted from shell casings, while the oil was taken from automobiles. See Schutzman, *Sefer Czenstochow*, vol. 2, pp. 131–134.

meat or fried chops from the barracks' oven. Sometimes I managed to cook a potato soup with real fat, which tasted wonderful, and the three of us ate it together. Such culinary activities were carried out in great secrecy from the Germans, with constant fear of the possible consequences. The *Werkschutz* often conducted raids and searches in the barracks, and we constantly heard tragic news. Once the *Werkschutz* shot a boy they found in the women's barracks. Another time, someone was shot for stealing bread. Some were sent to extermination camps. A woman was killed for evading work.

My brother and I decided to make some soap, partly for our own use and partly for sale. My brother bought some tallow from a Polish worker, but the *Werkschutz* caught him with the package during a search at the camp's entrance, took him to the guardhouse, and beat him so badly that he could not sit for several days. He walked with difficulty, even though I continuously applied cold compresses to his bruised and sore body. At that time, soap was worth its weight in gold and, despite everything, we boiled a large amount late at night on the barracks' stove, with the help of our *Stubenältester* (room master), who made sure that the *Werkschutz* did not catch us during the process.

Despite the great risk, people conducted various prohibited activities. Life proved stronger than all prohibitions, and the instinct for self-preservation inspired people to acts of creativity. Some traded in horse meat, smuggling it into the camp using clever tricks. Others sold vegetables, such as old Altman, who traded in onions, parsley, and carrots, storing all of this "merchandise" under a bunk mattress. There was one brave man, Lejzerowicz, who baked potato pancakes and sold them around the barracks, shouting "latkes, latkes" while carrying them on a tin tray. His pancakes were excellent and widely praised. Women cooked potato soup for a living, and these clandestine eateries persisted for some time despite the prevailing terror and constant manhunts and searches.

There were also some who managed to escape from the camp. Some succeeded, while others paid for their attempts with their lives. Michał Wajskopf, a young resident of Częstochowa, escaped from the camp and was caught by the Gestapo on the Aryan side and shot. There was also a surprising incident with a German foreman named Horn from the mechanical workshop, who helped a Jewish worker escape. However, when this was discovered, the foreman was sent to the Russian front. At the same time, another German foreman, Heisner, shot a Jewish worker, accusing her of evading work.

In late 1943, the Germans liquidated the Płaszów labor camp for Jews in Kraków, sending everyone to Auschwitz. A small number of prisoners—

mostly policemen and prominent Jewish people from Płaszów—arrived at HASAG, along with some SS men.[6] They tried to take control of the camp and announced the introduction of a very strict camp regime, the creation of a concentration camp, and the construction of gas chambers and a crematorium. For the time being, however, the power struggle was lost by both Płaszów Jews and the SS men, and management of the camp remained in the hands of *Werkschutzleiter* Herman and his staff.[7]

The management of the Judenarbeitseinsatz remained with Zylberszac and his few officials, among whom Krauze, who directed the workers' roll calls and kept the records and files of the Jewish prisoners, assumed the greatest importance. As a result of the influx of this new labor force from the Łódź ghetto and Płaszów, the number of prisoners in our camp increased considerably, so the Germans set up two branches of the HASAG munitions factory in the former textile factories of Warta and Częstochowianka. There, too, camps for Jewish prisoners were created, with the same administrative structure as our camp and the same extremely strict discipline. It was even said that the conditions in these camps were far harsher than ours, and the living conditions much worse.

6 According to Pietrzykowski, Płaszów prisoners were brought to Częstochowa in January 1944. See Pietrzykowski, *Hitlerowcy w Częstochowie*, p. 195; Jerzy Mizgalski, "The Jews of Częstochowa: A Short History," The World Society of Częstochowa Jews and Their Descendants, https://www.czestochowajews.org/old-czestochowa/jews-of-czestochowa/. See also Ryszard Kotarba, Kamil Budziarz, and Dorota Plutecka, *A Historical Guide to the German Camp in Płaszów 1942–1945* (Warsaw: Institute of National Remembrance—Commission of the Prosecution of Crimes against the Polish Nation, 2014), p. 37. On January 10, 1944, Płaszów changed its status from labor to concentration camp. The concentration camp continued to function until January 1945. As the Red Army was advancing, the Nazis began to dismantle the camp. The prisoners were sent to other forced labor camps, as well as to death camps. All children were deported to Auschwitz on May 15, 1944. The biggest transport left Płaszów on August 6, deporting 7,500–8,000 Jewish prisoners to Auschwitz-Birkenau. See Dean, *USHMM Encyclopedia of Camps and Ghettos*, vol. 2, part B, p. 865.

7 Upon the SS takeover of the camp, there were indeed rumors about gas chambers and crematoria about to be built, as the author mentions later.

CHAPTER TEN

DAILY LIFE IN HASAG

In the summer of 1944, due to the significant deterioration of the military situation, the defeats suffered, and the continuing retreat of the German army on the Russian front, the Germans closed their armaments production in Skarżysko-Kamienna and Pionki. These facilities were located in eastern Poland, and it seemed that the Germans recognized the danger in these areas. As a result, all machinery and equipment, along with the Jewish workers, were moved from there to Częstochowa and placed in the HASAG munitions factories in Pelcery, Warta, Częstochowianka, and the steelworks in Raków. The number of Jewish prisoners at HASAG rose sharply to about 11,000 people.[1]

Our camp became more crowded, living conditions worsened, and the regime and discipline grew much stricter, particularly because all these camps were now under the command of the former *Werkschutzleiter* of Skarżysko, Fritz Bartenschlager,[2] infamous for his cruelty. He was an

1 See Pietrzykowski, *Hitlerowcy w Częstochowie*, pp. 194–195; Mizgalski, "The Jews of Częstochowa: A Short History," The World Society of Częstochowa Jews and Their Descendants, https://www.czestochowajews.org/old-czestochowa/jews-of-czestochowa/; Karay, *Death Comes in Yellow*, p. 71.

2 Chief of the *Werkschutz* at Skarżysko was *SS-Haupsturmführer* Kurt Krauze, and Fritz Bartenschlager was his deputy. Karay, *Death Comes in Yellow*, p. 41.

extraordinary sadist and a murderer, for whom shooting a Jewish prisoner was an everyday occurance. He was known for arranging parties for the German foremen and *Werkschutz*, to which he would bring young, pretty Jewish girls whom the drunken Germans raped and then murdered without mercy after the party.[3] During the evacuation of Skarżysko, it was reported that Bartenschlager sent a large number of Jewish prisoners to the camps in Trawniki and Pionki.

The arrival of this large number of Jewish prisoners in our camp caused a great deal of confusion and disorder, which the Germans—even with the aid of the *Werkschutz*—were unable to control, despite their severe repression and harsh regime. They therefore used the previously established Jewish fire brigade, composed of prisoners, to maintain order and discipline. These firefighters wore blue uniforms and navy-blue caps, and many had the privilege of wearing leather-soled officer boots. The firemen were relieved from factory work and organized fire protection exercises almost daily both in the barracks and in the factory buildings. Adam Rotaub, a former fire-brigade instructor in a prewar linen and burlap factory, was appointed chief of the fire brigade in Gnaszyńska Manufaktura in Gnaszyn, near Częstochowa. Now, these firemen were being used by the Germans as auxiliary policemen to watch over and discipline the people arriving from Skarżysko and Pionki.[4]

The newcomers were temporarily housed in vacant factory halls, where living conditions were primitive. They slept in their clothes on the floor. The *Vorarbeiters*, who were also members of the fire brigade, were particularly zealous in their cleaning duties and in keeping order. They did not spare any pokes or brutal behavior toward the newcomers from Skarżysko, who were completely lost in the new camp conditions.

The behavior of some Polish workers, employed as hired hands in the HASAG factories, differed greatly from the reprehensible behavior of the fortunately scarce scum of the earth and socially marginalized in our camp. Many of them risked their lives to smuggle money and letters from the Aryan side for their Jewish workmates.[5] One such Pole, Jan Brust,

3 Bartenschlager's sexual crimes and subsequent murder of his victims are discussed in Karay, *Death Comes in Yellow*, p. 79.

4 Adam Józef Rotaub (1912–1982) was a teacher, historian, political activist, and city councillor. He was in charge of the HASAG-Pelcery fire brigade, which, as Kromołowski indicates, performed some police functions as well. See Sętkowski, *Częstochowa Jews: A Biographical Dictionary*, pp. 377–378.

5 Throughout his book, Kromołowski's criticism and frequent indignation toward

fled when he noticed an inspection being carried out at the entrance to the factory premises. During his escape, the *Werkschutz* shot and severely wounded him. Brust had money and letters for Jewish prisoners with him. He managed to destroy the letters in time, but the money was confiscated. Another time, the *Werkschutz* captured a Polish worker called Eugeniusz Nabiałek, who was sent to a concentration camp by the Gestapo. The Jewish doctor at the Raków ironworks, Dr. Lajzer Glatter, was also known for his noble behavior. He did everything possible to help the sick, suffering, and weak. Together with other prisoners, he was sent to a concentration camp, where he died.[6]

As for me, I got a new job. I was ordered to paint serial numbers on the barracks' bunks. According to a new order from the camp authorities, each bunk bed sleeping place was to be marked with the appropriate number. The Germans assigned this work to our *Reinigungskommando*, and since nobody else could paint pretty numbers, I was ordered to do it. Equipped with a light ladder, a can of black paint, and a brush, I walked around the barracks, painting numbers on the front boards of the bunks. The work was good: It was unrestricted, gave me a great deal of freedom, and, most importantly, allowed me to be in the barracks at any time of day, under cover, which was especially beneficial during autumn dusk and the cold winter, given my lack of clothing and shoes full of holes.

For all prisoners in our camp, the day began at dawn. During autumn and winter, it was still dark outside, and the yellowish light of the electric lamps shone in the barracks square. At 6:00 in the morning, the HASAG prisoners were assembled for roll call. On the vast barracks square, sleepless and exhausted people with pale faces—thin and dressed in wretched, dirty clothing, marked by the Germans with long red stripes—lined up in even rows. The outer garments were painted red to prevent prisoners from escaping. Initially, the workers lined up for morning roll calls according to

Poles give way to statements of appreciation, particularly for specific groups and individuals. However, he shows little tolerance for Jews who held privileged positions and mistreated their fellow Jews.

6 Jan Brust died of his wounds. Eugeniusz Nabiałek was sent to Gross-Rosen. He survived until the liberation by the Red Army. See Brener, "Resistance and Destruction in the Częstochowa Ghetto," pp. 158–162. Dr. Leon Lajzer Glatter (1910–1945) was either deported to Germany in January 1945 or murdered in the camp. See also Brener, p. 138; Sętkowski, *Częstochowa Jews: A Biographical Dictionary*, p. 161.

their place of work, but later, when the SS men from Płaszów took over,[7] they were ordered to line up in front of their sleeping barracks. When the entire camp was ready for roll call, they had to wait for the arrival of the *Werkschutzleiter* and his crew. Sometimes the wait was long and tiring, especially on rainy autumn days and in the winter. Ice-cold rain or snow fell, and the wind blew right through our scant clothing, making people shiver from the cold, rub their hands together, and stomp their frozen feet on the ground.

Finally, the Germans appeared and, assisted by the *Werkschutz* armed with rifles, and the Jewish officials from the Judenarbeitseinsatz, they began counting people, checking who was absent, and identifying anyone who was sick. During roll call, the deputy *Werkschutzleiter*, Stieglitz, paraded around with a tame parrot on his shoulder, which occasionally shouted "Judenschwein" (Jewish pig) in a throaty voice.

During roll calls, he made people throw their hats onto the roof of the barracks and then ordered them to climb up to retrieve them. This was not easy for the exhausted, freezing people, many of whom fell to the ground, much to Stieglitz's delight. However, they had to repeat their actions until their cap was on their head. The *Werkschutz* would show off by riding their bicycles, which they rode along the rows, running over people's feet under the pretext of leveling the ranks.

Finally, when the agony of the roll call ended, people marched toward the exit gate, where the *Werkschutz* again stood and beat with their truncheons those who forgot to take off their headgear when passing before them. At the same time, the night shift entered the camp. Exhausted by the hard work and after beatings from the foremen, they threw themselves onto their bunks fully clothed and fell fast asleep. The air in the barracks was stale. There was a specific stench of dirty rags and sweaty bodies, as well as the stench produced by the masses of bugs that prowled the barracks and human bodies. People often bathed in the camp bathhouse, but this did not generally improve the state of hygiene because there was no soap for washing and cleaning clothes.

I painted the bunk numbers with black, quick-drying paint. Walking around the men's and women's barracks, I reached the top bunk beds on

7 The SS took over the command of the prisoners on December 14, 1944. See Pietrzykowski, *Hitlerowcy w Częstochowie*, p. 195; Mizgalski, "The Jews of Częstochowa: A Short History," The World Society of Częstochowa Jews and Their Descendants, https://www.czestochowajews.org/old-czestochowa/jews-of-czestochowa/.

my portable ladder, which gave me a daily glimpse of the sad existence of the HASAG forced laborers in private, intimate conditions. The bunks were the only place where people could be alone, cry, and complain to their closest neighbors. Often people lay on their bunks, their backs bruised from beatings, with faces swollen from the blows of the foremen's fists, applying cold water compresses to any sore spots. Here also lay the sick with high fevers—those trying to avoid the camp hospital for as long as possible, fearing the Germans. Women in advanced stages of pregnancy also lay on the bunks, afraid to reveal themselves to the foreman, because the Germans often shot pregnant women. There were also women who secretly gave birth on the bunks in the barracks and hid their newborns in their beds to protect them from inevitable death.

Sexual intercourse also took place on these bunks, also in secret, and it was not uncommon for me to climb up my painter's ladder and retreat in embarrassment after seeing half-naked lovers entwined in loving embraces, immersed in each other and isolated from the world and people. Nature was asserting its rights even under these miserable conditions.

In the summer of 1944, to everyone's surprise, the German authorities permitted soccer games in the barracks square. This unexpected break in the camp's strict discipline was immediately the subject of speculation. Some maintained that the Germans were softening their harsh approach, that they would treat the Jewish prisoners more humanely, that the tragic period of physical extermination was over, and as a result, Jewish prisoners working for the German armaments industry as essential workers would be spared and might have a chance to survive the war. Others were far more cynical, saying it was a tactic aimed at reducing the Jews' vigilance before their imminent liquidation.

A group of camp dignitaries—mainly foremen—played soccer with each other on summer afternoons. It was an unusual sight. Against a backdrop of widespread poverty and terror, among the shabby, barefoot, and constantly frightened prisoners, a few well-fed, energetic people kicked a ball and scored goals using an improvised goalpost. Unsurprisingly, playing soccer was suddenly forbidden, the balls were confiscated, and people were forbidden to gather in the barracks square under penalty of death. The *Werkschutz* beat several prisoners passing through the square with their rifle butts. Hope dissipated like smoke.

News from the outside world, however, reached our isolated camp, which was surrounded by barbed wire. Occasionally, someone would surreptitiously read the government's *Krakauer Zeitung*,[8] or talk about news they had heard from Polish workers who had been listening to a foreign radio station. From these sources, we learned that the entire world was engulfed in a total conflagration. The bloodiest battles were still taking place on the Russian front. The German war machine threw millions of soldiers and thousands of planes and tanks onto this front. After their initial successes, the Germans suffered defeats, about which one could easily learn—reading between the lines of official reports of the Wehrmacht headquarters in the newspapers—where the planned withdrawal of the German army to other positions was increasingly mentioned.

The turning point on the eastern front was the Battle of Stalingrad. From January 10 to February 2, 1943, the German offensive there collapsed, and the Russian army broke off into its first major assault, which stretched the front from the city of Voronezh all the way to the Caucasus Mountains over a distance of 1,500 kilometers. The Russian army penetrated deep into the territory captured by the Germans for 150–500 kilometers in the direction of western Russia. After breaking the German blockade at Stalingrad, the Russian army moved forward, aligning the front line in the area of Diemensk and Vyazma. On July 5, 1943, the Germans launched an attack in the Kursk area and suffered a defeat. German armies were constantly retreating under the pressure of the victorious offensive. Russians captured the cities of Orel, Belgorod, and Kharkov, and in autumn 1943, they reached the Dnieper River.

The anti-fascist coalition was beginning to take shape, signaling that the world had awakened from its stagnation and recognized the necessity of a united armed struggle by democratic nations against the fascist Berlin–Rome–Tokyo Axis. The German barbarism and genocide committed by Hitler's hordes on Polish and Russian lands became a bell of terror. The world understood that only by defeating the fascist countries and through ruthless armed struggle could the nations of the free world be saved from fascist oppression and from the destruction of human culture and civilization.

Therefore, the anti-fascist coalition used all their economic means to support the Soviets in their fight against Germany. Transports of weapons, ammunition, food, and medicine were sent to the northern ports of Russia, mainly to Murmansk, under the protection of warship convoys, which were

8 *Krakauer Zeitung* was a German newspaper published in the General Government from November 12, 1939, to January 17, 1945.

sometimes destroyed by German submarines.[9] However, many reached their destination, supplying the Russian army with the weapons and materials necessary to continue the war. The anti-fascist coalition forces were making feverish preparations to open a second front and engage the German army on two sides.

In the first half of 1944, the Russian army smashed the Germans near Leningrad and Veliky Novgorod, as well as in the right-bank Ukraine—the west bank of the Dnieper River. The Russians liberated Odessa and Crimea. Finland, hitherto fighting on the side of the Germans, was eliminated from the war effort after a series of devastating defeats,[10] and by June 1944, almost all Soviet territory had been liberated from the German occupiers.

Italy also became a theater of unfavorable events for the Germans and the fascist Axis. On July 25, 1944, Mussolini's government collapsed, and he himself was imprisoned. The Italian Marshal Badoglio took power and signed a truce with the Western Allies on September 3, 1944.[11] In October 1944, Italy declared war on Germany, but German commandos freed Benito Mussolini, who established a partial fascist state in northern Italy, known as the Salò Republic.[12] Fighting continued throughout Italy.

In the spring and summer of 1944, the Russian army liberated Belarus, western Ukraine, parts of the Baltic countries, and the eastern areas of Poland. The Russian army advanced to the Narev River and the central Vistula region. They stood at the gates of Warsaw but watched the Warsaw Uprising and the systematic destruction of the city with indifference. The entire city of Warsaw lay in ruins.[13]

9 Arctic convoys were Allied naval operations during 1941–1945 that delivered vital supplies, weapons, and equipment to the Soviet Union via the Arctic Ocean route. These convoys, sailing from Britain and North America to the Soviet ports of Murmansk and Arkhangelsk, faced extreme weather, hazardous ice, and constant threats from the German navy, especially from U-boats, that used the wolf-pack tactic in which multiple German U-boats coordinated attacks on Allied convoys, overwhelming their defenses through simultaneous, concentrated strikes.

10 The Moscow Armistice between Finland on one side and the Soviet Union and Great Britain on the other was signed on September 17, 1944.

11 The Armistice of Cassibile was signed on September 3 but was made public on September 8.

12 The Italian Social Republic (known as the Salò Republic) was a state established in northern Italy that existed from September 1943 to April 1945. Governed by Mussolini and headquartered in Salò, it was under German influence until its collapse near the end of World War II.

13 The Warsaw Uprising, launched on August 1, 1944, was the largest military effort

All these events—especially the defeat of the Germans on the Russian front—did not stop them from continuing their merciless extermination of the Jewish population, not only in the territory of Poland but also in the occupied European territories. The Germans did not slow the pace of this extermination, despite talks on the matter with representatives of Jewish organizations in the United States and Switzerland.

The Germans were aware that the Western countries were anxiously watching the victorious advance of the Russian armies and were alarmed by the specter of a communist Europe. They sought to undermine the anti-Hitler coalition. In the spring of 1944, German authorities indicated that they might be willing to release a certain number of Jews and possibly halt further implementation of their genocidal plans. These offers, made to Jewish organizations, were intended to reassure public opinion, agitated by increasingly frequent reports of the murder of Jews in Poland, Russia, and other occupied European countries. Facing imminent defeat, the Germans sought to create more favorable conditions for negotiating with certain circles in the West.

An example of such a diversionary offer was the case of the Hungarian Jews. After occupying Hungary in mid-March 1944 and installing the Quisling Sztojany government, the Germans began organizing the mass deportation of the Jewish population to Auschwitz. Adolf Eichmann and his collaborators Wisliceny,[14] Krumey,[15] Hunsche,[16] Blecher, and others, who

undertaken by resistance forces to oppose German occupation during World War II. The noncommunist Armia Krajowa sought to liberate Warsaw from German occupation. The Red Army stationed nearby did not intervene, allowing the Germans to suppress the uprising over sixty-three days, resulting in massive destruction in the city and some 180,000 casualties, mostly civilians and over 15,000 insurgents.

14 Dieter Wisliceny (1911–1948) was an SS officer and deputy to Adolf Eichmann who played a central role in organising the deportation of the Jewish communities from Slovakia, Greece, and Hungary between 1942–1944. After the war, he testified at Nuremberg and his testimony was used during Eichman's trial in 1961. He was sentenced to death and hanged in Bratislava in 1948.

15 Hermann Alois Krumey (1905–1981), an SS officer and close collaborator of Adolf Eichmann who participated in the persecution and deportation of Jews in the Łódź, Poznań, and Zamość area as well as in Croatia. In Hungary, he played a central role in organizing the mass deportation of Hungarian Jews to Auschwitz-Birkenau in 1944. He was tried and sentenced to life imprisonment on August 29, 1969, for his role in the mass murder of Jews. The sentence was ratified on January 17, 1973, by the federal court in Karlsruhe, Germany.

16 Otto Hunsche (1911–1994) was one of the chief assistants to Adolf Eichmann in

had arrived in Budapest, led this operation, and the staff worked closely with the higher SS and police commander Winkelman. In mid-April 1944, after many anti-fascists and democratic activists had been arrested and deported to Mauthausen, they concentrated more than 300,000 Hungarian Jews into closed ghettos and labor camps. During this time, Eichmann met several times in Budapest with representatives of the Jewish Relief and Rescue Council (Va'ad Ezra Vehatzala), Joel Brand and Rezső Kasztner. Eichmann misled them with the promise of saving part of Hungary's Jewish population in exchange for a large ransom. During one conversation he supposedly declared the following to Brand:

> I am ready to sell you a million Jews. I will not sell you all of them. You could not collect that much money and goods. But one million—let it be. Goods for blood—blood for goods. You can take this million from Hungary, from Poland, from Austria, from Terezin, from Auschwitz. Wherever you want. What would you like to save? Men capable of fathering children, women capable of giving birth, old people, children? Sit down and speak.[17]

It was in this cynical manner that Eichmann, who already had the deaths of millions of Jewish victims on his conscience, put forward proposals masking his real plans. In doing so, he declared that his project had received Himmler's full approval, and in return for the release of 1 million Jews, he demanded the delivery of 10,000 trucks and various goods. In order to make this possible, Eichmann instructed Brand to travel to Constantinople, where

carrying out the deportation of Hungarian Jewry. He was sentenced to twelve years in prison in 1969 when Krumey received his life sentence.

17 See Alex Weissberg, *The Story of Joel Brand* (New York: Criterion Books, 1958). Kromołowski's quote is on pp. 1–2. These events have been discussed and interpreted in detail in several studies, especially by Yehuda Bauer. Acording to Bauer's interpretation of the entire sequence of events and parties involved, apart from Eichmann's role in the story, the SS—that is Himmler—sought to draw the Zionist leadership into efforts to split the Western Allies from the Soviet Union and secure a separate peace by engaging in ransom discussions in exchange for the cessation of deportations of Jews from West Europe and the Balkans. It is now clear that the Allies were initially prepared to keep channels of negotiation open, but abruptly terminated all contact in July. See the chapter "The Mission of Joel Brand," in Yehuda Bauer, *The Holocaust in Historical Perspective* (Seattle: University of Washington Press, 1978), pp. 94–155.

he was to present the offer to representatives of Jewish organizations and the Allied countries. If Brand agreed to the proposal, Eichmann promised to destroy the Auschwitz camp and deliver the first batch of 10,000 Jews to the Spanish border.

According to historians, including A. Eisenbach, Eichmann's proposal was pure blackmail. The Germans had already decided on their tactics toward the Hungarian Jews, and Veesenmayer had agreed on it with Eichmann.[18] In a letter to Berlin on April 3, 1944, he asked whether to begin the deportation action already or to wait until the offer of all Hungarian Jews to Roosevelt and Churchill—until the deceitful ruse to free part of the Jewish population in Hungary—had been conveyed to the governments of the United States and England.

Brand had several more conversations with Eichmann and his associates—Wisliceny, Krumey, and others, as well as with the Sipo and SD chief, von Klags and his deputy Klausnitzer. Finally, on May 14, 1944, Brand, accompanied by Bandi Grosz, departed for Constantinople. Grosz had long been an Abwehr agent and had served in the Sonderdienst since March 1944. After the war, it emerged that he had also been a double agent for British Intelligence.

The main role in this mission to Turkey was precisely played by B. Grosz, and he admitted in the heat of cross-examination during Kastner's trial in Israel in 1954 that the main purpose of the mission was to establish contact with representatives of the Western countries regarding the feasibility and conditions of a peace treaty with Germany, while Eichmann's offer to the Jewish organizations was camouflage to conceal the nature and purpose of the Budapest delegation's trip. This was a game played by Himmler, who realized that Germany was facing certain defeat. Realizing that Hitler would not make any concessions and would order the Germans to fight to its last soldier, Himmler sought a separate peace with the Americans and the British.

As a pretext for these talks, he used the matter of freeing Hungarian Jews from extermination, although their extermination was already a

18 Edmund Veesenmayer (1904–1977) was a German diplomat and an SS officer who became influential in Balkan affairs. Assigned to Zagreb in 1941, he helped implement the persecution and murder of Jews in Croatia and Serbia. In 1944, he was appointed Reich plenipotentiary in Hungary, where he worked closely with Adolf Eichmann and provided diplomatic cover for the deportation and destruction of Hungarian Jewry. After the war, he was convicted of war crimes and sentenced to twenty years in prison, but was released in 1951.

foregone conclusion. Indeed, the police authorities, not waiting at all for news from the delegation, proceeded to carry out the extermination. On June 6, 1944, the day the allied forces landed in Normandy, the Germans began deporting the Hungarian Jews, and by June 27, 1944, the gas chambers and the crematoria of Auschwitz had already devoured half a million Hungarian Jews. To accelerate the extermination, Rudolf Höss (the first camp commandant) returned to Oświęcim. In his testimony before the Nuremberg tribunal, Kastner also quoted the words he had heard from Eichmann around June 5–8, 1944, saying that they undertook an obligation to the Hungarians that not a single one of the displaced Jews would return alive.

After arriving in Turkey and handing over the offer, Brand reached an agreement of sorts with a Jewish Agency attorney, then made a trip to Syria, from where he left for Cairo, where he was arrested and interrogated by Intelligence Service attorneys. During this time, B. Grosz made contact with the military attaché of Western countries. In Cairo, Brand also had a conversation with I. Hirszman, the War Refugees Board plenipotentiary, and the British minister for Middle-Eastern affairs, Lord Moyne. The latter, when informed of the project to release 1 million Jews (who were threatened with extermination), said: "What will I do with a million Jews?!" Nevertheless, Hirszman edited a reply with Moyne and sent it to Himmler's plenipotentiary through the Budapest delegation's liaison officer in Istanbul. However, Hirszman did not reveal the contents of this reply!

In late June 1944, US Secretary of State Hull announced the punishment of all those responsible for the deportations of Hungarian Jews.[19] A relief action was also discussed. In fact, no such aid was given. Secretary of State Hull, in an attempt to justify the failure of this diplomatic relief effort, stated in his memoirs that the State Department did not have enough money or personnel to carry out the plan to contact and bribe the German officials who directed the extermination of the Jews.

Meanwhile, news of the Nazis' offer had leaked to the public. The Reuters agency, reporting on July 19, 1944, about the Nazi offer, admitted that the proposal had already been considered in London, but in its view, there was a belief in official British circles that it was merely an awkward attempt to create discord between the Allies. There was no hope that the British and American governments would accept this proposal, despite

19 See Gerald Reitlinger, *The Final Solution: The Attempt to Exterminate the Jews of Europe 1939–1945* (London: Vallentine, Mitchell, 1953), pp. 412–447.

their willingness to come to the aid of the Hungarian Jews. In spite of all this, the gloomy fact is that the American and British governments also indirectly contributed to the deportations of the Hungarian Jews, because they did nothing to help them.

We cannot know whether, at that time, hundreds of thousands of Hungarian Jews could have been saved from certain death for the goods demanded by the Germans. And where were the millions of American Jews, who showed complete indifference to these initial possibilities of rescue, at a time when Germany was already facing defeat and opportunities were opening up, even if only to bribe the Nazi dignitaries who had a decisive voice in the matter of the extermination of Hungarian Jews!

It is not impossible that, under these transactional propositions, the Germans concealed their camouflaged insinuations of gaining political profits. In the course of the great Soviet offensive, they could have been interested in achieving a peace treaty with their Western enemies and thus securing their occupation of most of the territories seized so far and saving Germany from Soviet communism and total destruction. They did not intend to make any peace negotiations with Russia, and only to fight. In the Jewish matter, however, the intentions and decisions of the Germans were quite clear. They did not plan to free a single Jew alive from their concentration camps, as evidenced by the action of transporting prisoners from the camps deep into Germany and shooting them en masse along the way, in the face of the approaching front. Even in the final months of the Third Reich, Hitler's leaders did not relinquish the physical destruction of the remnants of the Jewish population. They used these miserable Jewish prisoners, devastated by hunger and cruelty, for their political games, pretending that their actions were not devoid of humanitarian qualities.

An example of this is the camp of Theresienstadt, which also housed Jews deported from Denmark. At the end of June 1944, at the height of the genocidal operations against the Jews, Ribbentrop, with Himmler's approval, arranged for a Red Cross delegation to visit the camp in Terezin to facilitate secret talks with the Allies in Turkey. Members of this delegation were Frants Hvass of the Danish Foreign Ministry, Eigil Juel Heinigsen, chairman of the Danish Red Cross, and a representative of the Swiss Red Cross. The purpose of this visit was to show that even the elderly lived in this camp, and all the information about a barbarian liquidation of Jews could not possibly be true.

In the meantime, a short time after the departure of the delegation, 20,000 Jews were deported from Theresienstadt to Auschwitz, where they were exterminated until the very last in gas chambers. Himmler's promise to destroy the gas chambers of Auschwitz was a mere ruse. Indeed, the Germans began dismantling them in November 1944. They also burned the bodies of the victims and their documents of the crime. However, they were only obliterating the traces of genocide. This did not happen as a result of an alleged decision to halt the extermination of Jews, but because of the proximity of the front and the need to hastily withdraw from the area.

In discussing the extermination of Hungarian Jewry, Raoul Wallenberg's mission must not be forgotten. After arriving in Budapest in mid-1944 as attaché to the Swedish diplomatic mission, he began organizing an office for Jewish affairs, which was to collect information about the situation of the Jewish population, intervene with the local authorities, and provide material aid to the Jews. The letters of protection he issued to Jewish families and his charitable activities were tolerated by the Germans as long as his mission could be used for certain political purposes. Wallenberg, who stayed there almost until the end of 1944, had the funds of the American War Refugees Board at his disposal. It is difficult to say if his admittedly noble intention of saving a certain number of Jews was successful. What is known for certain is that during Wallenberg's stay in Hungary, the Swedish embassy in Berlin asked the German authorities to allow 400 Hungarian Jews who had Swedish documents, known as letters of protection, to leave for Sweden. The German authorities delayed answering, on the grounds that they would make a decision only after the matter of the Hungarian Jews had been definitely settled.

There is no certain information whether Wallenberg managed to save at least some of these Jews by sending them to Sweden; however, it is rumored that some Jews made it to Sweden thanks to Wallenberg's efforts. It is also known that Wallenberg was arrested by the Russian authorities after the seizure of Hungary by the Soviet army, that he was transported to a prison in Russia and never heard of again. The mission of the former Swiss President Musy should also be mentioned here. He came with his son Benoit to Germany, where he had a series of conversations with Himmler and Schellenberg about rescuing certain groups of Jewish families from the concentration camps, including women in Ravensbrück. Musy undertook the mission at the suggestion of Dr. Isaac Sternbuch, the Swiss ombudsman. As a result of these negotiations, an advance of 5 million Swiss francs was placed at the disposal of the Germans in a Swiss bank. In February 1945, in a new stage of the ongoing negotiations, a check for 20 million Swiss francs was handed over to a representative of the German authorities and deposited in a Swiss bank. There is no source information on whether the Germans released any groups from concentration camps. It is known, however, that they did not, even in the final months of the war, abandon their criminal policy of exterminating the Jews.

Retreating westward, they evacuated the concentration camps and executed tens of thousands of prisoners en route. For example, on January 18, 1945, the Nazis hurriedly evacuated the Auschwitz camp and of the approximately 58,000, mostly Jews, hardly anyone remained alive. At the same time, they evacuated Jewish prisoners from Buchenwald, a concentration camp deep inside Germany, and shot along the way those prisoners who, as a result of exhaustion, could not march further. There were many Jews from the Częstochowa HASAG camp among these Buchenwald prisoners who died, including my brother-in-law Tadzio (Dawid) Szmulewicz. Witnesses—former HASAG prisoners who were miraculously rescued by American troops—testified to this during the trial against the executioner of Częstochowa's Jews, Paul Degenhardt. Testimony was also given by a former Buchenwald prisoner deported there from HASAG in Częstochowa, Alfred Monhajt.[20]

Alfred Monhajt, Buchenwald survivor, 1945.

20 Alfred Monhajt became Kromołowski's brother-in-law after the war, when Kromołowski married Róża Monhajt.

CHAPTER ELEVEN

APPROACHING LIBERATION

The news of the landing of the joint American and British armies in Normandy, and with it the establishment of a second front against Germany on June 6, 1944,[1] reached us, the prisoners of HASAG, much later. We received the news with mixed feelings. On the one hand, it heralded the inevitable German defeat and thus brought joy, satisfaction, and a conviction that the day of retribution for the bestial extermination of the millions of Jews at the hands of the German murderers was approaching. On the other hand, we realized that the Germans would seek to liquidate their camps to erase any trace of genocide. It was rumored that the HASAG barracks and factory buildings would be blown up, and that the prisoners would be evacuated deep into Germany. Nevertheless, we closely followed the news of the Allied successes and Operation Overlord,[2] the Allied offensive in France. In August 1944, the Allies liberated Paris,

1 D-Day, June 6, 1944, marked the Allied invasion of Nazi-occupied France, with over 150,000 troops landing on the beaches of Normandy. This pivotal operation opened a Western Front, leading to the liberation of France and ultimately contributing to the defeat of Nazi Germany.

2 Operation Overlord was the codename for the Battle of Normandy, which began with the landing of the Allied forces in Normandy on D-Day.

Brussels, and Antwerp,[3] and later in October and November 1944, a second front drove the Germans out of Alsace and Lorraine.[4]

In December 1944, our camp was formally taken over by the SS and police forces. It was renamed the HASAG concentration camp and became a branch of the Auschwitz extermination camp. From the very beginning, strict discipline was introduced by the SS. No one was allowed to stay or gather in the barracks square. After the morning roll call, the prisoners marched out of the camp area in compact ranks; only in this way were they allowed to pass through the camp gate to work in the factory halls. SS men stood in front of the gate with rods in their hands, beating anyone in their vicinity.

Alongside them stood a newly appointed Jewish *Judenlagerleiter*—a thuggish renegade named Goldsztajn, brought from Płaszów by the Germans. Dressed in high boots and a police cap, he beat the prisoners and abused them in a truly sadistic way. At the gate, the Jews had to take off their caps, and the Kapo of each unit had to loudly state his name and report how many prisoners he was leading. If the report was made incorrectly or in a voice that was too soft, Goldsztajn would beat both the Kapo and his men with a truncheon he kept ready at hand. He did this far more efficiently, forcefully, and cruelly than the SS men, who stood by and watched the spectacle.

Goldsztajn demanded that people march evenly and in time, sometimes ordering them to march in place, lift their legs high, and pound the ground forcefully. This continued until the prisoners lost their strength, after which he would strike them on the head and back without restraint. People often fell to the ground, fainting from the blows and exhaustion. The return from work followed the same pattern: in full columns, accompanied by harassment, beating, and kicking.[5] At this time, we also heard a rumor that transports of striped uniforms worn by concentration camp prisoners had arrived, and that construction of gas chambers and crematoria was about to begin.

The Russian offensive began in January 1945. The 1st Byelorussian Front advanced toward Warsaw and Poznań, and on January 12, the 1st Ukrainian Front launched its attack. The Germans defenses were threatened

3 The Allies liberated Paris on August 25, 1944, Brussels on September 3, 1944, and Antwerp on September 4, 1944.

4 The liberation of Alsace-Lorraine continued into the first months of 1945.

5 On Goldsztajn, see Brener, "Resistance and Destruction in the Częstochowa Ghetto," pp. 163, 166–167.

with encirclement and defeat along the Vistula River, as their Kielce-Radom army formation was simultaneously surrounded. The Russian army's assault on Częstochowa included battalions of the 5th Guards Army, commanded by Colonel-General Zhdanov. The German defenses in the area were broken, and on January 15, 1945, troops captured Kielce. At the same time, the 5th Guards Army continued its successful assault on Częstochowa. The front advanced toward the city with terrifying speed, and the Germans did not grasp the seriousness of their situation, as was evident in their behavior.

Work in the HASAG munitions factories was carried out as usual on the morning of January 15, 1945. Only in the late afternoon did disorder begin to creep in. We noticed that many German foremen were missing, and there were rumors that they had fled the factory grounds. The foremen and technical managers who remained displayed great nervousness. They only talked to each other and paid absolutely no attention to the workers. People were agitated; something hung in the air. News of the approaching front spread from mouth to mouth. Reports came that the German personnel had already packed their suitcases and were only waiting for a signal from management to leave the factory. Airplanes roared overhead as they flew past the factory buildings, and some claimed to have seen red stars on their fuselages.

With my painting tools and ladder, I could walk around the camp quite freely. I saw the behavior of the Germans and the *Werkschutz* with my own eyes. Both panic and anxiety were clearly visible. At one point, two SS men from the camp command appeared in the barracks square. With loud whistles, they summoned Goldsztajn, who reported to them, out of breath. The Germans ordered him to wake up the night shift of the *Infanterie* department, and these prisoners were to report with their belongings. Armed *Werkschutz* appeared. They quickly formed ranks of prisoners and directed them to the freight cars, which were waiting on the factory siding. Panic and a stampede ensued: The Germans were evacuating the camp.

The *Werkschutz* led the half-conscious and frightened women from the night shift onto the train cars. They hurried them along, pushing them with their rifle butts. Cries and shouts of farewell were heard. The first evacuation train—consisting of a dozen or so freight cars filled with both women and men, escorted by *Werkschutz* and SS men—departed. Whispers circulated that our entire camp was about to be evacuated to Buchenwald concentration camp.

The early winter's night interrupted the evacuation, and for the time being, there were no new train cars. But it was said that the evacuation would continue the next day at dawn. Nobody slept that night. Everyone was nervous and anxious. News circulated in the camp, originating from the few German foremen who remained in the factory. Some said that the entire factory, including the barracks, would be blown up. Others feared that the Germans would throw incendiary bombs and grenades, and start shooting at the prisoners they had not yet evacuated. German anti-aircraft defenses swept the dark sky with their searchlights looking out for Russian planes. Yet all around, silence reigned.

The Germans resumed evacuating the camp early the next morning, January 16. The SS men and *Werkschutz* ran around the barracks, herding people into the square and ordering them to line up according to their workplaces. We could hear the sound of distant detonations, growing steadily closer and more frequent. According to the experts, these were the booms of artillery fire. The front had apparently reached the eastern suburbs of Częstochowa, where battles were now being fought.

Standing in the barracks square, I saw ranks of four being formed from the *Rekalibrierung* department. Among them I saw my brother-in-law Tadzio Szmulewicz standing with a bundle of his things, ready to go. I approached him and tried to persuade him to stay. "Don't go," I said. "Run away! I will help you hide in one of the barracks! The front is approaching, the Russians may soon drive the Germans out of the city and then we can save ourselves, regain our freedom. Evacuation is dangerous! They said they are going to take us to Buchenwald!" I tried to persuade Tadzio to stay, but he did not want to hide or run away. The Germans were going to blow up the camp, so those who remained would face certain death. He said that he wanted to go with his work friends and was afraid to risk escape, and that whoever arrived at the new work site soon would have a better chance of surviving. I understood that it would be impossible to convince him. Besides, perhaps he was right. It was difficult to predict what would happen in the next few hours and what kind of plans the Germans had for evacuating the ammunition factory. There were explosives everywhere, and one spark could cause a blast. In a single moment, this huge compound could turn into a pile of rubble.

I went into one of the *Judeneinsatz* warehouses. I felt at home there, because that's where I was often ordered to make various inscriptions, signs, and announcements. It was empty. In the storeroom, there was bread on the table, sliced into quarters. I grabbed two quarters and hid them under my shirt. I caught up with Tadzio as his column was moving from the barracks square. I gave him the stolen quarters of bread so that he would at least have some bread for the journey.

I squeezed Tadzio's hand, and we said goodbye in silence. I broke away from the *Rekalibrierung* group marching to the train cars, unnoticed by either of the two *Werkschutz* escorting the prisoners. Tadzio's silhouette vanished into the crowd. I never saw him again. After the war, one of his friends who had miraculously managed to survive told me that Tadzio, together with his fellow workers, was evacuated to Buchenwald, where he worked for some time. When the war reached Germany's original territories, the SS evacuated the prisoners from that concentration camp, driving them on foot deep into Germany. Tadzio, like many others, was murdered by the Germans. Exhausted by the long trek and weakened by hunger, he did not have enough strength to withstand the pace of the fast march. He was left behind, shot by the Germans. Tadzio Szmulewicz died a martyr's death on a German road at the age of just sixteen.

Returning to the events of that memorable day—January 16, 1945—in our camp: Amid hectic traffic and unceasing uproar, the Germans were constantly transporting Jewish prisoners in freight trains from the railroad ramp. People were evacuated according to factory departments. All of a sudden, I heard someone shout: "They are deporting the *Werkzeugbau*!" This department manufactured various work tools, and it was where my brother Heniek worked. I looked around the crowded barracks square and found my brother among the people lined up in a column of four. I decided not to allow Heniek to be taken away. I had to find a way for him to be pulled out of the column. If not, they would take him away, we'd be separated, and I might never see him again. We had to be together. He was the only one of my relatives still alive, the only survivor of my once numerous family.

Time was pressing on, and I had to do something. I rushed into the *Judeneinsatz*, thinking that I would ask one of the Jewish managers to intervene and remove my brother from the group. But no one was there. The office was empty. On top of the cupboard lay the armband with *Judeneinsatzkommando* written on it, which was worn by members of the camp leadership during roll calls. I snatched this armband and pinned it to the sleeve of my jacket. I left the office confidently, holding some papers in my hand that I had taken from the desk, and I pretended to be one of the members of the camp's command. The *Werkzeugbau* group was already standing in tight formation, waiting for the order to march out toward the train cars. My brother stood together with others in silent anticipation. I reached the *Werkschutz* and told him that the locksmith Kromołowski was urgently needed, because someone had slammed the door to the bread warehouse in the *Judeneinsatz* office, and no one could find the key, and the bread had to be distributed among the departing people. I pointed to my brother. "*Gut! Soll er gehen!*" (Good! Let him go!), said the *Werkschutz*.

I grabbed my brother by the arm and led him out of the ranks. After a while, we found ourselves in one of the barracks. I took off my armband and put it in my pocket. It might come in handy amid the ever-increasing chaos. We hid in a dark corner of the barracks and waited.

My brother did not object. He seemed to agree with me that, although risky, it was preferable to stay put in an attempt to avoid deportation. The sound of explosions echoed from some distance. Every now and then, we heard the roar of plane engines overhead, and with the naked eye, we could see the red star on the fuselage. Now it was certain—it was a Russian aircraft.

Henryk (Henio) Kromołowski, Alfred's brother, June 1946.

Dusk was falling. The barracks square was almost dark. Not a single electric lamp was burning. From far away, we could hear the din of voices, shouts, and shrill German orders. Several other people were in the barracks with us. Some, like us, had escaped from one of the transports, while others had not left the barracks at all, hiding beneath the bunks. Now the whole camp was drowning in darkness. The night was frosty, and the sky was starless. The sounds of explosions grew closer and closer. From time to time, the black sky was streaked with red, followed by a long, deafening rumble. Everything indicated that the fighting was nearby, perhaps even in the city itself. Our excitement mounted by the minute. Decisive moments were approaching. Yet it felt as if death was lurking all around. We felt like we were sitting on a barrel of gunpowder, ready to blow up at any moment.

Between the detonations, we heard the constant din of German voices and shouts. Evidently, the evacuation was still in progress. Had they forgotten about us? Had we managed to avoid deportation? No, they had not forgotten. Suddenly, a dark figure holding a flashlight stood in the open doorway of the barracks. I recognized him. It was the old *Werkschutz* Doroshenko, holding a rifle with his finger on the trigger. He was dressed in his black military coat and had a well-stuffed knapsack on his back. He shouted, "*Raus, alle raus*!" He order us to leave the barracks, and said that whoever did not come out immediately would be shot!

We exited slowly into the dark square. Doroshenko, shining his flashlight, searched every corner of the barracks, chasing the last few stragglers out in front of him. Darkness spread all around, but we could still see a crowd of people rushing toward the gate leading to the railroad tracks and the factory square. From there it was only a few steps to May 1 Street. We realized that the last transport of prisoners had just been evacuated. There were no more train cars, so the prisoners were being rushed on foot to the nearby Stradom train station, which was very close to the German border station. The *Werkschutz* shouted, "Forward, faster," pushing people forward with their rifle butts. Everyone was dressed for the road, wearing coats and carrying military rucksacks or suitcases. A German *Werkschutz* called Herman, also equipped for the road, ran through the barracks square. He fired a shot into the air with his revolver and shouted, "*Kinder, kommt mit uns!*" (Children, come with us).

The sounds of explosions were now very close. The sky was a purple-red, tongues of flames visible above. Somewhere nearby, something must have been on fire. The crowd pushed slowly forward, drawing closer to the exit gate. Suddenly, a thought flashed through my mind: Evacuation means death. The Germans are taking us away to kill us. No, I won't let them take me away. What will happen will happen here on the spot.

I took advantage of a convenient moment when the *Werkschutz* were in front of us and could not see us. Grabbing my brother by the hand, I whispered into his ear, "Let's run." Swiftly jumping out of the still-surging crowd, we dodged to the side and dashed into the dark depths of the barracks square, running toward the nearest barrack. I looked behind me. No one was chasing us. No one had noticed our escape. My brother and I rushed through the open door of the barrack, clung to the bunks, and covered ourselves with some kind of rug. We lay there motionless, side by side in silent anticipation of what would happen to us. Unbroken silence now reigned. No sound came from the barracks square, no shots or detonations.

After an hour or two, I decided to check what was happening outside the barrack to get an idea of our situation. I cautiously approached the open door and stuck my head out. The barracks square was empty. Not a living soul could be seen. There was complete silence. After some discussion with my brother, we decided to leave our hiding place and go to the factory square and the so-called colony, where some Polish administrative officials working for HASAG lived. We were also aware that in the event of evacuation, the Germans would probably blow up the entire facility. It was even said that the entire area had been mined by the Germans. However, a long time had passed since the last transport, and nothing suggested that the Germans' threats to destroy the plant would come true. Silence and complete stillness prevailed all around.

Filled with new hope, we walked carefully, hiding behind the barracks. Before us stood the wide-open gate of the camp. We lingered there, undecided and deep in thought. Should we go further, pass through the gate, and reach the factory yard—a forbidden area for prisoners, allowed only under German escort? Or should we wait for further developments? Were the Germans still on the factory grounds and in the colony? What should we do? Or perhaps, in a moment, the entire facility, including the barracks, would be blown up, and we would die under the rubble. But nothing happened. It remained quiet and empty. The night was dark, with only a narrow sliver of moon peeking from behind the clouds. It was cold yet windless.

Suddenly, the silence of the barracks square was broken by heavy footsteps. People passed through the gate, heading for the barracks. The clatter of treads and loud conversations could now be heard. They were Jews! Shreds of conversations in Yiddish reached us. Someone cursed loudly, someone laughed. We ran toward them and caught up with them, out of breath.

"What is going on? People, speak up. We just came out of hiding!"

"What do you mean, you don't know anything?" somebody's voice said. "The Germans escaped! There is not a single one of those bandits in the whole factory anymore! We are free! The Russians are occupying the city!"

People who had hidden in the factory halls before the evacuation were now running through the corridors, breaking down warehouse doors, looking for both food and hidden Germans. They had already smashed the weapon magazines near the guardhouse and seized rifles and pistols. Loud conversations and shouts of joy could be heard everywhere. Human figures emerged from barracks, from ditches, from nooks, from under the machines, and from factory cellars. These were prisoners who had risked their lives, who had hidden on the factory grounds, and had managed to avoid deportation. They had already heard the good news. Some stood dumbfounded, still in disbelief, while others were shouting joyfully, throwing themselves into each other's arms. Others cried loudly.

All around, the sounds of detonations spread—roars of single shots and the rattling of machine guns. The sky reddened with flashes of explosions. There was fighting in the city. Russian tanks circled the streets, pressing the German marauders, who fell dead in uneven combat. The German troops defending the city had long since retreated westward. The surprise of the Russian attack was so great that the Germans completely lost their arrogance and conceit, fleeing in panic before the armored forces and suffering heavy losses. Their entire defense collapsed abruptly. Even our German tormentors from HASAG fled in fear, driving the last transport of Jewish prisoners before them. And the few of us who remained could not believe our miraculous liberation. Are we really free? Can we go anywhere? Can we go out onto the street with impunity, walk in the city, enter the Aryan quarter?

It was hard to believe. My brother and I stood there stunned, holding hands and looking around. But there were neither SS men with pistols nor *Werkschutz* anywhere in sight, the German foremen with truncheons in their hands had disappeared, and we could not hear any German commands and curses. A miracle had taken place! We Jews were truly free! We had survived the hell of the German extermination campaign, and we were witnessing the defeat of our families' murderers!

CHAPTER TWELVE

THE WAR IS OVER

On the factory premises in the colony, there was a German canteen. It was a huge hall filled with tables and chairs, and there was a large buffet with a beer dispenser at the back. A huge portrait of Adolf Hitler hung on the wall.

When my brother and I—for the first time as free people—crossed the threshold of this room, which, until now, only Germans were permitted to enter, the entire canteen was already filled with Jewish prisoners of HASAG. Women and men in their prison garb, painted with red stripes, filled the tables. It was noisy. People were talking loudly, laughing and shouting. Many sat motionless, watching the crowd. Many women were crying.

All the mugs and bottles were hurled as projectiles. People smashed glass vessels against Hitler's portrait. The glass shattered with a clatter against the Führer's head, tearing the canvas of the painting. Shards of glass rained down everywhere. Someone smashed a chair against the stone tabletop and used a piece of wood to crack open a glass display case for snacks, of which nothing remained. Someone else was playing an incomprehensible melody on the piano.

Every now and then, figures appeared in the doorway of the canteen. They wore the hats and overcoats left behind by the Germans. Among the tatterdemalion HASAG prisoners, one figure appeared wearing a hat à la Eden—usually worn by Lüth, the factory director—and a navy-blue overcoat. He bowed with exaggerated politeness to left and right. Another wore a German *Werkschutz* cap with the peak torn off. People raided the Germans' apartments, robbing everything. Others walked around with guns—with rifles slung across their shoulders and pistols in holsters.

It was daytime. My brother and I left the half-destroyed canteen and went down the stairs, which were now covered with glass shards. We decided to leave our HASAG prison and go into town. Walking down the long, tree-lined avenue we knew so well, we saw that the iron factory gate stood wide open. No one stopped us from leaving. We went out onto May 1 Street, which was empty and still quiet in the gray dawn of that January day. We were free; yet, we were lonely, orphaned, and our hearts ached after nearly six years of torment and captivity, during which we were close to death at the hands of the Nazi executioners every day.

The huge House of the Prince, which had been occupied by various German offices during the war, was now on fire. Clouds of black, acrid smoke rose into the sky. On the corner of Wolności Avenue, embedded in the wall of a house, the giant, black wreckage of a German tank stood motionless, abandoned by its defeated crew.

There was not a living soul in sight. We walked along the empty street, holding hands. We decided to seek shelter with Stefan Maksymek, a former worker of our parents who, according to my brother's inquiries, lived on Warszawska Street. We walked through the empty, lifeless streets of the city, and on Wały Dwernickiego, next to the railroad track, we almost fell into the hands of a German patrol. Fortunately, at the corner of Jasnogórska Street, we looked to see if the way was clear, when we noticed two German SS men walking slowly down a completely deserted street. We immediately retreated and took shelter in a nearby gateway. We were alarmed by this. Apparently, not all the Germans had left the city. Perhaps there was still some fighting going on, and the Russian army had not yet captured the city. We did not know how to proceed or where to go. Homeless, hungry, and alone in our hometown without any family or friends, we were completely lost.

After much consideration, we decided to go to the Maksymeks anyway. We had no other friends here. Leaving the gateway of the house on Jasnogórska Street, we turned onto Wały Dwernickiego. The street was completely empty. It was already light outside. We walked through a tunnel under the railroad tracks—Kacapski Bridge—to Krótka Street, where many bloody selections of Jews had taken place. There we saw the corpses of German SS men and soldiers, who had been gruesomely crushed on the roadway by tanks. Some were nothing more than bloody shapeless masses crammed into ragged uniforms and boots. German helmets and various weapons lay scattered on the roadway. Further down the street stood an abandoned Russian tank, its tracks damaged and its gun barrel raised high. Apparently, fighting had taken place here between the advancing Red Army and the German garrisons defending the city, which, according to the German plan, was meant to become a fortress guarding the entrance to the German *Vaterland*.

The streets were still completely deserted, and we did not encounter any other human beings the entire way. When we reached the Maksymeks', who we found in one of the houses in Warszawska Street, we received a cold, unfriendly welcome. We were not invited to sit at the table, and we were not invited to sit down and rest. We were not even offered a piece of bread or a cup of tea, although we said we were hungry and cold. On the contrary, the Maksymeks urged us to leave both their apartment and the city immediately, as they claimed that fighting was taking place nearby and that the Germans would surely come back. They were also preparing to leave the city, because they felt it was safer in the countryside. We felt very bitter and were painfully affected by this lack of kindness from people who, once homeless and unemployed themselves, had experienced a friendly welcome from our parents, received work and housing from us, and for several years lived with us in close proximity under the same roof. Without saying goodbye, we left the inhospitable family and decided to head for the countryside as well.

Hungry and freezing, we walked along dirt roads, avoiding clusters of people. We headed toward the village of Mirów, where a man named Kupczyk lived. He was a friend of my brother's who owned a store, and he used to buy soap and kerosene from us. My brother, who worked in my parents' company, had visited him on business trips before the war and said that Kupczyk was a decent man and would offer us hospitality. On the way to Mirów, we came across a Russian supply convoy moving slowly along the road, consisting of hundreds of one- and two-horse wagons, carts, and carriages. The convoy was escorted by a squad of horsemen, armed with light rifles slung over their shoulders. The caravan followed in the wake of the motorized Russian army. No one accosted us or paid us any attention, and we trudged along the road in our jackets, badly tattered and marked with red stripes—clear evidence that we had come from a German camp.

Finally, we reached Mirów and found Kupczyk's house. I wouldn't say that Kupczyk was delighted to see us. He greeted us rather coldly, but offered us hospitality. We were given a plate of hot soup with potatoes, which we devoured greedily, eating a slice of cornbread. We told our host about our recent experiences. Finally, tired, we lay down on the kitchen floor and fell asleep. The next day, however, we decided to return to the city, somewhat discouraged by the cold reception from Kupczyk and his family. The peasants in Mirów also brought news that the Russian army had occupied Częstochowa and its surroundings, ousted the Germans, and forced them to retreat along the entire front line. The city was calm, and it was safe to move about on the streets. We needed a place to live and to rebuild our lives anew. We returned to the city, walking along the road in our prison garments, which aroused interest among the local peasants who passed us on foot or in carts.

Some passed us by with a friendly smile, greeting us with a nod of the head, while others showed clear signs of dislike. There were even those who threatened us with their fists and shouted hostile epithets, including "Jewish commissars" and "*Judokomuna*," among the mildest insults. Almost all returned from the city laden with sacks and household goods, apparently plundered from apartments abandoned by the Germans. Some carried furniture, cabinets, and chairs on horse-drawn carts, and two people even transported a piano.

The city was now bustling with traffic; people lined the streets, and a constant buzz filled the air, including music coming from the street loudspeakers. In our prewar apartment, we found some foreign furniture. Our home had been occupied by two refugee families from Warsaw. There was nothing there for us, so we went in search of any apartments abandoned by the Germans, which we found on the first floor of a well-maintained building on Kościuszko Street. We forced the locked door open with a strong kick. The apartment had several rooms but was completely empty of furniture, except for two iron beds without bedding in the middle of one room. We began searching the apartment for food when suddenly two Russian soldiers in fur hats, rifles in hand, entered. Without further ado, they ordered us to leave, saying simply, "*Pashli won*," and added by way of explanation, "*Zdies budiet ruskaja kamiendantura*" (Off you go; this will be the Russian headquarters). We left and resumed our journey.

After a long, arduous search, tired and hungry, we found an apartment consisting of a room and a kitchen in a nice villa set in a garden on Dąbrowskiego Street. We did not find much furniture, but there was a wooden bed with a mattress, a table, and two or three chairs covered with a red-flowered fabric of sorts. We claimed the apartment by locking it, and, exhausted, with empty stomachs and our bowels playing a march, we lay down to rest, wrapped in our prison jackets. Such was our first day of freedom. We felt that there was neither care nor interest in our fate as prisoners of German camps from the locals, who lacked neither food nor medical care—resources we ourselves lacked so desperately.

The next day, we ventured out again onto the city streets, hungry and freezing. The traffic was heavy with numerous, fully armed Russian soldiers. Some wore the red armbands of the military police and maintained order. Stores were closed, and restaurants and bars were shut down. The sound of military music came from the streets' loudspeakers, and Soviet propagandists screened the film *Chapayev* on the walls of a house on Śląska Street, next to the municipality building. Onlookers watched the Russian cavalry charging at the German cannons. We met some camp comrades who were still homeless. They told us that when they returned to their prewar apartments, where they even recognized their furniture, they were met with a hostile reception and chased away.

At the outbreak of the war, there were about 29,000 Jews living in Częstochowa. In April 1941, the Jewish population numbered over 35,000, and in September 1942, about 37,000. These numbers included only registered Jews. However, obtaining official registration was dependent on the consent of the German administration, so there were many unregistered Jews in the large ghetto. In Jewish circles, it was therefore calculated that in the month preceding the liquidation of the ghetto, there were about 48,000 Jews living in Częstochowa.[1]

When the 5th Guards Army finally occupied Częstochowa on January 17, 1945, there were 5,200 Jews who had survived the Holocaust, including 1,518 who had previously been permanent residents of the city. They were homeless, lonely people, for the most part without their families, who had been murdered by the Germans. Many of these people were ill, and a significant percentage were in a state of psychological depression. Almost all the HASAG prisoners required immediate medical attention and care. Despite this, no one took care of the fate of those unfortunate people at the time, and the general attitude of the local

1 See Rutkowski's summary of the estimated Jewish population in Częstochowa: December 1940—40,000; 1941—45,000; 1942 (before September 22)—48,000; April 1943—4,000; January 1, 1945—11,000; and January 17, 1945—5,200. See Table 3 in A. Rutkowski, "Martyrologia, walka i zagłada ludności żydowskiej w dystrykcie radomskim podczas okupacji hitlerowskiej," *Biuletyn Żydowskiego Instytutu Historycznego*, 15–16 (1955), p. 140.

society toward the Jewish victims of German barbarism was completely indifferent and often even hostile.[2]

We heard that there were potatoes lying in the cellars under the German canteen on Śląska Street, where the Europa Restaurant had been before the war. In an empty yard, we found a German cart, took bags from the basement of our villa, and went to get those potatoes. There was a big pile of potatoes in a large, dry cellar where some civilians were working. There were also some Soviet soldiers loading potatoes into sacks. We, too, loaded a sack full of potatoes and took our haul home. From the remains of broken furniture that we found in the yard, we lit a fire in an iron stove and cooked the potatoes in a large pot. We took off their skins and—without salt, because we did not have any—ate them hungrily. It was our first hot meal since our release from the German camp.

The mood among the few miraculously surviving Jews was somber. People did not know what to do with themselves nor how to conduct themselves in a country where people were clearly unfriendly to Jews. Most were determined to leave the country, either for Western democratic countries or Mandatory Palestine, from where we heard vague information about ongoing battles between Jewish military organizations against the Arabs, who sought to annihilate the Jewish population, following the example of Hitler and his criminal collaborators. The Arab leader, the mufti of Jerusalem, Al-Husseini, openly called for the murder of Jews, declaring holy war against them. More and more young Jews of both sexes left Poland, sneaking across the "green border" (through the forests on the Polish border) with the intention of immigrating to Mandatory Palestine and participating in the liberation struggle in the Haganah (the Jewish paramilitary organization in Mandatory Palestine).

An exodus of the remaining Polish Jews began. Many realized that it would be very difficult for Jews to live on Polish soil among the graves of the millions of victims of German barbarism and among people they felt were unfriendly, and even hostile, toward them. People fled from the bloody memories of the atrocities that had taken place in this land. They said that they could not live in the cemeteries, among the stench of Jewish blood, or tread on the ground that concealed the bones and remains of their families: parents, siblings, wives, husbands, and children. So, they sold their houses, factories, and more valuable possessions—which they had managed to recover as successors of their closer or more distant relatives

2 Kromołowski and his brother personally experienced this attitude when reaching out to their prewar Polish friends for food and shelter, as he describes.

or their own prewar property—to Poles for paltry sums of money and left for Western Europe, the United States, Australia, and, in overwhelming numbers, for the land of their forefathers, Mandatory Palestine.

I searched in vain for the grave of my wife Stella, murdered by the Germans in the small ghetto area. I knew from hearsay that she had been shot along with Helenka Tenenbaum and her brother on July 20, 1943, while working in the garden near the ghetto kitchen. I walked among the ruins of houses, in the yards and gardens, among the stumps of burned trees, but I found no trace of a grave. All that was left of her was the memory and the grief that contracted my heart. How can we go on living among these graves? No wonder people felt emigration fever. They thought of nothing else but leaving Poland as soon as possible.

More and more acts of violence against Jews, committed by Polish antisemitic militias, contributed greatly to this fearful mood.[3] This also happened in our town, and there were numerous incidents of Jews being beaten on the city's streets. Several armed men broke into the oil factory of Mojżesz Fajerman, a former HASAG prisoner, and shot at him with their revolvers. Fajerman hid behind barrels and miraculously escaped death. On another occasion, two men broke into the apartment of a Jewish doctor, Dr. Dobrzyński, late one evening and fired several shots. He managed to barricade himself in one of the rooms, opened a window, and called for help. The attackers fled. And Leon Borensztejn, a HASAG prisoner from Łódź, was shot dead in Narutowicza Square.

On July 4, 1946, an anti-Jewish pogrom took place in Kielce, the capital city of the province, to which Częstochowa was administratively subordinate. Its organizers spread false rumors that Jews had abducted a Polish child. The rumor spread rapidly in the city, and the gathered crowds started to drag Jews out of their apartments, beating and murdering them. As a result of the pogrom, which lasted several days and spread across Kielce and its surrounding towns, forty-three Jews were bestially murdered and over forty were seriously wounded. Among the dead was a former prisoner of the Częstochowa HASAG factory, Rembak, who had been thrown from the window of a speeding train traveling from Kielce to Koniecpol.

The Kielce pogrom continued amid the inaction of the authorities, the police, and the security organs. The murdered and beaten Jews, who had

3 An overview of anti-Jewish violence can be found in David Engel, "Patterns of Anti-Jewish Violence in Poland, 1944–1946," *Yad Vashem Studies*, 26 (1998), pp. 43–85.

just returned from the German camps, were not defended by anyone. Militia officers also participated in the pogrom, beating and murdering Jews, as evidenced by both Polish and Jewish eyewitnesses and by reports in the local communist party newspaper, *Gazeta Ludowa.* Among those arrested in the Kielce pogrom were five militiamen. On July 11, 1946, a court hearing took place: nine of the arrested were sentenced to death, including two militiamen. Whether the sentence was carried out remains unknown. In any case, it was never officially reported in the press. However, it is known that several leading officers of the militia and security service (Urząd Bezpieczeństwa, UB) were moved from Kielce to other cities, and, for a time, the head of the Security Office in Kielce was incarcerated in Mokotow Prison, where he supposedly belonged to the exceptionally privileged prisoners. Nothing is known about his ultimate fate.

It had barely been a year since the liberation of Poland from German occupation, and already Polish society in Kielce, as well as in other cities—in line with the infamous traditions of years gone by—demonstrated its newly regained national sovereignty by beating and murdering Jews.[4] And this was not the first time in the history of the 1,000 years of close Polish–Jewish relations. After World War I, when the Polish nation regained its independent existence after 150 years, it also seemingly began its political existence by beating and murdering the Jewish population.

On November 21, 1918, in just the third week after Poland's liberation from occupation by the three occupants who partitioned Poland, the newly formed Polish army staged a pogrom against Jews in Lwów. As previously mentioned, after the fall of the Austro-Hungarian Habsburg Empire, Lwów, formerly under Austrian rule, was occupied for a time by the Ukrainian army of Ataman Petliura. He quickly withdrew from the

4 As Kromołowski relates, the Kielce pogrom was triggered by a false accusation that Jews had kidnapped a Christian boy for ritual purposes. An angry mob, as well as soldiers and policemen, attacked Jews, shooting, stabbing, stoning, and beating them with planks, rifle butts, and iron bars. The violence resulted in the deaths of forty-two Jews and injuries to approximately eighty others. The pogrom highlighted the persistence of antisemitism in Poland, even after the Holocaust, as Jews attempted to return and rebuild their lives. This event contributed to a broader trend of Jewish emigration from Poland, as it underscored the ongoing dangers faced by Jews in the postwar period. For a reconstruction of the events in Kielce, see Bożena Szaynok, "The Pogrom of Jews in Kielce, July 4, 1946," *Yad Vashem Studies*, 22 (1992), pp. 199–235; Sara Bender, *In Enemy Land : The Jews of Kielce and the Region, 1939–1946* (Boston: Academic Studies Press, 2019), pp. 279–298.

city, which was then occupied by Polish legionaries under the command of the infamous Major Mączyński.[5] It was under his leadership that the soldiers organized a bloody pogrom against the Jews, who were considered for some unknown reason to be traitors.[6] For three days, from November 21 to 23, the pogrom lasted in the densely populated Jewish districts of Lwów, especially on on Żółkiewska, Gołuchowska, and Kazimierska Streets. Polish soldiers massacred innocent Jewish civilians of both sexes. They bestially murdered 71 people, women and men, and wounded over 100.[7] They burned to the ground the great synagogue of Lwów and thirty-eight Jewish houses, and across the entire Jewish quarter, property was plundered and destroyed. Polish officers stood idly by and watched the soldiers killing the Jewish population, raping Jewish women, and burning the synagogue.[8] The Germans seemed to have had a good example when they blew up the Great Synagogue on Tłomackie Street during the Warsaw Ghetto Uprising when it was their turn twenty-five years later.

The pogrom began with false news, later officially denied, that Jews were shooting at Polish soldiers from their homes. The same news was also spread by provocateurs in many other cities, where at the same time Polish legionaries and Hallerians organized pogroms against Jews. This was the case in Vilna, Płock, Pińsk, Częstochowa, and in many other Polish cities and towns, where Jews were murdered, their property looted, and houses and synagogues burned. I experienced the pogrom in

5 Czesław Mączyński was a Polish officer and the commander in chief of the Polish forces in the battle for Lwów in November 1918. Mączyński did not intervene to stop the violence against civilians. The degree of his responsibility is debated. See Maciej Kozłowski, "Poles and Ukrainians: Troubled History," *The Polish Review* (1988), pp. 271–293, especially p. 281.

6 Caught in a precarious situation in the Polish-Ukrainian fight over the city, the Jews declared neutrality. They were accused by Poles of siding with the Ukrainians. See Rachel Manekin, "L'viv," YIVO Encyclopedia of Jews in Eastern Europe, https://encyclopedia.yivo.org/article/1396 (accessed August 18, 2025).

7 According to historian Piotr Wróbel, over seventy Jews were killed. See Piotr Wróbel, "The Seeds of Violence: The Brutalization of an East European Region, 1917–1921," *Journal of Modern European History/Zeitschrift Für Moderne Europäische Geschichte/Revue d'histoire Européenne Contemporaine*, 1:1 (2003), pp. 125–149, specifically p. 138. According to Manekin, "L'viv," YIVO Encyclopedia of Jews in Eastern Europe, almost 100 Jews lost their lives.

8 For details on the violence and damage inflicted on the Jews in Lwów, see William W. Hagen, *Anti-Jewish Violence in Poland, 1914–1920* (New York: Cambridge University Press, 2018), pp. 123–172.

Częstochowa, my hometown, as a young boy, as described in the earlier pages of this memoir.

Very characteristic of that period was the fact that Polish socialists and the Polish intelligentsia, especially the leaders of the Polish Socialist Party, which played such an important role in liberating Poland from its occupants, did not react to the wave of pogroms. The same happened after World War II, when the so-called leading force of the nation, the Polish Workers' Party (PPR), kept silent and did not react to the wave of anti-Jewish excesses, culminating in the pogrom in Kielce in which it seemed that many PPR members directly or indirectly participated.

On the margin of the anti-Jewish pogroms after World War I, it is also worth mentioning the courageous and dignified behavior of the already then-world-famous Jewish painter Artur Szyk.[9] Outraged by the wave of pogroms and the indifference shown by the Polish intelligentsia to those bloody events, Szyk went to the commander of the military garrison in Łódź, Major Zbrożek, and, expressing his indignation and protest against the unpunished murder of Jews, renounced his Polish citizenship. On April 15, 1919, Jewish society in Poland was shocked by the tragic news of the pogrom in Pińsk. Polish soldiers under the command of Major Leszczyński dragged out thirty-five Jewish boys praying in the synagogue, lined them up against the wall of the monastery, and shot them.

Especially tragic was the situation of the Jewish population living in the eastern territories. Here, alongside the Polish army, Ukrainian troops under the command of former tsarist officers took part in the battles against the Bolshevik army. These troops, occupying a village or town, began their rule by beating, cutting off Jewish beards with bayonets, murdering Jews, and plundering their property. Particularly notable in the murder of the Jewish population were the Ukrainian gangs under the command of the notorious murderer of Jews, Stanisław Bułak-Bałachowicz, allied with the Polish military headquarters in Warsaw. When entering towns inhabited by many Jews, Bułak's bands, together with Polish legionaries, spread false news accusing the Jewish population of spying for the Bolsheviks, and under this pretext, the slaughter and robbery began. Old people, women, and children were not spared, and rabbis were murdered under the claim that they supported the Bolsheviks. The raging wave of pogroms did not

9 Artur Szyk (1894–1951) was a Polish-Jewish illustrator and caricaturist known for his detailed, illuminated manuscripts and political cartoons, especially during World War II. His works often depicted anti-Nazi and pro-Allied themes, as well as Jewish heritage and Zionism.

elicit the slightest protest from the Polish government, the headquarters of the Polish armed forces, or Polish society. What is worse, the pogroms against Jews took place with impunity before the eyes of the French military mission under General Weygand, who was visiting Poland and who rushed to provide financial and military aid to rebuilding the Polish armed forces—but no one from the French mission seemed to utter a word of protest against the unpunished spilling of Jewish blood. Anyway, as seen before, Europe and the world remained silent, pretending not to see or hear the cries of despair of the murdered Polish Jews, identical to what would happen twenty-five years later during the great extermination.

The crowning glory of Polish antisemitism during this bloody period of the emergence of Poland's independence after World War I was the order issued by the chief inspector of the Polish armed forces, General Kazimierz Sosnkowski, that all Jewish soldiers fighting on the Bolshevik front be immediately withdrawn from the ranks of the army and interned behind barbed wire in a military camp in Jabłonna near Warsaw. The order read: "Disarm all officers and soldiers of Jewish faith of the Polish army, take away their uniforms and shoes, and concentrate them under confinement and guard in the Jabłonna military camp."[10]

Whole trains of barefoot and nearly naked Jewish officers and soldiers headed for Jabłonna, the first camp for Jews on Polish soil. It even came to the point where two trains carrying interned soldiers collided with each other under unusual circumstances, resulting in many Jewish casualties. Even after the Bolshevik troops were repulsed from Poland (after the so-called Miracle on the Vistula),[11] the concentration camp for Jewish soldiers still existed, and over 10,000 interned officers and soldiers, including a

10 Thousands of Jewish soldiers—some volunteers, others enlistees—were interned between July and September 1920 at the Jabłonna army camp, near Warsaw, on orders from Military Affairs General Kazimierz Sosnkowski due to the hysteria over "Judeo-Bolshevik" sabotage of the anti-Soviet war. The conditions at the camp were terrible, characterized by lack of sanitation and hunger. See Hagen, *Anti-Jewish Violence in Poland*, pp. 379–386. According to Hagen, "Zionist parliamentarians archived an undated summary of Sosnkowski's order," p. 381.

11 The Battle of the Vistula, also known as the Miracle on the Vistula, was a decisive conflict fought in August 1920 during the Polish–Soviet War. Polish forces, under Marshal Józef Piłsudski, successfully repelled a Soviet invasion aimed at capturing Warsaw and spreading communist revolution across Europe. The battle turned the tide in favor of Poland, halting the Soviet advance and securing Poland's independence. The victory is considered a miracle due to the unexpected Polish victory despite overwhelming odds.

significant number of people from the professional intelligentsia, were imprisoned there.[12] Many dozens lost their lives due to illness and the extremely harsh camp discipline. A song was composed in Jabłonna by interned Jews to the melody of the legionary song, "We, the First Brigade," which ironically expressed all the bitterness and protest of the innocently imprisoned Jews against the military leadership of that time. This song was then sung by all Jewish youth in Poland in protest against pogroms and antisemitism.

The above historical reminiscences and parallels between the periods after both World War I and World War II on Polish soil may serve the obvious conclusion that not only the history of Polish Jews during the Middle Ages but also in modern times points to a permanent state of persecution, mayhem, pogroms, and bloody exterminations committed against the Jews. In some cases, historians and politicians boast of the nation's alleged religious and political tolerance toward Polish Jews throughout the centuries of their residence in Poland, but from my perspective and experience, this is simply a lie and falsification of historical reality.[13]

12 The actual number was probably 5,300 on September 5, 1920. Some allegations voiced at the time included higher numbers. There were fatalities, notably due to a derailed train that killed several soldiers. See Hagen, *Anti-Jewish Violence in Poland*, p. 386.

13 The history of Jews in Poland is exceptionally complex and cannot be reduced to a single narrative. For centuries, the Polish–Lithuanian Commonwealth provided conditions in which Jewish communities enjoyed far-reaching communal autonomy and experienced unprecedented demographic, economic, and cultural development, making Poland the largest and most important center of Jewish life in the world until the twentieth century. At the same time, this history unfolded within a region marked by continuous political upheavals, shifting borders, and recurrent military conflicts, as well as changing ethnic and confessional constellations. These factors contributed to persistent social tensions and to phenomena of anti-Jewish hostility. Holocaust historians such as Jan Grabowski, Jan Tomasz Gross, Barbara Engelking, and others have addressed an extensive phenomenon of anti-Jewish violence, denunciations, and different forms of abuse that came from the Polish Blue and Criminal Police as well as from local neighbors, thereby complicating idealized narratives of long-standing Polish tolerance.

CHAPTER THIRTEEN

STARTING AGAIN IN POLAND AND DENMARK

In the wave of emigration from Poland, there were not only Jews who had survived the Holocaust on Polish soil but also those who had endured the cataclysm of World War II in Soviet Russia and returned to Poland under the repatriation law. The latter fled Poland, claiming that they did not want to experience the communist "paradise" a second time, having had enough of the Bolshevik-Russia experience in the Soviet camps and prisons.[1] My few relatives who returned from Russia settled in Łódź and worked there. One of my cousins was a lawyer, another a dentist. Another cousin worked as a Russian language teacher at a teachers' seminary. However, they did not stay in Łódź for long. They immigrated with their families to Canada and Israel, and advised me not to hesitate to do the same. My mother's brother Górski came with his wife from the United States to visit us, and he too urged us to emigrate. He promised to help us in the United States or Israel.

1 After World War II, Poland became a Soviet satellite state. The Soviet-backed Polish Committee of National Liberation replaced the Polish government-in-exile, and communists consolidated power over Poland. By 1947, Poland was a one-party communist state, aligned with the Soviet Union.

However, neither I nor my brother could make the decision to leave. I was weary and worn out from my experiences in the ghetto and in the German camps, and I had neither the strength nor the courage to start all over again. My tragic experiences, the daily struggle for life, the loss of my beloved and those closest to me all caused a violent emotional and physical reaction. I felt ill, incapable of starting a new life in another country and unfamiliar surroundings. I therefore took the path of least resistance: I stayed in Poland and started a family there. I worked as a lawyer, and the years passed by.

Alfred Kromołowski and Róża Monhajt, HASAG survivors, shortly after their marriage, 1946.

Alfred Kromołowski, Częstochowa, Poland, 1948.

However, a series of events occurred that had a significant impact on the fate of the remaining Jewish community in Poland. From October 1956, Poland was ruled by the first secretary of the PZPR (Polska Zjednoczona Partia Robotnicza, Polish United Workers' Party) Władysław Gomułka, a typical representative of the national tendencies prevalent within Communist Party ideology, which sharply conflicted with its international character. This rise in nationalism was reflected in Polish patriotic traditions. National anniversaries were celebrated—more or less solemnly—including the 1000th anniversary of Polish statehood, the 600th anniversary of the founding of the Jagiellonian University, the 550th anniversary of the Battle of Grunwald,[2] and the 100th anniversary of the January Uprising, which would previously have been unthinkable, since the uprising was directed against the Russian occupier.[3]

In addition, Poland's economic situation was worsening. Workers' wages decreased, and the price of goods—especially food—was disproportionately high relative to workers' earnings. Discontent grew among the proletariat, whose standard of living was low. The USSR extracted various raw materials, coal, light industry products, and foodstuffs—especially meat—from Poland, leaving these goods in chronic short supply on the domestic market. Meat stores gleamed with empty hooks, and consumer goods, clothing, and footwear were expensive, with shortages keenly felt. The only reliable way to buy such goods was to bribe the sellers and buy them "under the counter."[4] Furthermore, Russia paid for Polish goods in rubles, which were worthless in the West. The party and Gomułka could not find a way out of this deteriorating economic situation. By its own admission, the gap between the party and the working class was growing, and the party's role as the nation's guiding force was waning.

Something had to be done to stop the rebellious workers from taking to the streets in protests and demonstrations, which, as early as

2 The Battle of Grunwald (1410) was a decisive conflict in which Polish-Lithuanian forces defeated the Teutonic Knights. The celebrations of the 1000th anniversary of Polish statehood took place between 1960 and 1966. The Battle of Grunwald was celebrated in 1960 as part of the millennial celebrations.

3 The January Uprising in 1863 was a Polish insurrection against Russian rule, aimed at ending occupation and regaining national independence.

4 Kromołowski refers to a state-run economic system, where store employees were part of the state apparatus rather than proprietors. During product shortages, these sellers exploited their access to goods by selling them at prices higher than those fixed by the state.

October 1956 in Poznań, had escalated into bloody riots against the Polish Communist Party.[5] Workers and peasants alike saw the Communist Party as the oppressor, holding the nation in check with threats of armed Russian intervention, as had occurred in Hungary and Czechoslovakia.[6]

Gomułka began fighting the so-called revisionists, seeing them as enemies of the system. In fact, this was a battle against almost the entire nation and its main bastion of opposition, the Catholic Church.[7] However, as it was impossible to persecute the entire nation, it was necessary to find a scapegoat to divert the workers' attention from the worsening economic difficulties. Gomułka found such a target for blame in the Jewish population.

After the victory of the Israeli army in the Six-Day War in 1967, there was consternation and clear dissatisfaction in the Communist Bloc, which traditionally supported the Arabs. The Arab states that fought in this war against the Jewish state—most notably Nasser's Egypt—were under Soviet influence, had been armed by the USSR with Russian weapons, and had benefited extensively from Soviet military advisers. Nasser did not hide the fact that the goal of his policy was to destroy the Jewish state and push the Jews into the sea. Syria, closely allied with the Soviets, and Jordan, also interested in annexing Jewish lands and destroying Israel, joined this holy war against the Jews. Military assistance was also provided by Iraq, which made no secret of its hostile intentions toward Israel.

To the amazement of the entire world watching this bloody wrestling match between the modern, Arab Goliath and the Jewish David—in lightning-quick actions by the air force and motorized forces, which lasted only six days, and the Jewish army fighting for its life and for the independence of the young state—dealt a crushing blow to all the Arab armies involved, almost completely destroying the Egyptian air force and its motorized formations in the Sinai Peninsula and forcing the retreat of the Syrian army, the Jordanian army and the Iraqi auxiliary troops. The

5 The 1956 Poznań protests, or Poznań June, was the first major uprising against communist rule in Poland, sparked by workers demanding better conditions, higher wages, and political freedom.

6 The Soviet interventions in Hungary in 1956 and Czechoslovakia in 1968 were military invasions to suppress uprisings and reforms challenging communist rule and Soviet dominance in Eastern Europe.

7 The Catholic Church successfully competed with the communist regime in Poland over the formation of Polish identity.

Israeli army took control of the entire Sinai Peninsula, consolidating its position over the Suez Canal and rendering it immobile for shipping, as well as the Golan Heights, from which Syrian soldiers had been shelling low-lying agricultural Jewish kibbutzim for years, and the West Bank of the Jordan River along with the eastern part of Jerusalem. After many years, Jews gained access to the Western Wall—the remnants of the walls of the Temple of Jerusalem, destroyed by the Romans, a site sacred to Jews but previously in the hands of Jordan, who denied them access to these and other holy sites of Jewish tradition.

In world opinion, the Israeli army's victory was perceived, above all, as a victory of Western democracy and Western weapons used by the Israeli army alone over the pro-Soviet Arabs who fought with Soviet weapons and equipment, under the instructions of Russian advisors. Along with the rest of the free world, the overwhelming majority of the Polish nation perceived the Israeli victory as a military and political defeat against the Russians. Thus, the Poles rejoiced and expressed their satisfaction by congratulating their Jewish colleagues and friends. They did this not at all out of love or sympathy for the Jews, but out of hatred for Russia, which was regarded in Poland as an occupying power and the cause of the economic crisis and of all the evils that had plagued the country since the outbreak of World War II.

This celebration of Israel's victory in Poland enraged the Polish communists, all the more so because Russian mass media were foaming with anger over the terrible defeat of their Arab protegées. The entire communist camp spared no words of condemnation for Israel and its army and echoed the Kremlin's line that the Jews were Zionists, nationalists, racists, and fascists who had committed aggression against innocent and defenseless Arab states—similar lies for which the Kremlin is internationally well known.

The Polish communists, headed by Gomułka, decided to exploit these events in the Middle East for their own benefit and reached for the tried-and-true methods of deceiving the working class: By pointing to the Jews as the cause of all evil, they found an easy victim to offer as prey to the angry mob. Gomułka said things like the Jews are the enemies of the system, the cause of all evil, that Jews are Zionists, nationalists, traitors and revisionists, that in Poland they held high positions in administration, trade, and industry, they were in the party, the government, and the army, and that they deliberately did a bad job and led the Polish state to economic collapse. He claimed they were the fifth column of capitalism seeking to overthrow the communist system.

Gomułka stood in front of the Polish television cameras, loudly and indignantly quoting all of these trumped-up, deceitful accusations against Polish Jewry. He spoke of Zionists, but he meant Jews. He accused them of celebrating and rejoicing over Israel's victory over the oppressed Arab nations, which is exactly what only enemies of the regime and traitors do. This was all the Polish antisemites needed. There was a loud upheaval in the press, on television and radio, accompanied by a flood of anti-Jewish articles in Communist Party newspapers, information bulletins for communist luminaries, and secret circulars of the Central Committee of the PZPR. The slogan of the day became the fight against Zionism and revisionists—the fight against Jews.

Polish communism, modeled after its "big brother" in Moscow, turned out to be as antisemitic as Stroński's former National Democracy, as well as Rydz Śmigły's OZN or the National Polish Party. From party headquarters, it was proclaimed that the student riots at universities, anti-government revolts, and workers' demonstrations were also the vile work of Zionists and revisionists, the fruit of the propaganda of the "fifth column." A widespread campaign against the Jews began. The militia (the official police force) and ORMO (Ochotnicza Rezerwa Milicji Obywatelskiej, Volunteer Reserve of the Citizens' Militia) distributed leaflets with antisemitic content during student demonstrations, which apparently said things like, "Down with the Moishes! Moishes to Palestine! Moishes, out of Polish universities! Throw Moishes out of their high positions, because they are the fifth column, enemies of socialist Poland." The antisemite minister of the interior, General Mieczysław Moczar, led the party's militia to fight the Jews.

Arrests began among students and leaders of student demonstrations. A few of them were of Jewish origin, from mixed Catholic-Jewish marriages, but they had no connection to Jewry, let alone Zionism. The party and government officials' campaign against so-called revisionism did not spare the Polish creative intelligentsia. Not only students but also many professors who had joined the student movement—demanding greater democracy, freedom of speech, the abolition of censorship, and wide-scale economic reforms to rescue the country from its critical situation—were expelled from the universities.

Among them was Professor Leszek Kołakowski, who was stripped of his chair and forced to leave Poland for preaching liberal views. The uproar among workers and anti-government student demonstrations was heavily influenced by the events in Czechoslovakia, where in January 1968, Antonín Novotny was removed from the Communist Party leadership, and

Alexander Dubček was elected. Liberal communists, seeking to establish "communism with a human face" and independence from Moscow's dictates, were allowed to take power.

Both the Prague Spring and the workers' and students' upheavals in Poland were suppressed with an iron fist, assisted by the army and the militia. In Poland, the UB and militiamen beat demonstrating students with truncheons, and the central party authorities ordered the removal of Jews from leadership positions. A large-scale purge began. Directors of unions, departments, senior state and party officials, and factory directors were ousted from their posts. Scientists, magazine editors, and Jewish journalists were fired. Often, this was done brutally and in a manner deceptively reminiscent of the Nazis' methods during the recent occupation. It was reported that a Jewish director was loaded into a sack, taken away from the plant or institution in a wheelbarrow, and thrown into the street gutter. Among others, this was how the director of the Industrial Construction Union, Gershon Tolion, elevated to this position by the party's will, was removed in Częstochowa. The backgrounds of various prominent party and state officials with Polish surnames and first names were scrutinized, and whenever any trace of Jewish origin was discovered, the individual was mercilessly dismissed.

Party dignitaries, prewar communists, political prisoners who had spent years in Sanacja prisons for their communist leanings, prisoners in the camp of Bereza Kartuska, and participants of the fights in Spain were rapidly ousted from their posts under the pretext that they had Zionist convictions—although it was known that they consistently opposed the Zionists and distanced themselves from Jewry. High-ranking secret security officers, military men, participants in the liberation battles on the trail from Lenino to Berlin, members of government, and all sorts of apparatchiks were thrown to the pavement because they were Jewish, even though they, too, swore that they had long since renounced their Jewish roots and any connection with Jewry. Polish communism bared its fascist claws, demonstrating that it could employ the old tsarist methods against the Jews, as had been done by the Black Sotnia and the German genocide perpetrators.

In August 1968, the allied communist armies of Bulgaria, the German Democratic Republic, Poland, and the USSR rolled their tanks into Czechoslovakia and, with fire and iron, suppressed the Czech patriots' movement calling for reforms and democracy. There were Jewish communists among them who paid with their lives, or ended up in prison or in exile for the fight for communism with a human face—the very opposite to the communism in the Soviet Union and the countries that were part of the Warsaw Pact.

In Poland, a new exodus began in March 1968, driven by the campaign against Jews. This time, Jewish communists—yesterday's builders of communist Poland—fled the country en masse. They fled with their Crosses of Merit, Virtuti Militari, Orders of Lenin, and Red Stars of the Heroes of the Soviet Union, which had been earned in the ranks of the Soviet army or the Polish army. They fled to Israel, as well as to other places, as stateless persons. They received Israeli visas, paid for with Israeli funds, but their Polish citizenship and the right to return to the country to which they had devoted their blood and final strength were revoked. This is how communist Poland thanked its faithful Jewish comrades for their contribution to rebuilding the country they (erroneously) believed would become their homeland.

Among this mass of communist refugees was Stanisław Wygodzki, a former prisoner of Bereza Kartuska and Rawa Ruska, who spent half his life in prison for his beliefs. A writer and publicist, he became a symbol of the Jewish communists from the "Gomułka emigration" to Israel. Wygodzki confronted Soviet-style communism, pouring out his bitterness over disappointed hopes in numerous publications and leaving no thread of mercy for his former comrades from Poland and Russia. Thousands of Jewish Communists, like Wygodzki, left Poland for Israel, Western Europe, America, or Australia, where, as political refugees, they took advantage of the right of asylum and started their lives anew as free people.

Non-partisan Jews and Jewish youth also immigrated to these countries, seeking work and a livelihood in the West and in the free world—something they had been denied in Poland. But, above all, they sought an atmosphere of freedom, without ethnic and religious persecution. At the time of this writing, they were still regarded as strangers and guests in the country in which they were born. Undoubtedly, the majority of Polish Jews who emigrated during the Gomułka era went to Israel, where they found cordial attention from government authorities, moral and material support in building a new life for themselves, and, most importantly, an atmosphere of freedom and genuine equality of rights. The right to return to the land of their ancestors welcomed the weary wanderers, exiles, and victims of massacres and pogroms, offering them not only a breath of freedom that can flourish only in one's home, but also restoring a sense of dignity and human worth, felt solely in their newly reclaimed, ancient homeland.

This unstoppable wave of emigration also included my children. My daughter Halina, after graduating from high school and passing her matriculation examinations, left for Israel. There, in the ancient homeland, she graduated from the Bezalel Academy of Art and Design, got married, and gave birth to two boys—real Israeli *sabras*, Guy and Noam. My children and grandchildren are living happily in their new homeland, breathing freely and not experiencing persecution or degrading persecutions. They are building their future with hard work and responding to enemy threats and attacks with dignity, arms in hand, guarding their independence like all free people in the world.

A few years later, my son Jerzy left Poland for Denmark, where, after obtaining political asylum, residence, and a work visa, he began his higher education at the University of Copenhagen. He, too, did not want to remain in Poland as a domestic foreigner, constantly being exposed to antisemitic persecution and demeaning personal attacks and invective because of his Jewish background.

The two of us, my wife and I, remained alone in our spacious apartment, which had once teemed with the exuberant and impromptu energy of our children's youth. We waited for letters and news, consumed with longing and memories—not only of our family life with our children, but also of the tragedy of the Holocaust. My wife, who came from a Jewish family in Częstochowa, also lived through this period in the ghetto, the labor camp, and the HASAG concentration camp, where the Germans murdered her parents and immediate family. It became more and more difficult for us to live in this atmosphere of loneliness, in an environment with so few Jewish families like ours. This was all the more painful because my brother Henryk, the only surviving member of my family, sadly died in January 1970 at the age of fifty-five, deepening my despondency and grief.

Given these circumstances, we began to take our son's pleas for us to immigrate to Denmark both more seriously and positively. There, we could obtain refugee status and enjoy a very acceptable standard of living. Nothing was holding us back in Poland. All ties between us and our home country had long since been crushed. With no close or extended family in Poland and feeling unwelcome in Polish society, we lived among the graves of murdered Polish Jewry, in sorrow, haunted by memories of the past and deprived of any joy in life. My health was also failing, and I was no longer able to run my law practice, forcing me to retire. As a result, our material situation deteriorated significantly, which, given the prevailing high prices and permanent shortages of basic foodstuffs, made our daily lives increasingly difficult. We therefore decided to leave and reunite with our son in Denmark. Later, there was also a realistic prospect of reuniting with our daughter's family in Israel.

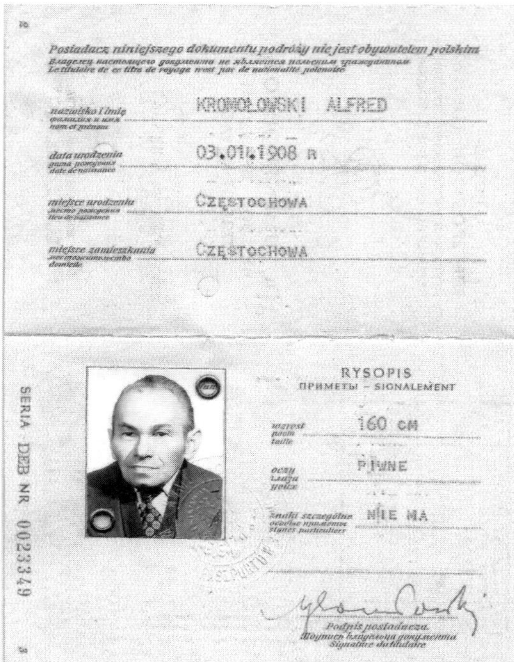

Posiadacz niniejszego dokumentu podróży nie jest obywatelem polskim

nazwisko i imię: KROMOŁOWSKI ALFRED

data urodzenia: 03.01.1908 R

miejsce urodzenia: CZĘSTOCHOWA

miejsce zamieszkania: CZĘSTOCHOWA

RYSOPIS

ПРИМЕТЫ – SIGNALEMENT

wzrost: 160 CM

oczy: PIWNE

znaki szczególne: NIE MA

Podpis posiadacza

SERIA DEB NR 0023349

Alfred Kromołowski's travel document, issued on September 30, 1976, for emigration to Denmark. At the top, it reads: "Holder of this document is not a Polish Citizen."

We quickly liquidated our affairs in Częstochowa, packed our belongings, and, equipped with a travel document—deprived a priori of Polish citizenship—and with Israeli and Danish visas in our pockets, we left for exile on a bright, autumn day. We left Poland, where many generations of our families had lived their entire lives, with feelings of regret and disappointment, bitterly felt by those expelled from their homes and homeland. Under the threat of being refused permission to leave, the organs of the Citizen's Militia forced us to sign the preprepared renunciation of Polish citizenship—seemingly another manifestation of antisemitism and hostility that the Polish state had shown toward

Jews on countless occasions and that accompanied us from birth nearly to death.

To our indescribable joy, our children were waiting for us on the platform of the train station in Copenhagen. How warm and welcoming it was after so many years of separation! We were greeted with bouquets of flowers from our son and his fiancée, and from our daughter, who had flown in from Israel especially for this occasion. With their help, we quickly completed the necessary formalities with the Danish authorities and were accomodated in a Copenhagen hotel with full board.

We received an extremely warm and friendly reception from the Danish authorities, as well as from the semi-official Dansk Flygtningehjælp (Danish Refugee Council) organization, established specifically to take care of refugees. Soon we were granted political refugee status with the right of asylum. We were provided with modern, functional housing and material support. The Danish municipal authorities surrounded us with friendly care, also offering us medical assistance and demonstrating an understanding and humane approach to all aspects of our lives.

Alfred Kromołowski in his study, Częstochowa, Poland, 1972, taken by his son, Jerzy, a few years before leaving for Denmark.

Halina Hamou, with her son Guy and her grandson Michael—Alfred's daughter, grandson, and great-grandson in Israel.

Jerzy Kromołowski—Alfred's son—a screenwriter and film director, living in Los Angeles, California, with his wife, Mary Olson-Kromołowski. They have one son, Daniel, Alfred's grandson.

Halina's son Noam—Alfred's grandson—with his wife Yael in the United States.

AFTERWORD

As I write these memories and reflections, thirty-eight years have passed since the bloody and tragic events in Poland, of which I was not only an eyewitness but also one of the victims. Before my eyes, the vivid and vibrant world of Polish Jewry—which for nearly 1,000 years had created indelible works of spiritual and material culture in Polish lands, contributed greatly to the development of the entire Polish nation, and made a significant impact on world progress—was annihilated. While this world has disappeared, its graves and cemeteries remain.

In this memoir, I have tried to depict as accurately as possible, against the backdrop of pivotal political events, the experiences of three generations of Polish Jews—members of my family and people close to me in my native town of Częstochowa. One thing is indisputable: All events and tragic experiences recounted here are absolutely true, as are the characters who appear in them. The three Jewish generations mentioned here, though they lived in different periods, share a common thread of tragic experiences: the suffering caused by constant persecution due to their Jewish origin within the environment in which they lived.

The thorny, bloody crown of these sufferings of the Jewish people on Polish soil was their extermination at the hands of German murderers. I have often wondered why in numerous historical studies and descriptions of those times the nomenclature of Nazis or Nazi perpetrators under the sign of the swastika is generally used, while the name Germans is often avoided. But history has passed its judgment on the Germans, and they themselves are trying to dry the Jewish tears of pain by paying reparations to the victims miraculously rescued from their torture and extermination camps. It is impossible by any means to erase these bloody pages of history just as it is impossible to bring back to life the millions of innocent Jewish victims of the German genocide.

To bear witness to a truth so tragic and cruel, I have written these pages as an eyewitness testimony of these terrible events, so that the memory of the Holocaust and the biological destruction of nearly half of the Jewish people by German executioners will endure as a grave warning and a reminder for future generations. No more fascism and racial hatred! No more extermination camps and concentration camps! Never again the shedding of innocent blood because of differences in religion, race, and nationality!

And to those people who still doubt the bloody facts of genocide and allow themselves to be deceived by criminal agents of international antisemitism:[1] Let them go to Poland, where every child will show them the Auschwitz slaughterhouse of Jews and many others, with its gas chambers and crematoria—the place of extermination of innocent people. In the Auschwitz Museum, they will see thousands of personal effects[2] that the Germans took from their victims before herding them to their deaths in the gas chambers. Let them go to the cemetery of Treblinka, where the Germans murdered hundreds of thousands of Jews[3] in the gas chambers and dug their graves; let them visit the Jewish cemeteries in Polish towns and cities, where the graves of a huge number of Jewish men, women, and children are located;[4] let them finally visit the museum of the Jewish Historical Institute and read the archive of Emanuel Ringelblum[5] offering firsthand accounts of the great extermination of the Jews.

1 Kromołowski refers to the phenomena of Holocaust denial and Holocaust distortion globally attested both at the time of his writing and in the present day.

2 The list of gruesome trophies at Auschwitz is long and horrifying including suitcases, pans, pots, glasses, prayer shawls, dolls, brushes, artificial limbs, shoes, human hair, and more.

3 As mentioned earlier, between July 1942 and September 1943, some 870,000 Jews were murdered in Treblinka. See Silberklang, *Gates of Tears*, p. 252.

4 Along with the industrial murder of Jews in the death camps, the local murder of Jews in their hometowns took place on a scale just as horrifying. One of the most common places of mass executions of Jews was the local Jewish cemetery, often located on the outskirts of town. In other cases, Jews were murdered in the town and taken to the cemetery to be buried or murdered in the forests and buried in the pits dug by themselves prior to their death.

5 The Archive of Emanuel Ringelblum, also known as the Oyneg Shabes Archive, is a clandestine collection of documents created by a group of Jews in the Warsaw

More than forty years have passed since the annihilation of the Jewish community in my hometown, Częstochowa, and the annihilation of 6 million Jews, murdered by the Germans. However, I believe that the lessons have not been learned from these terrible historical events, and the consequences have not been realized. Antisemitism unfortunately continues to spread, fueled by the enemies of the Jewish people.

Since the proclamation of the Jewish state, the State of Israel, bloody wars and terrorist attacks—against the victims of the death camps and those who managed to survive Hitler's onslaught, against their children and grandchildren, within Israel and in the Diaspora—have not ceased. Antisemitism has only changed its name. Today it has taken the name of anti-Zionism, but the objects of its attacks are the same Jews who, after the massacres and pogroms in Poland, Russia, Western Europe, and the Arab states, have taken refuge in the country of their ancestors, where they are trying to secure a peaceful haven for themselves and their children.

Fortunately, the Jewish people have awakened from its long lethargy of passivity and, like the warriors of Israel and Judah, and like Judah Maccabee, are fighting with arms against its enemies, defending the national independence of a homeland regained after long centuries. Israel's modern army is now the guarantor of Israel's independence and the security of its citizens. My children and grandchildren in Israel live, and will live, as free people in a sovereign homeland, without extermination and humiliating persecution of the kind their fathers and grandfathers have suffered. May a day come when all Jewish children find a peaceful haven in their homeland, Israel!

L'shana haba b'Yerushalayim! (Next year in Jerusalem)[6]

Alfred Adam Kromołowski
Copenhagen, May 17, 1983

ghetto during World War II. Led by historian Emanuel Ringelblum, the archive preserved testimonies, diaries, official decrees, and other materials documenting the daily life, suffering, and resistance of Jews under Nazi occupation. Hidden in metal boxes and milk cans, parts of the archive were discovered after the war and remain a key resource for Holocaust research.

6 This is said at the end of the Passover *seder* and at the end of the Yom Kippur prayer service.